Maren Tomforde

The Hmong Mountains:
Cultural Spatiality of the Hmong in Northern Thailand

Southeast Asian Modernities

edited by

Christoph Antweiler, Rüdiger Korff,
Frauke Kraas, Boike Rehbein, Jürgen Rüland,
Judith Schlehe, Susanne Schröter,
Hermann Schwengel

Volume 5

LIT

Maren Tomforde

The Hmong Mountains: Cultural Spatiality of the Hmong in Northern Thailand

LIT

Cover: Hmong people in a neighbourhood square in Mae Sa Mai, Thailand, 2002. Background: The silhouette of the Doi Inthanon, the highest mountain in Thailand. © Maren Tomforde

The publication of this book was supported by the Deutsche Forschungsgemeinschaft (German Research Foundation).

Bibliographic information published by Die Deutsche Bibliothek
Die Deutsche Bibliothek lists this publication in the Deutsche Nationalbibliografie; detailed bibliographic data are available in the Internet at http://dnb.ddb.de.

ISBN 3-8258-9313-8
Zugl.: Hamburg, Univ., Department Kulturgeschichte und Kulturkunde, Diss., 2005

A catalogue record for this book is available from the British Library

© LIT VERLAG Hamburg 2006
Auslieferung/Verlagskontakt:
Grevener Str./Fresnostr. 2   48159 Münster
Tel. +49 (0)251–62 03 20   Fax +49 (0)251–23 19 72
e-Mail: lit@lit-verlag.de   http://www.lit-verlag.de

Distributed in the UK by: Global Book Marketing, 99B Wallis Rd, London, E9 5LN
Phone: +44 (0) 20 8533 5800 – Fax: +44 (0) 1600 775 663
http://www.centralbooks.co.uk/acatalog/search.html

Distributed in North America by:

Transaction Publishers
New Brunswick (U.S.A.) and London (U.K.)

Transaction Publishers
Rutgers University
35 Berrue Circle
Piscataway, NJ 08854

Phone: +1 (732) 445 - 2280
Fax: + 1 (732) 445 - 3138
for orders (U. S. only):
toll free (888) 999 - 6778
e-mail:
orders@transactionspub.com

To Norbert

CONTENTS

Acknowledgements	ix
Maps	xiii
Figures	xiii
Acronyms	xiv
Equivalents	xv
Notes on orthography	xvi

INTRODUCTION — 1

PART ONE: THEORETICAL APPROACHES AND CONTEXT IN THAILAND — 21

1 Towards a Theory of Cultural Spatiality — 21

Are cultures emplaced?	22
Approaches to cultural spatiality	32
Summary	55

2 Contested Spaces in Thailand — 58

The politics of Thailand	60
The ethnic mountain groups within Thailand	61
Development of Thai politics of conservation	64
Disputed citizenship rights	66
Increasing state control over geographic space	68
Protected landscapes and its repercussions for local communities	72
Conflict over forest and mountain spaces	75
Changed perceptions of the environment	77
Extension programs in the mountains	81
Summary	82

PART TWO: RESEARCH AMONG THE HMONG — 86

3 In the Field: Contextualising Research — 86

- Context of the research — 86
- Living and research conditions — 87
- Multisited research — 90
- Intracultural variation — 93
- Local communities as research units — 95
- Methodology — 97
- Methods in the field — 99

4 The Research Sites: Mae Sa Mai and Ban Phui — 101

- Mae Sa Mai — 103
- Ban Phui — 116
- Political units in Mae Sa Mai and Ban Phui — 123
- Summary — 129

5 "Flying Like Birds": Hmong Origins, Migration, Sedentarisation, and a Life in the Diaspora — 132

- Hmong origins in China — 133
- Always on the move? Hmong migration and processes of sedentarisation — 138
- The Hmong diaspora — 143
- Summary — 147

6 Hmong Cosmological Spaces and Religious Practices — 150

- Hmong cosmology: View of the world — 153
- Shamans and other religious experts — 165
- Religious practices: Hmong rituals — 173
- Conversion to other religions — 183
- Summary — 188

7 Hmong Social Organisation: The Simultaneity of Social Proximity and Socio-Spatial Extension   191

"One-house people" (*ib yim neeg*)   194
"Brothers from one family" (*ib cuab kwv tij*)   198
Patrilineal clans and subclans   202
The village community   210
"Maleness is Hmong and Hmong is maleness":
Gender differences   213
Spatial dimension of social networks and Hmong endosociality   221
Social relations among the Hmong of Mae Sa Mai and Ban Phui   223
Summary   236

8 Positioning of the Hmong: Ethnic Identity, Interethnic Contacts, and Prospects of the Hmong Youth   240

Hmong-Thai identity and relations   244
Hmong perceptions of and relations with the Karen   248
The Hmong youth: Living in two worlds   252
Summary   259

9 Transformations, Outside Influences, and Socio-Spatial Dimensions of Hmong Economy   261

Transitions in the Hmong traditional resource use system   262
Poppy substitution, development projects and international companies   269
Transformations in the Hmong economy   273
New forms of agriculture in Mae Sa Mai and Ban Phui   275
Economic survey data   281
Further economic activities   303
Household income and expenditures   311
Summary   317

10 Hmong Perceptions of the Environment and Spatial Orientation	**323**
Traditional relation to the landscape and natural phenomena	327
Self-critique and dilemma of development	330
Declaration of protection areas and changed environmental awareness	332
Traditional and new forms of conservation: Sacred forest areas	337
Spatial orientation	345
Summary	348
11 Rhythm of Spatiality: Important Village Settings	**351**
The house	353
The neighbourhood square	369
A ceremony in the village	376
Trips to mortuary rites in a neighbouring village	382
The trip to a market in the lowlands	390
The world outside of Thailand	393
Summary	396
CONCLUSION: THE HMONG MOUNTAINS AND THE CONSTITUTION OF HMONG CULTURAL SPATIALITY	**401**
APPENDIX:	
HMONG VILLAGES VISITED IN NORTHERN THAILAND	**421**
BIBLIOGRAPHY	**433**

ACKNOWLEDGEMENTS

In a period of globalisation and ever-increasing generation of information, the "slowness of ethnographic data collection" has become more and more difficult, unaffordable, and, in part, even stigmatised. Slowness seems not modern; it is ill-suited to high-tech communication and information systems. The rapidity of information generation and distribution renders only recently obtained data out-of-date and confronts anthropology with a serious dilemma. The discipline used to anchor its identity and status in thorough research. However, funds for long-term studies have become scarce and professions like journalism increasingly undertake short-term studies about ethnographic topics that replace more in-depth work.[1] Anthropology cannot present up-to-date, current data about its topics, but rather "medium-term" historical collections about cultural phenomena. These do not belong entirely to the past or future, but account for how things have just been and shape the present and future. In light of this dilemma, I appreciate that I was given the moral and financial support to conduct a "traditional", long-term field research "of the old school" variety that enabled me to accrue in-depth data.[2]

I wish to express my grateful thanks to the numerous institutions and people that supported my endeavour to conduct long-term ethnographic fieldwork. I want to express my deepest gratitude to my supervisor, Prof. Roland Mischung of the Department of Social and Cultural Anthropology (University of Hamburg), who supported my research in manifold ways. Prof. Mischung accompanied my studies as a critical but instructive teacher.

---

[1] George Marcus presented a paper on the topic "Can We Still Afford the Slowness of Fieldwork?" at the Department of European Anthropology, Humboldt University in Berlin, Germany on 10th June 2003. He emphasised that researchers are no longer accorded esteem based on the reception given to their work by other anthropologists but rather on the basis of their reception from other constituencies like journalists and politicians. According to Marcus, this influences the topics that are now studied and the length of fieldwork.

[2] The terms "traditional" (and "modern") are not understood here to describe essentialist and static socio-cultural phenomena but are, for the purposes of my argument, used conventionally to outline certain trends.

He introduced me into his former Karen and Hmong research sites in northern Thailand in 1995, gave me invaluable insights into processes of "cultural learning" during my fieldwork and backed my research with constant advice, confidence, and immeasurable assistance in obtaining financial funding. While I conducted research among the Hmong, from April 2001 until March 2002, Prof. Mischung visited me for a period of three weeks in the Hmong village Ban Phui. During his stay, he assisted my work by gathering data about village history and genealogies and depicting a map of Ban Phui. It was a unique experience to conduct research together with an experienced anthropologist, who introduced me to new anthropological aspects and approaches. I am deeply thankful for these special and supporting circumstances, which made it possible for me to conduct research of a kind that is rarely possible today.

The support of the German Research Foundation (Deutsche Forschungsgemeinschaft) made the fieldwork and writing of this thesis financially feasible. I gratefully acknowledge this support. I am also indebted to the German Academic Exchange Service (DAAD), which provided me with a grant for a previous one-year research visit to two Karen communities in northern Thailand (April 1999-March 2000). This prior research formed an essential basis for my fieldwork among the Hmong, providing valuable insights into various aspects of life among northern Thailand's ethnic mountain groups.[3]

Next to my supervisor and funding institutions, I wish to mention the numerous people who have participated in this thesis in many ways. The encouragement, assistance, and care of many have helped me to complete this book. I cannot thank anyone here whom I have not thanked before. However, some people need to be named. Their help was central in accomplishing my work. To start with, there is no adequate way to express

---

[3] From April 1999 until March 2000, I conducted a one-year course of fieldwork on a similar topic in two Karen villages northwest of Chiang Mai in northern Thailand. Selected results of this work have been published, which also incorporate some of the results of the Hmong study (see Tomforde 2003, 2003a).

Acknowledgements

my sincere gratitude to the Hmong people of Mae Sa Mai and Ban Phui. I owe my warmest thanks to all the villagers who paid attention to my project, helped, informed, taught, and enthusiastically shared their experiences and thoughts with me during my fieldwork. I especially wish to thank Win Huj Yaj for his outstanding help as field assistant and interpreter, as well as his extended family and lineage for their hospitality and patience. Without their support and understanding, my research would not have been possible. Special thanks goes also to key informants Txwj Xaab Yaj, Nplaj Thoj Xyooj, Nyaj Sua Yaj, Vaam Zeej Xyooj, Yeeb Yaj, Mailas Yaj from Mae Sa Mai and Mbua Yim Yaj, Nyaj Xeeb Yaj, Chuv Tuam Yaj from Ban Phui. I also wish to thank my dear Karen friends, especially Nahkomò Kitjaroonchai and her family, for their companionship, teaching, and helpful insights throughout the past ten years.

I am grateful to the National Research Council of Thailand for the complete freedom given to me in pursuing my project in northern Thailand. Special thanks also to my Thai colleagues Prof. Anan Ganjanapan, Dr. Prasit Leepreecha, Dr. Pinkaew Laungaramsri, Dr. Chumpol Maniratanavongsri, and Prasert Trakarnsuphakorn for their time, expertise, and advice, as well as for providing me with facilities, access to libraries and contacts in the field. The cooperation of Dr. Andreas Neef and his team from the Thai-German "Uplands Program" gave me further organisational support and valuable multidisciplinary exchange.

During my stays in Chiang Mai, valuable discussions and debates took place with international researchers Dr. Robin Roth (human geographer, Canada), Dr. Katharine McKinnon (human geographer, New Zealand), Lotte Isager (anthropologist, Demark), Dr. Berit Kaae (human geographer, Denmark), and James Peters (anthropologist, U.S.A.). I am deeply thankful for this academic inspiration, which was vital during fieldwork and provided me with invaluable insights into the Thai context.

After research, Katja Hintz, Karoline Lehmann, and Dirk Hüttenrauch converted my hand-written fieldwork data into computer documents and helped assemble the bibliography. I wish to express my gratitude to them.

Acknowledgements

This thesis took written form while I was first working at the Department of Social and Cultural Anthropology (University of Hamburg) and then at the Social Research Institute of the Bundeswehr. I wish to acknowledge the generous and stimulating atmosphere of both Institutes. The support of several people enabled me to finally complete this book: Prof. Jörn Thießen; Jörg Keller, whose constant encouragement, patience and statistical calculations were invaluable; and Carola Reinholz, who was of great assistance in preparing the manuscript. I am also indebted to my friends and colleagues Birgit Luig, Katja Duehlmeyer, Dr. Nina Leonhard, and Dr. Heiko Biehl for their stern, but helpful comments on a previous version of the thesis. I also wish to extend a special note of appreciation to Patricia Szobar, who emended and smoothed my English in many ways.

There are, as always, others who contributed much in the way of moral support and encouragement. Among these are my family, dear friends, and, most of all, my husband who accompanied me during parts of my stay in the Hmong villages and proofread this work. Without his presence, assistance, enduring patience, and emotional support, the fieldwork and completion of the thesis would not have been possible. This work is dedicated to him with love.

MAPS

Map 1:	Map of Thailand with research sites	59
Map 2:	Research Area: Chiang Mai and northern Thailand	102
Map 3:	Mae Sa Noi Watershed	105
Map 4:	Mae Sa Mai	109
Map 5:	Ban Phui surroundings	118
Map 6:	Ban Phui	120

FIGURES

Figure 1:	Cosmos depicted as a mouth	155
Figure 2:	Synthesis of Hmong Cosmology	156
Figure 3:	Geomantically correct siting of a Hmong village	163
Figure 4:	Important persons	225
Figure 5:	Social relations with other ethnic groups	230
Figure 6:	Trips to other cities (Mae Sa Mai and Ban Phui)	233
Figure 7:	Trips to other cities, separated by gender (Mae Sa Mai and Ban Phui)	233
Figure 8:	Trips to rituals in other Hmong villages	235
Figure 9:	Crops grown in fields larger than 0.25 rai (Mae Sa Mai and Ban Phui)	291
Figure 10:	Relation of cultivated land size (litchi) to revenues in Mae Sa Mai	295
Figure 11:	Relation of cultivated land size (cabbage, onion) to revenues in Ban Phui	296
Figure 12:	Gross margin calculation for two Hmong villages near Chiang Mai	313
Figure 13:	House patterns	355
Figure 14:	Male seating order during ceremonies	379
Figure 15:	Spatial division of a Hmong house during mortuary rites	387

ACRONYMS

Au.Bau.Tau	=	Thai acronym for *Aung Karn Baurihan Suan Tambol*, "management organisation of the subdistrict"
BAAC	=	Bank for Agriculture and Agricultural Cooperatives
BP	=	Ban Phui
FAO	=	Food and Health Organisation
FEBC	=	Far East Broadcasting Company
FORRU	=	Forest Restoration Research Unit
GTZ	=	Gesellschaft für Technische Zusammenarbeit
HAMP	=	Highland Agricultural Marketing and Production
IMPECT	=	Inter Mountain Peoples Education and Culture in Thailand Association
MSM	=	Mae Sa Mai
NGO	=	Non-Governmental Organisation
RFD	=	Royal Forestry Department
RP	=	Royal Project
UN	=	United Nations
UNDP	=	United Nations Development Program
USAID	=	United States Agency for International Development
WWF	=	World Wildlife Federation

EQUIVALENTS

Currency

39 baht = 1 Euro

Due to inflation, the exchange rate changed constantly during my research. The value given is the mean average value.

Area

1 *rai* is equal to 1.600 m^2, or 0.16 hectares, or 0.395 acres

1 *ngan* is equal to 400 m^2

NOTES ON ORTHOGRAPHY

Hmong orthography

For Hmong orthography, I have used the Romanised Phonetic Alphabet (RPA) developed and refined by Linwood Barney, William Smalley and Yves Bertrais in 1953 in Louang Prabang for "White" Hmong (Bertrais 1964; see also Heimbach 1979). Final consonants indicate the following eight tone values: high (-b), high falling (-j), intermediate (- no ending consonant), mid rising (-v), ordinary low (-s), low guttural (-g), lowest glottal stopped at the end (-m), and the rarely used low rising tone (-d). Final nasalisation is denoted by double vowels such as in the word *Hmoob* for Hmong, pronounced with a high tone. The consonant "x" is pronounced like the English "s".

The dialect groups of Thai Hmong are usually called "White" Hmong (*hmoob dawb*) and "Green" or "Blue" Hmong (*moob ntsuab*). The script was invented for White Hmong, which is most widespread in written accounts of Hmong language (for a Green Hmong dictionary see Lyman 1974). In theory, the script should work equally well for both White and Green Hmong, but in practice there are some differences. For this reason, Green Hmong in the United States have called on linguists to develop a separate system for their dialect. My Hmong interpreter and assistant Win Huj Yaj, being himself a Green Hmong, has primarily learned the White Hmong script, which he uses in most of the cases. For this reason, most Hmong terms in the course of this book appear in White Hmong, despite the fact that fieldwork was conducted among Green Hmong and transliteration exists for some Green Hmong terms. The Hmong people interviewed are cited in the words of my field assistant and interpreter, since he translated their comments sentence by sentence. Hmong names are spelled with their tonal marks.

Thai orthography

Several different systems exist for the transcription of Thai. Since Thai terms do not play a central role in this book, I follow none of these standardised systems but do apply the common spelling system. Unfortunately, I could not incorporate Thai language publications into this work because I do not read Thai fluently. In the bibliography, Thai names appear according to their surnames, not first names, as in conventional usage.

INTRODUCTION

The villages of the Hmong people where I conducted my one-year field research (April 2001 – March 2002) are located in the northern Thai highlands amid cultivated fields and protected forests some distance from the main traffic routes. Every now and again, when I needed time to write up my notes or take a break, I went to certain spots in the settlements where I could enjoy the landscape and quietness of a hot summer day. I would sit on a large stone at the side of a litchi plantation just outside the village, enjoying the view over the fields and forested slopes that stretched down into the lowland area towards Chiang Mai. Or, I would sit on a stool in front of a Hmong friend's house that provided a good view of the cultivated mountain slopes surrounding the village and try, from a distance, to make out the ever-changing crops in season at the time. Very often, I would also relax under a shady jackfruit tree on the small village square, joining a number of Hmong women stitching and chatting the afternoon away, taking pleasure in their company.

Sitting in one of these places, enjoying the landscape, the company and the atmosphere, I was acutely aware that *my* perception and appropriation of the surroundings and situations most likely differed from those of the Hmong villagers (see also Wassmann 1992).[4] The landscape and situations we initially see and experience and the space "produced through local practice and which we come to recognise and understand through fieldwork and through ethnographic description and interpretation" (Hirsch 1995: 2) are not identical (cf. Amanor 2002: 126; Schechner 2002: 619; Gow 1995:

---

[4] Perception is the product of taking in a stimulus, passing this stimulus on as a sensory impression, and evaluating this stimulus by the brain. Learned, "sedimented" experiences influence how and what we perceive. Sensory consciousness is always structured by our culture, as Constance Claasen (1991: 59) has shown (cf. Beer 2000: 6).

43-44). In this respect, British anthropologist Peter Gow (1995: 43), who has conducted fieldwork in Brazil, writes: "Being able to see Amazonia has nothing to do with sight as naïve perceptual experience." Spaces, whether geographical or socially enacted, are endowed with meaning; a meaning closely related to practice and experience that is not merely perceptible by sight.

This difference between "unreflexive forms of experience" (Bourdieu [1972][5] 1996: 86) and the form of "experience beyond everyday" (Hirsch 1995: 4) correspond both to landscapes and more generally to all spaces of human action and interaction. When I look at mountain fields with lush, green dry rice plants slightly bending in the afternoon sun, I find them beautiful. A Hmong villager who looks at the same scenery might have totally different associations, connected to his own experiences and background: For example, he might contemplate the hard work it takes to till the soil or be concerned about the yields needed to supplement the family's subsistence. Whereas I sit among a group of embroidering Hmong women and enjoy their peaceful chatter, these women might experience the situation very differently: For example, they might think of conflicts among villagers; feel socially obliged to join the women in the square instead of taking time to rest; or worry about the painstaking work involved in embroidering the family's clothes for the next Hmong New Year's festival. When I sit at the corner of the litchi plantations stretching towards the lowlands, I see the area as part of a Hmong village located near Chiang Mai in the North of Thailand, about 9.000 kilometres away from Germany. A Hmong farmer might have completely different associations, perceiving the area as part of a Hmong village in the vicinity of several other Hmong communities where members of his clan live. These villages in turn form part the "Hmong Mountains", which extend from the original homeland in China to Vietnam, Laos, Thailand, Burma and other countries around the world which host

---

[5] When citing influential texts that have been reprinted and/or translated, the date of the original edition is given in brackets.

Hmong diaspora groups (see also Tapp 2002a: 13; Geddes 1976: 232).[6] This work aims to understand the ways the Hmong are alive to, experience and give meaning to the world around them.

When we look at landscape or experience a situation, we do *not* perceive the spaces we live in and are part of neutrally. Instead, we instantly and usually unconsciously link our surroundings to a multiplicity of socio-culturally shaped experiences, values, and ideas. People establish very specific and different relationships with the spaces they inhabit. The nature of the relationship between people and spaces depends on "objective" conditions of the spaces that are potentially and actually used and inhabited, or imagined.[7] It also depends on "subjective" perceptions, symbolic connotations, and meanings that are linked to the space. Perceptions and meanings of spaces are both the infrastructure and the result of "culture" because culture provides the human agent with the resources to make sense of and classify "the world around us" (Durkheim and Mauss 1963).

One focal point of contemporary discussions in anthropology and related disciplines deals with the nature of connections between spaces and places on the one hand, and with culture and socio-cultural identities on the other. Faced with dissolving boundaries, a vanishing of the unity of culture and locality as well as of places and local conditions, anthropologists must determine which relation exists between cultures, social groups, and the spatial (Kokot 2000: 192). People perceive of places in very varying ways, imbue spaces with different meanings, and are "alive to the world around

---

[6] According to Nicholas Tapp (2002a: 3, 10), the Hmong are a "classic refugee diaspora", rather than a "labour" or "trade" diaspora. This is because the diaspora Hmong have formed a "community of suffering" morally united by a deep nostalgia about their loss of "homeland" in China. The "dominant identity narrative" (Julian 2003: 125) among the Hmong worldwide can be described as a quintessential "refugee story". This includes a loss of a book and the violent background of the group's dispersal from China. In chapter five this is described in more detail. For the nine common features of a Diaspora see Robin Cohen 1997: 26 (cf. Dorsch 2000, Tomforde 1997)

[7] Eric Hirsch (1995: 4) states that space (in contrast to place), and representation (in contrast to image) have a perceived "potentiality" ("the way we could be"). The purest form of potentiality is emptiness itself. For example, in many regions of the world, sacred sites and places are physically empty or largely uninhabited, and situated at some distance from the populations for which they hold significance (see also Bourdieu [1972] 1996: 2).

them" differently (Basso 1996: 54). Analysing these perceptual differences gives insight into apparently contradictory processes of dissolving boundaries and increased interconnections on the one hand and the increased importance and interconnectedness of the local with worldwide change on the other (Kokot 2000: 193, see also Dracklé and Kokot 1996: 13). Cultural identities are shifting due to profound global changes; these identities can mentally reunify people across vast distances and prevent people such as the Hmong from being isolated in "local, minoritized pockets around the globe" (Schein 2004: 287). Henk Driessen writes in this regard:

> "[T]ransience is one of the most striking characteristics of the world at the close of the second millennium. [...] In sum we have to deal with the changing identity of object and subject, with issues of power, authority, voice and signature." (Driessen 1996: 291, 293)

In other words, it has become increasingly important to do justice to the fact that cultures, identities, and spaces are no longer (and may never have been) identical with geographical locales. As a result, it is necessary to formulate concepts of spaces and places in terms of social relations because the spatial should, inter alia, be conceptualised as "social relations stretched out" (Massey 1996: 2). One way to conceptualise spaces is to regard them as closely linked to socio-cultural practices, as both the outcome of action as well as the medium or structure of action. This approach is inherent in the term "cultural spatiality".[8] Already in the 1970s, geographer Henri Lefebvre ([1974] 1996: 6, 143) drew our attention to the fact that space is lived before it is perceived, and constituted before it can be "read". Lefebvre underscores that cognitive or conceptual space cannot be dissociated from "lived" space and can no longer be understood as an object. Rather, it needs to be seen as closely related to human action. German philosopher Martin Heidegger (1986: 102) also emphasises that spatial order and the spatiality of all things are derived from human action. Contemporary theoretical approaches to

---

[8] For an early ontology of spatiality see geographer John Pickles 1985: 156.

space therefore understand space as a conceptualisation of physical-material reality *and* as a medium through which a relationship between socio-cultural and physical-material conditions is created (Werlen 2003: 7). This approach, applied throughout this book, views space as more than something physical and external to the social context and social action. Instead it includes, as cultural spatiality, the constitution, appropriation, and experience of spaces through socio-cultural activity (Hesse 2003: 91-92, Dickhardt 2001: 21-22). Spatiality is an immediate part of every human culture; it is a symbolic and symbolising medium of action and a system of social order, communicative action, classification, values and appropriation of spaces (Hesse 2003: 93).

Conceptualising spatiality as an aspect and outcome of socio-cultural practice enables the social scientist to see places and spaces as integral parts of the constitution, appropriation, and experience of the world people inhabit and are alive to. It opens up alternative ways of viewing the lifeworld of a people because all spaces and places - either real, imagined or potential - that constitute parts of a society's actions can be included in the analysis of a group's spatiality. The concept of cultural spatiality is useful in the sense that it (a) includes all facets of a people's socio-cultural practice, (b) includes all real, imagined and potential places, interconnections between people and areas and interrelations between the past, present and future, as well as between the living and the dead, and (c) provides an approach to spatial structure as it is constituted through human experience and practice.

The main objective of the book is to analyse the cultural spatiality of the Hmong inhabitants of two communities in northern Thailand, where I conducted ethnographical fieldwork from April 2001 until March 2002. The study of cultural spatiality, first and most of all, necessitates an ethnographical research that assesses the group's culture as holistic as possible, the emphasis laid on practices and structure related to the spatial. The manifold topics that need to be tackled to gain an understanding of the ways the Hmong are "alive to the world around them" and of their cultural spatiality include the Hmong people's history of migration, (religious) worldviews and ritual practices, social and economic activities and its spatial dimensions, political structures, social (inter-ethnic) relations and networks, gender and age differences, behavioural patterns, everyday actions, future perspectives, as well as people's norms, wants, needs, and values.

Theoretical approaches to space

Even though theoretical studies on space have increased rapidly within the past two decades, ethnographic accounts that deal with the local constitution of cultural spatiality, perceptions and experiences of spaces and places are still few numbered. Concerning a theory of spatiality in anthropology, theoretical and methodological examination of the topic spatiality is still in its initial phase (Dickhardt and Hauser-Schäublin 2003: 18, 22; Dickhardt 2001: 14, 24-25; Feld and Basso 1996a: 4-6; cf. Gupta and Ferguson 1997c: 2).

In most anthropological studies in the past, space was to be an intuitive term, not a theoretically analysed and methodologically developed research concept. In other words, space and group perceptions of space were not incorporated as an active analytical variable (Hirsch 1995: 1-2; Geertz 1988: 4-5, see also Soja 1989). For the past two decades, the literature on space and place has increased rapidly. The result was the elaboration of the spatial approach, including an attempt to develop a "theory of cultural spatiality". The expanding field encompasses an extensive, interdisciplinary range that includes professional photographers, social anthropologists, human geographers, psychologists, archaeologists, and historians, to name only a few.[9]

Theoretically as varied as the questions they ask, authors on space and place include scholars who emphasise postmodernist fragmentation and deterritorialisation (e.g. Clifford 1997; Olwig 1997; Waters 1995; Appadurai 1991). They also include scientists who insist that grand theory (of Marx and Gramsci, for example) remains crucial to the understanding of the changing

---

[9] For a good critical review of diverse approaches to space and place as part of a "new" regional geography, see Benno Werlen, 1997.

territoriality of the contemporary world (e.g. Harvey 1995). Researchers and practitioners who are concerned with cultural spatiality, built environments, political geographies, and other aspects of the spatial realisation of human social and cultural life now exist in great numbers (e.g. Dickhardt and Hauser-Schäublin 2003; Winslow 2002; Dickhardt 2001; Roß 2001; Rapoport 2002, 1982; Gupta and Ferguson 1997, 1992; Hauser-Schäublin 1997; Feld and Basso 1996; Hayden 1995). In the often theoretical treatises, spaces and spatiality are now widely understood as constituted, appropriated and experienced by people and their actions, as spheres shaped through cultural difference, historical memories, social organisation and praxis.

In the 1990s, studies on space and spatiality were closely linked to postmodern discussions about the emplacement of culture in times of globalisation, transnationality and deterritorialisation.[10] Within the field of anthropology, for example, Arjun Appadurai's concept of "global ethnoscapes" (1991: 192) has been very influential in the globalisation debate.[11] Appadurai relates "ethnoscapes" to the cultural reproduction of groups, which can no longer be easily localised but instead have become increasingly connected to a global distribution of persons, groups, relations and imaginations characterised by motion and interactivity. In other words, within "the landscape of the global cultural flow, it is apparently no longer possible to study culture as a discrete closed system." (Yamashita 2003: 3)

---

[10] I agree with Lewellen's valuable examination of the phenomenon "globalisation" in relation to anthropology: "Indeed, there are many definitions of globalisation – late capitalism, post-Fordism, post-modernity, space-time compression, and so forth; some of these suggest a quantum break with the past, others a smooth evolution. What is important to the anthropologist is that the links, both obvious and subtle, be recognized, articulated, and theorized in relation to the lives of real people. Unlike dependency and world-system theories, implicit in any definition of globalisation is the idea that localization, regionalisation, and globalisation are all part of the same system, or, if one finds the term "system" anachronistic, at least that the different levels are mutually and possibly dialectically interrelated. The bird's-eye view problem disappears altogether; global and local are one." (Lewellen 2002: 75)

[11] Appadurai speaks of multiple dimensions of landscapes, including people, media, technology, finance, and ideology, each of which he calls a "–scape". Scapes make up the "building blocks" of "imagined worlds" that bind individuals in relationships beyond bound places such as neighbourhoods or nation-states (Appadurai 1991: 33). Scapes thus express the fragmented, discontinuous, and heterogenous character of postmodernity.

Akhil Gupta and James Ferguson (1997a: 2-3, cf. Gupta and Ferguson 1992) stress that cultural places have never been closed entities. Instead, they have always been part of "interconnected spaces", and tendencies of deterritorialisation have always been connected to tendencies of reterritorialisation, giving new meaning to uniquely constituted places. Karen Olwig and Kirsten Hastrup (1997: 11-12) developed this approach further, pointing out that both unique localities and typical "cultural sites" like temples and family homes are cultural institutions that are important in the constitution of socio-cultural structure - also and perhaps especially in times of globalisation. Despite these valuable conceptualisations of spatiality, these distinct theoretical and methodological concepts have not yet been integrated into a comprehensive theoretical framework in anthropology as Michael Dickhardt and Brigitta Hauser-Schäublin (2003: 19) emphasise.[12] These two German anthropologists (Dickhardt 2001; Hauser-Schäublin 1997, 2003) have worked towards the development of a "theory of cultural spatiality" as the starting point for an extensive social and cultural scientific discourse on spatiality (Dickhardt and Hauser Schäublin 2003: 18).[13]

I agree with Deborah Winslow, who believes that "part of being here is a sense of there" (2002: 156). As the example of the Hmong communities studied shows, people can be part of "here" and of "there" and do indeed

---

[12] More advanced attempts to develop this theoretical framework in geography and sociology have been based on works of Michel Foucault (e.g. [1967] 1991), Henri Lefebvre (e.g. [1974] 1996) and Anthony Giddens (e.g. [1984] 2001). See for example publications by geographers Allan Pred 1983, 1990; Benno Werlen 1995, 1997, 2003; and Nigel Thrift 1996, 2003.

[13] Recent conferences on space elucidate the current relevance of the topic to the social sciences and reveal that a great number of scholars have participated in the attempt to develop a sound theory of space. See, for example, the conference "Passages: On the Global Construction of Locality", 14th to 15th November 2003 in Berlin, Germany, and the conference "Locating the Field: Metaphors of Space, Place and Context in Anthropology", 29th to 31st March 2004 in Durham, England, attended by more than 60 scholars from around the globe who discussed diverse approaches to the spatial (see http://www.theasa.org./asa04 for a downloadable conference booklet with abstracts). Since 1998, the journal Space and Culture had brought together interdisciplinary theoretical work on social spaces of everyday life.

have a sense of how their own place fits within larger spatial systems of Thai society and the world (see also Driessen 1996: 287; Geertz 1996: 262).

People constitute and experience their identity in delimitation to the "other" as well as by acting from their position within and in relation to larger systems. In other words, despite processes of globalisation and deterritorialisation and changes in spatial order and behaviour, most people still identify with localities; indeed, they relate to localities, perhaps more than ever, with a creativity and variety that often includes the meso and macro level, as well (Benko 1997: 23-26). Boundary-exceeding cultural currents are integrated and incorporated into specific local cultural contexts. These connect the local to the global and vice versa (Hannerz 1996: 28, 175-177).

The concept of cultural spatiality

The spatiality approach can provide a number of valuable insights. First, it can provide a new perspective on the global, regional, and local, while shedding light on all spheres of social relations. Second, it can contribute to an improved understanding of the way these spheres are linked and how they affect one another. In other words, one advantage of the spatiality approach is that movements and contacts to all spheres (for example, the "outside" and the supernatural) as well as to imaginary and potential places and spaces are integrated into a broad socio-spatial analysis of the culture. Anthropological research today needs to go beyond simple dichotomies of local versus global, provincial versus cosmopolitan, static versus mobile. In this regard, the concept of cultural spatiality extends our understanding of locality, community, and other real, imagined and potential spaces involved in socio-cultural practice. It focuses on various social and political processes of place to describe "embodied practices that shape identities and enable resistances" (Gupta and Ferguson 1997a: 6; cf. Shields 1997: 198). For example, as the discussion of my field data shows, the Hmong create their own world by integrating and transforming influences from the global, national, and regional levels into inherent aspects of their own culture. In spite of the fact that the Hmong regard themselves as part of a larger diaspora community and maintain extended clan networks, local places in Thailand are nonetheless of utmost importance. They are fundamentally an intersection of moving bodies and are defined essentially by the set of movements and actions that take place within it. As Shinji Yamashita (2003: 5) correctly notes, even translocal cultures cannot exist without a place, "indeed there is no culture without place. Culture has to be localized." Via their specific relationship to places and their larger cultural spatiality, most Hmong are socio-culturally "anchored" in Thailand even though, as an ethnic minority, they exert little power over socio-economic and political domains and spaces that are largely dominated by the majority society.

For Michel de Certeau (1980: 208), a place is an immediate configuration of positions. It implies stability. Places have not lost their significance in times of globalisation and transnationality (cf. Rössler 2003: 212). Processes which initially appeared as a deterritorialisation of life contexts and a loss of meaning of places and distances ultimately turn out to be an alteration of the role of places and spaces rather than a loss of fundamental meanings of the spatial. Possibilities for spatial actions have changed, but the fact that human action is always also spatial action has not (Dickhardt and Hauser-Schäublin 2003: 16; see also Hengartner and Kokot and Wildner 2000: 11). Cultural spatiality thus needs to be regarded as a main component of the recent reality of cultures, which are increasingly delocalised and interconnected but at the same time re-localised in a new fashion. The concept of spatiality helps to transcend the superficially marked boundaries between territories, villages and cities, the spheres of the living, the ancestors and supernatural beings, and ethnic groups and nations within a broad spectrum of human notions and actions (Rössler 2003: 212). New experiences of mobility, migration and communication link distant places and alter the spatial allusion of groups and actors. Through an increasing and unprecedented interconnectedness of places, people and experiences, life realities and identity constructions assume a multilocality in which the interconnectedness of reference points becomes important (Dickhardt and Hauser-Schäublin 2003: 15).

As my research of the Hmong exemplifies, the villagers have always been and remain interconnected to spheres outside their villages, regions and even countries via trade, mass communication systems, tourism, government and development programs and through an influx of national and international researchers (cf. Jónsson 1998). For example, a Hmong woman who leaves her village in the mountains only five times per year can nonetheless be actively connected to the world market through the lilies or tomatoes she plants and sells to traders, can have friends in Canada through visiting tourists and researchers, and can remain informed about international developments via television and radio. In spite of the Hmong's increasing interconnectedness, the local remains of vital importance. For Ulf Hannerz (1996: 27), the local enters into dialogue with global, boundary-exceeding cultural flows "in which a variety of influences come together, acted out perhaps in a unique combination, under those special conditions." Thus globalisation is not a phenomenon "out there", but rather the sum of various alterations, interconnections and paraphrases that are present and expressed in our everyday life, not only in New York, London or Berlin, but also in the mountain areas of northern Thailand.

It is the virtue of the spatiality approach that it can simultaneously incorporate both "here" and "there", the local level and the (sometimes imagined) other levels – local, regional, national, global, even supernatural – into the present, past and future. The spatiality approach can take the extralocality and interconnectedness of societies and cultures into account and is thus able to provide an integrative method to bridge local and larger frames of analysis in accordance with anthropology's long tradition of contextualisation (Burawoy 2000: 26-27). The relatively new approach of cultural spatiality provided me with an alternative but nonetheless genuinely anthropological concept to reconstruct and interpret life worlds that are situated in multidimensional local, regional, national, global spaces as well supernatural spheres.

Following this argument, Hmong cultural spatiality can only be understood within its formative history and its interconnections. These include, for example, other Hmong groups in the diaspora, neighbouring societies, the wider world, the "Otherworld" of the supernatural agents. In their temporal interconnection, they include the ancestral past and perceptions of the future. By means of their socio-cultural structures and everyday practices, the Hmong "situate" themselves in time and space and constitute a spatiality that differs from the cultural spatiality of neighbouring societies such as the Thai and Karen. In fact, Hmong social networks, despite their spatial attenuation, are marked by "endosociality" (Friedman 1997: 287), meaning that the networks are largely exclusive to the group and characterised by a close social proximity of their members.

The theoretical approach to cultural spatiality, as explained in detail in the theoretical chapter of the book, is a holistic approach. It includes socio-cultural activity and symbolic meaning, in the past, the present and future, in specific localities and in imagined or potential places for action, in a local place and in a distant place, in the sphere of the living and the sphere of supernatural agents. This embedded approach examines not only actual social contacts and practices but also cognitive and potential ones that might be understood as located outside the groups' reachable boundaries. Only an analysis that attempts to examine interactions at all these levels, their meanings, interpretations and aspects of further action, can fully illuminate the cultural spatiality of a people. The researcher is thus confronted with the task of practically assessing human practices and spatial structures at all relevant levels in the field.

The empirical study of settings

One way to empirically assess spatial action and structure in the field is to apply the concept of setting, mainly developed by Amos Rapoport (2002).[14] According to Rapoport, a setting is a place or a zone in known or imagined space that is associated with specific activities and purposes (Rapoport 2002:

---

[14] Rapoport's paper was first published in Tim Ingold's first edition (1994) of the "Encyclopedia of Anthropology", which meanwhile is in its fourth printing.

462). Places are transformed into settings via social activities of various kinds. Members of a society possess implicit knowledge, which enables them to "read" their built environment and thus to know how to behave in specific settings. This embodied knowledge provides for a reciprocity of perspectives among people using a particular setting. Settings thus consist of common understandings of spatial arrangements and behaviour. These socially structured spaces help to organise human interaction (Crabtree 2000: 3).

Even though the setting concept is relatively straightforward, the reconstruction of spatially differentiated everyday behaviour in its various settings is not a trivial task. This is all the more the case because symbolic, communicative, temporal, gender and generation specific features must be taken into account. Historical experiences, current contexts, outside influences, and socio-economic, political and legal conditions must all also be considered. The entire system of settings and their meanings result in a complex image of spatially structured lifeworlds. The settings relevant for a group may be summarised into subclasses and classes that constitute, in their totality, the cognitive map or mental model of a group.

People are not always aware of the spatial structure they inhabit and the culturally specific meanings of their mental models even though they govern their daily existence. For the ethnographer, formalised social institutions are much easier to observe than normalised structures that exist on the cognitive level. Yet within these phenomenal elements, embodied practices, and interactional competences of a group is located the inherent social structure of the world as it is acquired via perception and experience (Grøn 1991: 114). The researcher nonetheless must always remain aware that spatiality forms only *one* potential resource for social organisation and structure alongside many other possible structuring social processes. The concept of spatiality can thus, along with other approaches to social processes of structuration and social praxis, be used to comprehend social formation and other human concepts (cf. Tanner 1991: 39).

Mental model: The Hmong Mountains

A mental model reflects the world as it is imagined by a group, and cannot be regarded as a one-to-one image of the physical, material or social environment. Rather, a mental model includes internalised representations of the spatial lifeworld. These models should be externalised as "re-representations" in the course of participant observation that pays special attention to pervasive discourses and spatial topics among the group under study.

My central thesis is that the cognitive map or mental model through which Hmong understand their lifeworld is represented by the concept of the Hmong Mountains (*hmoob ntshuab roob*), a concept that is more or less unconsciously established among my subject group even though the term is employed directly in village discourse.[15] Discourses are always linked to a set of practices, although both discourse and practice may change and develop independently. In other words, the practices inspired by a given discourse are not inextricably bound to the discourse and vice versa, although they can mutually influence one another (Thayer 2000: 208). When a Hmong villager is asked by a Thai lowland farmer or a member of another ethnic mountain group "Where are you from?", most Hmong respond "from the Hmong Mountains," even if their village is only a forty minute drive from Chiang Mai, one of the largest cities of Thailand. The Hmong term *hmoob ntshuab roob* is also frequently employed by Hmong villagers to describe the spaces they inhabit in a cognitive and practical sense. Expressions like "In the Hmong Mountains, we do things in this way", and "Our life is in the Hmong Mountains" are frequently voiced.

The Hmong Mountains is a cognitive concept, a model that was thoroughly investigated during fieldwork and will be elucidated in its full dimension in the course of this book. In the brief outline of the concept, it is important to emphasise that it includes, in geographic terms, the

---

[15] See also Jürg Wassmann's (1993: 35) accounts on the difficulty of externalising knowledge and models regarding daily walking routes of the Yupno on Papua New Guinea.

mountainous areas of South China, Vietnam, Laos, Thailand and Burma. At times it might also include other (partly lowland) regions of current Hmong settlement in, for example, Australia, France, North America and French Guyana. In addition to describing what is often an imaginary geographical terrain belonging to the Hmong, the Hmong way of life in the mountains includes many socio-cultural features that are inherent in the concept. It is a model that provides the stateless Hmong with an area they can call their own and helps to draw ethnic boundaries between Hmong and Thai lowland society on the one hand and between the Hmong, originally from China and spread over Southeast Asia, and other ethnic mountain groups with a different background on the other. When places like the mountainous areas of the Hmong habitat are actively perceived and incorporated within embodied practice, the physical landscape becomes connected to the mental model, the cultural landscape of mind (Basso 1996: 55; Stock 1994: 323-325; Agnew 1993: 263).

Outline of the book

This book is organised into two parts: The first part discusses theoretical approaches and the context of ethnic mountain peoples in Thailand. The second part analyses my research among the Hmong and ethnographic data I acquired in the field in order to understand the group's spatiality. Those readers mainly interested in the Hmong might want to concentrate their reading on this second part of the book.

In chapter one, a theoretical chapter on culture and spatiality, different methodological contemplations are discussed. These include the question whether culture remains a viable concept and whether cultures continue to have an abiding emplacement in an age of globalisation and deterritorialisation. A clear definition of culture and its relationship to spaces and places is essential, particularly because the concept of culture underlies theoretical approaches to spaces and cultural spatiality. Most studies on space have drawn in some fashion upon Pierre Bourdieu's and Anthony Giddens' "structuration school of thought". I therefore discuss their central ideas before embarking upon an outline of new approaches towards a "theory of cultural spatiality". Processes of spatial structuration are then described as *cultural* processes of structuration while cultural practice is conceptualised as practice innately connected to the *spatial*. In order to illustrate and elucidate the theoretical ideas, selected empirical examples from the Hmong research are already integrated in this part of the work.

Chapter two outlines the context for the Hmong and other ethnic mountain groups in Thailand, with special emphasis on contested spaces and contested resources. This chapter provides the reader with the necessary background to understand the overall setting, opportunities and impediments confronted by the Hmong and other minority groups in Thailand. Since I conducted a previous study in two Karen communities in the northern Thai Doi Inthanon Nationalpark (April 1999 – March 2000), my examples mainly draw from the Hmong and the Karen, the two groups with which I am most familiar. The discussion in this chapter focuses primarily on the expansion of control by the Thai state and other national and international agencies across the historically formed geopolitical space of northern Thailand, and the repercussions for the ethnic groups that live in these areas. Before environmentalist discourse and the awareness of growing environmental problems slowly reached Thailand in the 1970s, the forested mountainous areas of northern Thailand were perceived as uncivilised and wild habitat. Ethnic groups inhabiting this region were judged accordingly. As a result of the influence of international environmentalism and politics and of the rapid degradation of natural resources, "modern" ideas, which begin to conceive of natural resources as valuable "national assets", have gained widespread public and media support in Thailand. As a result, the ethnic mountain groups who live in the remaining forest areas are generally seen as "intruders" in a geopolitical space they have long occupied, in some instances dating back even before the foundation of the Thai state. In other words, in a process of "nature-making", geographical space in Thailand has become politicised, and peripheral peoples have become in many instances marginalized.

The second part of the book discusses the research among the Hmong and my ethnographical findings. When necessary, these are compared to data acquired by other scholars. The aim is to provide the reader with an understanding of contemporary Hmong culture as experienced in two Hmong villages from April 2001 until March 2002. Chapters three through ten provide the ethnographical background data necessary to comprehend Hmong cultural spatiality and the mental model of the Hmong Mountains, understood as a representation of the Hmong spatiality. Chapter eleven then outlines the "rhythm of Hmong spatiality" expressed in daily routine and in the cycle of recurring daily, weekly and monthly activities, events and rituals by way of examples from the village setting.

The second part of thebook starts with chapter three. This chapter relates to the context of the empirical study in two Hmong communities in the mountainous North of the country. In addition to a description of living and research conditions, the methodology, the ethnographic methods, and research strategies which I employed, are discussed. Since the ethnographer functions as the "main research tool" during fieldwork, the context of my fieldwork is discussed in detail to provide an insight into the background of the conditions of the study as well as to enable an assessment of the results.

Chapter four provides general information on the two primary research sites, Mae Sa Mai and Ban Phui, for a better understanding of the history, political organisation, developments and main characteristics of contemporary Hmong villages. It also serves as contextual information for the research results.

Chapter five examines the origins of the Hmong in China and the long history of migration from this "ancestral home" to countries of Southeast Asia and other parts of the world. It is explained why the Hmong can be defined as a diaspora group, and which strategies have been chosen, especially in the United States, to maintain Hmong cultural identity translocally as well as transnationally. Especially in the first half of the twentieth century, the Hmong in Thailand followed patterns of migration that permitted the practice of pioneer swidden farming for opium poppy cultivation. These repeated movements to new land gradually came to a halt after the 1960s. The subsequent decades have been marked by processes of sedentarisation as well as new resource use systems.

The aim of chapter six is to approach Hmong spatiality by an analysis of Hmong religious structures and practiced forms of beliefs in the two research villages. Included in this chapter are expositions of Hmong cosmological spaces and forms of geomancy, an overview of the functions of the religiously trained specialists, and an outline of the most important aspects of Hmong rituals. Elucidating the Hmong religious structures and practices provides an understanding of the way the Hmong people perceive the world in cosmological terms and the way they relate between the spheres of the living and the supernatural, the past, and the present.

Chapter seven explains the different levels of social organisation that are closely linked to Hmong kinship categories. I demonstrate the importance of household and family structure, understood as the symbolic representation of the cosmos, and of the lineage and clan relationships as they help the Hmong to simultaneously maintain social proximity *and* a wide spatial extension of the Hmong within Thailand and other countries around the globe. The scope of these endosocial networks is discussed following the examination of general gender differences that touch upon all spheres of Hmong socio-cultural structure and praxis.

Chapter eight complements these results by elucidating the interethnic positioning of the Hmong within Thailand. I show how the Hmong draw boundaries between themselves and other groups such as the Thai or the Karen. Identity formations and future perspectives of the Hmong youth are integrated in this chapter to highlight possible generational differences between the old and the young, and to provide an outlook on potential future developments.

In chapter nine, a substantial part of the book is devoted to past and present transformations of Hmong economic structures and practices and the socio-spatial dimensions of the Hmong economy. The transformation in natural resource practices is elucidated in its relationship to other economic activities. This reveals how the Hmong relate to their physical environment. It also demonstrates the extent to which Hmong practices are formed by outside influences. Finally, I discuss which potentials and impediments for social action are inherent in economic structures of Hmong society. The analyses contained in this chapter help to understand the socio-spatial scope of Hmong economic activities and the ways the Hmong people relate to Thai society and the "outside world".

In chapter ten, it is then argued that the villagers of the research sites have undergone a change in environmental awareness, partly due to new sedentarised forms of settlement. The Hmong today thus relate differently to their land and natural resources than only two to three decades ago. The change in environmental perception is described using the example of the "sacred tree" (Hmong: *ntoo xeeb*) ritual, which has been redefined by the Hmong for resource conservation. To understand a group's cultural spatiality, it is important to analyse how the natural environment is perceived and practically understood, and to examine how people spatially orientate themselves within it. Orientation systems reveal aspects of cultural conception of the world because they constitute fundamentally different strategies of spatial conception. These focus, for example, either on ego-centred configurations, or on geo-centred orientations within a larger frame of reference like a landscape.

In chapter eleven, "the rythm of spatiality" and relevant settings of the Hmong communities studied are discussed, including their implications for spatial practice. These important prototypical settings, where the majority of village activities take place, include the household, the neighbourhood square, trips to mortuary rites in neighbouring villages and to the lowlands and the world outside of Thailand. The latter is mainly a largely imaginary setting for the majority of the villagers studied. Nonetheless, it has an impact on practices and (spatial) perceptions among the Hmong. The description of the different settings illuminates typical behavioural patterns connected to these "locales" that result in spatial structuration and vice versa. Insights from the analysis of settings shed light on the ways Hmong cultural spatiality is constituted.

The conclusion summarises my findings on Hmong spatial structuration principles and socio-cultural practices, which, by means of their dialectic relationship, constitute cultural spatiality. The main hypotheses of the book – namely that a representation of a typical mental model of the Hmong can be seen in the concept of the Hmong Mountains – is substantiated by the accumulation of results from the treatise's chapters. The concept of the Hmong Mountains demonstrates that the Hmong spatially constitute their own lifeworld in a manner that permits the maintenance of cultural identity in spite of their stateless, legally landless, and "fluid society" (Michaud 2004: 6) in Thailand.

PART ONE: THEORETICAL APPROACHES AND CONTEXT IN THAILAND

1 TOWARDS A THEORY OF CULTURAL SPATIALITY

In the course of this chapter, the terms culture and spatiality are defined and discussed to provide the basis for the examination of Hmong cultural spatiality in the empirical part of the book. Since a group's spatiality is defined here as both an element and an outcome of socio-cultural practice, the ambiguous term "culture" and its relation to space and place must be analysed prior to the theoretical discussion on space and spatiality. Given the complexity of the cultural and spatial topic, it is impossible for this book to reconstruct the entire, ongoing debate on culture and space. Instead, I discuss the concepts of culture and space in order to permit understanding of the relationship between the spatial and the cultural and provide insight into the development of a theory of cultural spatiality. My aim is thus not to describe all existing definitions and concepts of culture and space, but instead to formulate, within my ontological beliefs and relational understandings, the concepts of culture and space in order to arrive at a theoretical approach to cultural spatiality. In the empirical section, I then apply this approach to the ethnographical data assessed in the two Hmong villages.

In the following, I first discuss the anthropological debate on the utility of the concept of culture, and especially the debate on the emplacement of culture. In order to ontologically and epistemologically site my work in the field of anthropology, I describe my conception of culture and how it relates to spatial, and then proceed to examine the debate about spaces and places in the social sciences. I refer to the cornerstones of Bourdieu's and Giddens' "structuration school of thought" and proceed to a discussion of new developments toward a theoretical approach to cultural spatiality. Amos Rapoport's concept of setting is described as a substantial contribution to the assessment of cultural spatiality in the field and thus as an important contribution to the development of the theoretical approach. The accumulated meaning of important classes of sites and locations constitute the mental models that structure the internalised representations of the spatial lifeworld of a group such as the Hmong.

Are cultures emplaced?

In the past three decades, critical discussions on the character of the anthropological object and appropriate approaches to it have led to challenging questions on problems of representation, of authority, of accountability and to a fundamental rethinking of the concept of culture (Melhuus 2002: 79; cf. Kuper 2002: 143).[16] Proponents of feminist theory, postmodernism, and critical theory have reconsidered some of the basic tenets of the anthropological field. They have correctly pointed out the problematic nature of some aspects of anthropology, including the concept of culture. The problem within anthropology is no longer a debate on the existence of multiple definitions for the concept of culture. Instead, the recent debate questions whether the concept of culture, often labelled as an example of essentialist thought, is of any intellectual value whatsoever (Rubel 2003: 6-9). Such theorists have often called for the abandonment of the concept of culture, which is understood as outdated, in part also because of its conceptual bias that is closely linked to the dominance of nationalist thought in Western countries and to the contested notion of "whole cultures"

---

[16] This debate started with Geertz's article on the Balinese Cockfight (1972), an exemplary text for a "thick description", in Geertz's terms (1973). Even though this article has been the subject of a great deal of criticism for failing to represent local perceptions – a claim that Geertz made for anthropological texts – it has triggered a critical evaluation of ethnographic and anthropological texts as texts. Among the most influential are the collection of essays by Clifford and Marcus 1986, and Marcus and Fisher 1986, as well as Edward W. Said's (1978) critique on western perceptions of the Orient.

(Hastrup 2002: 27; cf. Kokot and Tölöyan and Alfonso 2004: 4; Rapport and Overing 2000: 93, Rodseth 1998: 55; Gupta and Ferguson 1992; Kahn 1989). Fredrik Barth (2002: 29-32) also criticises the concept of culture that led anthropologists to suppress variation in favour of models and overall patterns. The outdated approach to culture, Barth believes, impedes the development of generative models of social action, which he understands as an important research objective. Scholars who do not want to abandon one of the central concepts of anthropology thus argue for a fundamental transformation and revision of former ontological approaches to culture.

Cultural or culturing?

In order to escape the dilemma of an overly bounded concept of culture and its inherent essentialist character, Alan Barnard and Jonathan Spencer (2003: 142) want to replace the noun "culture" with the adjective "cultural". Tim Ingold (2002: 330) also argues for a revision in the idiom, opting for the adjective form or the verb "culturing", which he argues places a stronger emphasis on cultural practices than on culture as a delimited "object": "It might be more realistic, then, to say that people *live culturally* rather than that they *live in cultures*." (Ingold 2002: 330, italics in the original). Scholars critical of old approaches call for the overdue recognition that the concept of culture should be strongly related to practice in order to combine the perceiving and the acting agent. They thus conclude that it is necessary to openly acknowledge the important relationship between symbolic meaning and practice, between mind and body, between actor and action, and between concept and performance (cf. Rapport and Overing 2000: 97).

Symbolic formations only acquire meaning through action. Meaning, and thus culture, arises in the sphere of social action – in form of an "acted document" – in socially and historically contingent form rather than via relations of abstract entities in structural contexts (Geertz 1973: 10). Culture is thus a publicly acted document that acquires its specific meaning through interpretative acts of symbolically acting people. Approaches to cultures as processes of culturing, permit a synthesis between the symbolist meaning system and mental representations and concrete actions and behaviour, which is believed to be constitutive of meaning. Actors and embodied actions are no longer seen as passive instruments in a representational view of the body, and actions are no longer perceived as unconscious results of underlying structures of shared symbolic meaning. Instead, actors and their actions move to the centre of approaches to cultural phenomena (Friedman 1994: 206; cf. Hastrup and Olwig 1997: 3).

Rather than remaining wedded to a concept of culture as a conceptual structure comprised of representations of reality to orient, direct, and organise action in systems, we should understand culture as a constant flux of continual re-creation of "living, experiencing, thinking, affectively engaged human beings who follow [...] particular lifeways" (Rapport and Overing 2000: 96). Whether or not one replaces the noun "culture" by the adjectival "cultural" or the verb "culturing" is less important than revising a concept of culture as a complex whole. Instead, culture should be understood as an ideational notion, as one element among many in a more expansive class or category of phenomena - human action. Ideas are made immanent, operative, and, to a degree, intersubjectively accessible, only in necessary combination with other aspects and dimensions of existence. In their totality, these aspects – which include social relationships, will and purpose, and material context – comprise social action (Barth 2002: 35). This new approach to cultures or to culturing, which emphasises social action as a central constituent of any cultural phenomenon, is also useful to the assessment of spatiality. As shown below, spatiality is understood as constituted by the dialectic relationship between structures and cultural practice.

The concept of culture and ontological approaches to the culture concept are thus a contentious topic within anthropology. So, too, is the question of who may legitimately represent culture from "the native's point of view". The result has been a "crisis of representation" in ethnography, in the words of George Marcus and Michael Fischer (1986: 8). Postmodernists like the

American cultural theorist James Clifford argue that only people from within a culture can present their culture since "every version of an 'other', wherever it is found, is also the construction of a 'self', a process of self-fashioning" (Clifford 1986: 23-24). According to Clifford, an anthropologist is not able to describe a local culture, but only to "re-represent" the way of life of others. The question of the legitimate representation of a culture, the image that the outside world is to be given of that culture and its people, and the issue of who has the authority to create this representation, is a political issue that always involves power relations, as anthropologists have attempted to address in recent decades (Rubel 2003: 15; cf. Mischung 1999: 170-171; Duncan 1993: 40-47, 53-54).

A growing body of studies on culture within anthropology and many other disciplines emphasise the problem of how to define the difference between culture as a lived life, culture as re-representation or an invented construct, and culture as an analysable object (Paerregaard 1997: 39; cf. Hastrup 1993: 175). Culture is lived and acted by people, reconstructed by the researcher, and often consciously employed by people who wish to construct cultural identities. Nonetheless, Kirsten Hastrup and Karen Olwig (1997: 3) argue that the concept should not be discarded entirely, but rather should be "reinvented, as it were, through an exploration of the 'place' of culture in both the experiential and discursive spaces that people inhabit or invent." They understand the "siting of culture" (Hastrup and Olwig 1997: 11) as a dynamic process of self-understanding among people around the world, which also repositions the anthropological object. In other words, the concept of culture is not only transformed by heightened emphasis on human action but also by the incorporation of interrelations and constituted (real or imagined) spaces (see also Gowan and Ó Riain 2000: xii). Cultures are no longer - if indeed they ever were - characterised by homogeneity and boundedness. Instead, it is now acknowledged that cultures interpenetrate and emerge from one another. They are characterised by spatial extension and an interconnectedness on many levels. To give a concrete example of how interconnectedness needs to be included into anthropological studies, migrants or "travellers" (Clifford 1997: 39) who belong to a group but spend most of their time geographically separated from it, should nonetheless be seen as part of the communities studied since they often influence and reshape their home communities and vice versa.[17] Migration and travelling may even be a strong parameter in the self-definition of a people. For example, among the Hmong studied in northern Thailand, a number of villagers work outside their home area for months on end and many children spend most of their school year in distant locales in the Thai lowlands. These travellers and children might not be physically present in their village for more than one or two weeks per year. Nevertheless, they are regarded as important members of the communities, and they define themselves as such as well. Movement, connection to other places and interrelationships should thus always be one focus of anthropological studies. It is an important aspect of social life and of cultures that affects people in various places over an extended period of time. People do not need to be firmly settled in one location to be a member of a group. But does that mean, in an inversion of this argument, that cultures are completely unbound in place or space?

How do cultures relate to places?

A longstanding debate in theoretical anthropology is whether or not people are naturally (primordially) rooted in particular places. As a result of debates on globalisation and deterritorialisation and an apparently increasingly interrelated world, the "rootedness" of cultures has come under increasing attack (Lovell 1998: 1). Are cultures thus no longer sited in particular locations, but foremost characterised by transnationality?[18] Does cultural practice no longer involve particular places but take place in undefined

---

[17] For example, Deirdre McKay (2003) has conducted a valuable study on remittance economies in the northern Philippines that illuminates how remittances sent home by female Filipino overseas contract workers transform the landscape and resource use systems of local Filipino communities.

[18] According to Michael Kearney, transnationality describes a phenomenon in which "processes are anchored in and transcend one or more nation-states" (1995: 548).

spheres? Has the study of cultures concentrated so much on the interconnections of people and cultures that a "rootedness" or an emplacement of cultures is now a concept of the past?

In contemporary anthropology, two competing accounts of human relations to place and space exist. In fact, the polarisation of these two positions is indicative of the major dilemmas facing current anthropological theory. One approach to the human relation to places and spaces is expressed in the transience, the rootlessness, the migratory, the diasporic, the out-of-placedness that is believed to increasingly characterise populations, communities, and individuals around the world. James Clifford (1997: 7), for example, understands the social world of people as increasingly entangled. Clifford has been much criticised for his concept of vague and modern "contact zones" (Weiner 2002: 26). However, his belief that globalisation has led to homogenisation and loss of cultures on the one hand, but also to emergence, invention and "revitalisation" of the cultural on the other, has been widely accepted (Clifford 1988: 19).

The second concept of culture and its relation to places is represented, for example, in the contributions to the volume "Senses of Place" (Feld and Basso 1996). The authors of this volume attempt to detail the many dimensions of intimacy, knowledge, familiarity, history, and the attachment to particular places. This approach underlines that humans are centrally "beings in-place and em-placed, and that all of the other conventional aspects of social and cultural life are also varieties of events and practices bound to places" (Weiner 2002: 21).

Is it possible to reconcile these two seemingly contradictory views of extreme interconnectedness on the one side and human attachment to particular places on the other? Even before colonisation, communities were linked over great distances by routes along which objects, myths, and cult practices travelled and were exchanged. People were connected through the interchange of objects, languages, stories, and humans themselves and were intimately and anonymously entwined (Singer 1997: 18-19; King 1995: 8-10). Diaspora and migration seem to have been with us for a long time, in all parts of the world, as diaspora communities of the Jews and Chinese around the world and the Hausa in West Africa exemplify (Yang, Kou 2003: 273; see also Kokot 2002; Tomforde 1997). However, the great scale of this constant movement must be balanced with another major phenomenon of human existence – the tenacious and long-term locality that was on the basis of these movements and also created them. "[I]f the 'indigenous' already had their travelling cultures and contact zones, no less do we Westerners have had and still have our sedentariness and extreme localism, our embodied, instilled, and enstilled neighbourhoods and precincts of the everyday." (Weiner 2002: 26) Akhil Gupta and James Ferguson (1997b: 39) correctly conclude the debate on the question whether cultures are emplaced with a warning not to concentrate on either side of the argument:

> "We need to give up naïve ideas of communities as literal entities [...] but remain sensitive to the profound 'bifocality' that characterises locally lived existences in a globally interconnected world and to the powerful role of place in the 'near view' of lived experiences." (Gupta and Ferguson 1997b: 39)

In spite of the justified critique of what was once an overly rigid and essentialist concept of culture bound to particular localities, I agree that the importance of localities for human cultures cannot be negated. Instead, the interconnectedness of cultures and their peoples and the relation to (potential and imagined) spaces and places must be taken into consideration in the study of cultures and cultural practices (cf. Korff 2003; Otto and Driessen 2000; Barth 1969). Processes of reterritorialisation and relocalisation have already drawn our attention to the fact that individual and collective identities, contexts of meaning, and social networks can expand over several spatial or even temporally separated localities without losing their connection to certain places. James Weiner, for example, emphasises that "the inward space of the mind" (Weiner 2002: 26) cannot be seen as detached from the "sensual and embodied terrain" of emplaced human beings who are socially "enspaced". Weiner believes that James Clifford and

Towards a Theory of Cultural Spatiality 29

contributors to "Senses of Place" (Feld and Basso 1996) are largely indifferent to the latter. As my example of the two Hmong communities underscores, cultures have not become deterritorialised but instead are, as they might have always been to some degree, connected to more than only one locality through their socio-cultural practices.

Many people's everyday life is characterised by interfaces within diffuse and ambiguous relations between the local, regional and the global. Within this framework, individuals and groups reconstitute new contexts of spatiality and reproduce the way they conceive of themselves via dynamic processes of "place making" and "siting culture". By means of their social practice and interrelations, people define how this spatiality is constituted for their group and what is (potentially) an element of it. People thus find and constitute a place for themselves (Hastrup and Olwig 1997: 11-13). As explained in detail below, the Hmong people studied have constituted a place for themselves in Thailand, which can be seen to be represented in the mental model of the Hmong Mountains. This concept includes the concrete Hmong villages as well as (unknown) other Hmong places in the mountains, lowlands and other countries, potential places of action, and spheres of the spiritual beings "above the sky" and "underneath the earth". The concept of the Hmong Mountains exemplifies how the Hmong have constituted their own place in the world, which coincides with actual physical locations and includes interfaces that help to counter the experience of the lack of a "Hmong country" and the experience of marginalization in Thailand (cf. Rössler 2003: 213).

The example of the Hmong clarifies that humans primarily exist in a specific relationship to certain spaces – be they real in a material sense, experienced through social practice, cognitively constructed, or imagined and constituted through the sum of all former categories (cf. Rapoport 2002: 485). Social groups constitute their "inner" and possibly unbounded cultural sphere in clear distinction from the "outer" sphere of the "other" (cf. Long 1996: 50). Our understanding of culture has correctly shifted from the concept of a distinct lifestyle practiced by a territorially restricted group of people to a composite concept involving different, interconnected yet distinct life forms among people around the world. Processes of deterritorialisation and globalisation, while they have occasionally been exaggerated, have drawn our attention to the fact that cultures are not necessarily discrete, bounded, homogeneous, and stable systems, but instead are in contact with other cultures and can incorporate more than one locality. It is now widely acknowledged that societies are increasingly multicontextual and multicultural, as are individuals. As a result, life at the local level includes more than one (spatial) frame of reference and often appears more fragmented than in the (idealised) past (Otto and Driessen 2000: 11-12).

A group's spatiality is thus based on creative resources generated from local culture and from the experiences with interfaces and interconnections with other cultures. I thus acquiesce with Arjun Appadurai (1991: 196, 209) that people's "cultural spaces" do not always coincide with actual physical locations. However, I do not agree with Appadurai that the world merely consists of deterritorialised *ethnoscapes* and that cultures must thus be understood as disconnected from real existing localities. Instead, local places and "cultural sites" are still of historical and social significance as focal points of identification for people who, in their daily lives, are involved in a complex web of relations of local, regional, national and global dimensions (Hastrup and Olwig 1997: 11; see also Lang 2003). Ted Lewellen (2002: 81) argues that globalisation, in contrast to distinct cultural entities, is nothing more than context (see also Burawoy 2000: 32-35). In the future, acknowledging global links may be as routine in contextualising any study as describing the setting of fieldwork.

The aim of the book is to demonstrate that mental models such as the Hmong Mountains are one way to establish culture "on site" – the exact nature of this site, its extent and its relation to real or imagined localities is elaborated in my empirical section. The Hmong, as an ethnic minority in Thailand, are "seeking place" in a country where they are numerically marginal, thereby creating cultural difference and a specific cultural identity.

Socio-economically and politically disadvantaged peoples like the Hmong attempt to use processes of siting culture as a device to maintain identity and to insure group survival. Marshall Sahlins describes this process as a "more or less self-conscious fabrication of culture in response to imperious outside 'pressure'" (1993: 16). Local peoples do not attempt, and do not have the power, to overthrow the global order. Rather, their "inventions and inversions of tradition can be understood as attempts to create a differentiated space within it" (Sahlins 1993: 20).

In summary, the focus of anthropology has turned away from bounded entities and realities towards the diversity of ways in which humans establish and live their social lives. Instead of conceptualising cultures as naturally given facts, the role of the agent and its embodied praxis is emphasised. Because of the increasing possibility for interlinkage, the emplacement of people and cultures, and the role of localities for cultures have been disputed (Kokot and Tölölyan and Alfonso 2004: 1). Instead, debates about deterritorialised (ethno-)*scapes* have long determined discourses about cultural spatialities. The deterritorialisation and globalisation debate has rightly alerted us to the fact that cultures and peoples are increasingly interconnected and can also be characterised by a relation to multiple (potential and even imagined) spaces and places. However, in spite of this interconnectedness, localities have not lost their salience for peoples and their cultural practices.

My concept of culture is that it is *both* knowledge, symbolic meaning and habits of thought, *and* social praxis, interactions on several levels, communicative behaviour, and physical-material objects. I am convinced that cultures have, indeed, an abiding emplacement, no matter which form (real, imagined or potential) these places and the people's relation might be. I agree with Tim Ingold that people live culturally, meaning that cultures are part of an evident *activity*. Symbolic meaning and knowledge cannot exist without social practice. In other words, culture is structured through symbolically laden praxis, which is achieved and lived by people as socio-cultural agents.

At the centre of an approach to a "theory of cultural spatiality" also stands social praxis and culturally active people. This approach, as most scholars working on spatiality conceive it, is based on the works of Pierre Bourdieu's habitus concept and Anthony Giddens' structuration theory. In the following, the main concepts of space are differentiated, and then the "structuration school of thought" is briefly discussed, and finally supplemented by contributions to a further development of a theory of cultural spatiality. In the field and in the analysis of my ethnographical data, I combined these theoretical approaches with Nigel Rapoport's concept of setting ([1994] 2002), which enabled me to "practically grasp" the "nature of cultural spatiality". The study of settings permitted insight into cultural spatiality because cultural forms are articulated in daily social interaction and receive their meaning from this largely symbolic action.

Approaches to cultural spatiality

> "Where there is space, there is being."
> (Lefebvre [1974] 1996: 22)

As is true for the concept of culture, there is no universally accepted definition for the term "space". On the contrary, space has been transformed into a widely used idiom with multiple and often incompatible meanings (Nigel Thrift 2003: 1; Dickhardt and Hauser-Schäublin 2003: 22; Ingold 2002: 330; Rapoport 2002: 478; Massey 1996: 250; Soja 1980: 210). Consequently, *the* space does not exist. Instead, there are a great variety of space concepts.[19] The geographer Doreen Massey (1996: 146) believes one of the main outcomes of the debate on globalisation and deterritorialisation is that scholars are increasingly uncertain about the precise meaning of spaces and places and of the way "we relate to them". However, in a time of contested "rootedness of cultures", it is more important than ever before to

---

[19] For an overview of the development of different approaches to space within anthropology, see Schoenfelder 2000.

ascertain how people, societies and human cultures are related and relate to places and spaces.

> "An anthropology whose objects are no longer conceived as automatically and naturally anchored in space will need to pay particular attention to the way spaces and places are made, imagined, contested, and enforced." (Gupta and Ferguson 1992: 19-20)

Within the diverse definitions of space, it is possible to distinguish two main approaches in contemporary social science.[20] The first is a conventional concept of abstract space, while the latter is an alternative concept of human space. The conventional concept of abstract space departs from the assumption that space is a neutral thing, an objective container. Space, activity, and event are seen as separate from each other and as only contingently related. This view regards space as a simple surface for action, an abstracted geometry that is detached from meaning. Space is understood as universal and existing as a neutral container for people, their activities and cultures everywhere and anywhere in the world in the same manner (Tilley 1994: 9; cf. Giddens [1984] 2001: 110; Entrikin 1991: 134; Appadurai 1988: 39). This interpretation of space could permit, for example, the relative locations of cities and transportation routes to become the object of statistical analysis. This abstract space might be visible, for example, in large human-made plazas, or in looking down from an airplane at a urban pattern of roads. However, space is rarely encountered in such a "pure and abstract" fashion (Relph 1985: 25). While Western built spaces or environments tend to be geometric in design, non-Western societies may instead structure their spaces in social, ritual, or symbolic ways that might not be assessable by an abstract space approach (Rapoport 2002: 461).

Especially when focusing on practice and action, space cannot be simply seen as an object or "container", but must be considered as a

---

[20] For the distinctive ways "interpretative communities" of the social sciences relate space and culture to each other, see John Agnew (1993: 251-260).

conceptualisation of physical-material reality and as a medium that creates a relationship between socio-cultural and physical-material conditions. Space is more than physical and external to the social context and social action. It is instead a medium created *by* society. According to geographer Benno Werlen (2003: 7), space needs to be approached as a formal-classificatory phenomenon. It is formal as it relates to content characteristics of material conditions, and classificatory as it permits descriptions of social order and organisation (see also Entrikin 1991: 5-7). As such, space, or, more precisely, spatiality, entails opportunities and barriers for action and social communication, which are related to the physical-material and to the socio-cultural realm (Werlen 2003: 7). Spatiality is a basic aspect and a result of human action and interaction. The philosopher Immanuel Kant (1787: 59-70) was convinced that space could not be reduced to mere relations between objects. According to Kant, space (and time) is not an *a priori* category, but needs to be viewed as a mental frame of reference independent of objects. Similarly, Emile Durkheim ([1912] 1994: 11, 31) already demonstrated in the early part of the twentieth century that the experience of space is always socially constituted.[21]

Despite the long history of philosophical debate on space and spaceness, it is only since the 1980s that social scientists have started to actively reconceptualise space by recognising that space is not an unchanging given (Levinson 1992: 8). In the 1990s, anthropological interest in spatial concepts shifted to the construction of landscape as one of the primary sources of involvement for the establishment of human belonging and emplacement (Bender 2003, 1995; Hirsch 1995; Tilley 1994; see also Descola and Pálsson 1996).

---

[21] At the beginning of the last century, Emile Durkheim ([1912] 1994: 29-31) opened up the prospect of exploring and documenting a vast range of radically different space-time worlds – as opposed to metaphysical speculation – through empirical field research. At this early stage, Durkheim ([1912] 1994: 31) courageously proposed a correspondence between social structure and the society's notion of space and spatiality. For example, if an ethnic group's camps are laid out in a circle, it is most probable that their notion of cosmological space is also circular because spaces are structurally similar to the social form of a society.

In discourses on space, it has now been widely acknowledged that space itself may be primordially given, but the organisation, use, and meaning of the spatial is a product of appropriation, constitution, social translation, embodied action and experience (Lefebvre [1974] 1996: 77; Weichhardt 1990: 12; Soja 1980: 210). The geographer Edward Soja (1980: 211) speaks of the "socio-spatial dialectic", meaning that the spatial is socially and the social spatially constituted. This socio-spatial dialectic is part of the definition of the term "spatiality" employed by scholars like Michael Dickhardt (2001: 7-9) and Benno Werlen (2003: 3); it stands for spaces that are constituted, appropriated, experienced, formed, and imbued with meaning, or imagined by humans via social action. The term "spatiality" emphasises that the meaning of spatial dimensions of human life conditions are themselves constitutive. In other words, human beings both organise space and at the same time are organised by space (Rapoport 2002: 461).

As such, the spatial is involved in *action* and *experience* and cannot be divorced from it. It cannot exist apart from the events and activities within which it is implicated (Gupta and Ferguson 1997a: 4; Basso 1996: 54). Spatiality combines the cognitive, the physical and the emotional into a feature that may be reproduced but is always open to transformation and change (Lefebvre [1974] 1996: 86-87; Tilley 1994: 10). This concept of spatiality is not yet prevalent within alternative approaches to human space, even though it was introduced to the field of geography by John Pickles in 1985. However, all approaches to human space contribute in some fashion to the development of a theory of cultural spatiality. Amos Rapoport (2002: 483), for example, prefers the term "spatial organisation" when emphasising that behaviour and activity systems are organised relative to human spatial organisation of physical-material space. Henri Lefebvre's "Production de l'espace" ([1974]; translated edition 1996) continues to be influential in the debate. Lefebvre questions previous ontologies that conceptualised space as "empty space" or a container ([1974] 1996: 7, 44). Instead, he ([1974] 1996: 48-52) organises his understanding of space within occasionally analytically disputable separate concepts, including absolute space, abstract space, contradictory space and differential space (cf. Gregory 1997: 204; Shields 1997: 200-201). However, at the core of Lefebvre's spatio-analysis approach are the concepts of production and the act of producing *social space* ([1974] 1996: 26, 66-67).[22] Henri Lefebvre importantly underlines that social space is *lived* before it is *perceived*, and *produced* before it can be *read*, and thus emphasises that mental and conceptual space cannot be dissociated from "lived" space ([1974] 1996: 6, 143).

> "(Social) space is not a thing among other things, nor a product among other products: rather, it subsumes things produced, and encompasses their interrelationships in their coexistence and simultaneity – their (relative) order and/or (relative) disorder. It is the outcome of a sequence and set of operations, and thus cannot be reduced to the rank of a simple object. At the same time there is nothing imagined, unreal or 'ideal' about it as compared, for example, with science, representations, ideas or dreams. Itself the outcome of past actions, social space is what permits fresh actions to occur, while suggesting others and prohibiting yet others." (Lefebvre [1974] 1996: 73, parenthesis in the text)

Henri Lefebvre's conceptualisation of social space alerts us to the way it is structured and connected to rules about what is appropriate and expected in specific places. Space, he demonstrates, is directly related to patterns of social relations and social organisation and can be thus seen as part of a group's spatiality. Social relations thus possess a spatial dimension: they are inscribed into space and, at the same time, also produce that space (Lefebvre [1974] 1996: 182-183; cf. Hauser-Schäublin 2003: 84). Lefebvre ([1974] 1996: 191) comments on the basic duality of social space as always "both a

---

[22] As shown below, Pierre Bourdieu (1991) also refers to socially appropriated physical space by the term "social space". Geographer Rob Shields (1997: 186) argues that this term has become too ambiguous to be used: the reflexive character of the "production" and "perception" of space, for example, is often lost. He prefers the terms "cultural spatiality" and "spatialisation" because they include the cognitive and the practical habitus in the Bourdieusian sense (Shields 1997: 192, 194, 198). See also Jürgen Jensen 2004: 36-38.

field of action [...] and a *basis of action*" (italics in the original); it is at once an *actual* given and a *potential* locus.

We learn from Lefebvre that the spatial reflects social organisation and can itself be understood as an unconsciously created graphic display of the behavioural aspect of social organisation – unconscious because spatiality and its importance for the organisation of everyday life is largely unnoticed by a society's members (cf. Rapoport 2002: 462; Crabtree 2000: 10; Bourdieu 1991: 27; Tanner 1991: 21). Instead of being uniform and unchanging, the spatial is contextually constituted by human experiences and is expressed in an ensemble of subspaces, settings and places (Tilley 1994: 11).

The concept of spatiality, which is prefigured in Henri Lefebvre's (e.g. [1974] 1996) and Michel Foucault's (e.g. 1986, 1991) ontological notions on "other spaces", gained increasing salience in theoretical treatises on space. Most approaches that reconceptualise the spatial by relating it to social practice and social organisation in order to reach an understanding of human spaces are founded in some fashion on Pierre Bourdieu's "theory of practice" and Anthony Giddens' "theory of structuration" (Niranjana 2001: 36-37).[23] Along with Henri Lefebvre and Michel Foucault, Pierre Bourdieu and Anthony Giddens have employed a similar yet distinctive approach to practice and space to facilitate a shift away from a concept of space as mere physical form (cf. Dear 1997: 49). Instead, their conceptualisations of space demonstrate that the spatial is very much the substance within which social life exists. The importance of Bourdieu's and Giddens' approaches to contemporary theoretical debates on space cannot be overemphasised, as the German anthropologist Michael Dickhardt (2001: 59) notes.[24] The geographer Allan Pred (1983: 45) speaks of a "structuration school of thought"

---

[23] Bourdieu's and Giddens' approaches are not discussed in detail here since they have been sufficiently elaborated elsewhere (e.g. Dickhardt 2001: 12-17; Werlen 1997: 141-214; Thrift 1996: 1-50).

[24] Praxis-based theories elaborating on the work of Pierre Bourdieu and Anthony Giddens have become canonical in anthropology in the last decade, and new ethnographies regularly draw on a corpus of ideas about the routines of social life and their relationship to bodily dispositions, linguistic discourses, power relations, and social structures (Moore 1996: xi).

when discussing Bourdieu's theory of habitus and practice and Gidden's theory of structuration.[25]

The structuration school of thought

Giddens' and Bourdieu's theories of "social praxis as structuration" reject structural determinism and structural realism and permit the spontaneity of "free" subjects. The conception of "praxis as structuration" instead includes concepts of structure, structuration and agents that are correlatively linked to each other. This relational approach enables the researcher to constitutively analyse subjectivity and to relate it to objectivity. Bourdieu ([1972] 1996: 82-95) employs the concept of "habitus" and his theory of practice, which he also applies to the study of spaces. Anthony Giddens employs a theory of structuration and a stratification model of action. This model is always related to the knowledgeability of the actors who draw upon different forms of knowledge as "techniques of 'doing' social activity" (Giddens [1984] 2001: 22), which allows people to react to and influence a diverse set of social circumstances.

In addition to the importance of past experiences for the formation of habitus, Bourdieu ([1972] 1996: 167-170) emphasises the dialectic between the objective and subjective, between outer and inner structures, as both appropriate one another. Structures are thus understood as acquired and simultaneously reproduced through action. In other words, social action produces structures while actions are structured. This insight leads to the contention that habitus is the "structured structure" (Bourdieu [1972] 1996: 90). However, the dialectic between structure and praxis cannot be simply understood as a circular phenomenon that is simply reduplicated. It can be questioned or reformed during times of crisis when old habitual structures

---

[25] Geographer Nigel Thrift (1996: 68) also includes R. Bhaskar and D. Layder in this "structurationist school". Those authors are not further discussed here; for a discussion on their writings, see Thrift 1996: 67-78.

can successively give way to new ones that are better adapted to outer structures and prerequisites of the agents.

The structured structure or habitus is inscribed into the bodies and minds of humans as an internalised, implicit program for action. As such, habitus can be described as embodied culture – as existing prior to self-conscious reflection, it sets limits to thought and chosen action.[26] Informants cannot describe their habitus in the course of an interview, even if they wished to do so. It is thus necessary to distinguish between implicit, unintentional, unconscious and explicit knowledge. Implicit memory, in contrast to explicit memory, cannot be reproduced verbally, but is nevertheless a form of cultural competence that influences action. (Bourdieu [1972] 1996: 89)

According to Pierre Bourdieu (1991: 32), it is also the habitus that forms the habitat since the habitus forms specific preferences for a more or less adequate use of the habitat. Bourdieu emphasises that economic, cultural and social capital, as the most important forms of capital, are needed to access a locality and to be part of a habitat formed and appropriated through habitus. How spaces are accessed, appropriated and experienced depends on the kind of capital an actor has at her/his disposition.[27] Bourdieu (1991: 32) writes that a city – Paris, for example – is experienced by an actor according to her or his capital: The perception and appropriation of the city and its settings take completely different forms for, for example, the wealthy and the poor, for the French people and for immigrants, for Parisians and for tourists.

Different appropriation of spaces exists both because of differences in capital and because of the plethora of social markers. In a diversified city like Paris, these markers, built and passed on by social agents, indicate and delimit the spaces available to members of different groups. Artefactual cues such as benches in a park invite people to recline, for example, serve as

---

[26] Scholars like Shigeharu Tanabe and Charles Keyes (2002: 4) argue that embodied practices are, indeed, reproduced and transmitted through Bourdieusian habitus, but that not all socially constructed remembering activities can be reduced to objective structures.

[27] In other publications, Bourdieu discusses (see e.g. [1979] 1996; 1985) other forms of capital, including symbolic capital, political capital, educational capital and bodily capital.

guides to expected behaviour and as aids for "wayfinding in the built environment" in the highly differentiated setting of the city (cf. Ingold 2002: 335-336). All people have a certain capital at their disposal which determines and is also determined by their spatiality: their spatiality depends on the form of the capital, and the habitus of the actors, the areas of the city that are used, for what purpose and at what times they are used. In other words, it depends on how the habitat is appropriated and experienced. (Bourdieu 1991: 32)

In other words, the ability to constitute a distinct spatiality through material or symbolic appropriation of goods distributed in space depends on the economic, cultural and social capital an actor has at her or his disposal (Bourdieu 1991: 30). Power over space is determined through acquisition of capital (cf. Massey 1996: 4). As will be confirmed in the empirical section, the Hmong communities studied in Thailand who do not possess legal land titles only have cultural and social power over their terrain. The land does not legally belong to the Hmong, but it is still an element of their spatial concept of the Hmong Mountains as constituted through social, ritual, agricultural and other forms of cultural practice. The major form of Hmong social capital is the widespread clan network, which allows the Hmong to constitute an alternative spatiality within and beyond Thailand. To summarise Bourdieu's ideas on spatiality, the habitus does not only influence the way a habitat is structured and appropriated by means of the actors' capital, but also the way physical spaces are socio-culturally constituted (Bourdieu 1991: 27).

Anthony Giddens's approach to structure, structures and practice does not emphasise the role of past actions and experiences to the same degree, as does Bourdieu's concept of habitus, although Giddens also discusses the structuration of social systems. Structure is seen as both *medium* and *product* of the practices it organises. According to Giddens ([1984] 2001: 16; 25-29), action and structure are closely related to each other in a "duality of structure" (see also Thrift 1983: 29).

> "The structural properties of social systems are both medium and outcome of the practices they recursively organise. Structure is not 'external' to individuals: as memory traces, and as instantiated in social practices, it is in a certain sense more 'internal' than exterior to their activities in a Durkheimian sense. Structure is not to be equated with constraint but is always both constraining and enabling." (Giddens [1984] 2001: 25).

Structure has thus to be understood as the *result* of actions and as such cannot have any meaning apart from what it attains through action. Following this notion, structure is not itself a competent actor. Just as languages can only acquire actuality through the process of speech, structure can only attain reality through actions of social agents. Correspondingly, structure does not constitute what we do, but constraints or enables what we *can do*.

Anthony Giddens ([1984] 2001: 25) speaks of a duality of structure when emphasising that structure is both product and medium of structuration and that structure and action are connected through a relation of reciprocal necessity. Yet this duality of structure should not be conceived merely as a simple "reproducing circle". Giddens places greater emphasis on the constituting contribution of individuals, as human agents, for social praxis than does Bourdieu. Giddens believes that any given practice is structured by the skills of individuals required to reproduce praxis. These skills can also be transformed according to conditions and needs (Giddens [1984] 2001: 171). However, a distinction must be drawn between the way that actors interpret the meaning of their own words and actions, and how other actors interpret these verbal expressions and activities. Discrepancies might arise because practices are based on knowledge of which actors may or may not be consciously aware (Giddens 1987: 100-107; 1979: 64).

Space and time relate to broader aspects of social systems since human interaction is always "situated" in time and space (Giddens [1984] 2001: 110). Anthony Giddens ([1984] 2001: 111) critically connects his theory of structuration to the "time-space-geography" espoused by the geographer Torsten Hägerstrand (1975), who argues that sources of constraint over human activity are posed by the body and the physical contexts in which activities take place; these constraints limit behaviour across time and space. Giddens ([1984] 2001: 164) regards the extension and "closure" of societies across time and space as problematic, since he conceptualises societies as both permeable and loosely conveyed across time and space. The example of the Hmong villagers studied in northern Thailand, who indeed act across time and space, will demonstrate the forms that Giddens' ([1984] 2001: 171) "time-space distanciation" assumes in practice. In contrast to Hägerstrand and his colleagues, Giddens believes that the time-space distanciation constraints human actions because it withholds some possibilities of human experience but at the same time it is enabling others. Spatial boundaries indeed do exist in locales, understood as the settings of interaction, but may be overcome by other means of social praxis (Giddens [1984] 2001: 171). Similar to Amos Rapoport, Giddens understands locales as a combination of physical-material properties, human artefacts and human interaction and thus as important elements in constituting contexts of interaction (Giddens [1984] 2001: 118).

What can Bourdieu and Giddens teach us about the spatial?

To briefly summarise Bourdieu's theory of practice and habitus, Bourdieu underlines the dialectic between the objective and the subjective and between structure and practice. Structure is acquired through actions of social agents and is, at the same time, reproduced through these actions. The outcome of this dialectic process, the habitus, is understood as the structured structure formed through actions of the past. The body plays a central role in the mediation between structure and actions, which mutually influence one another. According to Bourdieu, physical spaces, as habitat, are appropriated through habitus and the embodied practices of this habitus. A dialectic relationship also exists between physical-material and socially appropriated physical spaces, because the physical-material has an impact on the way it is appropriated by actors. In return, appropriated physical spaces as socio-cultural constructs based on habitus form the physical material. To assess or socially appropriate physical space, social actors require economic, social or cultural capital. Through this capital, actors exert (symbolic) power over socially appropriated spaces, which are materially and symbolically structured. Bourdieu's approach teaches us that spatiality is appropriated and constituted through the embodied actions of actors, which stand in a dialectical relationship to structure. Structure is formed through past actions and experiences, but this structure also has an impact on actors and actions in the present and the future. According to Bourdieu, to access a group's spatiality, it is first necessary to analyse the habitus of its actors; it is the habitus that determines the way spaces are appropriated and structured, which in turn structure the habitus.

Giddens also understands structure as both medium and product of the practices they organise. He thus speaks of a duality of structure. Structure only acquires reality through actions by social agents; it does not exist by itself but only as an enacted entity. Structure restricts and enables what we can do, and structure is, as inherent knowledge, an important condition for action. The totality of social practices and institutionalised routine activities can be summed up us the praxis of a society. Social praxis, as the human socio-cultural form of existence – broadly understood to include its meaningful circumstances, such as practices, relations, contexts, events, and broader properties of social systems – is generated during the institutionalised course of routine activities. These routine activities can be studied in locales that are physical regions involved in action and are the frame for action. Locales and time are connected to a time-space continuum that, as structure, are part of action and also delimits or enables action. To study spatiality, it is important to assess the characteristics of this time-space continuum and how it enables and delimits action.

To conclude, Bourdieu and Giddens have, with their specific approaches, inserted the term praxis at the centre of socio-cultural theory and have enabled a relational conception in the social sciences. They have developed a fundamental ontology of the socio-cultural. In relation to space and spatiality, Bourdieu's and Giddens' work demonstrates that space is not only relevant as a physical-material element of processes of symbolic forms but also as practically appropriated and embodied spatiality. Both scholars emphasise that spaces are constituted through structured social practices, which form spatiality but which are also reproduced through the spatial. Thus the nature of spatiality, like culture, can only be understood by means of a praxis-theoretical perspective. Of course, places and knowledge about past events are extremely important for social action, as they indirectly constitute specific activities and meaning. Social forms employ spatial and temporal aspects to attain specific social, cultural and economic aims. Spatial organisation and the meaning of spaces, which are closely connected to context and action, are thus important elements in the attempt to understand social processes.

New approaches

While the 1990s were determined by debates about globalisation and deterritorialisation and the construction of realities, the new millennium has augured a more distanced, less emotional debate on the consequences of globalisation and the anthropological object. Time and research have shown that new relations are built and lived while old ones are not necessarily abandoned, but instead preserved or transformed to meet new requirements. Scholars like the German anthropologists Michael Dickhardt and Brigitta Hauser-Schäublin (2003) abandoned the emotive elements of the debate on the global and local and instead have embarked upon a pragmatic attempt to fashion a theory of cultural spatiality, since a theory and a proven methodology is still lacking in spite of the volumes that have been written on space and spatiality.

Theoretical questions about the nature of cultural spatiality, and questions about how socio-cultural phenomena can be spatial without being reduced to old, bounded concepts like places, are urgently in need of analysis. Answers can be formulated along Bourdieu's and Giddens' structuration theory, which was first applied to a concept of spatiality by the German geographer Bruno Werlen (1997). Michael Dickhardt (2001) has developed this approach further, in part in collaboration with Brigitta Hauser-Schäublin and the authors of their edited book on "Kulturelle Räume – Räumliche Kultur" (2003, "Cultural Spaces – Spatial Culture"). This edited volume is, as a combination of theoretical essays and case studies, an important contribution to the development of a theoretical and methodological basis for the study of cultural spatiality. It is the major aim of anthropologists like Michael Dickhardt, Brigitta Hauser-Schäublin and Nina Glick-Schiller as well as scholars from other fields, like the geographers Nigel Thrift (2003) and Benno Werlen (2003) to interpret, represent and deduce the meaning of spatiality for human existence.

As Bourdieu and Giddens have already emphasised, the study of the spatial can allow alternative insights into human phenomena by opening up a relational rather than a dual view of the world. This relational view does not oppose subjectivity and objectivity, action and structure, but rather relates these aspects in a dual constitution. Central to this theory is the *praxis* that constitutes reality. Spatial order and the spatiality of things are, as Martin Heidegger claimed ([1927] 1986: 102), derived from human actions and human use of spaces. Spatiality thus needs to be studied on the basis of spatial behaviour because spatiality is an aspect and a result of actions (Werlen 2003: 4).

Michel de Certeau demonstrated in 1986 (page 117) that "space is a practiced place". Practices overlap and thus intersect and blur the boundaries of places and spaces so that *in practice*, for example, east and west, north and south may be one. For example, as the analysis of Hmong spatiality in the empirical section demonstrates, mountainous areas of China, Vietnam, Laos, Thailand, and other areas outside Asia, are "joined-up spaces" (Thrift 2003: 7) and elements within the mental model of the Hmong Mountains. Thus anthropologists should define a place and the field of work not primarily in terms of a locality, but as the field of *practices* and *relations* that are significant to the people involved in the study. This allows an examination of both the nature of non-local relations and the way in which they mould and in turn are moulded by the different localities to which they are connected (Hastrup and Olwig 1997: 8).

Spatiality is also important for the structure of memory and for the consciousness of the historically derived relation of one's own group towards the outside world (Rössler 2003: 199; Mecklenbräuker et al. 1998: 44; Singer 1997: 127). Coordinates of memory are time and space. Memories are not only connected to specific times but also to specific places. Thus, experiences are localised. If one thinks of a specific place, one generally thinks of the personal or group memories connected to this place. For example, when Hmong lineage members jointly visit their ancestors' graves in the forests of former settlement areas once per year, they not only connect to the gravesides, but also to their forefathers and their histories. These places are important mnemonic devices that link the Hmong to their past and the Hmong to each other in the present. Places can change, not only because they are not static and do not always remain the same, but also because social relations lined to these places and memories are susceptible to transformation (Singer 1997: 127). However, identification with the spatial, in whatever fashion it constitutes a group's cultural spatiality, is generally of great relevance for personal, social and cultural identities. The multilayered term "identity" can in this sense be defined as a spatial term describing a localised sense of belonging, in whatever form this locale may take (Werlen 1997: 116; cf. Weichhardt 1990: 23-24; Giddens [1984] 2001: 171).

It needs also to be emphasised that each movement in space is always a movement in time. Temporality is, like spatiality, a fundamental dimension of human praxis and human existence, which Giddens has described via his concept of time-space distanciation. Just as holds true for the term "space", many divergent ontological concepts also describe the category of "time". Time may be understood, for example, as linear or circular, as homogenous or qualitatively differentiated, or as abstract or concrete (Dickhardt 2001: 18-19; Hesse 2003: 93-94; cf. Ingold 2002: 337; Ardener 1993: 6-8; Foucault 1986: 23). The example of the Hmong shows that their belief in rebirth entails a conceptualisation of time as circular and including (re-)birth, life, death and afterlife (Symonds 2004: 4). The Hmong's cultural and temporal-spatial praxis does not only extend to different (horizontal and vertical) spaces but also to different times: The past and the present are interconnected to form one dimension, mediated by the ancestors as vital actors both in the past and present.

Important insights for the development of a theory of cultural spatiality are provided in Michael Dickhardt's thesis (2001), which contains a valuable combination of an ontology of cultural spatiality substantiated with empirical data from Fiji. Most anthropological works on space to date, except for the contributions in Dickhardt and Hauser-Schäublin (2003), have either concentrated on theoretical deliberations or on field data, and not linked the theoretical and methodological approach to ethnographical insights to form a single, comprehensive theoretical account of spatiality. On the basis of Bourdieu's and Giddens' praxis-theoretical structuration school of thought and Ernst Cassirer's conception of symbolic forms, Dickhardt tries to fill this gap by developing an ontology of society, culture and space that renders the socio-cultural and spatial mutually conceivable.[28] He argues this is necessary (2001: 21) since space is more than just an abstract, homogenous and isotropic extension or a qualitatively defined place. Instead, space is only conceivable as *spatiality in cultural praxis*, spatiality conceivable only in its duality as product and medium of practical structuration. The prerequisite for

---

[28] Dickhardt supplements Bourdieu's and Giddens' praxis theory of structuration with theoretical reflections on culture according to Ernst Cassirer's conception of symbolic forms. Cassirer's philosophical reflections on symbolic forms will not be recapitulated here (see Dickhardt 2001: 36-63), but form an integral part of the discussion of Dickhardt's approach to cultural spatiality.

this theory is understanding "praxis as structuration" since, following Bourdieu and Giddens, a structural deterministic view needs to be abandoned in favour of a perspective of free spontaneity of bondless subjects. Concepts of structure and practically active agents need instead to be correlatively interconnected (Dickhardt 2001: 14).

Subjectivity and objectivity have to be conceptualised as always constituted through practical action. These actions mediate, by means of structuration, between subjectivity and objectivity. Dickhardt concludes that subjectivity and objectivity are mutually constituted through the mediation of human practice (Dickhardt 2001: 14-15). The spatial can be experienced as part of this subjectivity and objectivity, and as part of this context of mediation. In this perspective, space is part of human praxis. It is only conceivable as constituted spatiality of praxis, while praxis constitutes spatiality. It can thus no longer be viewed as an entity unconnected to practically active people. Following Bourdieu's concept of embodied actors, Dickhardt (2001: 20, 59) points out that agents are always, by means of their corporeality, extended in space. The principal spatial extension of all socio-cultural praxis can be derived from this corporeality of the actors, as it forms the primary instance of the constitution of praxis. Praxis thus always needs to be understood as situated praxis that generates spatial contextuality and makes use of this contexuality to generate praxis (Dickhardt 2001: 21). As the discussion of Hmong cultural spatiality exemplifies, it is the people's corporeality that constitutes spatiality, whether through concrete actions observable to everyone or the trances of the shaman who is linking the human and the supernatural spheres. In addition to these situated practices, the Hmong also constitute spatiality and supplement the extension of Hmong spatial dimension by means of their belief in potential spaces that lie beyond their practical current reach that are nonetheless, like, for example, China or the United States, integrated into the group's mental map of the Hmong Mountains.

To conclude, at the centre of the theoretical approach to a theory of cultural spatiality stands the notion that a group's cultural spatiality is as much constituted by embodied practices and interrelations between people and locales as it is an aspect of these actions. Spatial structure and human practices are thus linked by a dialectic relationship, and spatiality is constituted through this dialectic. In other words, spatiality is product and medium for spatial structuration. This perception of spatiality needs always to be conceptualised as *cultural* spatiality since it is the means and product of *all* cultural practices, no matter what form they take.

This approach toward a theory of cultural spatiality provided the basis for my own anthropological study of the Hmong's spatiality that I fully develop in the empirical part. To extend existing approaches of cultural spatiality and to make an ethnographical assessment of spatiality feasible, Amos Rapoport's (2002) concept of setting, similar to that of Gidden's locales, is applied to the empirical study of Hmong spatiality in Thailand. This concept of setting is especially helpful "for taking" the theoretical concept of cultural spatiality into the field and for empirically ascertaining embodied structure in praxis.

In the following, Rapoport's approach to space and settings is elucidated and supplemented by other scholars' findings to develop a more practical understanding of senses of place and mental models.

The concept of the setting

As noted above, according to Amos Rapoport (2002: 462), a setting is a place or a zone in known or imagined space that is associated with specific activities and purposes.

> "It follows that what happens (or does not happen) in some settings greatly influences what happens in others. Unless the extent and nature of the relevant system of settings have been discovered, specific spaces or parts of built environments cannot be understood or studied." (Rapoport 2002: 463)

A setting is not important for its spatial expansion but only for the way it is related to actions by social agents. Settings and their cues define situational rules for penetration and appropriate behaviour, and are a specific dimension of cognitive domains (for example, sleeping area, bathhouse, store, church). The ongoing patterns of behaviour depend on cultural codes and are usually elicited by the cues marking the setting: Settings and their culture-specific behavioural codes structure spaces and hence help to organise them (Rapoport 2002: 484).

It is important to note that a setting is not necessarily identical with a specific place or locality like a village, building or room. Instead, a place or locality might at different times be transformed into a different setting through a specific group of people and their activities. For example, the neighbourhood square in the Hmong village turns into different settings requiring different modes of behaviour according to the people, the activities and the time span involved in the usage of the square area. As explained in more detail in the empirical part, the square is, for example, used by different sets of people during the day, each group of people necessitating special forms of conduct. As Amos Rapoport (2002: 463) writes: "Settings have according to specific situations and time, different rules and all together make up the cultural landscape of a people." To combine the cultural spatiality and settings approach and to make the theoretical concept of spatiality practically comprehensible, it can be concluded that cultural spatiality is constituted by classes of settings that include people, their behaviour, actions and symbolic meanings as "non-fixed elements"; furniture, plants or make-shift components of rituals as "semi-fixed elements" and, last but not least, buildings, streets or crop fields as "fixed elements" (cf. Dickhardt and Hauser-Schäublin 2003: 28).

A place can turn into a different setting when different individuals use it at different times and require different behaviour. For example, a Hmong house can be the living quarter of an extended family for most of the year. However, it can also, when necessary, be turned by shifts in furniture and through the attendance of numerous visitors, into the central ritual place of mortuary rites. To clarify the difference between a setting and a place, a place is always a specific locality. For some peoples, such as the Hmong, distant or more abstract mythical places in the sky or underneath the earth may also exist. The fact that people may have never seen such places is irrelevant, and makes these places no less real; people have an idea or a picture in their mind without actually having physically experienced such places (Tuan 1977: 92; cf. Ellen 1996: 16). For example, many Hmong have specific notions about their "ancestral homeland" in China without ever having visited the country. Thus, places are concrete points in the physical, mythical, or imagined environment of a people. These places are not only contexts for action but are endowed with specific meaning and have to be seen as a physical-material component of spatiality.

A setting is not only made up of a place or places but first and foremost of the people and their social practices, their behaviour, and the meanings they attach to their cultural praxis. Thus the conceptual differentiation between places and settings helps to distinguish between concrete material and imagined localities (places) and their socio-cultural constitution in the form of settings which encompasses places *and* the people, their embodied practices, modes and symbolic meaning of behaviour, emotions, constraints and opportunities for behaviour, and time span.

Anthony Giddens also makes use of the term setting, at times interchangeably with the term locale: "'Locale' carries something of the connotation of space used as a setting for interaction." (1979: 207) For Giddens ([1984] 2001: 118-119), place and setting are also two different phenomena that need to be examined separately. The geographical term "place" is something exclusively physical whereas the term "setting" relates to the notion of the contextuality of social practice. According to Giddens, a setting is a specific, action-oriented aspect of space which has a certain order or pattern of material conditions and interacting individuals or groups. A setting is a social "event" with a specific meaning, normally localised on a time-space basis:

"A setting is not just a spatial parameter, and physical environment, in which interaction 'occurs': it is these elements mobilised as part of interaction. Features of the setting of interaction, including its spatial and physical aspects [...] are routinely drawn upon by social actors in the sustaining of communication." (Giddens 1979: 207)

These locales or settings can be seen as an essential element of structuration processes since they influence an agent's access, control and capacity for action. In other words, the physical-concrete structure is included in practices as a framework of practices that has produced this structure in the past. However, one should be aware that principles of structuration inherent in settings cannot be seen as an unchanging given, because they only acquire meaning when actors practically connect to them. Therefore, a certain form of interdependence exists between spatially articulated practices and their permanent sedimentation in structuration (Giddens [1984] 2001: 110-115).

Settings are interconnected through people who partake in them and who move from one setting to another. Brigitta Hauser-Schäublin (2003: 46) speaks of an everyday topography made up of the spaces of everyday action. Within this topography, which is characterised by the perceptions, meanings, values and aims connected to it, people are culturally active as agents. Their actions are manifested as social relations, which are typical for the structure of a society. Through the concentration of actors in socio-spatial settings, which assigns social roles and certain forms of behaviour to the participating actors, the existing social order is reproduced (Hauser-Schäublin 2003: 48). Rapoport (2002: 484, 488) extends this idea by summarising the settings relevant for a group of people into classes and subclasses. In total, all the classes with their subclasses and specific places can be summarised as a subjective, cognitive mental map or mental model whose contents reveal the organisational structure of the cultural spatiality of a group.

Mental models of the spatial lifeworld

A typical mental model of the spatial lifeworld of a Hmong villager might, for example, contain the following partially overlapping categories of settings: the house, the village, neighbouring Hmong villages, the fields, the forests, the mountains, nearby markets, the district city, the distant (mostly only imagined) capital, China, and the Western world. Within these categories, specific components are associated with certain qualities (cf. Giddens [1984] 2001: 118). For example, in a Hmong house, the door and the main hearth bear special importance. Within the village, the house of the shaman of one's own clan can be imbued with special meaning; in the district city, the noodle shop, the market place and the district administration offices might seem particularly important and are visited for differing purposes, require varying modes of behaviour, and are experienced in diverging ways. In forests, specific behavioural patterns are required according to the nature of a locality, whether it is profane or sacred, and according to the time this locality is visited, whether during a ritual or on another day. For example, the Hmong avoid the area of the sacred tree above their village for most part of the year. Once a year, the tree is visited by representatives of all households to ritually pay tribute to the supernatural agents connected to the tree.

Mental models are built in our minds, *inter alia*, through the collection, structuring, processing and retrieval of information about our spatial practice. The product is a structural representation of the way a person views the world. Since this mental model reflects the world as it is imagined, it cannot be seen as a one-to-one image of the physical-material or social environment. A mental model includes internalised representations of the spatial lifeworld (cf. Piaget and Inhelder 1967: 454). These models need to be externalised in order to be seen and understood. This task is difficult because an outsider, for example an anthropologist, might not be able to easily describe these cognitive representations. Instead, only re-representations of these difficult to approach mental models can be captured.

In other words, we will always only be able to approach these models but never be able to fully comprehend them.

Mental models are simplified models of the reality lived by a certain group, which permit interpretations and predictions of events and connections (Roß 1997: 182). These "unconscious theories" allow people to fit new elements into existing systems. Norbert Roß (2001: 22) who has studied mental models of the rainforest of the Lacandon Indians in Mexico, suggests that these models do not have to be completely conclusive, nor are they completely conscious representations of the world. We can speak of "cultural models" if these concepts or ideas are shared, to some extent, by all members of a group. These shared cognitive representations in the minds of individuals build part of a group's culture. This does not mean that each member of a group has to completely conform to all elements of the model.

These models are abstract and, as typical for abstract knowledge, cannot be easily captured in interviews (cf. Brown 2002: 171). During my fieldwork among the Hmong, I could not simply ask people about their mental model in interviews. Instead, I had to thoroughly study important subclasses and classes of settings, and had to be so deeply involved in these settings as a participant observer so that I also, to a certain extent, myself embodied Hmong cultural practices. After months of fieldwork, I had learned how to behave in specific settings and knew which forms of actions were expected, possible or completely unacceptable. The sum of the meaning of the most important settings and classes of settings were slowly disclosed to me in the course of my empirical study when I finally, step by step, gained an image of the content of the Hmong mental model. Mental models of a group's spatiality such as the Hmong Mountains are neither naturally given nor are they static. Rather, the mental model is part of a group's social and cultural knowledge that has to be learned, embodied and experienced in practice. The model is always susceptible to change and can also be lost.

A mental model based on the people's actions and their way of "being alive to the world around them", as seen among the Hmong in northern Thailand, can also compensate for a lack of control over physical, political and economic environment and constitute a reality of its own which is not merely constructed but is based on people's actions, on the (micro to macro-level) context of these actions, and their symbolic meaning (cf. Blu 1996: 217). The Hmong, as an ethnic minority group in northern Thailand, cannot exert much political power over their territory nor are they in the possession of legal rights for the land they inhabit and till. They are thus under pressure to imagine their own "Hmong specific landscape" in relation to all the material and social practices and representations in which they participate. Some of these they control, and some, they do not. Nevertheless, the Hmong confront the spatial representations and localising practices of larger-scale social formations, such as of the Thai society or the world-market, as creatively as they can. They thus keep with their own agendas and reveal themselves as more than mere respondents of the diverse external influences (cf. Winslow 2002: 162). The enacted and embodied model of the Hmong Mountains helps the Hmong to constitute a spatiality of their own within Thailand. Despite the legal landlessness, it keeps the Hmong from being a people without a "sense of place" existing in an anonymous space. Cognitively and practically, they appropriate and constitute their physical-material environment by means of their capital in the Bourdieusian sense, imbue it with meaning and thus gain "power" in a relative sense of the term over their surroundings (Feld and Basso 1996a: 10-11; Ellen 1996: 5; Agnew 1993: 263).

Summary

In the course of the chapter it has been shown that, in past decades, not only the concept of culture has been questioned, abandoned altogether and redefined, but also the relation of cultures to places have been contested on the basis of the argument that globalisation and boundary-exceeding interrelations result in a delocalising effect for cultures. These notions, closely related to postmodernism and critical theory, have by now been countered by arguments that it is still legitimate to maintain a concept like culture but that the relation between symbolic meaning and practice, between mind and body needs to be more explicitly acknowledged, and by arguments that no human culture exists without relation to the spatial. Instead, people and their cultural practices are always dialectically connected to spatial structure: Social agents constitute spatial structure by means of their cultural practice while at the same time their practices are influenced by the spatial. Through these practices, people find and constitute, according to their economic, social and cultural capital, a place for themselves in the world. This place might not be identical with a certain locality but might be characterised by physical-material, potential and imagined places *and* people's actions, experiences, expectations, memories, thoughts, their (boundary exceeding) social relations and their mental models based on the former categories (cf. Lefebvre [1974] 1996: 88; Hirsch 1995: 1-2). Spatiality is involved in action and experience and cannot be divorced from it. The spatial forms both the medium and the outcome of action, both constraining and enabling it.

For most people, their village, town or neighbourhood in large cities is not just a place where they go about their daily activities but is also a place where they relate, where they have networks of friends, relatives and acquaintances, where they acquire a cultural frame of reference to interpret the social world around them. This place, with all its connotations and meanings, is where people are socialised as human beings. In other words, people continue to be profoundly attached to particular places, which have socially endowed and shared meanings that touch on all aspects of life and help shape people's identity via this attachment to a specific locality. These places, including potential and imagined localities, will always maintain their meaning for social actors as long as they are connected to their actions, and as long as they are part of an enacted spatiality.

Looking more closely at "empractised spatialities" of groups like the Hmong, one can gain an understanding of the aspects and meanings underlying these cultural spatialities which, for example, influence mundane reality, pose chances and barriers for social action, influence use and neglect of potentialities, and affect people's outlook on and position in the world. The way the spatial is structured and organised influences daily behaviour and can involve support or restrictions for certain actions. To look behind the meaning of spatiality is to better understand a group's motivations that might not be apparent at first glance or that might not seem rational to an outsider.

Researchers need to focus on the fact that the spatial is not only imagined or constructed but rather appropriated and constituted through social action and imbued with meaning through past experiences. A thorough understanding of social praxis, including its spatial-temporal dimension, is the prerequisite for an assessment of a people's spatiality. The concept of setting allows the researcher to delimit, group and categorise centres of human activity in the field, and to include all forms of socio-cultural practice, no matter where or when it takes place. In addition, processes of production of difference in a world of culturally, socially, and economically interconnected and interdependent levels need to be closely explored. For example, since the Hmong belong to an ethnic minority group in Thailand, the assessment of the Hmong way of siting culture also has to include the economic and political conditions of the meso- and macro level that are transformed and connected to the local mundane reality.

The following chapter deals with contested spaces in Thailand and demonstrates that northern Thailand is involved in a number of meso and macro level, socio-economic and political processes and as such is appropriated and used quite differently by actors like the Thai state, lowland society and the ethnic mountain minorities. For example, the northern Thai mountainscapes used to be viewed by Thai lowland society as the "natural other" or the untamed wilderness. As in the past decades the Thai perception of the environment has been culturalised and the activities of production naturalised (Ellen 1996: 8), the northern mountainous areas and its forests now belong to a valued landscape that needs to be protected for its biodiversity and natural resources.

2 CONTESTED SPACES IN THAILAND

Important aspects of conditions for ethnic mountain peoples in Thailand are discussed in this chapter.[29] The aim is to situate the Hmong in a wider context with reference to the geographical environment, the historical milieu and to the meso (regional) and macro (national and international) settings in Thailand (see also Schweizer 1999: 7). It is important to understand the context for ethnic mountain groups in Thailand in relation to the influences, rules and regulations that are similar for all minority groups in northern Thailand. Special emphasis is placed upon (international) environmentalism and Thai politics of conservation. These have, in recent decades, greatly influenced policies and resource management agendas in the North, triggered a conflict over spaces, and affected perceptions of ethnic mountain groups by Thai majority society. In this chapter, the Hmong are conceptualised as one group within the constellation of ethnic minorities in Thailand and thus are contrasted to Thai lowland society. In a later chapter on Hmong ethnic identity and interethnic contacts (chapter eight), I will demonstrate that the Hmong also define themselves as an element of Thai society.

---

[29] This chapter is based on a paper presented at the Second International Conference of Asian Scholars, Freie University Berlin (9-12 August 2001), which was published in the Journal of Southeast Asian Studies (Tomforde 2003).

Map 1: Map of Thailand with research sites

Source: http://www.thailand-ticket.de, own alterations

The politics of Thailand

Thailand, as the kingdom of Siam has been called since 1939, is the only regional state in Southeast Asia that has not been directly colonised by the Europeans. Since the bloodless "revolution" by a group of military officers and elite civilians in 1932, Thailand has been a constitutional monarchy with the King as the head of state (McCargo 1997: 6). The King embodies the chief commander of the defence forces and heads the Buddhist religion, thus demonstrating the unity of the Thai nation state (Bünte 2000: 41). King Bhumipol Adulyadej, who has been on the throne since 1946, has over the past decades exercised a unique personal authority that has succeeded in mitigating the political assertiveness of the military in the events of "black May" 1992, when the military fired into a mass of 200.000 demonstrators calling for more democracy (Vatikiotis 1996: 53-55). Through the King's intervention, a further escalation of the conflict or even a civil war was prevented. The military has long enjoyed a very powerful position in the Thai political order: Between 1932 and 1973, the military and bureaucrats ruled in a coalition of "bureaucratic polity" over affairs in the state, including several coup d'état (Bünte 2000: 27; McCargo 1997: 6). Since then, (semi-)democratic regimes have been in power in Thailand, interrupted by another period of military rule in 1991-1992. Prime minister Thaksin Shinawatra, in office since February 2001, leads the country in a populist way and is called, as the owner of the most important Thai media, the "Berlusconi of Thailand". His government rules the country in an almost authoritarian fashion, with the reckless "war on drugs" and elimination of political enemies in the South of Thailand as the most prominent examples (Buchsteiner 2004:3).

Popular political participation in Thailand is limited, as Thai politics and parties are characterised by an increasing commercialisation, patronage system and corruption. Especially the votes of the rural population are bought. After the elections, they are obligated by patronage and clientelistic relationships to the representatives (Kessler 2005: 12; Bünte 2000: 45-47).

The administration of Thailand is strongly centralised; Bangkok is its socio-economic and political centre. The state is divided into seventy-six provinces (*changwat*), 811 districts (*amphoe*), 7.409 subdistricts (*tambon*) and about 67.582 villages (*muban*) (Bünte 2000: 42). Thailand has a population of about sixty-three million, primarily composed of ethnic Tai whose religion is the Theravada branch of Buddhism (Leifer 2001: 37; cf. O'Connor 2000). The ethnic mountain groups, who mainly settle in the northern Thai provinces, make up a little more than one percent of the total population (Gravers 2001: 18).[30]

The ethnic mountain groups within Thailand

Ten ethnic mountain groups, of which most are divided into subgroups with different names, cultures and languages can be found in northern Thailand: the Karen, Hmong, Lahu, Akha, Mien, H'tin, Lisu, Lua', Khmu, Mrabri (Tribal Research Institute 1995: 5). The total population of these groups in North Thailand was estimated in 1997 to amount to 774.316 people, of which the Karen form the largest group with 353.574 members and the Hmong the second largest group with 126.300 members. The Hmong constitute approximately 0.20 percent of the national population (Sathitpiansiri and Suebsaeng 2001: 1, 17; see also Culas and Michaud 2004: 71; Kunstadter 1983: 17). Despite the location of most villages in areas distant from the state's centre in Bangkok, one cannot speak of remote ethnic mountain communities who constitute closed, isolated and undifferentiated entities (McKinnon and Michaud 2000: 6). These groups are, on the contrary, influenced and formed through political, economic and ideological input from Thai lowland society, through the impact of world economy and

---

[30] In the ethnographic literature, the terms "ethnic mountain group", "ethnic minority" and "montagnard" are preferred over the term "hill tribe" to designate ethnic groups living in the mountainous areas of South East Asia. For discussions about proper terms and concepts applicable to these peoples, see Renard 2001: 79-80; McKinnon and Michaud 2000: 5-9; McCaskill and Kampe 1997: 50; Gray 1995: 56; McKinnon 1989: 307. In this thesis, the term "ethnic mountain group" is employed.

international politics, through missionaries of various congregations from all over the world, through national and international development, research projects, and through neighbouring ethnic groups, mass media, and tourists (cf. Tanabe and Keyes 2002: 9-10, 14; Jónsson 2000: 223; Durrenberger 1996: 2-5).

All ethnic mountain groups in Thailand are, to varying degrees, integrated into larger – and ultimately global – economic, cultural and political systems. Yet, to go beyond simple dichotomies of local versus national/global, historical relationships, policies, laws and majority-minority issues need to be studied as well (cf. Jónsson 1998: 195, Geusau 1983: 244-246). Especially in regard to the constitution of spatiality at the local level, it is imperative to show how Thai politics and economy have developed and have successively increased their power over mountain spaces, thus affecting livelihoods and settlement areas of ethnic mountain groups. These processes and developments, closely related to (international) environmentalism, are addressed in this chapter. The various socio-economic relationships that transcend spatial boundaries on the local level, which connect the local to meso (regional) and macro (national/international) levels and which take the apparently external and transform it to an internal social situation are discussed via the example of the Hmong in the empirical part of the book. A deeper understanding of coping strategies and reactions of the Hmong to outside influences and demands and their mechanisms for transforming these influences along their own terms is provided. The analysis demonstrates that links between the levels are multifaceted; in combination with group specific cultural and social structures and practices these result in a spatiality specific to the Hmong.

The ethnic mountain peoples live in constant contact and exchange with Thai majority society. As a result, elements are appropriated from the dominant culture, yet their meaning is transformed to fit the group's culture and needs. Sometimes cultural elements are transformed through ironic juxtapositions in a subversion and challenge to Thai majority culture. A constant ambiguity between, for example, Hmong and Thai culture can be observed: On the one hand, through their generations of residence in the Thai state, many Hmong people understand themselves as Thai citizens and sometimes conceive of their cultures as subculture of Thai culture. On the other hand, ethnic mountain groups such as the Hmong live as minorities in Thailand and as such have to deal with racism, discrimination and unequal access to all kinds of resources.[31] As minorities, they are marginalized in many ways: geographically, politically, culturally and socially, economically and environmentally (Rigg 1997: 118; Jónsson 1996: 184). These circumstances result in a subliminal and sometimes even open opposition to the dominant society. This ambiguity and existing conflict potential between ethnic mountain groups and the majority society does not only exist in Thailand but can be found in countless instances in Asia and in other parts of the world. As nation-states have progressively expanded their sphere of influence and territories, as natural resources become scarcer and thus more valuable, conflicts between ethnic minority peoples and nation-states have multiplied around the globe. These conflicts usually concern land rights, control over resource management, and citizenship (Renard 2001: 51-56; Rigg 1997: 117-118; Jónsson 1996: 181-182; Colchester 1995: 62-65).

In Thailand, relationships between Thai society and its ethnic mountain groups must especially be seen in relation to the Thai view of "wilderness" and its natural resources. State forestry and demarcation of forest reserves, partly triggered by international debates on environmentalism and numerous international development programs, have had a substantial impact on environmental awareness, led to different treatment and legislation of forest

---

[31] The term "minority" relates to both the scale and the form of organisation in the total social system. An ethnic minority may be defined as a group that is politically non-dominant, and which exists as an ethnic category. Although the term minority usually refers to inferior numbers, in the professional literature it denotes political submission. The majority does not only possess the political power; it usually controls important parts of the economy, and, perhaps most importantly, defines the terms of discourse in society. Language, codes of conduct and relevant skills are defined and mastered by the majority (Nohlen 1991: 461). It is important to note that a group can be a minority in relation to a state and a majority society, but at the same time maintain a majority status in another setting, as is true for the Karen, the largest ethnic mountain group in the mountainous areas of northern Thailand.

and mountain areas, and different perceptions of its inhabitants, the ethnic mountain groups (cf. Delang 2002: 490-493; Jónsson 1996: 191).

Development of Thai politics of conservation

Through globalisation, rapid mass communication systems and experiences of pollution across national boundaries, people around the world have become sensitised to the global scale of locally produced environmental problems. It is an important assumption of international environmentalist discourse, in accordance with the United Nations, that environmental problems must be viewed on a global scale, even though major disagreements exist over appropriate policies to tackle ecological problems and over the role of economic development in specific local contexts. Keeping in mind that environmentalism as an analytical concept encompasses a large range of meanings, environmentalism is here understood not only as a collective response to environmental degradation but also, given the wide range of socio-political interests and value systems involved, as a multifaceted social and political phenomenon. Environmentalism is a discourse that involves a struggle over crucial natural resources and over the symbolic power to define how environmental problems should be solved. As a discourse, it both reflects and influences social, economic and political processes (Isager 2000: 4; Hirsch 1997: 1; Milton 1993: 1-2).

In Thailand, environmentalist debate and policy are clearly influenced – though not necessarily determined – by the rhetoric and interests of global environmentalist discourse led by governments, international organisations and movements which are still mostly dominated by European or North American countries (Isager 2000: 12). Environmentalism in its existing forms lies at the centre of conflicting perceptions of ecological problems and their causes, and solutions and the parties responsible (Milton 1996: 32-33).[32]

---

[32] Kay Milton's study provides a good overview of the variety of forms of environmentalism, which cannot be discussed in detail here.

The global debate influences Thai environmentalism in many ways, including its ideas, information, political demands and, last but not least, financial resources. However, the global discourse is also affected by "regional discourses" like Thai environmentalism, and there is little doubt that Thai scholars have contributed to a global social scientific understanding of the relationship between environmental policies and social and ethnic identification processes. Due to the geographically and socially unequal distribution of costs associated with ecological problems, environmentalism in Thailand has become highly politicised and inscribed within the broader political debate over ethnic minority rights (Ganjanapan 1997: 202-222; Hirsch 1997a: 16-20).[33]

Ethnic minority groups inhabit many parts of Thailand that have been turned into protected areas by the state over the past three decades and are thus particularly affected by environmentalist discourse.[34] Minorities such as the Hmong have only limited access to political power and thus to ways of actively influencing Thai environmental policies according to their own ideas of a viable future. Instead, their local farming practices involving the use of forests and forest products have been marginalized as a result of state control over forest areas (Isager and Ivarsson 2002: 397). As a consequence, ethnic mountain groups, in cooperation with Thai lowland farmers, have been attempting to regain control over their natural resources through a people-oriented Community Forest Bill (cf. Ganjanapan 2003: 137-139). Fifteen years after it was first drafted in 1990, the bill has yet to be passed by Parliament. One reason for the long debate over the final draft can be found in the fact that other urgent issues need to be resolved first; these include land rights, equal access to education and jobs, citizenship rights and the legal status of communities settling in protected areas. If these problems

---

[33] An overview of the financial issues of development and environmental change is given in Jonathan Rigg 1995.

[34] About fifty per cent of total land area in Thailand is state-owned and managed. This fact has significant implications for local – lowland and mountain – people who cultivate the land, as well as for other major issues such as water supply, energy and the conservation of biodiversity (Sato 2003: 345-346).

remain unsolved, they threaten to undermine the main principles of the community forest bill (Sato 2003: 345; Vandergeest 2003: 29-31; Vaddhanaphuti and Aquino 1999: 8; cf. Iorns Magallanes and Hollick 1998: 1-2). The new national "people's constitution", ratified in 1997, includes articles on government accountability and transparency as well as participatory approaches to development. Articles 46, 56, 76 and 79 give individuals and communities the right to participate in the management of their local natural resources (Muanpawong 2000: 43; Vaddhanaphuti and Aquino 1999: 8). As yet, these rights have not been fully granted to the people. Instead, the Thaksin Shinawatra government continues to circumscribe individual rights to enforce "law and order policies", turning Thailand's path again in the direction of an authoritarian regime. International Human Rights Groups estimate that at least 3.000 people were killed in the course of Thaksin's harsh war against drugs in 2002 and 2003 (Kessler 2004: 3). This war, in which suspected "drug dealers" and other "disturbing" elements were put on police black lists, primarily targeted areas in northern Thailand, and thus included villages of the ethnic minority groups.

Disputed citizenship rights

In the nineteenth century in Siam and the northern Kingdom of Lanna, the concept of majority and minority as such did not exist. Instead, there were only peoples who had less or more access to power, and who had more or less direct connections to ruling groups of the kingdoms (Renard 2001: 53; Durrenberger 1996: 12). During this era, mountain groups such as the Karen maintained close relations with the ruling powers of the Lanna Kingdom and were linked to lowlanders as elephant drivers, loggers, soldiers, scouts, taxpayers and suppliers of forest products and rice (Isager 2001: 97; Gravers 1994: 22; Mischung 1984: 38; Keyes 1979: 31-54; Marlowe 1969: 53-68; see Leach 1954 for the documented importance of upland groups in lowland polities in Burma). Certain ethnic mountain minorities were still "revered as 'original holders of the land' by the valley-dwelling wet rice cultivating peoples, who had established political dominion over them" (Tapp 1989: 73). The importance of mountain peoples for lowlanders disappeared slowly by the end of the nineteenth century as the British and French colonial powers extended their influence in Thailand to regulate the teak industry, the domestic and international market for non-timber forest products declined, and a centralised Thai nation-state was in formation (Jónsson 1996: 169, 176-179; cf. Tanabe and Keyes 2002: 11; Isager 2001: 103-104).

After 1939, when the country's name was changed from Siam to Thailand, a specific Thai identity slowly emerged with Buddhism, the nation, and the monarchy as its most important pillars (see Renard 1994: 658). Ethnicity started to become a more important and problematic issue. Thai identity is still relational and can only be discerned by who adheres to the cornerstones of "Thainess" (loyalty to the King and the Thai nation and adherence to Buddhist ideology) and against those defined as non-Thai (Reynolds 1989: 137).

Despite earlier efforts to grant ethnic mountain groups citizenship and to incorporate them into the Thai nation, in past decades the many changing governments have repeatedly halted and changed these efforts, leaving numerous mountain dwellers without citizenship. From the beginning of a constitutional monarchy in 1932, a date which is often seen as the beginning of the modern Thai state, until 1972, Thai citizenship was available to all persons born in Thailand (cf. Renard 1994: 661). From then on, citizenship rights were severely restricted, and limited to people whose paternal grandfather could be proven to be Thai and to those residing in legal villages. For people who could not prove their Thai ancestry and legal settlement, citizenship was revoked. Applying for citizenship became hard when a justified claim could not be proved with legal papers. Only since 2000, with provincial officers maintaining more authority in granting citizenship, has it has become easier for ethnic mountain groups to become officially naturalised (Renard 2001:52-55; Sretthachau and Jarernwong 1999: 4-7). It is estimated that of the 774.316 people belonging to settled ethnic mountain groups (in contrast to the many refugee people in Thailand), only sixty to seventy per cent have Thai citizenship. These numbers are only estimates and are not absolutely reliable. Nonetheless, for many people belonging to ethnic mountain groups, citizenship remains a very important socio-economic and political issue (Vandergeest 2003: 20, 29; Vaddhanaphuti and Aquino 1999: 1).

Increasing state control over geographic space

About thirty years ago, nature in Thailand was still equivalent to dangerous wilderness and opposed to Thai culture, civilization and nation (Ganjanapan 1998: 151). People living in this wild and uncivilized habitat were judged accordingly (Davis 1984: 81-83).

> "As forests changed from being a source of various important products to being a contested resource, uplanders lost their importance to lowland rulers and came to be viewed as an intrusive element in the forests." (Jónsson 1996: 179)

The rather negative view of natural habitat has changed in the last decades, not only as a result of international environmentalism and politics, but also as a result of the fact that natural resources have been degraded to such an extent that they must be urgently valued and protected (Isager 2000: 12-17; Jónsson 1996: 186-187). It is estimated that about twenty percent of the original state's forest cover still exists (cf. Isager and Ivarsson 2002: 398). If counter measures are not effective, logging companies and increasing industrialisation will endanger these remaining forests.

Looking back at the history of state control over resources, the emergence of commercial state forestry and the establishment of the Royal Forestry Department (RFD) in 1896 in Thailand were linked to a successive appropriation of geographic space in terms of territorial claims over forest land outside private ownership throughout Thailand (then known as Siam)

(Isager 2001: 103-104).[35] For much of its early history, the RFD was concerned with the management of log extraction as an important source of revenue for the Thai state (Hirsch 1990: 167). Peter Vandergeest (1996: 159) is convinced that the assumption of control over the forest landscape and its resources was a necessary aspect of the creation of the modern Thai state. He calls this process of state annexation of peripheral forest land the "territorialisation" of state control over natural resources, whereby the state attempted to control people and their actions by drawing boundaries around a geographic space and prescribing specific activities within these boundaries (Vandergeest 1996: 159; cf. Cooke 2003: 267). State authorities can arbitrarily produce and manipulate space and space is always part of a political process (Pile 1997: 3). A further way of enhancing Thai state control over mountain spaces was building strategic roads into remote upland and highland areas of the country, which opened up a new frontier for arable farmland, and the establishment of Thai schools and other state institutions in these areas.

In order to legitimise the appropriation of geographic space by the state, environmental politics in Thailand have developed in connection with Western institutions (cf. Iorns Magallanes 1998: 212-219). For example, the latest Thai Forestry Sector Master Plan of 1993 was drawn up in connection with the World Bank's Tropical Forestry Action Plan. The enforcement of the ban on shifting cultivation in the 1960s was based upon the Food and Agriculture Organisation's (FAO) assumption that population pressure and swidden agriculture were the main cause of deforestation of Asian landscapes (Forsyth 1999: 23; Taylor 1998: 29-30; cf. Lakanavichian 2001:

---

[35] Thongchai Winichakul (1994) has written an excellent book on the creation of nationhood through mapping in Siamese times from the 19th century until the beginning of the last century. This geographic mapping, imposed by the British and French colonial powers of the neighbouring countries, played a decisive role in the emergence of the geo-body of nation in a "new kind of Siam" and still influences the perception of Siam and the roots of the Thai people today. The new, fixed territorial boundaries also had repercussions for ethnic mountain groups such as the Karen, who were deprived of a role in determining relationships on the frontiers; Karen chiefs, who had been vassals to the Siamese courts, became irrelevant when the administration of land was turned over to Siamese officials (cf. Walker 1992: 21; Keyes 1987: 20).

122). This ban is particularly enforced in northern Thailand's numerous national parks and wildlife sanctuaries, mainly affecting ethnic mountain groups who can no longer practice their traditional farming methods.[36]

During the period of modernisation beginning in the 1950s in Thailand, the suppression of upland and highland cultivation commenced (Isager 2001: 106-108). Migratory cultivation began to be viewed as problematic since this local form of agriculture was seen to be competing with the State's commercial expansion of logging activities and extraction of timber. Furthermore, this kind of agriculture was and continues to be regarded by Thai forestry administration and public as an uncontrollable and undisciplined use of forestland (Renard 2001: 5). In opposition to this seemingly "vague" resource use, the vast and permanent yet predictable clearance of forest through mining or road construction companies is accepted as part of the country's development. Arable land and self-defined management of resources in mountainous areas have been further jeopardised for ethnic mountain groups since the 1970s when landless Thai peasants started to enter into the mountainous areas in their search for fertile land (Kunstadter 1978: 202). Land scarcity and resource depletion in northern Thai mountains are additionally enhanced by the large influx of refugees escaping warfare in Burma (Ganjanapan 2000: 83-86; Geusau 2000: 126; England 1997: 65).

Thailand's economic development since the 1950s was, apart from the Asian crisis that began in 1997, one of growth accompanied by a tremendous expansion of industrial activity and rapid integration into the world market in

---

[36] Recent studies on shifting cultivation in Thailand show that swiddening practices described in older texts are not longer practised. Strengthened forest and watershed laws, a population increase, and commercialisation have led in short rotational cycles, when shifting cultivation is practised at all. In many areas, farmers have instead turned to intensive cash crop cultivation (Maniratanavongsiri 1999: 116-119; Ganjanpan 1998: 71-76; cf. Schmidt-Vogt 1999). For a good scientific debate about positive and negative ecological aspects of shifting cultivation, see for example Masipiqueña et al. 2000: 177-212; cf. Fox 2000.

general, and of manufacturing in particular (Coxhead and Jayasuriya 2003: 54-62, 193; Ganjanapan 2003: 126-127; cf. Scrase and Holden and Baum 2003: 272-273). Deforestation of large areas is doubtless connected to this development and modernisation along the Western model (Lakanavichian 2001: 119; Iorns Magallanes and Hollick 1998: 2-5). Deforestation of vast terrains, loss of biodiversity, water contamination and soil degradation are more related to agricultural expansion, cash crop production and logging concessions than to increased agricultural production in the mountainous areas. Yet ethnic minority groups are still blamed for today's continuing forest degradation (Isager and Ivarsson 2002: 400; Taylor 1998: 21-24).

To tackle environmental problems and protect remaining natural resources, Thailand follows the two principles of wilderness thought prevalent in the United States. These are the principles that wilderness has to be large and continuous and the principle that all human intervention is damaging to the preservation of diversity (Ganjanapan 1997: 213-214).[37] Legal mechanisms for enforcing conservation in Thailand were introduced with the enactment of the Wildlife Conservation Act in 1960 and the National Park Act in 1962. In the latter year, Khao Yai, northeast of Bangkok, was officially declared the first national park. Conservation through the establishment of conservation areas in Thailand has been supported financially and technically by international agencies including FAO, UNDP, USAID and the World Wildlife Federation (Tomforde 2003: 350).[38]

---

[37] In the past decades, a belief in the need to think about ecosystems in a more pluralistic fashion has become increasingly dominant. Ecosystems are now regarded as dynamic and continuously changing, and the importance of humans in their development and functioning is better acknowledged. International conservationists have begun to acknowledge the need for community participation and collective use and management of natural resources in rural areas (Chatty and Colchester 2002: 8-9). Unfortunately, representatives of the RFD, who mostly represent a top-down transfer of technology model of conservation, do not always share these efforts.

[38] From 1989 on, the amount of land officially declared as conservation forests increased rapidly, and now comprises up to seventy-nine per cent of the country's total area. Core conservation areas like national parks; wildlife sanctuaries and forest parks make up thirty-four per cent of the country's total area (Lakanavichian 2001: 120).

The U.S. American conservationist concept of "green islands" has been turned into a means to prove to the world community that Thailand is able to advance "progress and civilization".[39] Thus protected areas are not only valued as natural ecosystems but are also seen as part of a technology necessary for the modernisation and acceptance of the country along international standards (Laungaramsri 2001: 64-65; Vandergeest 1996: 168). The official logging ban of 1989 is generally seen as a turning point in Thai forestry and as the beginning of a new era of conservation.[40] Yet it does not allow direct local dependence on the forest and its resources because these are still to be controlled and managed by the state. As in many other countries, the commitment to environmental protection has not led to meaningful solutions for forest conservation in Thailand. On the contrary, the environmental agenda is supported by lip service, while issues which challenge economic imperatives are not tackled (England 1997: 53).

Protected landscapes and its repercussions for local communities

Throughout the last century, the Thai state has progressively taken over the administration of resources and land rights, with no recognition or respect for customary rights of ethnic mountain groups, some of whom had arrived in Thailand - fleeing wars, population pressures and persecution in Burma, China or Laos - before the Thai nation state was founded (Gravers 2001: 17;

---

[39] It is much disputed whether the Thai conservation model has succeeded in halting the rapid degradation of the country's natural resources. Commercial interests still play an important role in national politics, which is committed to economic growth, including privatisation of business and free international trade. These principles collide with an effective and sustainable protection of the biosphere (England 1998: 258-260).
[40] As a result of constant pressure from several conservationist NGOs on the Thai government, this logging ban was achieved. Nevertheless, illegal logging still continues, sometimes even with the tolerance of government or military officials (Vaddhanaphuti and Aquino 1999: 3; England 1997: 61).

cf. Jónsson 1996: 181-182).[41] However, incursions on lands long used by ethnic peoples, by the state and (logging/mining) companies do not only occur in Thailand but throughout Asia and elsewhere in the world (Coxhead and Jayasuriya 2003: 84; Gray 1995: 48-49).

Under the present forest policy, the RFD has the sole authority to manage and control forest and watershed areas, as any land that is not private property belongs to the public domain (Banijbatana 1978: 56). The government generally does not recognise rights to collective property such as land and forest and does not officially acknowledge traditional forms of common property owned and managed by local villagers (Leepreecha 2004: 338). To date, government and RFD policy has aimed at dividing the country's forest areas into so-called "use forests" and "conservation forests". The forest conservation areas are demarcated as national parks, wildlife sanctuaries or priority watershed areas where human use of natural resources is limited or totally prohibited. As a result, approximately twelve million people, or over 12.000 lowland and mountain communities, have been enclosed in protected areas, almost half of them situated in northern Thailand (Vaddhanaphuti and Aquino 1999: 3; cf. Vandergeest 1996: 167). The demarcation of protected areas by the RFD and insecure land tenurial rights still result in a fear of resettlement for many ethnic mountain people who now live in forest reserves or in areas to be designated as such in the future (Ganjanapan 2000: 176-180; cf. Iorns Magallanes 1998: 200-201). In most cases the people have not been asked to participate in the definition of boundaries of the protected areas. Instead, people have been seen as a major obstacle to the protection of the environment (personal communication with Dr. Thanhikorn, RFD Bangkok, 23.03.2001).

By establishing the National Forest Reserve Areas, settlements within these areas have become illegal under current forest law (Corlin 2000: 107).

---

[41] For example, groups such as the Karen and Mrabri have lived in Thailand for centuries, while the Hmong and Mien belong to the more recent immigrants (Gravers 2001: 17). The Lua' are believed to have lived in northern Thailand before the arrival of the first Tai groups (Isager 2001: 108).

This means that villagers residing inside these regions live in a state of constant contradiction: Their villages are illegal by forest law but at the same time officially registered as legal settlements at the Ministry of the Interior (Sathitpiansiri and Suebsaeng 2001: 13; cf. Charoenpanij 1989: 465). This contradiction in law exemplifies the fact that each governmental department has its own policy towards ethnic mountain groups depending on whether the mountain areas are seen as the locus of valuable natural resources, of reputable development projects, or as the destination of international tourists seeking the exotic (cf. Bhruksasri 1989: 15-21). Villages within protection areas whose residents still do not have full Thai citizenship rights are particularly vulnerable to eviction by the RFD since their home is not recognised as a traditional settlement. People living in protected areas are thus marginalized on their own land. Their (subsistence) activities are endangered through strict rules that can turn them into prosecuted criminals if they do not follow the laws.[42] Prohibited conduct in forest protection areas include the collection of non-timber forest products, cutting of trees, hunting, night-fishing, building of tar roads with construction vehicles and the "import" of any house building materials into the area. These interdicts affect all aspects of the ethnic mountain peoples' everyday lives and require strategies to bypass them to make life in the protected areas viable. A continued upward movement of landless Thai peasants into mountainous regions since the 1970s has accelerated land problems in that area (cf. Turton 1976: 122).

In forest conservation areas, only wet rice or cash crop agriculture on long existing fields are regarded as a proper method of natural resource

---

[42] More than once during my fieldwork in northern Thailand, Karen and Hmong villagers were arrested by RFD personnel for illegally cutting wood in forests that customarily were classified as village terrain. The villagers were detained in prison for a number of days and were fined up to 20,000 baht.

management (cf. Renard 1994: 663; Kunstadter and Chapman 1978: 7).[43] Fields cut or burned in the forest for dry rice or mixed fruit and vegetable cultivation are not regarded as "proper land management", and thus no land titles are granted even when these fields have been in use for centuries (Colchester 1995: 69). Instead, disincentives for ecologically sound, long fallow periods are given: Fields in the forests that have been fallow for more than three years and which thus have a fairly good vegetation cover may no longer be cut or burned. They are to be totally abandoned for natural resource protection purposes (Dirksen 1997: 344). As a result, Karen farmers, for example, who traditionally had fallow periods of up to twelve years are forced to shorten these periods to less than three years in order not to loose their already vague land use rights.

Conflict over forest and mountain spaces

Thai conservation policies have mostly turned forests and mountain areas in northern Thailand from productive into consumptive landscapes. These policies heighten social tensions especially in northern Thailand, where rural lowland Thai and ethnic mountain groups rely on natural resources for farming. Pinkaew Laungaramsri (2001: 3) talks of a "war of space" which has been triggered through new policies and the (re)drawing of maps and boundaries. Peter Vandergeest (2003: 22-23), arguing from a standpoint closely related to political ecology[44], contends that administrative mapping and extension of state control have produced and reinforced spatio-ethnic distinctions and thus the racialisation of the inhabitants of this geographical

---

[43] See O'Connor's (1996) article for a good discussion of the role of wet rice agriculture for rule and power in Thailand. Peter Vandergeest (2003: 21) argues that the majority societies of Thailand, Laos and Malaysia are convinced that paddy cultivation is the only "natural" way of land use, while the shifting cultivation of the countries' minorities is judged negatively as "unnatural". This assumption "racialises" the thinking about the groups' agricultural practices (see also Tapp 1989: 65).

[44] Political ecology focuses on power differentials with respect to resource use, and on environmental problems like pollution in relation to colonialism, poverty, racism, and injustice by linking the situation of politically suppressed people to the global environmental crisis, global economic disparities, and global demography (Krauß 2001: 40-47).

space. Thus, state power operates through the mapping of social inequalities into spatial categories that are produced through cultural contestation. Socio-economic and political control of geographical space and ethnic minorities go hand in hand. Ethnic mountain groups are increasingly caught in a contested space, also because of the growing environmentalism among Thai (especially urban middle class), who adopted the Western idea of nature as a recreational space, devoid of people (Gravers 2001a: 60; Hirsch 1997a: 20-22, 25; Lohmann 1993: 187).

Conflicts between ethnic mountain groups and lowland majority Thai over contested spaces have already erupted more than once (Vandergeest 2003: 27). One well-known example is the 1998 conflict in Chiang Mai's Chom Thong district (where I conducted my research among the Karen). In that incident, Thai lowland farmers and activists grouped together to burn a Buddhist pavilion in a Hmong village and close the roads of the Doi Inthanon National Park, which is mainly inhabited by Karen and Hmong people, for a number of days.[45] Lowland activists claimed that they sought to remove the ethnic mountain groups from the Chom Thong watershed because of their alleged responsibility for destroying the forest and causing water shortages during the dry season (personal communication with Khun Bunta, Head of the District administration in Chom Thong and member of the "Chomthong Watershed Conservation and Environment Association", 25.03.2000; see also Laungaramsri 1999: 108-110).[46] On the other hand, ethnic mountain groups, in cooperation with several NGOs, have also organised themselves to demonstrate publicly for secure land and settlement rights, Thai citizenship and active participation in local resource management (see also Evans 1999). For example, rallies by the "Assembly of the

---

[45] See Laungaramsri 1999 for detailed analysis of the conflict.
[46] Not all Chom Thong inhabitants supported these activities, especially the traders who make a living selling their products to the Karen and Hmong in the Park. Since at least the 1997 Asian crisis, Thai traders (of TV/DVD/stereo sets, motorbikes, furniture, household goods, foodstuffs, etc.) have started to visit mountain villages regularly to sell their products, if necessary on a loan basis. Since mountain communities increasingly engage in cash crop cultivation, obtain surpluses, and are willing to spend money on industrially made products, the mountain regions have turned into a worthwhile market for lowland Thai traders.

Poor" and other NGOs like the Northern Farmers Network bring together hundreds and thousands of members of diverse ethnic mountain groups and lowland farmers. The rallies take place annually in front of government buildings in Chiang Mai and Bangkok to push for governmental negotiations on the most urgent problems (Vaddhanaphuti and Aquino 1999: 1; cf. Jónsson 1996: 192; Lohmann 1993: 189). One such demonstration in May 1999, taking place at the beginning of my Karen fieldwork, almost ended in bloodshed when armed RFD personnel were called in by the government to disperse the demonstrators (personal communication with the Karen scholar Prasert Trakarnsuphakorn, 22.6.1999).

Changed perceptions of the environment

Connected to the country's rapid social, economic and political changes since the 1950s, "modernised ideas" about nature have developed to become an inextricable part of modernisation in the Thai nation-state. Especially since the 1980s, forest conservation and protection of wildlife have become issues of state and public concern because of the widespread international anxiety over the condition of Southeast Asia's rain forests and alarming extent of national forest destruction (Isager 2001: 33; Iorns Magallanes and Hollick 1998: 2-3).

> "Many influential people from Bangkok, Chiang Mai or other major cities support environmentalist groups operating in the highlands, or they donate money to Buddhist temples in rural areas. For one thing, this suggests how Thai environmentalists apply principles of Buddhism to conservation. More significantly, it shows that the *meuang* elite nowadays accepts that *paa* is part of the modern civilized Thai state [...]. Conserving the forest has become a new way of making merit among the *meuang* elite." (Isager 2001: 110, italics in original)

The Thai term *paa (theuan)*, formerly representing a concept close to "nature", historically designated forestlands on the fringe of the Thai civilized space. The term was used for untamed and unsocialised forested wilderness, which, inhabited by spirits, demons, and wild animals, stood in clear contrast to the civilised *meuang* (city, state, political entity).[47] Today, the term *thammachat* (environment) is preferred to *paa theuan*. *Thammachat* is less derogatory than the older term and represents the "tamed and clean" nature which is now valued as an integrated part of the modern nation state (Ivarsson 2001: 34, cf. Stott 1991).

Shifting state attitudes and environmental practices have resulted in a change in the (mostly urban) discourse of Thai concepts of forest and nature. The long tradition of environmental awareness amongst forest monks and Buddhist principles such as the love of nature have, along with Western environmentalist ideas, come to play an important role in forest and wildlife conservation ideas in Thailand (Ivarsson 2001: 33-34; Hirsch 1997a: 33; Jónsson 1996: 186).[48] Whereas *paa* (nature) was formerly conceived as being wild, untamed and outside the sphere of the civilised city/political entity, forests and nature now constitute accepted parts of the modern nation-state. As such, forests and nature have been cognitively transformed into "natural resources", objects to be protected from human destruction as well as measured, calculated, mapped and appropriated in forms of legally declared protection areas open to tourist activities but closed to production (Jónsson 1996: 187, 191; Renard 1994: 660; Stott 1991: 144-50; cf. Falvey 2000: 15-18). The number of tourists in protected areas in many cases exceeds that of the local population, as the example of the Doi Inthanon National Park illustrates, while ethnic mountain groups are seen as the major

---

[47] David Wyatt (1984: 7-9) gives a precise definition of the historically, ritually and politically meaningful term *meuang* in his historical account of Thailand.

[48] In Thailand and in other Buddhist countries, a Buddhist ecology movement has developed in the past years. Buddhists involved in this movement regard their religion as critical for providing practical as well as moral guidelines for ecological conservation. At the heart of this movement are the so-called "ecology monks" (Thai: *phra nak anuraksa*), who serve as the movement's leading figures by their active engagement in conservation activities (Darlington 1998: 1-6; see also Taylor 1997; Tambiah 1984).

threat to natural forests and their agricultural activities viewed as destructive.[49]

"To the extent that they grant access to some (e.g., ecotourists) while restricting the access of people who depend on the land to survive (e.g., limiting productive activities to external notions of traditional hunting and gathering), reserve areas may become an additional constraint on access to land, exacerbating conflicts on the use of key resources and accelerating the environmental degradation they seek to halt." (Painter 1995: 15-16)

Since the logging ban, Thai environmentalist discourse has generally perceived and portrayed forests as fragile, vulnerable and susceptible to extinction while shifting cultivation and village settlements have been depicted as the ultimate menace to these "national assets". This rhetoric has gained widespread public and media support, resulting in socio-economic tensions and new perceptions of the people inhabiting these areas. Within the last decades, "Thai policies toward its minorities have varied from indifference to condescension to repression" (Durrenberger 1996: 12).

The term "hill tribe problem" (Thai: *pan haa chao khao*), which is widely used in Thai media and speech, embodies the prevalent notion that problems of forest destruction are closely linked to the so-called *chao khao* (hill tribes) (Vandergeest 2003: 26-27; Renard 2001: 47; Renard 1994: 662; Vienne 1989: 47-49). Moreover, the term *chao khao* is pejorative and misleading because it suggests a clear dichotomy between Thai lowlanders and peoples from the mountainous areas. The term is nonetheless firmly established in daily Thai speech (Sathitpiansiri and Suebsaeng 2001: 3; Walker 1992: 17). The association of "hill tribes" and "forest destruction" is part of a discourse in which the Thai public unquestioningly uses both terms as if they were

---

[49] Around 700,000 visitors travel to the Doi Inthanon National Park each year. The peak tourist season is from December to February during the cold season and in April, when up to 300,000 people come to the Park within a few days to celebrate the Thai New Year (personal communication with Khun Anusit, Superintendent at the Doi Inthanon National Park Headquarter, 18.02.2000; see also Kaae and Toftkaer 2001: 182-183).

synonymous. The official discourse on hill tribes clearly subsumes all mountain groups within the same category, regardless of their distinctive histories, cultural identities and their own understanding of socio-cultural belongingness. Marginalization of peripheral peoples is thus an integral part of the process of nature making in Thailand (Laungaramsri 2001: 5). Blaming ethnic minority groups for forest depletion is a consequence of the politicisation of space that largely ignores the groups' (long) history within Thailand and actual ecological consequences of their agricultural activities. State notions regarding the mountainous areas have become the key to the country's ecological integrity and disregard the severe environmental problems that permeate the entire country (Sander 2000: 143-153, see Sathirathai 1995: 42).

The environmental discourse in Thailand however, does not assess all ethnic groups – even those subsumed under the category hill tribe – in a uniform way. Environmentalism has entailed new and even positive perceptions of ethnic mountain peoples, although older and more negative stereotypes still persist (Isager 2001: 111). More differentiated views might distinguish between "good" and "bad" peoples such as the Karen and Hmong. While Karen people are generally seen as submissive, backward, ecological and benign, Hmong people are placed at the other end of the scale, mediated as aggressive depleters of resources (cf. Tapp 1986: 47-48; see also Safran 2004: 19). The contrasting "good and bad model" informs the Thai ideological view of desirable, "proper hill tribes" (Laungaramsri 2001: 54; Gravers 1994: 27). In contrast to the Hmong, labelled "destroyers of nature", the Karen are viewed in positive terms as "forest conservationists" whose traditional cultural values allow them to coexist in a sustainable way with their natural environment. However, as Michael Gravers (1994: 21) argues, ethnic categorisation for the Karen, as positive as it may be, can also have negative repercussions, particularly in situations where they are no longer able to live up to their public image as indigenous forest conservationists.

Extension programs in the mountains

Yet in many regards, the impact of the Thai environmentalist discourse and its subsequent changes have been similar for most ethnic mountain groups in the sense that agricultural systems have changed from shifting cultivation to permanent paddy and/or cash crop cultivation through the ban of shifting cultivation, the input of national and international development organisations and public pressure. As a substitute for illegal shifting cultivation inside protection areas, development agencies have promoted the cultivation of formerly unknown cash crops such as cut flowers, cabbage, beans, zucchini, onions, strawberries, peaches, persimmon, litchis or coffee (Renard 2001: 57-65).

The first development programs were begun as poppy crop substitution and counter-insurgency programs, followed by highland development programs aimed at the agricultural, educational and health development of ethnic groups living in the mountainous areas of northern Thailand.[50] By 1983, there were no less than sixty-one different agencies at work in the northern Thai mountains (Renard 2001: 45-50, 70-71; Walker 1992: 16). The most important government program is the Royal Project (RP), initiated by King Bhumibol Adulyadej in 1969 and supported by universities and various international agencies including the United Nations Development Program. The Project's objectives are to improve the livelihood of the people, stop poppy cultivation and preserve the forest (Royal Project no year: 1-8). As the main poppy cultivators in northern Thailand, the Hmong have been one of the primary target groups of the Royal Project, yet other

---

[50] Highland development began in the 1950s with the aim of providing general welfare services in remote and poverty stricken mountain communities (Chandraprasert 1997: 84; Chotichaipiboon 1997: 98). Since the late 1960s, the emphasis of extension work turned to a replacement of opium poppy (*papaver somiferum*) cultivation. Opium was declared illegal in 1958 by the Thai government under military rule, but it was not until 1984 that the government began to eradicate poppies (Sathitpiansiri and Suebsaeng 2001: 6; Renard 2001: xi, 174). For a comprehensive study of opium poppy cultivation, its decline, and highland development programs, see Ron Renard's study (2001).

groups like the Lahu or Karen also benefit from its financial, technological and personal inputs.

In the past, official development programs and foreign-aid development agencies active in the northern Thai mountains paid more attention to the eradication of opium poppy and economic development than finding viable solutions for sustainable development in the mountainous areas. The result is clearly seen in the increased commercialisation of this area and problems such as water shortages, contaminated water and soils or the high use of agro-chemicals (Ganjanapan 1997: 211-212). Another negative aspect of these programs lies in management regimes that have been imposed too often by national and increasingly international authorities who have no basis in local environmental knowledge. The management of natural resources is first and foremost a question of social relations, a means of regulating people's access to these resources (Kalland 2000: 328). However, the RFD, in cooperation with development agencies, upholds the right to supervise and determine the management of resources within protection areas. Living as minorities within the Thai state on land legally owned by the state, ethnic minority peoples cannot freely decide how to use their natural resources any longer. Many restrictions imposed by the state aggravate this situation (cf. Banijbatana 1978: 56). Apart from these constraints by the government, lack of arable land, high population densities and the outwards migration of youth further limit and challenge the traditional use of local land (Taylor 1998: 47-48).

Summary

The overall situation of ethnic mountain peoples in Thailand is not very favourable because these groups are not viewed or treated as Thai citizens with equal rights. Instead, they face problems, obstacles and racism dealing with both the Thai authorities and public. Ethnic mountain people have to fight for the most basic human rights, such as equal treatment by government agencies, equal access to power, education, job opportunities and health services, not to speak of equal access to secure land. Prejudices and discrimination are still prevalent; the mountain people's periphery is geographical as well socio-economical and political. These peoples do not wield much political or economical power over the mountain spaces they inhabit. Resource management systems are imposed from the Thai state, which legally owns the land and development agencies.

Politically, the marking off of ethnic groups in Thailand is used to cement the cohesion of the Thai as "us" in contrast to "them", "them" not included in the Thai nationality concept. Ethnic mountain peoples are not only excluded from the Thai majority due to their different culture, belief systems and their still doubted loyalty to the Thai nation, the King and Buddhism (Isager 2001: 109). They are also excluded because they populate areas which have become increasingly important for the Thai state and public, which have become more environmentally aware during the past decade. Ethnic mountain peoples are blamed for the destruction of Thailand's valuable natural resources in mountainous areas. In addition, mountain people's traditional farming methods are generally viewed as destructive (Forsyth 2001: 81-86; Sathitpiansiri and Suebsaeng 2001: 2; Rigg 1997: 119; Tapp 1986: 49).[51] It is thus almost ironic that the spaces which only a few decades ago were seen as a dangerous and unwanted wilderness have now turned into valuable assets for the country, populated by "third-class citizens" who cannot be easily resettled any longer due to an overall scarcity of fertile land for cultivation (Lohmann 1993: 185-186).

To account for some of the dynamism of the landscape (political, socio-economical and ecological) of Thailand, rapid degradation of resources, water shortage and laws that strictly regulate resource use within protected

---

[51] For examples from other Asian countries, Africa and South America, where peasant farmers are also depicted as a threat to the environment and resources "due to low living and intellectual conditions in addition with backward working methods" (Vietnamese Ministry of Agriculture, cited in McElwee 2002: 307-308), see Chatty and Colchester 2002: 7; Montoya 2002: 21 and McElwee 2002:307.

areas are seen as problems which do not only affect ethnic mountain peoples but also lowland Thai farmers. Farmers in the rural periphery in Thailand, whether from the lowlands or the upland and highlands, are confronted with similar problems. When mountain people and lowland farmers live and cultivate within the same watershed, a common usage of scarce resources such as forests or water can lead to open conflict, as the Chom Thong example clearly demonstrates. However, relationships between the Thai lowland and the mountain areas are not only characterised through open conflict and racism, but have instead developed during the past centuries from strong cooperation between servants and rulers, to opium trade relations, to social welfare and development approaches for minorities to conflicting approaches towards the groups today. That is to say, problems and conflicts between ethnic minorities from mountain areas and the Thai state and public exist on a general level whereas, on the concrete local level, interaction and intermixing occurs, as the empirical part of this book emphasises. Moreover, many groups have settled in Thailand for generations and identify themselves, apart from their own affiliation to their own group, as Thai citizens (whether they have a legal title or not). Born and raised in Thailand and educated in Thai language in Thai schools, especially young people believe they belong to the Thai state to a certain degree. Anthropologist Edmund Leach (1954: 10) describes this ambiguity of belongingness very aptly when he writes (relating to the Kachin in Burma) that "an individual may belong to more than one esteem system, and that these systems may not be consistent" (1954: 10).

Confronted with a minority status, with constraints imposed from the outside and development inputs on local resource use systems, with the rapid transition from low scale/subsistence agriculture to commercialisation of the landscape and livelihoods, ethnic mountain groups find their own terms for reacting to these changes and influences. Local people try to find strategies to deal with new social and cultural circumstances, adapting to the new without letting go of the old entirely and thereby creating a sense of continuity with the past in a rapidly changing world. In the following empirical part of the treatise, data collected in two Hmong communities will be described and analysed to demonstrate how these people, as local actors and decision makers, constitute their own spatiality within the larger context in Thailand.

PART TWO: RESEARCH AMONG THE HMONG

3 IN THE FIELD: CONTEXTUALISING RESEARCH

This chapter aims to contextualise my research to provide insight into living and research conditions, my choice of research sites, the motives behind the multisited research, my applied methodology, and the database I acquired during research. I was first introduced to the study of ethnic mountain groups in Thailand through a one-month student excursion in 1995, organised by my supervisor to Prof. Dr. Roland Mischung (University of Hamburg, Germany) to his own former research sites (see Mischung 1984, 1986, 1990) in Doi Inthanon National Park in northwestern Thailand.[52] The purpose of the excursion was to provide practical training to ten students of anthropology, including my husband Norbert and me, in ethnographical field methods (see Tomforde and Placzek 1996). During my stay in a Karen village, I was drawn to fieldwork and to the people of northern Thailand.

Context of the research

Main research for this book was carried out from April 2001 to March 2002 in the Hmong village of Mae Sa Mai in the Doi Suthep-Pui National Park and in Ban Phui in the Pang Hin Fon Forest Reserve. Mae Sa Mai is located about forty kilometres northwest of Chiang Mai. Ban Phui is located approximately 110 kilometres southwest of Chiang Mai and about twenty kilometres west of Mae Chaem (see map two). In my selection of villages, I hoped to find two Hmong communities that would be sufficiently dissimilar

---

[52] For a discussion of Mischung's work on the Hmong see Postert 2004: 50-51.

In the Field: Contextualising Research 87

to provide a broad understanding of Hmong life in Thailand. My explorations of possible Hmong research sites included visits to more than twenty Hmong villages in northern Thailand in the two months before I started fieldwork. This provided me with an early insight into Hmong village structures, and similarities and differences among villages. Mae Sa Mai and Ban Phui were finally chosen because they differ in a number of aspects, including size, infrastructure, religious composition, and interethnic contacts.

Living and research conditions

I began my research in the village Mae Sa Mai, located near the provincial capital of Chiang Mai, in April 2001.[53] Following a nine-month stay in Mae Sa Mai, I moved along with my male Hmong translator, Win Huj Yaj, to the village Ban Phui, which is located approximately twenty kilometres west of Mae Chaem and 110 kilometres southwest from Chiang Mai.[54] In both villages, I conducted semi-structured interviews on topics relating to household data, resource use systems, social network data, religious ideas and beliefs. I also observed and participated in multiple settings in the two villages, although the important initial phase of "cultural learning" (Mischung 1988: 79) took place mainly in Mae Sa Mai. Nonetheless, during my stay in Ban Phui I collected important research data, including comparative data that provided a more complex understanding of Hmong cultural practices.

---

[53] In Mae Sa Mai, I cooperated with the "Uplands Program", a Thai-German interdisciplinary research project by the University of Hohenheim on "Sustainable Development in Mountainous Areas in Southeast Asia". Researchers from this program, who include agro-economists, soil scientists and biologists, visited the village on a daily basis and provided me with valuable insights from their disciplines. I, in return, mediated between the villagers and the researchers when intercultural problems occurred.

[54] My assistant's Hmong name is Raav Huj Yaj. His family members address him using classificatory kinship terms, while his wife calls him Huj. I mostly called him by his Thai nickname "Win", which my assistant had already used when he had worked for six years for a U.S. protestant organisation that ran one of the Hmong refugee camps along the Thai-Laotian border. He now prefers to be called Win Huj by friends.

My translator and field assistant, Win Huj, was a thirty-seven year old resident of the village Mae Sa Mai, married and the father of three children. During my research, my assistant and his family still lived with Win Huj's parents, his younger brother's nuclear family, and his younger sister and her son, for a total of sixteen people in one household. I rented the house next to my translator's family home. This house belongs to Win Huj's elder brother, who lives with his family and works in the nearby town of Mae Rim in the Thai lowlands. During my research, Win Huj had to fulfil his many duties as husband, father and son, and his duties as *Phu Yai Ban* (Thai for village head). Despite the fact that I slept in a separate house, I was part of my assitant's large household, spending much of my time in their house, sharing meals with my host family, and participating in many activities and excursions with the family and with other lineage and clan members. During our stay in Ban Phui, Win Huj and I rented a house belonging to the Thai Social Welfare Department, which was empty and unused for most of the year. This made it possible for us to avoid the need to stay with a family for a three-month period. Especially given that there were two, and at times three of us when my supervisor Roland Mischung visited, this would undoubtedly have been a strain to hospitality. Nonetheless, I was still able to integrate into the village community, because the majority of the villagers belong to Win Huj's Yang clan (White Hmong: *Yaj*, Green Hmong: *Yaaj*), the clan into which I had been adopted. Many Ban Phui villagers had already met or heard of Win Huj through clan meetings, and some villagers even had been connected to my assistant's family for decades.

My husband also played an important role during my Hmong research. His presence, especially at the beginning of my fieldwork, was important for my assistant and for me since we both had to guard our reputation as faithful spouses. It was also important that I maintain my reputation as a respectable married woman. Only after most of the villagers had seen and met my husband did it become acceptable for Win Huj and me to be seen in the village together, and to travel to other locations. During the first days in Mae Sa Mai, my husband and I were adopted by the *Yaj* shaman and the village elders into the *Yaj* clan. Clan membership made it possible for my husband, and for me as a woman, to be seated in the hierarchically correct locations at the table during formal clan gatherings and rituals. In many ways I was treated as a man or respected visitor during my research stay, which conferred upon me a neutral gender role (see also Symonds 2004: xliv). My gender changed according to situation and to the people I was spending time with. The women accepted me as a companion and female friend, whereas the Hmong men accepted me as a clan member of "neutral gender" interested in Hmong culture and knowledge. Because the men did not want me to learn exclusively about the female side of Hmong culture, which they deemed to be of lesser importance, they consciously introduced me into as many aspects of "proper" Hmong cultural practice and knowledge as possible.

In general, research and living conditions in the Hmong villages were ideal for my purpose, though not without their difficulties. Working closely together with an assistant and spending most of the day and night in close proximity with a large number of people, I often had to make compromises. My translator and host family also had to adjust to my „western peculiarities" and me – their life had been "invaded" by my research and me. In some instances it was difficult to cope with the constraints of fieldwork – to not be able to sleep when tired, to never be alone, to eat unfamiliar foods, not to be near my family and friends, and to not be able to do sports to keep physically fit. Even though these circumstances were onerous at times, I felt compensated by the many valuable experiences I had and the unforgettable time that I spent with Hmong villagers, some of whom are still dear friends today.

When I set out to conduct research among the Hmong, I naively believed I would be able to learn the Hmong language since I had already learned Karen and Thai. Very soon, however, I realised that I did not have the aptitude to learn yet another language thoroughly. Moreover, Hmong, with its eight tones, was a greater challenge than Karen, which only has four tones. During my Hmong research, I thus mainly used Thai to communicate with Hmong villagers; indeed, some Hmong villagers even use Thai to communicate among themselves, especially in villages like Mae Sa Mai, which is located near the city. Because of Ban Phui's proximity to many Karen villages, many Ban Phui residents are fluent in Karen. This made it possible for me to communicate in Ban Phui with a combination of Hmong, Karen and Thai. Of course, members of my host family and the lineage tried to teach me as much Hmong as possible. Eventually I acquired rudimentary knowledge of Hmong, including largely idioms, everyday language, and terms relevant to my research. Nonetheless, my imperfect knowledge of the Hmong language undoubtedly made it more difficult for me to analyse complex symbolic structures.[55]

From February until March 2003 and in March 2005, I again visited the Hmong villages for several weeks. In addition to my wish to see my Hmong friends again, the purpose of the visits was also to present my research results to the villagers. I believed it was important to return with what I had learned during my fieldwork and to discuss my insights with the villagers. I hoped thereby to discover whether or not they agreed with my results, and how their own ideas about the findings might differ from my own. The outcome of these discussions have been integrated in the analysis of field data presented in this book.

Multisited research

In addition to my fieldwork in the Hmong villages, I occasionally conducted interviews with representatives of national and international governmental and non-governmental institutions in Chiang Mai and with scholars at Chiang Mai University. My goal was to ascertain connections between the Hmong villages and Thai institutions, national organisations, and international organisations. My research in northern Thailand was also

---

[55] Only few non-Hmong anthropologists who work on the Hmong do indeed speak Hmong fluently as it requires more than one or two years of research to learn the language (Tapp 2004: 21).

In the Field: Contextualising Research 91

carried out in cooperation with other social scientists who worked with or about ethnic mountain groups and provided me with information about other regions and circumstances.[56] My connections with a national and international group of researchers in Chiang Mai made it possible for me to participate in discussions about topics relating to ethnic mountain peoples and provided me with a great deal of information and insight into the Thai context.

Some scholars argue that research findings from participant observation are only applicable to the fieldworker's particular location in both time and space. This raises the question whether research results are valid only for the particular area under study, but unreliable for understanding anywhere outside the immediate location of research. Indeed, the local group of social scientists debated this issue more than once.[57] In the course of our discussions, we realised that even those of us who were studying the same ethnic group at the same moment in time often arrived at divergent research experiences and data. For this reason, it appears that general statements about all members of a culture are true in some instances, but false in others.

In developing my research design before starting fieldwork, I decided to conduct a multisited study. Like other anthropologists who have conducted such research, I hoped to take advantage of the close proximity of mountain villages and ethnic groups in the region and the reasonably good infrastructure, which made it possible to conduct multisited research without onerous travel (see also Mischung 1990; Cooper 1984). The methodological approach also entailed acquiring data from more than one village and

---

[56] Because of Thailand's ethnic diversity, the ease of obtaining research permits, and a relatively good infrastructure, a large number of national and international researchers choose the northern Thai mountains as research sites. This has turned the city of Chiang Mai into a centre for research cooperation and information exchange, conferences, and non-governmental organisations (see e.g. Korkeatkachorn and Kiatiprajak 1997: 128-172). As a result, a researcher, student group, or a research team sent by the government or a non-governmental organisation has visited even many of the remote villages. This is also true for my two villages (see Leepreecha 2001).

[57] Adam Kuper (2002: 148) also notes that drawing on the reports of other scholars working in the same area enables the ethnographer to leave behind conventional boundaries for more liberal ones and to learn from other researchers' perspectives and experiences.

visiting many others, which meant that my methodology was at least partially adapted to current conditions and interconnectedness on the local, regional, national and global level. Thus my research design was chosen to do justice to the reality that local cultures and societies are not closed entities but rather influence and are influenced by many outside factors and interconnections. Also, by conducting research in more than one location, I was able to better understand and compare diverse socio-cultural practices in their relation to the spatial. This methodology also heightened my awareness of differences among different age groups, between men and women, and between the two villages studied. When I worked in one village, I learned and understood more about the others, and at the same time better comprehended the scope of the Thai context in which the two focal villages are embedded.

In conclusion, I chose a multisited research approach in order to become familiar with and compare data from at least two villages and thus gain better insight into variations of Hmong culture.[58] In addition to studying the selected key villages and the larger issues of the Thai context, I also planned to visit as many other Hmong villages as possible. In part this was because I hoped to learn as much as possible about intra-cultural variation. However, I also wanted to learn as much as possible about the different locations that were important to the village inhabitants of my primary research sites. Whenever possible, I accompanied villagers from my primary sites when they travelled to other locations. According to James Clifford, anthropologists "traditionally" sited themselves in villages, focusing on and emphasising only the "localised" culture while failing to pay attention to the ways in which the villages were linked to the wider world beyond their borders (1997: 19) Instead, Clifford argues, while examining a culture's centres in the local village, community, and neighbourhood, researchers should also

---

[58] Fredrik Barth (2002: 32) regards the study of variation as a central task for anthropology. He defines "variation" as the emergence of new and divergent instances of social action out of pre-existing ones. Nicholas Tapp (1996: 94) also believes that variety and diversity are fundamental rather than secondary phenomena of cultures.

pay attention to a culture's farthest range of displacement and imagining (1997: 24-25). The challenge for the researcher, especially for researchers working on issues of spatiality, is to explore the nature of cultural experience in as many sites relevant to the population in question as possible (Rubel 2003: 11; see also Dracklé and Kokot 1996: 7). Since individuals often travel beyond their centres of living, it is important for these travels to be incorporated into the anthropological focus, a fact that has often been neglected in research. The spatiality approach allows these movements and external contacts, and sometimes imagined or potential places and spaces, to be integrated into the analysis of the focal communities.

Intracultural variation

The majority of cultural institutions, as collective social facts, are in fact shared within a group. However, individual cultural institutions do indeed differ from case to case. Among the Hmong, for example, one of the most important cultural institutions is the mortuary ritual, and the template for what constitutes proper Hmong mortuary rites is broadly accepted. However, in the nineteen mortuary rites that I attended during my Hmong fieldwork (the majority in Mae Sa Mai), I observed that the mortuary rites were not, in fact, identical. Instead they varied greatly. Some rites were conducted along traditional lines, some omitted traditional features, some displayed syncretistic features, some were adjusted in a pragmatic fashion to accommodate scarcity of funds or to reflect the age, gender, or personal history of the deceased or his or her family. Despite this variation among mortuary ceremonies, they all had certain elements and meanings in common, as I touch upon in chapters six and eleven.

The example of Hmong mortuary rites again demonstrates that the dialectic of anthropological research results in a middle ground that is far more than a compromise, but is in fact absolutely central to its subject. Intracultural heterogeneity and variation *need* to be mentioned and discussed by the researcher as an element of every study. They should not be omitted in an attempt to selectively search for a pattern of culture (cf. Descola and Pálsson 1996: 12). Indeed, Fredrik Barth argues that the study of variation is one of the key tasks of anthropology (2002: 32). Barth defines "variation" as the emergence of new and divergent instances of social action out of pre-existing ones. He further asserts that an anthropologist can hope to discover *some* functional imperatives, *some* normative pressures, *some* deep structural patterns, *some* effects of the relations of production on life chances, and *some* shared cultural themes in ranges of local institutions. These exist, nonetheless, surrounded by variation (Barth 2002: 32). Taking variation seriously entails a radical ontological shift, the realisation that variation must be recognised as a property of human ideas and human actions (Keesing 1987: 161). Thus any attempt to understand ideas and actions must acknowledge this pervasive and characteristic feature. "Variation appears empirically to be ubiquitous, and it poses a general theoretical challenge to any and every account of meaning and social action." (Barth 2002: 29-30)

Variation and culture change are relevant issues in the analysis of my data for several reasons. First, my multisited methodology and scientific exchange with colleagues conducting research on similar topics among ethnic mountain groups in neighbouring areas in northern Thailand had made the variation among cultural practices more visible. Second, local Hmong culture tends to undergo rapid transformation, particularly because members of younger age groups are increasingly active across Hmong, Thai, and other settings.[59] This contributes substantially to intracultural change and variation. Intracultural variation and culture change are phenomena that spark repeated discussion among Hmong villagers themselves as well.

The process that determines which variables are selectively retained in Hmong culture is value-driven. Simply put, people choose among the options according to their perceived and valued (or devalued) consequences.

---

[59] A few Hmong from Mae Sa Mai have already travelled to countries where Hmong relatives live, including France, China and the United States.

Change occurs as a result of the choices that people make, even in the face of the traditional authority of elders, as the Hmong data below demonstrates. This process can be defined as cultural selection by choice, a free election among variables. This is opposed to cultural selection by imposition, in which variables are imposed upon a society, as happened when swidden agriculture and the cultivation of opium poppy was outlawed in Thailand (Durham 2002: 203).[60] Culture needs thus to be regarded as a phenomenon constantly undergoing transformation and adaptation. Since ideas and behaviours change over time, cultural systems evolve as changes occur in the relative frequency of the variants (Hastrup and Olwig 1997: 8).

Anthropologists face a difficult task in finding a balance between acknowledging variation and change, and locating patterns and continuities that order social life. One solution to this dilemma would be to give up the idea of explaining a group's entire "culture", and instead focus on human actions, human lives, representations, and meanings. The cultural spatiality methodology attempts this latter focus. It analyses individual and group action, and places them in relation to a complex world.

> "It is precisely by shifting the gaze from generalising about culture to giving a reasoned account of people that anthropologists are able to capture the reality of cultural things. Just show how cultural images, knowledge, and representations are deployed, and sometimes created, by situated persons with purposes, acting in complex life situations." (Barth 2002: 32)

Local communities as research units

In addition to choosing multisited research, I also selected my research units in order to enable analysis of variation and culture change. The two communities I selected are small enough units to permit anthropological

---

[60] In 1958, the Thai government started to launch an anti-opium campaign, which was supported by the United Nations beginning in 1971. However, many Hmong villages continued to grow opium poppy for commercial reasons until the mid-1980s (cf. Tapp 1989: 19).

study, and are units that are recognised as such by the subjects themselves. The two communities constitute a collective system, fulfilling the key definitional features described by George Peter Murdock, namely common residency and face-to-face association ([1949] 1967: 79). Other defining characteristics of the communities are the existence of a self-definition of the social collective and their common language. Even though anthropologists have posed fundamental questions regarding the status of village communities as viable research units, pointing out that this is a conceptualisation that risks imposition from without, I agree with the Hmong people that their villages are important elements of social organisation at the local level (Roß 2001: 15; cf Tapp 1989: 5). However, it is useful to keep in mind that notions of community often refer *both* to a demarcated physical space and to clusters of interaction. For this reason, anthropologists should see their field of work both in terms of place, and as a field of *practices* and *relations* that bear significance to the subjects of the study in question (Cromley 1999: 54; Gupta and Ferguson 1997b: 36). The empirical section of this study documents how the two communities studied are constituted and linked to a set of locations where the majority of interactions of interest take place, and how they are interconnected with other spaces.

As a result, the villages as units of study are not defined as closed entities. Instead, they are conceptualised to include socio-economic networks, contacts among people, and spheres outside the village boundaries.

Many of the elements that constitute the day-to-day reality of village life can be localised elsewhere. These locales include, for example, the provincial city of Chiang Mai and the capital, where political decisions are made and Hmong market their products. It also includes the district town where children attend school, supplies are purchased, doctors are consulted, children are born in the hospital, and inhabitants of other villages and areas are met. Thus Hmong village life and culture is also localised outside the settlement area, especially in places where people attend school, work, and visit relatives. Hmong village life and culture are also connected to and influenced by other parts of the world via modern communication systems, trade and international organisations. The constant flow of people, knowledge, symbols, money and assets appears increasingly to dissolve the physical and cultural boundary of the village. For this reason, I agree with Martin Rössler, who writes about cultures as localised between the concrete village site and the totality of a not entirely comprehensible and assessable outside world (2003: 178). Clearly delineated and delimited entities such as villages, ethnic groups and nations no longer exist. Instead, individuals and groups reproduce in a dynamic process of place making and siting culture such cultural contexts. In so doing, individuals and groups create interfaces between their own concrete life worlds *within* the larger environment, including the global dimension (Rössler 2003: 213). Interfaces among the diffuse and ambiguous relationships between the village, the region, the nation and the world, as they exist within daily reality for most people today, are constantly in the process of construction, transformation and re-actualisation. For this reason, village communities are not themselves autonomous. Instead, as Bronislaw Malinowski noted as early as 1944, village communities are elements within the larger web of relations that defines a society and its relationship to other societies (pages 50-51).

Methodology

My basic methodological approach is analytically inductive (cf. Robinson 1951). During and after fieldwork, I examined the data I had collected from the two villages to deduce the principles of the constitution of cultural spatiality among the Hmong (cf. Bryman and Burgess 1994: 4). My methodical approach is indebted to grounded theory, which I define as an approach toward data analysis in which the theoretical assumptions are seen to emerge from the data (cf. Bryman and Burgess 1994: 7, on this approach, see Bogdan and Biklen 1982). Since it is the essence of the holistic anthropological methodology, from the beginning of my research, I attempted to remain open to the full range of information and to all kinds of people in the field (see Schweizer 1999: 6-7). In other words, *during* data collection, I continually engaged in preliminary analysis to refine the study's focus, reviewed field notes to consider whether I might be able to develop new and fruitful questions and categories, wrote memos about my findings in relation to a variety of issues, and explored emerging ideas. In my analysis *after* the completion of fieldwork, I focused on the development of a coding and node system, using QSR Nud*IST (now called N6) software.

Since I was aware of the pitfalls of grounded theory and the fact that the translation of grounded theory into action during and after research in the manner envisaged by Barney Glaser and Anselm Strauss (1975), Barney Glaser (1992), Anselm Strauss and Juliet Corbin (1990) is difficult to accomplish, I used grounded theory as a frame of reference for data analysis, no more and no less. This open-ended approach made it possible for me to remain as receptive as possible for unanticipated events and issues both before and during research. It also allowed me to keep an open mind about my ultimate research results, and whether I would even be able to analyse and put words to how cultural spatiality is constituted and characterised. Ultimately this receptiveness to new categories and ideas that arose within fieldwork proved immensely valuable to my analysis. For example, the category of the Hmong Mountains only became apparent to me in the course of my fieldwork. I was then able to collect additional data on this newly ascertained category in order to understand its nuances and consider its relationship to other categories of spatiality. I thus define the category Hmong Mountains as a "core category" that contributes to the development of a more effective theory of cultural spatiality (Strauss and Corbin 1990: 116). According to Ian Dey (1999: 10-13), grounded theory's central goal is transcending the particularity of a setting to arrive at substantive theories (as opposed to an abstract theory such as structuralism) and to provide generalisations about specific contexts to explain human phenomena.

Methods in the field

Numerous "classical" anthropological methods and techniques have been applied in fieldwork. These include participant observation, the implementation of semi- and non-structured interviews with individuals and focus groups, and the use of questionnaires.[61] They also include documentation of genealogies, local histories, architectural styles, local taxonomies, local knowledge of topics such as land use and traditional medicine, activity protocols, network data, and maps. Finally, they include exchanges about sites and locations, religious and political rituals, and proverbs, stories, and myths. I conducted a survey about all relevant socio-economic household data in twenty-nine Mae Sa Mai households and in twenty Ban Phui households, and used a structured questionnaire to obtain social network data from thirty people in both Mae Sa Mai and Ban Phui.[62] In selecting the households and people for structured data acquisition, I made sure to include women and men from all clans and age groups as well as poor, "middle" and rich households in order to have a diverse selection despite of the small sample size (see also Lang, Challenor and Killworth 2004). With a thorough and careful study of the important every day settings at the centre of my data collection, the "methodological toolbox of anthropology" (Bollig, Pauli and Schnegg 2000: 73), applied judiciously and adjusted to the specificity of the situation, proved to be useful to encircle the cultural spatiality of the Hmong.

---

[61] As I accompanied villagers and participated in their daily activities, including work in the fields and trips to the nearest town, countless free-flowing conversations took place. These provided me with valuable insight into the villager's beliefs and problems, their perceptions of the past, present and future, and the important and controversial issues within the community. These conversations and unstructured interviews often resulted in more valuable information than in the (semi-)structured interviews, when informants "tried to say the right things".

[62] Survey and social network interviews generally took more time (two to three hours) in Mae Sa Mai than in Ban Phui (one to two hours). This was due to the more complex activities of many Mae Sa Mai residents, which has a great deal to do with the proximity of the city of Chiang Mai. For this reason, in relative terms and in regard to village size, fewer interviews could be conducted in Mae Sa Mai than in Ban Phui. As the results presented in chapters seven and nine exemplify, data ascertained reflects the different structures and practices of the villages in spite of the small sample size.

As I worked to reconstruct the mental models that typified my subjects, I also paid attention to the observable symbolic, communicative, gender- and time-specific characteristics of places and settings. For example, I asked informants to accompany me on walks through the villages, fields, forests, nearby towns, and other areas of interaction and explain their key characteristics and meanings. I also joined Hmong villagers in their many travels to marketplaces in Chiang Mai and other towns, to mortuary rites, to other ceremonies, and to Hmong relatives in nearby villages. In so doing, I immersed myself in Hmong "time-space rhythms" (Burawoy 2000: 4). In order to include "voices from the field" (Diedrich 1999: 9-10) and to allow the people "speak for themselves", I quote directly from statements made by my subjects in semi-structured interviews and informal conversation. Some of my interview subjects asked to be named in my book. Others did not wish to be identified; their names have been omitted.

Since activities are always spatially situated, an explication of the ways in which activities are accomplished reveals much about the social organisation and structure of spatiality. As a method of "systematic illustration" (Smelser 1996: 95), faithfully describing "just what" people did in specific settings proved a very successful technique. Here my focus was on the ways people conducted their activities, interacted with each other, and employed the layout of site and space as a matter of course in carrying out their activities (see also Crabtree 2000: 9; Geertz 1996: 260). To deepen my knowledge and understanding of these settings, I recorded daily activity protocols of five households and recorded fifty-eight personal social networks. Due to time limitations, I was not able to record all the social networks of inhabitants of the two villages. Instead I was forced to select a representative cross-section of the villager's social networks for my analysis (cf. Schweizer 1996, 1989). The results of the study of settings are discussed in detail in the final chapter of the book on important village settings. They are also touched upon in various other chapters, including the discussion of the Hmong economic system and the prospects of Hmong youth.

4 THE RESEARCH SITES: MAE SA MAI AND BAN PHUI

In this chapter, the history and the key features of the two main sites in my study, the Hmong villages Mae Sa Mai and Ban Phui, are outlined. My discussion of Mae Sa Mai is more detailed for several reasons. First, Mae Sa Mai was fundamental to my research because that is where the largest portion of my fieldwork was conducted. It is the village where I was first introduced to many aspects of Hmong culture and underwent the most critical stages of "cultural learning". In Mae Sa Mai, I was adopted by the Yang clan and their network of clan relatives and friends. Second, Mae Sa Mai is much larger than Ban Phui, and its data and background information is thus comparatively more complex than that of Ban Phui. Third, the example of Mae Sa Mai details a number of characteristics of the "typical" Hmong village, which do not need to be repeated for Ban Phui. In the chapters that follow, my analysis and interpretation is largely based on data gathered in Mae Sa Mai. This data, however, holds also truth for other research sites and even other Hmong settlements that I visited, unless I have made a note to the contrary. When there are obvious differences between two villages in my study, I emphasise these differences in my analysis and discussion.

In order to ensure that my results would not be determined by specific local and structural features of a given locale, I chose research settlements that differ from one another in key structural, economic and social aspects. Mae Sa Mai (MSM) is a fairly large village with a population of 1.750. It is located near the provincial city of Chiang Mai and characterised by predominantly perennial cultivation. In contrast, Ban Phui (BP) is relatively small, with a population of 520. It is focusing primarily on cabbage and red onion cultivation, and is located twenty-eight kilometres from the small district town of Mae Chaem and 110 kilometres from Chiang Mai.

Furthermore, both villages differ from each other in a variety of other variables: location within a National Park (MSM)/location outside a park (BP); target of large development projects (MSM)/minimal extension work (BP); heterogeneous household income structure (MSM)/homogeneous household income structure (BP); problems with drugs (MSM)/few problems with drugs (BP); electricity throughout the year (MSM)/electricity only during rainy season (BP); interethnic contacts primarily to lowland Thai (MSM)/interethnic contacts primarily to Karen (BP).

Map 2: Research Area – Chiang Mai and northern Thailand

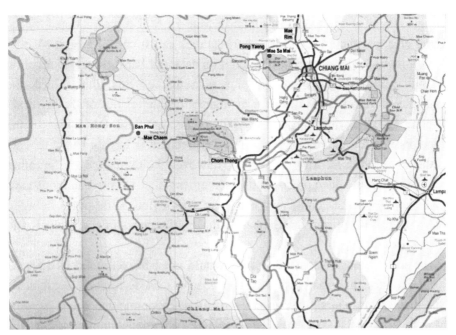

Source: Globetrotter Travel Map (Asia Books Bangkok), own alterations

Mae Sa Mai

In 1930, Hmong founded the village of Pakha, which is lies in the mountains to the south of Mae Sa Mai where Yunnanese Chinese had established an opium trading post. Pakha was largely abandoned in 1960 when most villagers moved north to Mae Sa Kau (Thai for "Mae Sa old", a river running through Mae Sa Kau and Mae Sa Mai is called "Mae Sa" in Thai) in their search for arable land.[63] This village was later abandoned in a four-kilometre move to the north to a location with a better water supply and closer proximity to the national road in order to facilitate opium marketing. This new village was called Mae Sa Mai (Thai for "Mae Sa new"). White Hmong of the Thao clan had lived in the vicinity of Mae Sa Mai for twenty years prior to the village's official foundation. The location of present day Mae Sa Mai is believed to be on the grounds that formerly were the site of four or five White Hmong homes. Four founders officially established the village itself in 1965: Ntxoov Kuam of the Thao clan, Blam Tswb and Vaas Yis (Win Huj's father's father) of the Yang clan, and Nyum Ntsum Teem of the Xiong clan. The village founders purchased part of surrounding land from Thai lowland farmers from Pong Yaeng with a payment of four horses, although no official papers document this transaction. Many of the neighbouring Hmong villages were also founded around this time, and have remained there since (see list of villages in the appendix). The early village settlers did not intend these villages to be permanent settlements. Instead they planned to exploit the area's natural resources for as long as possible and then move to join relatives in different, better locations (see also Mischung 1986: 92). In their biographical accounts, the informants repeatedly mentioned that migrating Hmong always followed in the path of relatives so that they would never live in a location with no lineage members, and where they would form the minority clan. By the end of the

---

[63] One of the four villages that Robert Cooper (1984) studied between 1973 and 1975 was Pa Nok Kok, a neighbouring village of Mae Sa Mai. More than one third of Mae Sa Kau's population moved to Pa Nok Kok, while the rest of the families mostly settled in Mae Sa Mai (Cooper 1984: 70-73).

1960s, it became evident that the era of "great migrations" had ended, and it would no longer be possible to move entire villages with the same frequency (see Mischung 1986: 96).

In the first years after the establishment of Mae Sa Mai, the majority of the households belonged to members from the Yang and Thao clans. These clans had arrived from Burma via Mong Khong (Chiang Dao District), moved south to Nong Hoi Kau, continued to Doi Samoen (Mae Chaem District), and then returned to Nong Hoi Kau and Mae Sa Kau (later Mae Sa Mai). After 1970, this area underwent a large influx of Xiong clan relatives who had been born in Burma and arrived from Doi Samoen in waves of "migrating communities" that consisted of parents, married sons, brothers and affinal kin. These newcomers had followed the Xiong clan village founder and his kin in a search for land suited to opium poppy cultivation. Others had followed Yang clan members with whom they had lived, intermarried, and migrated within the Doi Samoen region. At roughly that time, a number of Yang families resettled once again to join their kin in nearby Doi Pui.[64] The Yang clan is still the majority clan in Doi Pui today. These were also the years when a number of members of the Hang clan began to settle in the village. This pattern of migration into and out of the area established the relative proportion of clans in Mae Sa Mai that has continued into the present day.

---

[64] Hmong informants emphasised that these moves were not considered "movements", but rather short-distance relocations of minor importance (see also Cooper 1984: 58).

The Research Sites: Mae Sa Mai and Ban Phui 105

Map 3: Mae Sa Noi Watershed

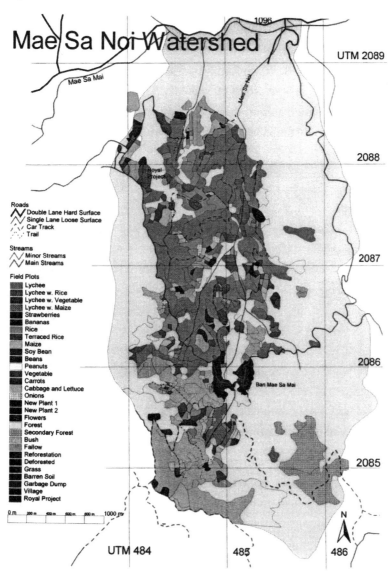

Source: The Uplands Program, 2002

Village characteristics

The village of Mae Sa Mai is located at an elevation between 1,125 and 1,200 meters above sea level in the Mae Sa Noi subcatchment on the northern slopes of the Suthep-Pui mountain range. This catchment forms a branch valley of the Mae Sa River. Administratively, the village is located in the Pong Yaeng sub-district (*tambon*), the Mae Rim district (*amphoe*), and the Chiang Mai province (*changwat*). The city of Chiang Mai is located thirty-seven kilometres southeast of Mae Sa Mai. The village is accessible

Mae Sa Mai from above

by a five-kilometre road, started in 1972, half of which is paved. The road links the Mae Rim-Samoeng highway to the village. Driving on the unpaved section near the village is difficult and dangerous in the rainy season because of the steep slopes alongside the road. The small Thai lowland town of Pong Yaeng, which has a small market, is located at the intersection of the national highway and the road to the village. The district town of Mae Rim is located halfway between Chiang Mai and Mae Sa Mai. Several other Hmong villages are located in the vicinity of Mae Sa Mai. Of these villages, Pha

The Research Sites: Mae Sa Mai and Ban Phui 107

Nok Kok, Bouak Chan, Nong Hoi Kau and Nong Hoi Mai are nearest in geography and accessibility. The area contains no villages populated by other mountain groups.

Mae Sa Mai is located at the base of two mountains, which frame the village to the southwest and southeast. The village fields are mainly located on the northern and eastern downhill slopes, and on and beyond the southwestern mountains. Most of the fields are accessible within ten to thirty minutes via foot, car, or motorbike. Most of the mountain slopes around the village are cultivated, mainly with litchi trees. The mountain to the southeast, directly "behind" the village, is densely forested with a fifteen-year-old secondary woodland. This area contains the sacred *ntoo xeeb* tree, where the greatest local divinity is believed to reside.[65] The reforested area is a designated conservation zone under the protection and management of the villagers themselves. A total of 2.408 *rai* of forestland is near the village.[66] Approximately 1.875 *rai* are under cultivation, with about 1.100 *rai* of litchi cultivation, 600 *rai* of various vegetables and 175 *rai* of dry rice (information provided by the Mae Rim District Office in May 2001; see also map three).

To the northeast of the village lies the "Queen Sirikit Botanical Garden", which contains several state-owned research stations and official reforestation land. During my research, the villagers and the Botanical Garden staff were involved in a land dispute that arose after the Garden expanded its boundary into an area formerly occupied and cultivated by Hmong villagers. The villagers had already had a number of conflicts and tensions with government officials about borders and land management, especially after the 1974 declaration of the Suthep-Pui National Park, which annexed the village into the Park and its resource policies.

The facilities in Mae Sa Mai include a primary school, a childcare centre, a Buddhist temple, two churches, offices of the Social Welfare Department

---

[65] The *ntoo xeeb* ritual tree and ritual is explained in more detail in chapter ten.
[66] One *rai* equals 1,600 m^2, 0.16 hectares, or 0.395 acres.

and the Thai-German "Uplands Program", several small shops run by Thai and Hmong, a nursery, a small gas station. A guesthouse erected by state agencies opened after my research stay (April to December 2001) and closed again in 2004. The village area includes three small forested areas, which are deliberately left unspoiled to function as "empty spaces" for the outdoor mortuary rites that immediately precede burial.

On the official administrative level, the village is represented by one village head (Thai: *Phu Yai Ban*) and four deputies (Thai: *Phu Chuey*), two officers for financial administration (called *Au.Bau.Tau.* in Thai; the acronym stands for *Aung Karn Baurihan Suan Tambol*, or "management organisation of the subdistrict"), nine state-related committees (on topics like administration, development, security, education and culture, health, and social services), two "unofficial" committees initiated by the villagers (a youth group and a "perennial trees group"), and several informal women's groups. In 1996, the village was divided into six administrative sections, each with section leaders and committee members in charge of administrative and development issues. In 2004, the inhabitants divided the village into two separate settlements. The administrative sections one and two, populated largely by the Xiong clan, now are part of a new village called "Mae Sa Noi" (northern Thai for "Mae Sa small"). The four remaining sections continue to belong to Mae Sa Mai. The purported reason for the council of elders' decision to divide Mae Sa Mai was that it had grown too large to be governed by a single headman. However, the separation made it possible to settle a long-standing conflict between the Xiong clan and the three other clans. In addition, the two villages would now be able to request more governmental aid for the building of roads, water tanks, and pipes. Prior to the separation, funds had been unevenly distributed in the village because the official lowland administration had considered the village as a whole rather than the individual sections in funding decisions.

The Research Sites: Mae Sa Mai and Ban Phui   109

Map 4: Mae Sa Mai

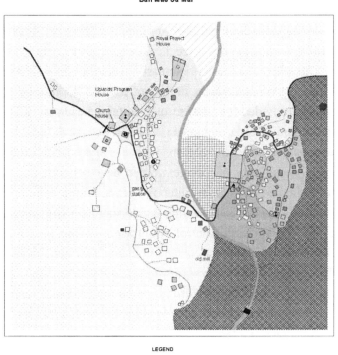

Ban Mae Sa Mai

LEGEND

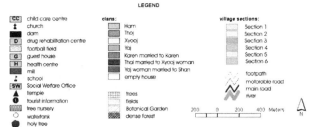

CC child care centre	**clans:**	**village sections:**
church	Ham	Section 1
dam	Thoj	Section 2
D drug rehabilitation centre	Xyooj	Section 3
football field	Yaj	Section 4
G guest house	Karen married to Karen	Section 5
H health centre	Thai married to Xyooj woman	Section 6
mill	Yaj woman married to Shan	
school	empty house	footpath
SW Social Welfare Office		motorable road
temple	trees	main road
tourist information	fields	river
tree nursery	Botanical Garden	
watertank	dense forest	200 0 200 400 Meters
holy tree		N

Source: own survey

In 2001, the village had a population of 1.750 people, (887 men, 863 women).[67] This population was divided into 340 families living in 196 houses. The majority of the Hmong population belonged to the Xiong (*Xyooj*) clan, with ninety-four houses. The Thao (*Thoj*) clan had forty-seven houses; the Yang (*Yaj*) clan had thirty-two houses; and the Hang (*Ham*) clan was the smallest with twenty-three houses (see also Leeprecha 2001: 43-44).[68] The village population had increased from 560 inhabitants in 1974 to 750 inhabitants in 1980, 1.600 in 1998, and 1.750 at the time of my research in 2001 (data provided by the former village headman Kasem Xyooj, personal communication 17.02.2001). The women gave birth to their first child at approximately age eighteen, with a standard deviation of two to three years. The majority of village women bear between three and seven children until the end of their reproductive years. Villagers believe that birth rates will begin to decline in the future due to state family planning programs and increased use of birth control. Contraceptive methods included oral contraceptives, hormonal injections and implants, and sterilisation (mostly of women).[69]

In the past, clan and lineage groups in Hmong villages tended to settle near one another (Culas 1994: 12). In Mae Sa Mai, villagers continue to follow this residence pattern, as is evident in the village map. However, construction space has become scarce, so adult children who move out of

---

[67] The actual population of Mae Sa Mai was difficult to ascertain because children lived at boarding schools in the lowlands and about 300 adults (about 17 percent of the total population) lived and worked for most of the year in other parts of Thailand. These people, most of whom sent remittances back to Mae Sa Mai, are still regarded as members of the village community and are thus included in population statistics.

[68] For a detailed list of Hmong clan surnames as mentioned in the Hmong literature see Kao-Ly Yang (2004: 211-212). The list reveals the many and often diverse spellings existing for clan surnames in both White and Green Hmong. Clan names in the course of this thesis are given in White Hmong (see also note on orthography above).

[69] As Peter Kunstadter (2000: 188) has pointed out in his analysis of data from a demographic survey of twenty-six Hmong communities, a substantial and rapid decline of fertility among the Hmong can already be seen to have taken place since the early 1980s. Motives for reducing fertility include land shortages; the declining need for labour in a market oriented crop economy, and increased educational expenses for children (see also Kunstadter 2004: 378-379).

their parents' homes are now forced to build homes some distance away from their closest kin, occasionally even at the village border. The beginnings of this pattern of spatial dispersal of close kin within the village were already evident in the 1970s, according to Robert Cooper (1984: 45). In the past, Hmong built their houses on the ground with materials such as bamboo or gras. Today most houses are built with heavy, wooden support beams, including a strong centre beam. The floors are built of packed earth, while most of the roofs are made of corrugated iron.

Of the 196 households in Mae Sa Mai, 114 observe the "traditional Hmong religion", sixty-two households are Protestant, fifteen households are Seventh Day Adventist and five households are Catholic. The observers of the traditional Hmong religion are assisted by four shamans (one male and one female from the Xiong clan, one male from the Thao clan and one male from the Yang clan) and by several ritual specialists. One aspect worthy of note is that religious affiliation was always listed for entire households, not for individuals. This is due to the fact that all household members typically observe the religion of the head of the household. Thus, if a Catholic woman marries into a household headed by a member of the traditional Hmong religion, she will change her religious affiliation and her clan membership, as I describe below. In the household survey interviews (n=29), none of the village households claimed to observe Buddhism, even though the monk, who has lived in Mae Sa Mai since 1971, stated that more than seventy percent of the villagers were Buddhist. This statistic is also quoted by the Thai administration in official village documents (see e.g. Mae Rim Agricultural Extension Office 1999: 20). The monk argues that this high figure for the percentage of Buddhists is justified because many villagers visit his temple with offerings for important Buddhist rituals such as *Khao Phansa, Ok Phansa, Visakhabucha* and *Thod Phapa*. However, it must be noted that temple visits do not necessarily reflect belief in Buddhism. Instead, the villagers may be paying respect to a village authority, as is customary in traditional Hmong culture. When questioned about her motives for visiting the temple, Zuam Yaj, a woman of thirty-two years, stated:

"We have to pay respect to the monk because he's lived in the village for such a long time. We want to show that we are loyal to Thai values because we live in Thailand and are not only Hmong, but also Thai." (Source: field interview, H-C-MSM 19)

Institutional pluralism in the village

Because of its proximity to Chiang Mai and its large size, Mae Sa Mai is known in northern Thailand as an important "model" village for a variety of development projects, including the replacement of opium poppy cultivation, the promotion of socio-economic development, and the implementation of state agrarian policies via agricultural incentives and extension activities (Tapp 1989: 20). The villagers tend toward scepticism about the effectiveness of these projects. This is confirmed by secondary data, which demonstrate that there has not been significant progress in land security, health and education services, and/or poverty alleviation (see Renard 2001: 90). For example, the FAO (Food and Health Organisation) headed "Mae Sa Integrated Watershed and Forest Land Use Project" which ran from 1973 until 1981, was largely ineffective. Other initiatives include, for example, the project headed by the Border Patrol Police of Thailand, who arrived in the village in the 1960s to carry out a counter-insurgency policy targeting communist influence in rural and mountainous areas. The Tribal Public Welfare and Development Centre established an extension station in Mae Sa Mai in 1974; a health centre began to falter in the 1990s and shut down entirely in 1997. In 1970, King Bumiphol visited the village to promote the Royal Project. In 1980, the United Nation's Highland Agricultural Marketing and Production (HAMP) project introduced new crops into the Hmong economy, including potato, cabbage, litchi, coffee, and red beans. One year later, in 1981, soldiers were sent to the village to enforce the "opium ban" and suppress poppy cultivation.

The Royal Forestry Department, the Royal Project, the Department of Agriculture, the Land Development Department, the Royal Irrigation

Department, the Chiang Mai University Faculty of Agriculture, and the Chiang Mai's Maejo University Soil Fertility Project are still intermittently active in the village, working to develop the village's economy and integrate its inhabitants into the Thai state. The Bank for Agriculture and Agricultural Cooperatives (BAAC), founded by the government in 1996, and the Royal Project both provide small loan credits to Hmong farmers. Since the majority of the plans promoted by the national and international agencies active in Mae Sa Mai entail largely top-down efforts and little direct participation, the villagers have tended to loose track of the various projects. Many villagers are still unclear about the objectives of the past and current projects, and the results of these development projects have been modest at best.

In addition to remaining the focus of a variety of development projects, Mae Sa Mai is also the subject of a number of small and large-scale research projects. Students from Chiang Mai's Mae Jo University and Chiang Mai University are often sent to "hill tribe villages" to obtain practical training in the application of research methods. A number of large-scale research institutions are still active in Mae Sa Mai. These include the Thai-German "Uplands Program" and the Yale University's School of Medicine. The British-based Forest Restoration Research Unit (FORRU), which cooperates with villagers to reforest the surrounding mountain region with local tree species, has been active in Mae Sa Mai since 1996. FORRU also runs a village nursery that conducts research on the germination of native forest tree species and conducts environmental education (personal communication with Dr. Stephen Elliott, 05.05.2001, see also Elliott et al. 1998). A number of anthropologists have also visited and studied the village; Prasit Leepreecha (2001) was the first Hmong anthropologist to conduct a study (on kinship and identity) in Mae Sa Mai.

Until the end of the 1980s, there was also a small tourist resort in the village. The RFD, however, urged the Thai owner, who also runs the popular Mae Sa Elephant Camp in the Mae Sa Valley, to close the resort because it had never obtained permission to operate within a National Park. While it was in operation, the resort employed several male villagers. These men learned some English and German, which they continue to use in their souvenir business.[70] Very few tourists visited Mae Sa Mai during my months of research, probably because the settlement is too close to Chiang Mai to be a destination for the "adventurous hill tribe trekking tours" to "remote" areas. However, a few Western tourists did visit the village at night to obtain drugs such as metamphetamine and heroin.

Drug related problems

Mae Sa Mai has long been known for its problems associated with opium smuggling and, more recently, with heroin and metamphetamine trafficking. During my research, the villagers estimated that approximately five to seven percent of residents were involved in drug-related issues, which they regarded as a problem for the entire village. The majority of the villagers felt themselves negatively affected by Mae Sa Mai's poor reputation, and even more so by the conflicts and divisions created by drug-related issues and problems in the settlement. Many inhabitants noted that it was necessary to protect property from addicts; the village had several AIDs cases caused by the reuse of dirty needles; a number of drug addicts were incarcerated, which left (semi-)orphans behind to be cared for by relatives (see also Symonds 2004a: 366). In order to tackle these drug problems, in 2001 the villagers cooperated with the Mae Rim police station to establish a twenty-four hour control post at the village entrance gate designed to keep key drug suppliers out of the village. In addition, the villagers inaugurated an anti-drug program with a large ceremony in which inhabitants publicly vowed to join in the fight against drugs. This program was launched in cooperation with the police and the regional administration office.[71]

---

[70] I learned about this former tourist resort in the village when, a few months after I had been in Mae Sa Mai, one evening my Hmong neighbour and teacher Vaam Zeej Xyooj wished me a "Gute Nacht" (good night in German), revealing that he could speak some German.

[71] On the day of the inauguration of the anti-drug policy a woman from the Xiong clan killed herself with a pesticide overdose. It was widely supposed that she did not believe that members of her clan would all follow the policy. She feared the wrath of the "spirits of the village" and the ancestors to whom allegiance to the policy was vowed.

The issue of drugs is also prominent in Mae Sa Mai because of the increasing problems across Thailand. At a national narcotics conference held in Chiang Rai in 2001, it was estimated that about 700 million metamphetamine pills were smuggled into Thailand from Burma or produced directly in Thailand. Authorities stated that they were able to seize only roughly fifteen percent of the rapidly increasing supply. The remaining amount reaches users among Thailand's population of sixty-three million. Drugs have also made inroads into the mountain communities. For ethnic mountain groups who are affected by land scarcity, poor education, and difficult access to lowland employment, the illegal metamphetamine trade is a quick, albeit dangerous, route to riches. In 2001, approximately half of the people incarcerated in northern Thailand were members of drug trafficking groups, nearly all convicted on narcotic charges (Sathitpiansiri and Suebsaeng 2001: 12). According to the anthropologist Ron Renard (1997: 324-325) the large-scale international development and poppy replacement programs are themselves an element in the ongoing drug issues in mountain villages because the projects focus on supply reduction to benefit their own countries while largely ignoring problems of socio-economic development in Thailand (see also Barrett 2003: 1616, 1629; Uhku 1997: 625-627; Vienne 1989: 46-47; Kesmanee 1989: 70).

When I first learned that Mae Sa Mai had a drug problem, I questioned the village's suitability for anthropological fieldwork. Illegal drug traffic and use can distort data in unpredictable ways, and trafficking and addiction can also lead to social problems. In my search for appropriate research villages, however, I discovered that the more than twenty Hmong villages I visited were to a greater or lesser extent all affected by Thailand's overall drug problem. Even in Ban Phui there were rumours of drug use and trafficking that were, as are all rumours, difficult to assess. Undoubtedly drug issues to some extent have affected my data. However, life in Mae Sa Mai is not only determined by drug problems, as my data demonstrates. Instead, life in Mae Sa Mai is primarily defined by the fact that the majority of the villagers try to lead a quiet existence, and work hard for a living, and try to keep their Hmong culture alive.

Ban Phui

Ban Phui was founded in 1972 by three lineages of the Yang (*Yaj*), Kue (*Kwv*) and Chang (*Tsab*) clans, who were members of the Green Hmong.[72] The ancestors of these three lineages migrated from northern Laos to Thailand in the end of the nineteenth century (*Yaj* and *Kwv*) and the

Ban Phui from above

beginning of the twentieth century (*Tsab*). Until the 1920s, they lived south and southwest of the "Golden Triangle" in northern Thailand. This region's natural habitat was particularly suited to the Hmong's economic system and thus attracted numerous Hmong settlements. After a period of relative immobility with only minor relocations, the Hmong began to migrate further south in the 1920s and 1930s. Population increase and extensive farming had

---

[72] Most of the following information is based on data acquired by my supervisor, Roland Mischung, who visited me for three weeks in February 2002 in Ban Phui and assisted my research by conducting interviews on local history.

resulted in serious degradation of the region's natural resources. The majority of new villages were founded in the vicinity of Karen (and Lua') villages in order to take advantage of the local rice market and of cheap labour for poppy field cultivation. Although Ban Phui was not officially founded until 1972, members of the Yang clan had lived in the area since 1950, while members of the Kue and Chang lineages had resided there since the late 1950s. In decades to follow, these settlements underwent only small-scale relocation within the region. Hmong people purchased land around Ban Phui from the Karen and from lowland Thai owners who had already cleared and cultivated the area. Apparently, White Hmong had already settled in the region before the Second World War, but had departed abruptly in 1960 in search of the "Hmong King" in Thoeng (described in greater detail below). Unlike the White Hmong from the Doi Inthanon region, these Hmong villagers did not return to their abandoned fields in Ban Phui but instead founded new villages near Chiang Rai.

Contrary to traditional practice, villagers of the three founding lineages did not encourage relatives to join them in Ban Phui. By the beginning of the 1970s, Hmong in northern Thailand had realised that land was becoming scarce and sedentarisation was unavoidable. For this reason, land resources needed to be divided with care. While families from the three founding lineages received good, fertile land in Ban Phui, the "latecomers" obtained only inferior acreage. As a result, apart from two Yang households, all of the latecomers left Ban Phui again within a few years' time. Thus, except for the two Yang households, all current Phui residents are members of the founding patrilineages.

Map 5: Ban Phui surroundings

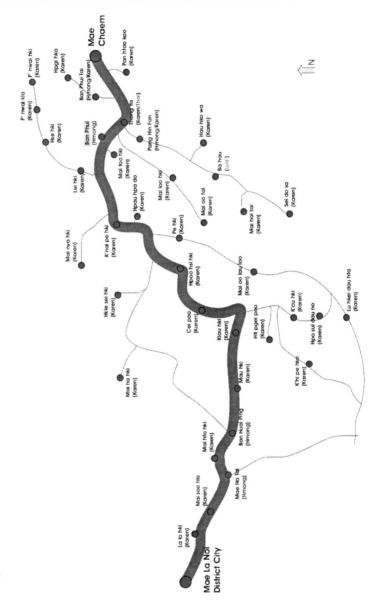

Source: Drawing by Chuv Tuam Yaj, Ban Phui, 15 March 2002

The Research Sites: Mae Sa Mai and Ban Phui

Village characteristics

Ban Phui is located at an elevation of approximately 1.180 meters near the small settlement of Pang Hin Fon. It is about twenty kilometres from the district town of Mae Chaem (about forty minutes by car) and 110 kilometres (or approximately 2.5 hours by car) from Chiang Mai. The road linking Mae Chaem and Ban Phui is partially paved, and is used by the nine Karen villages and two other Hmong villages located near Ban Phui. Two small villages inhabited by the Lua' ethnic group are also reasonably close to Ban Phui. Unlike Mae Sa Mai, where the main road ends in the village, and where the other mountain villages can only be reached via small dirt roads, the paved road that runs through Ban Phui continues to other Karen villages to finally end in the town of Mae La Noi in Mae Hong Son Province.

The Chiang Mai-Mae Hong Son provincial border runs west of Ban Phui through a mountainous region. Some of the village's fields are located in the Mae Hong Son Province. To the south of the village lies a mountain approximately 1.500 meters in height. Its slopes were declared protected forestland in 1989; the sacred tree also lies in this area. The fields to the east, north and northeast are mainly planted with seasonal cash crops like cabbage and red onion, and perennials like litchi.

Map 6: Ban Phui

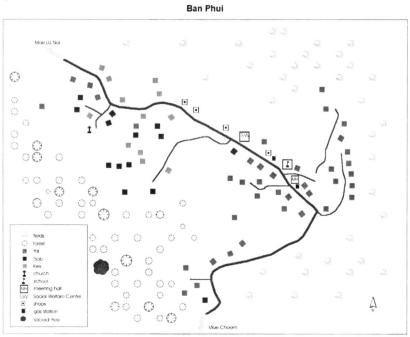

Source: Roland Mischung, February 2002, own alterations

With a Green Hmong population of 510 people divided into sixty-five households, Ban Phui is one of the smaller Hmong villages. With thirty-nine households, the Yang form the majority clan in the village. The Chang clan includes fourteen households, and twelve households belong to the Kue clan. As the village map shows, the village structure also reflects the distribution of the three patrilineages; the households of each lineage are each largely clustered together into one part of the settlement. Topographically, the village is divided into two parts: The section near the road that enters the village from Mae Chaem is largely populated by the Yang clan, while the section near the main road behind the small shops is largely populated by the

Chang and Kue clans. The small Protestant church, which is attended by five households (four from the Yang clan and one from the Chang clan), is also located in this section. Sixty households observe the traditional Hmong religion. The village has two female shamans, one woman from the Chang clan who is thirty-five years old and one woman from the Kue clan who is fifty years old. Four older men consider themselves ritual experts or "priests". Apart from one informal resource protection committee and the official village committee that includes the village headman, two deputies and one *Au.Bau.Tau.*, there are no other committees in Ban Phui.

Like many Hmong communities, Ban Phui is surrounded by a number of "satellite" Karen settlements. During the days of opium poppy cultivation, Hmong and Karen sited their villages near one another. Karen farmers settled near Hmong villages in order to work as day labourers in the poppy fields. The Karen were paid daily in opium, which led to a relatively high rate of opium addiction among Karen men. The Hmong sought the proximity of Karen villages to purchase surplus rice, fire wood and homespun blankets and to employ Karen day labourers (Tapp 1989: 14). For reasons of "pride", as some informants explained, Hmong villagers in the past and today refuse to work for other ethnic minority groups. Today the Hmong in Ban Phui still employ Karen farmers as well as the technically illegal but less expensive Shan and Chinese immigrants from nearby Burma (about seventy kilometres away "as the crow flies").

There are frequent disputes between Karen and Hmong villagers near Ban Phui over land issues. The Karen claim that the Hmong have encroached upon their land, which they wish to buy back because of growing land scarcity. Hmong farmers argue that the Karen do not need as much land because they grow mainly paddy rice and only a few cash crops like strawberries and a limited selection of vegetables in the dry season. The Hmong, in contrast, have their fields in year-round cultivation. As one Hmong man commented about the land disputes: "We arrived here after the others, but the Hmong think in bigger terms, not just in terms of small rivers and small mountains. That's why we need a lot more land than groups like the Karen or Lua'." (Source: field interview, H-S1 88)

Projects in the village

The Royal Forestry Department declared the entire area around Ban Phui a *Phaa Sa Nguan Haeng Chaat* (Forest Protection Area) about ten years ago, and plans to turn it into a national park in the near future. The inhabitants of Ban Phui and neighbouring villages hope to prevent the establishment of a park in fear of more stringent resource management restrictions. As the village headman Mbua Yim Yaj noted, it is easier to protest the establishment of a national park in a settlement area now than it was ten years ago. This is a result of the improved relationships between the Hmong and Thai officials; both sides appear to have become more accustomed to dealing with one another. In addition, Ban Phui and many other Hmong villages have initiated conservation measures of their own accord in hopes of improving their relationship with the RFD and forestalling the establishment of additional protection zones by the state, as well as the prospect of resettlement away from sensitive mountain and watershed regions (see chapter ten).

During my period of research, only the RFD and the Mae Chaem Administration Office were directly involved in village affairs.[73] The Thai officer (who was rarely seen not intoxicated) employed by the Social Welfare Department visited the village sporadically at best. His extension work, which he also carried out in neighbouring Karen villages, was largely ineffective. The NGO Care was active in the village from 1995 to 2000, mainly promoting the cultivation of persimmon trees. In contrast to Mae Sa Mai, which is located in a complex institutional and political arena, Ban Phui is a "remote" village in that few outside institutions pay attention to the small rural settlement or attempt influence, nor is it a tourist destination. A

---

[73] Unlike the Mae Rim Administration Office, the staff from the Office in Mae Chaem could not provide me with numbers about the total area of land believed to belong to the village of Ban Phui and the division of land into forest land, cultivation land and land for the settlement site. The villagers were also unable to provide exact numbers.

female Japanese anthropologist conducted two years of fieldwork in the village, from 1995 to 1997, but has not been heard of again. To my knowledge, to date she has not published on her work in the village in English.

Political units in Mae Sa Mai and Ban Phui

Most the literature on Hmong society and culture states that Hmong political organisation is rudimentary and not worthy of lengthy mention. In spite of the absence of formal and official political leaders in Hmong society, informal heads rule from the level of the nuclear family to the sub-clan level. In addition, like any settlement beyond a certain size in the mountains or lowlands, every Hmong village in Thailand has a *Phu Yai Ban* (Thai for headman) and a *Au.Bau.Tau.*, elected by the villagers every five years. These representatives mediate between the community and the Thai administration in the lowland subdistrict and district towns. Here I shall briefly sketch the forms of traditional and new political organisation that exist in Mae Sa Mai and Ban Phui.

Traditional organisation

To understand Hmong society, it is important to distinguish between leadership in the mundane sphere and leadership in the "spiritual" or supernatural sphere (Geddes 1976: 94). In this chapter I will discuss the former aspect of leadership, reserving a discussion of spiritual leadership for chapter six. An informal leader rules many levels of Hmong social organisation, from the nuclear family, to the household, the lineage, and the subclan. Most of the leaders are male; the rare exceptions occur when a husband dies and the oldest son is too young to become the head of the household. In such cases, the widow can be the head of the household until the oldest son takes over. When problems arise within one level of social organisation, the leader of that level first tries to arrive at a solution in cooperation with other respected men. If that fails, then the leader turns to the next level of the hierarchy. Thus, for example, a problem that cannot be solved at the household level will be turned over to the leader of the lineage. When possible, disputes are settled directly by the parties involved, their own leaders, or the leaders of the next level. If the informal leaders are unsuccessful, the elders and occasionally the village headman intervene (Saykao 1997: 2; Ovesen 1995: 25).

The lineage leader is probably the most powerful and influential leader in Hmong society. He is the only person who has the ultimate authority and responsibility over an entire group. The lineage leader is chosen by the lineage's elders on the basis of his knowledge of Hmong ritual, his ability to care for the lineage's spiritual life, and his ability to unite lineage members. Lineage elders also have an important function as the spiritual leaders of the kin group because of their knowledge of the proper worship of the clan and lineage spirits (Ovesen 1995: 31).

There are at least two leaders at the subclan level. The subclan leader is selected by the elders of the unit on the basis of his personal qualifications in order to preside over the subclan and solve conflicts. Sometimes the subclan does not have a leader, but is instead run by a council of elders that gathers when a problem or issue arises. The second leader at the subclan level is the religious leader. He is selected for his ritual knowledge and other spiritual skills, and his role is confined to the religious sphere.

There is no formal structure at the clan level. As at the lineage and subclan level, knowledgeable elders are important representatives of the group and make major clan decisions. Hmong typically display great respect for age and seniority, which is also demonstrated by the cult of the ancestor worship. The elders require respect, emotional and practical support from the young, while the young seek guidance and knowledge from the elders. This mutual relationship serves to fulfil physical, social and spiritual needs and enables both sides to perform the functions expected of them by Hmong society (Lee no year: 1).

The Research Sites: Mae Sa Mai and Ban Phui

At the interclan level in a village, a council of elders (*sab laj nrog kwv tij*) convenes in times of crisis to deal with serious political matters. Since Hmong society has no juridical apparatus, clan elders also exercise control over clan members and convene to control deviant. During my research tenure in Mae Sa Mai, the Xiong clan was the largest, and had four members in the elders' council. The other three clans, which were smaller, sent only two elders each. The council elders are selected by the clan's elders in accordance with four traditional criteria: "spirituality", knowledge of rituals and oral history, authority in their own clan, and ability to mediate with other clans. In the smaller village of Ban Phui, all elders of the three clans convene in case of conflict. This means that the positions of lineage elders, subclan elders and village council elders can overlap. The elders' council is an important authority in the village, and must be consulted for decisions that affect the entire community (for example, punishment of a criminal, long-term hosting of outside guests, interference by Thai authorities into village matters).

The elders also maintain something akin to a village court. For example, if a villager is caught shooting a bird in the forest protection zone, stealing a chicken from a neighbour, or harassing a woman, the village elders gather to jointly decide upon the fine. The Hmong prefer to arrive at a solution within the village, but when, as happened in one case in Mae Sa Mai, the thief is not willing to return the stolen item or pay the penalty, he or she is turned over to the local Thai lowlands police and charged under Thai law (see also Cooper 2004: 426-428).

At the interclan level on a macro scale, only a few historical figures might be said to have attained the status of interclan leader. For example, General Vang Pao was a Vang clan member who played a key role in the unification of the Hmong in Laos from the mid-1960s to the mid-1970s. General Vang Pao's accomplishments in the Vietnam War are famous among Hmong around the world (Saykao 1997: 3). The Hmong also have historically longed for a Hmong King. This longing to create a more "satisfying culture" (Dunnigan 1986: 47) under a unified and powerful leader might also be understood as a chiliastic movement. At the start of the twentieth century, for example, a messianic Hmong hero named Paj Cai, who claimed to be possessed by the spirit of the Hmong Emperor (*huab tais*), wanted to establish a Hmong kingdom in Laos (Tapp 1989: 95). According to Hmong legend, *huab tais* is "the great ruler" or "the legendary Hmong King", but can also mean a godlike creature or the "Lord of the Sky" (Smalley and Vang and Yang 1990: 13). Within the Hmong belief system, anyone with true leadership abilities also possesses supernatural qualities (Lee 1996: 8-9). In 1960, messianic rumours led many Hmong in northern Thailand to leave their village in exodus to the Thoeng district in Chiang Rai Province, where they hoped to find the Hmong King who would rescue them from suffering and misfortune and reward them with gold and silver. Suspicions later arose that the Communist Party of Thailand propagated these rumours. When their search for the King proved unsuccessful, most Hmong returned to their abandoned villages (Tapp 1989: 78-79, 98). In my research sites, the inhabitants had not left the villages in pursuit of these messianic rumours, which had mainly been spread among the White Hmong and not the Green Hmong.

Official representatives

Before the new constitution of 1997, village headmen ususally remained in office for a long number of years. Since the amendment of the constitution, the villagers elect the *Phu Yai Ban* for a five-year term. Depending on the size of the settlement, the headman is supported by an official village committee made up of one to four *Phu Chuey* (representatives) and one *Au.Bau.Tau*. All of the officials receive formal training for their positions and uniforms to be worn at formal meetings at the subdistrict and district offices. Mbua Yim Yaj, a fifty-five year old elder and the village headman from Ban Phui says about his position:

"I am working between two cultures. At the Thai administration, I fit into the Thai system. When I am back in the village, I am part of the traditional value system and pressures again. The elders chose me twelve years ago. I represent the village to the outside. I am chosen for as long as the others and I want me to be headman. In the past, shamans or ritual experts were also headmen but nowadays mostly young men are elected. Every New Year, the villagers come to my house to request their blessing and show their respect by prostrating [*pe tsao*]." (Source: field interview, H-JB 42)

When village headmen are elected, they are not necessarily chosen by all villagers, but as in the case of Mae Sa Mai, by the elders' council. At the beginning of my fieldwork in Mae Sa Mai, my Hmong assistant, Win Huj, was chosen by the elders' council to replace the village headman, Kasem Xyooj, who had resigned from office. Kasem was torn between his own Xiong clan, some of whom were involved in drug related problems, and his official tasks as *Phu Yai Ban* and representative of the state. His obligations towards clan members prevented him from cooperating effectively with the national police to combat the illegal drug trade. Many villagers in Mae Sa Mai believe that the Xiong clan is most involved in heroin and metamphetamine trafficking. This assumption has led to conflicts between the four clans and the elders in the past, with the result that no headman has remained in office for more than two years. My assistant and his family were not pleased that the elders had chosen Win Huj to become the new headman. Finally, however, my assistant submitted to the elders' pressure, only to resign from office nine months later. His reasons for resignation were numerous. He had attempted to tackle the drug problem by cooperating with the police and implementing an anti-drug policy, which ultimately failed. He also realised that the monthly headman's salary of 1.500 baht was not adequate compensation for the workload, and did not cover the many expenses of a *Phu Yai Ban*, who is required to play host to many guests. Most importantly, Win Huj felt torn between his Hmong clan affiliation and his official state obligations.

Often general conflicts and power struggles arise between the elders and the new Hmong representatives who work for the Thai administration. Elders are not willing to give up part of their authority to the younger men, who are typically between thirty and fifty years of age. According to Hmong norms, the young should respect the elders and not command over them. Most of these younger men received some form of formal education, are literate in Thai, and know how to behave in official Thai settings. These facts qualify the younger men for the position of village headman and committee member, and provide them with a much greater power than Hmong men of their age possessed in the past. "Modern" Hmong leaders require access to resources within Hmong society as well as within the "broader political order" (Dunnigan 1986: 43). Elders and official representatives frequently are confronted with disputes and competition over power issues. As Peev Yaj, a woman from Ban Phui who is thirty years old, notes, some villagers are confused about whose authority to follow:

"The elders belong to the last generation. They aren't educated, and they don't know how to relate to the outside. There is opposition between the traditional elders and the new leaders, they are not unified. Both sides go different ways. We ask ourselves whom we should obey: the elders or the officials? We have to submit to the elders and recognise them but we also have to go the official way. That gives us headaches." (Source: field interview, H-C-BP 3)

Nplaj Thoj Xyooj, an important elder from Mae Sa Mai, describes the conflict as follows:

"The elders are true to Hmong tradition but we do not live in our own country. We are Thai citizens and have to follow the Thai law. I think that the Hmong elders and the Thai system have to work together and complement each other. When the elders do not know some things, the Thai system can step in. I am happy that both systems can support each other." (Source: field interview, H-WP1 26-27)

Despite an underlying conflict between the traditional institution of the elders' council and the modern institution of the village headman and his official committee, the elders' council and the *Phu Yai Ban* jointly arrive at important decisions in both Mae Sa Mai and Ban Phui. For example, when an American Hmong film crew came to Mae Sa Mai to ask permission to produce a Hmong love story in the village, both the elders' council and official village council convened. The request was ultimately turned down because the California Hmong were not seen to behave according to the standards of morality, including showing respect towards the elders and behaving in a reserved manner. Instead, the California visitors displayed boastful behaviour, which many villagers criticised as un-Hmong (see also Tapp 2002: 101, 106). When I wanted to start fieldwork in Mae Sa Mai and Ban Phui, I also had to introduce myself to both institutions to inform the male representatives about my research. After I was questioned about my personal background, aims and attitudes, I obtained permission to live and work in the two Hmong villages.

Summary

The village of Mae Sa Mai, located near the cities of Mae Rim and Chiang Mai, was one of the largest in the province before the 2004 division. Its main characteristics are: The village is close to regional markets, has large litchi plantations, has electricity for most of the year, still has many (inter-)national projects active in the village, has many diversified village committees, is connected to a Royal Project station, and has drug-related problems. Because of these problems and the tensions between the majority Xiong clan and the three other clans, the village has been divided. In the past, village tensions would have resulted in the migration of a section of the village, which is no longer possible. Instead, the villagers tried to solve their difficulties first at the village level, in some instances, as with the drug problems, with the help of Thai institutions. Because this did not appear sufficient, the village was divided administratively. Despite these inner-village conflicts, Mae Sa Mai villagers work to strengthen the villages' political standing in dealings with Thai officials. This strength is particularly important given that the state continues to expand its influence on mountain spaces by controlling resource use systems (MSM) and founding national parks (BP).

Both of the villages are integrated into the Thai political system, with the result that new positions of power have been added to the traditional Hmong system, leading to further changes in the village's power structure. Mae Sa Mai is also greatly influenced by national and international institutions but has thus far managed to withstand drastic culture change, as my comparison of socio-cultural practices in Mae Sa Mai and Ban Phui below will demonstrate.

Ban Phui is more "remote" than Mae Sa Mai. Geographically as well as in its infrastructural connections, the village is located far from the northern centre of Chiang Mai. In comparison to other Hmong settlements, Ban Phui is a relatively small village, surrounded by many Karen communities. Inner-village conflicts appear to be less of a problem, perhaps because the settlement is divided into sections in which each clan or lineage of the village founders has its own space. Land disputes appear mainly to occur between the Hmong and their Karen neighbours, in part because the Hmong think in "bigger terms than just small rivers and small mountains". The Hmong method of permanent cash crop cultivation requires large land areas, and the Hmong self-understanding is still linked to "think large" in terms of territory, as they did when migration was still possible. This is particularly true in the case of Ban Phui, in spite of the village's comparatively remote and isolated location as one of three Hmong villages in a territory largely dominated by the Karen.

This chapter outlined the two research communities, focusing on their political structures and relations to the wider Thai context in Thailand, in order to provide a better understanding of the research background and the main characteristics of Hmong villages today. In the following chapter, Hmong origins in China, the southward migration, and the repeated pattern of resettlement within Thailand, which is connected to the Hmong system of pioneer swidden farming, will be discussed. Hmong history is closely linked to migrations and movements of entire villages and clan segments. In spite of processes of sedentarisation that have arisen since the 1960s, this fact continues to influence the way the Hmong constitute cultural spatiality today. The Hmong in Thailand are part of a diaspora dispersed over five continents, symbolically anchored by a common understanding of a homeland in China. This symbolic homeland provides for a transnational Hmong identity and a strong sense of belonging to a spatially unbound diaspora community.

5 "FLYING LIKE BIRDS": HMONG ORIGINS, MIGRATION, SEDENTARISATION, AND A LIFE IN THE DIASPORA

"An analogy could be with a flock of birds of a socially inclined mountain species, each bird representing a household. Sometimes a whole flock settles together. Sometimes it is scattered in smaller groups. Sometimes the main part of the flock is in one place but there are a few smaller groups picking on the outskirts. Solitary birds are rarely seen. Those, which do forage on the outskirts of the flock, will often rejoin it to stay with it or just to share its companionship for a while. Sooner or later, when food is exhausted in the area, the whole flock flies off to seek new mountainsides, passing over the territories of alien species in between. They may not all keep together. Some fly away to join other flocks from which perhaps their mates have come." (Geddes 1976: 88)

In "Migrants of the Mountains: The Cultural Ecology of the Blue Miao (Hmong Njua) in Thailand" William Geddes develops an analogy of the Hmong as a socially cohesive species of bird (1976: 88). Because of new forms of permanent settlement, this analogy is no longer completely accurate for the Hmong of Thailand. However, Geddes's analogy summarises Hmong patterns of migration and agrees with my Hmong informants that Hmong flew "like birds" in the days when they were still able to migrate on a large scale. In spite of changed patterns of settlement, migration and its freedom of movement are still regarded by the Hmong as an "important aspect of the Hmong way of life", as Hmong villagers, both old and young, repeatedly told me.

Hmong origins in China

Although the origins of the Hmong remain a matter of debate, there is today nearly universal agreement that Hmong originated in China, a theory that is supported by evidence from a wide variety of traditional Hmong oral lore and sung poetry (see for example Johnson and Se Yang 1992; Lue Vang and Lewis 1990: 93-107).[74] The shamanic practice of spiritually sending off the souls of the deceased to guide them to a final, ancestral resting place in China also supports this theory of origins (Leepreecha 2001: 70; Schein 1999: 701).[75] Some scholars even believe the Hmong are the "aboriginal Chinese", basing their argument on documents that mention Miao as one of the indigenous peoples of ancient, pre-feudal China (Tapp 1989: 18). This latter notion, however, must be regarded as extremely questionable in view of the fact that the ethnonym "Miao" as it appears in Chinese annals does not refer to a "genetic-linguistic group" with distinct culture traits (Lehmann 1967[76], cited by Tapp 2001: 9, cf. Leepreecha 2001: 56). Moreover, no archaeological evidence exists to sustain this theory. Both in the past and to a certain extent today, the term "Miao" has been employed in a very imprecise manner to refer to 'barbarians' or to non-Han Chinese peoples (Tapp 2001: 9; Leepreecha 2001: 25-27). The term "San Miao" (Three Miao), designating "barbarian peoples", receives its first mention in

---

[74] Sources on the Hmong are quite numerous and increasing rapidly. A first good overview of the literature on the Hmong can be found in Nicholas Tapp's 1989 study (198-201). In 1996, Christina Smith published a selective, annotated Hmong bibliography that includes works published between 1987 to 1995. Mark E. Pfeifer, director of the "Hmong Studies Resource Centre" in Saint Paul, Minnesota (USA), has also compiled a bibliography of publications on Hmong culture that concentrates mainly on the American Hmong but also includes works on Southeast Asia and other parts of the world from 1996 to 2003 (http://hmongstudies.learnabouthmong.org/worpub1996pr.html). Nicholas Tapp (2004) further discusses the state of Hmong studies until the year 2004 while, in the same volume, German anthropologist Christian Postert (2004) gives an overview of German and Austrian anthropological publications on the Hmong.

[75] On the first day of mortuary rites, the *qhuab ke* (showing the way) ritual, which is often regarded as the key to Hmong cosmology, is performed to guide the soul of the dead person to his or her birthplace, retrieve the placenta, and then follow the path of migration of ancestors to rejoin the ancestors in China (Symonds 2004: 193-238).

[76] This author is missing in Tapp's bibliography, so the original publication could not be cited here.

chronicles dating from approximately five thousand years ago (Peters-Golden 2002: 77). In his attempt to reconstruct the history of the Hmong, Yih-Fu Ruey (1972: 142), who has conducted research on the Hmong people of Sichuan, differentiates between three broad periods in the approach to Miao in Chinese history: first, the period of the "legendary" Miao between 2300 and 200 B.C., in which Miao are regarded as one of the ancient legendary ethnic groups of China; next the "age of the unidentified" Miao, dating between 200 B.C. and 1200 A.D., during which the term Miao is taken to refer simply to "man" or to southern "barbarians" more generally; and, finally, the third period from 1200 A.D. to the present, during which it is reasonably certain that the term Miao refers to an ethnic group, and includes the Hmong as one of the four major Miao sub-groups. Because of these uncertainties regarding the origin of the Miao, it is impossible to speak of an original and genuine Miao culture. What remains clear is that Hmong, as one sub-group of the Miao, made their first unambiguous appearance in Chinese chronicles dating from 1200 A.D. The Hmong's ethnographical outline can be traced without breaks to the eighteenth century, a timeline that has served as the historical backdrop for Hmong studies (cf. Ruey 1972: 146).

Already under the "Yellow" Emperor Huangdi (around 230-210 B.C.), the Miao clashed with the Han and retreated to the south along the Yangzi River (Schein 1999: 702; Yang Dao 1992: 258; Geddes 1976: 6-8). From the eighteenth century until the beginning of the twentieth century, numerous large Miao "rebellions" against the centralised Han authority took place in the southwest region of Hunan, Guizhou, and Sichuan. These "messianic" rebellions revolved around issues of political subordination and land resources. Ultimately the revolts led to a partial migration of Hmong to the southwest. According to the French missionary François Marie Savina, the Hmong strived for independence from foreign rule and struggled on behalf of notions of royalty and sovereignty under Hmong leadership (1930 [1924]: 259-260). The hope was that the true Hmong king would be found to free the entire people (see also Tapp 2001: 36). The final event related to the search for a messianic leader among the Hmong in Thailand was reportedly the 1960 exodus of Hmong, especially White Hmong, in response to rumours of the appearance of a Hmong king. These kinds of chiliastic movements also exist among other southeast Asian mountain minorities who struggled to restructure their politically and economically marginal position by religious means (Mischung no year: 10). With respect to marginality and discrimination, the Hmong in China are recognised as one of the fifty-six officially registered "national minorities" in China, known as *minzu* (Culas and Michaud 2004: 63; Vang 1998: 10; see also Tapp 2004: 17-18). Chinese *minzu* policy is still a way of positive discrimination and a category which does not exist *next* to the Han-Chinese majority but *apart* from the majority people. Indeed, "Miao-zi" is still a derogatory term used for the uncivilised "other" (Tapp 2001: 37). Its Thai derivative, "Meo", is also pejorative and offensive to many Hmong in Thailand (Lee 1996: 3). Hmong themselves prefer the term "*Hmoob*" which stands for "man". Many informants in the survey sites also claimed that the term means "free people"; a definition that is based on an inventive but misleading translation linked to processes of Hmong cultural identity formation within Yang Dao's (1975) and Sucheng Chan's (1994) publications (Tapp 2004: 20).

Returning to the early history of the Miao and Hmong in China, overpopulation and the continued suppression of Hmong groups by Han Chinese from the eighteenth until the early twentieth centuries led both to assimilation among some Hmong segments, and an exodus toward the southwest across the Chinese border into uninhabited forests and rugged mountain areas by other Hmong elements (Ruey 1972: 149-151; cf. Géraud 1993: 35). Among other reasons, the Han settlement and subordination of the Hmong, and the Hmong search for fertile and arable forestland, led to their transformation into mountain dwellers or montagnards (Culas 2000: 33; McKinnon and Michaud 2000: 11). These migrations into mountainous terrain, which included both large-scale refugee exodus movements and small-scale, deliberate relocations of individual families, resulted in a further division of the Hmong into sub-groups, each of which developed customs, dialects and styles of dress different from their ancestors in China (cf. Cooper 1986: 28). The Hmong in China were and remain divided into five main Hmong sub-groups: *Hei Miao* (Black Hmong), *Hung Miao* (Red Hmong), *Ch'ing Miao* (Blue Hmong), *Pai Miao* (White Hmong) and *Hua Miao* (Flowered Hmong). The names of the different sub-groups generally refer to the colours of the Hmong skirt worn by that group's women (Lue Vang and Lewis 1990: vi-vii).

The Hmong in Thailand, who are divided into White and Green Hmong sub-groups, are believed to be descended from the *Pai Miao* (White Hmong) who lived in the mountainous areas of Western Guizhou, South Sichuan and Yunnan in the late eighteenth and early nineteenth century (Mischung no year: 16).[77] White Hmong (*hmoob dawb*) and Green Hmong (*hmoob ntsuab*) dialects have a common origin and are mutually intelligible (Cooper 1984: 51; see Bertrais 1978: 1-5). The minor socio-cultural differences between the White and Green Hmong people in Thailand have blurred even further due to intermarriage and other forms of cultural mingling. In the case of the White Hmong of Mae Sa Mai, who are a village minority, they have largely adapted their customs, dress and dialect to the dominant sub-group.

The issue of the origins of the Hmong is thus a matter of intense debate. So, too, are the origins of the Hmong language. However, the majority of scholars agree that Hmong is a member of the Miao-Yao language family. The relationship of the Miao-Yao language family is itself uncertain, but it is believed to be a sub-group of the Sino-Tibetan language constellation (Ratliff 2004: 147-148; Tapp 2001: 9; Matisoff 1983: 65; cf. Lemoine 1972). The Hmong language does not have an authentic Hmong script or writing system. A number of myths have arisen to explain the absence of written documentation of Hmong origins. According to these myths, the books

---

[77] The White Hmong women customarily wear blue pants for everyday, and white skirts or pants for New Year; the Green Hmong wear blue batiqued skirts, which also include other colours such as bright green, pink, or red. In the Hmong language, they are called *hmoob ntsuab* because of the colour of the indigo dye used to batik the fabric of the skirt. *Ntsuab* is usually translated as "green", but when it refers to the dialect group, it is translated as "blue" because of the deep blue (*xiav*) colour of the skirts (Lue Vang and Lewis 1990: vi-vii).

written in Hmong were lost, either as a result of Han Chinese encroachments on Hmong territories, or during the exodus from China to the former Indochina, or because they were eaten by hungry rats and cows (Schein 1999: 701, Cooper et al. 1996: 42; Tapp 1989: 94, 122-123). Under Han Chinese rule, the Hmong were forbidden to speak or write Hmong. For this reason, Hmong women often allegedly embroidered clothing with Hmong characters. Around 1976 in the Ban Vinai refugee camp in Thailand, Hmong women began to design "storycloths" that reproduce the narrative of traditional mountain village life and the loss of homeland. The storycloth embroidery relates accounts of war, exodus and refugee life, and has become central to the representation of diasporic identity among the Hmong in Asia and abroad (Julian 2003: 127; cf. Ovesen 2004: 464).

Because of the erosion of memory and the process of development of the embroidered characters, the Hmong script is believed to have undergone successive transformations only to be ultimately lost. In my interviews with Hmong informants, this loss of literacy was associated with the loss of the China homeland and the Hmong's overall low economic and political status in Southeast Asia. The symbolic importance of writing and books in turn contributed to the high level of support my Hmong informants gave to the project of writing about their culture. My research was regarded as another welcome contribution to the list of publications on Hmong culture in Thailand (see also Tapp 1989: 127).

Hmong culture in Thailand should be understood as *one* specific variant of Miao culture, which originated in China but underwent significant transformation and development after migration. Another important consideration is that the Hmong were also in close contact with the Han Chinese and the Yi, which both influenced Hmong culture in China.[78] Han

---

[78] The term "Yi" refers to the Tibeto-Burman speaking population of Southwest China and former northern Indochina and includes groups such as the Lisu, Yao, Akha and Naxi. Apart from the Han-Chinese, Yi was, next to the Chuang and other Tai groups, one of the main cultural groups among whom Hmong lived in south China and who affected and were affected by Hmong culture (Tapp 2001: 12).

influence is particularly evident in the Hmong system of patrilineal clan descent, mortuary rites, practices of geomancy, and even the Hmong language (cf. Geddes 1976: 11; Ruey 1960: 147). It may well be the case that the Hmong in Thailand, Laos, and Vietnam have been more able to preserve their "traditional" culture than the Hmong in modern-day China. However, the so-called traditional Hmong culture in Thailand cannot be said to represent Hmong culture overall. Rather, it is only a single cultural variant that derives historically from Miao peoples of nineteenth-century Central and West-Guizhou. Moreover, Hmong culture in Thailand has been subject to transformation, development and adaptation to new circumstances in the course of migration and settlement (Tapp 2001: 14; Mischung no year: 16).

Always on the move? Hmong migration and processes of sedentarisation

As they migrated south to seek refuge from conflict with Chinese imperialists and arable land for cultivation, Hmong crossed the border into Southeast Asia, settling in what is now Vietnam, Laos, Thailand, Burma (Myanmar) and even the Tibetan state of Mi-li (Tapp 1989: 18; Bernatzik 1947: 21-26). The first Hmong migrants reportedly arrived in northern Vietnam between 1660 and 1740. The first arrival of Hmong people in Laos is dated between 1815 to 1820 (Culas 2000: 33-35; Yang Dao 1992: 264; Quincy 1988: 56; Mottin 1980: 47).[79] The "migrants of the mountains", as William Geddes (1976) has termed the Hmong, were not concerned with national borders. Instead they paid much greater attention to clan and affinal attachments. These affiliations allowed the Hmong people to travel within strong clan networks that even today link Hmong in distant locales in foreign countries. Indeed, the Hmong culture has long been imbued with a migrational pattern, partly as a result of their Chinese exile, and partly because of the Hmong system of semi-sedentary swidden agriculture. This

---

[79] For a critical discussion of the reliability of dates of the earliest arrival of Hmong in the Indochinese Peninsula see Culas and Michaud 2004.

does not mean that the Hmong migrate because of a "genetic or culturally determined *wanderlust*" (Ovesen 1995: 76, italics in original). Instead, in their search for new settlement territories and arable land, the Hmong can be seen to follow their proverb: "There is always another mountain." This territorially unbound way of life thus partially compensated for their stateless status. The volume edited by Sucheng Chan, *Hmong Means Free* (1994), which is based on Hmong émigré accounts from Laos and the United States, exemplifies the continuity of the fundamental notions of freedom that the Hmong demonstrated already in the China uprisings (see also Géraud 1993: 402).

In their search for new areas of settlement, White and Green Hmong began to arrive in Thailand from Laos as early as the 1870s. According to local village histories and biographies from my areas of research, this migration continued within Thailand for several decades as the Hmong searched for regions suited to their pioneer swidden farming system (Culas 2000: 37-39; Tapp 1989: 17). Every three to fifteen years, the decline in yield and soil fertility reached the point that sections of villages and even entire villages moved in search of new arable land (Kunstadter 2000: 174; Mischung 1990: 265; Keen 1978: 210; Grandstaff 1976: 197; Geddes 1970: 3-4). Hmong informants recall these times in idealised fashion either as events they experienced personally, or from accounts told by their parents and grandparents about the period of freedom when the "Hmong flew like birds". Due to land scarcity, state policies, and economic hardship, this former freedom has largely been lost and has instead been transfigured in memory in a romanticised fashion. As a result, villages that were long sites of Hmong settlement but were then abandoned still figure prominently as topographic and social reference points for many Hmong people. These places are closely bound to lineage history, kin networks, and to the ancestors who are buried there, and many Hmong continue to visit the locations in the annual *hawm ntxaas* rituals each April.

A large number of Hmong fled Laos for Thailand beginning around 1975. The U.S. Central Intelligence Agency had extended the Vietnamese war into a "secret war" (Yang, Kou 2003: 276-277) in Laos, in which the Hmong fought under the Hmong military leader Vang Pao against communist groups in northern Laos.[80] Many Hmong joined the operation in hopes that cooperation with strong allies like the United States and France would secure their position in Laos (Ovesen 1995: 10; Yang Dao 1992: 267-270). The *Pathet Lao* communist party gained control of the country in the early 1970s and finally assumed power in 1975. At that point, the Hmong became key targets for retaliation by the Laotians. Many Hmong then became political refugees in the Unites States, Canada, Australia, France, Germany, Argentina and French Guyana (Chan 1994: 46-48).[81]

The Hmong who had fled to Thailand from Laos lived for many years in refugee camps on the Thai-Laotian border. In 1992, nearly 50.000 Hmong refugees still lived in these camps, of which Ban Vinai was the largest and most well known. The majority of these refugees hoped either to return to Laos, to stay in Thailand permanently, or to migrate to a third-asylum country (Fadiman 1997: 165-169; Yang Dao 1992: 270; Cooper 1986: 24; see Tapp 1986: 44). About 7.000 Hmong refugees elected to return to Laos even though they were restricted to the lowlands and prohibited from returning to their home villages. According to reports and personal communication with Hmong, approximately 15.000 Hmong, who did not want to stay in Thai villages or return to Laos, where they feared further repression, fled to the vicinity of the Tham Krabok Monastery in the North of Bangkok from where, in 2005, many people have migrated to the U.S.A.

---

[80] At present, Vang Pao is still an acknowledged, partly mystified, leader of the Hmong diaspora. He currently lives in Santa Ana (California, U.S.A.) and symbolises the resistance basis of Hmong identity. Another important figure is Hmong scholar Yang Dao, the first Hmong man to receive a PhD (in France). Yang Dao now lives in St. Paul (Minnesota, U.S.A.), the "diaspora centre" of the overseas Hmong (Julian 2003: 126).

[81] I have had personal contact to one Hmong family in Germany, who informed me that about eighty Hmong who arrived from Laos in 1979 live in two villages near Stuttgart, Germany. See also Tou T. Yang's (2003) article on these Hmong families in Germany, who were actually intended to emigrate to Argentina. Tou T. Yang is a Hmong American who served as a major in the U.S. Army while stationed in Germany, where he learned about the Hmong community. This community is the least known of all Hmong diaspora communities in the West (Yang, Kou 2003: 280). For an anthropological study that focuses on cultural and social change among Hmong in French Guyana, see Géraud 1993.

(cf. Yang, Kou 2003: 277; Fadiman 1997: 169). Hmong anthropologist Prasit Leepreecha (2001: 33) has collected data from a variety of sources about Hmong global population estimates today.[82] According to these and other authors' estimates, seven million Miao (who include the Hmong subgroup) live in China; 790.000 Hmong live in Vietnam; 316.000 in Laos; 250.000 to 300.000 settled in the United States; 126.300 in Thailand (not including the estimated 15.000 refugees from Laos who live in Thailand without official authorisation); 25.000 in Burma; 10.000 in France; 3.000 in French Guyana; 2.000 in Australia; 800 in Canada; eighty in Germany; and about thirty Hmong are reported to live in Argentina. (All figures are approximations.) In Thailand, the Hmong population has more than doubled over the last three decades, making them the second largest ethnic mountain group (Culas and Michaud 2004: 7, 83; Kunstadter et al. 1991: 110).

The population growth among the Hmong, and among other ethnic minorities and the Thai majority, has led to a scarcity of arable land not under governmental protection in northern Thailand in the past decades. In the 1960s, Hmong villages were still quite small, averaging approximately 400 inhabitants, and roughly fourteen persons per household. At that time, the largest Hmong village had a population of 600 (Keen 1978: 210). Because of patterns of migration to new fertile land and primary forests suited to pioneer swidden farming, an ordinary village spent only roughly one decade in a single location. Meanwhile, however, swidden agriculture went into decline and was ultimately banned. Coupled with the end of the opium-poppy based economy, the conversion to commercial agriculture, the increasing dependence on exterior markets, the monetarisation of the village economy and economic exchange, and the establishment of forest preserves, all made it far more difficult for the Hmong to relocate their villages. As a result, the Hmong in northern Thailand underwent a process of

---

[82] These population numbers must be regarded as vague estimates, which have been compared and adapted to figures in other publications (see e.g. Yang, Kou 2003: 276; Ovesen 1995: 9; Géraud 1993: 99). Although they are imprecise, the population statistics provide a rough distribution of the Hmong across the world.

sedentarisation (Michaud 1997: 222; Tapp 1989: 30; Cooper 1979: 173). Indeed, this successive process of sedentarisation among the Hmong began as early as the 1960s. Many of the villages I visited during my fieldwork in northern Thailand had existed at their current location for decades (see appendix). However, the Hmong did not consciously choose permanent settlement. Rather, it was a necessity imposed by land scarcity, outside pressure, and state policy (Mischung 1986: 96, 130). Since the 1970s, the Royal Forestry Department has been actively engaged in working to "replace forest and keep these nomads fixed in one place" (Tapp 1989: 35). The forest protection policy went hand in hand with the overall aim of the state to control remote mountain areas and co-opt them economically into the national market and geopolitically into the state. Other measures to extend state control over mountain regions and compel permanent settlement of the Hmong minority included the erection of state outposts, the construction of Thai schools, and the extension of road infrastructure. As I explain below, the most important consequence of sedentarisation was the necessary shift from migratory swiddening to permanent cash crop cultivation within local resource use systems (cf. Michaud 1996: 271).

According to Nicholas Tapp (1989: 25), Hmong migrations have not come to a complete halt in spite of processes of permanent settlement. Tapp conceives of the migration of Hmong within Thailand as part of a long-term pattern of migration that has lasted for thousands of years and has spanned the region from northern China to southern China, Indochina, Thailand and Burma, and western countries like the United States and Australia. In recent times, this migration has also entailed a move from rural mountainous areas to urban settings like Chiang Mai and Bangkok. As the following chapters demonstrate, the Hmong rely on their extensive clan networks to move quite freely across Thailand to take advantage of job opportunities and visit relatives. Although these movements are not as wide-ranging as the large-scale migrations of the past, they nonetheless underscore that Hmong can and do continue to travel, relying on Hmong kinship structures, in order to pursue better living and economic opportunities.

The Hmong diaspora

Authors like Kou Yang (2003), Roberta Julian (2003), Louisa Schein (2004, 1999), Nicholas Tapp (2004; 2002a, 1989), and Gary Yia Lee (2004; 1996) all have written about the "Hmong diaspora" and their dispersal from China to Southeast Asian countries and to other parts of the world.[83] The Hmong-American diaspora in the United States is probably the most widely known. The US Hmong community has a "Hmong Resource Centre" in Saint Paul (Minnesota), a newsletter, several Internet information sources, and a number of journals, including the "Hmong Studies Journal", the "Hmong Forum" and the "Hmong American Journal" (cf. Yang, Kou 2003: 292-293).[84] In Los Angeles, a large New Year celebration is held on December 26, which is visited by approximately 30.000 to 40.000 Hmong from across the country. In the United States, Hmong political and cultural activists consciously attempt to unite Hmong into a transnational coalition. Here the (internet) sources and institutions cited above constitute only a single element of the project of "identity management" (cf. Julian 2003: 141). These activists and "cultural entrepreneurs" aim for a conscious mobilisation and redefinition of Hmong ethnicity along diasporic terms (see also Safran 2004: 17). The outcome is what Benedict Anderson has described as an "imagined community" (1983: 15), or a community that transcends spatial boundaries (Schein 2004: 273; Schein 1999: 723; cf. Cohen 1979: 185-187). This imagined community reconstitutes and re-enacts the past for the younger generations in an effort to mediate the history of expulsion from China and later from Laos, and "the *agon*, the tension, between past and present" (Tapp 1989: 190, italics in the original). Since 1995, a yearly "Hmong National Conference" has provided a forum for the exchange and

---

[83] See also William Geddes (1976: 10), who compares the Hmong to the Jews. He believes that the preservation of Hmong identity during the long history of migration is even the more notable because the Hmong lack "the unifying forces of literacy and a doctrinal religion" (see also Yang, Kou 2003: 273). In case of one of the other Thai ethnic mountain groups, the Akha, Leo Alting von Geusau (2000:142) also speaks of a diaspora.

[84] Information about these institutions, sources, and links to other groups can be found on http://www. hmongcenter.org.

dissemination of information, networking, and the discussion of contemporary issues (Yang, Kou 2003: 290-291).

The Hmong diaspora in Thailand is not nearly as prominent as the one in the United States. Because the Hmong have lived for many years as an ethnic mountain minority in Thailand, the larger public does not perceive them as a diaspora group with a history of dispersion. Moreover, the Hmong in Thailand do not portray a public image of a diaspora group in the manner of the Hmong in the United States. However, in spite of the absence of unified leadership and powerful cultural entrepreneurs with the resources and ability for large-scale efforts, the Hmong in Thailand, especially in the cities and at the universities, have also organised into non-governmental organisations (NGOs) and interest groups in an attempt to promote Hmong culture in Thailand outside of the Chinese homeland. One popular event organised by groups like the Hmong Association and the Inter Mountain Peoples Education and Culture in Thailand Association (IMPECT)[85] of Chiang Mai was the big New Year Celebration in the year 2000, organised to strengthen Hmong identity and "diasporic consciousness" in Thailand. The celebration, held in the municipal stadium in the middle of Chiang Mai, lasted for several days. Hmong from across Thailand and from neighbouring countries and overseas attended the celebration. During a break in my Karen fieldwork, I was able to attend and admire the large and colourful variety of Hmong costume on display.[86] At the celebration, relationships among far-flung kin were renewed, the latest information about Hmong topics was exchanged, potential marriage partners were considered by the young and their parents, and a translocal Hmong identity was displayed to the Thai and multinational visitors.

---

[85] The "Inter Mountain Peoples Education and Culture in Thailand Association" (IMPECT) is a Chiang Mai based NGO founded by members of ethnic mountain groups. The Association's objectives are to develop and strengthen local leaders, community organisations and networks to enable mountain groups to find their own solutions to problems (personal communication with Karen scholar Prasert Trakarnsuphakorn, former head of IMPECT, 20.1.2000 in Chiang Mai).

[86] Louisa Schein (2004: 280-282) argues that the many existing Hmong costume styles are a "a prime example of the kinds of cultural flow that transnationality has precipitated".

This transnational Hmong identity is largely based on a common notion of the Hmong homeland (cf. Dunnigan 1986: 45). This homeland is also referred to as *ntuj khaib huab* in Hmong rituals such as the ones performed at the New Year and at mortuary rites. Regardless of how the land is imagined or constituted, it serves as a symbolic anchor and immensely powerful unifying symbol for the Hmong in Thailand and in other countries around the world (Fadiman 1997: 13-14; see also Gupta and Ferguson 1997b: 39). For the Hmong in Thailand, this homeland is typically located or imagined in China. For the Hmong of the overseas diaspora, who often have multiple geographical connections to countries like China, Laos, and Thailand, the homeland is more likely to be located in Thailand than in China or Laos as these countries are less accessible for visits.[87]

"[…] that homeland is as much, if not more, a product of discursive construction as it is a geographic site" (Schein 1999: 699). This homeland is not envisioned as a territory but rather as "a social space in which all people can be together" (Ovesen 2004: 464). The multiple images of a real or imagined Hmong homeland function, among other things, as political capital, as a symbol for "genuine" traditions, and as a justification for the hopes of a "Hmong nation". Images of a Hmong homeland are influenced and disseminated in Thailand via Hmong videos produced by Californian Hmong filmmakers in Thailand and China. The videos are an important representation of a unified Hmong identity and culture created within "Hmong-America" (Schein 2004: 277-280; cf. Julian 2003: 130; Lee 1996: 31). The videos, which were very popular among the Hmong in my area of research, convey an extremely romanticised and rural image of "original" Hmong culture in China. Many Hmong also watch daily Chinese soap operas on Thai television. As Maiv Las, the thirty-four-year-old wife of my Hmong assistant, Win Huj, noted, "Chinese culture had greatly influenced Hmong people. But the Hmong in Thailand have already lost parts of our

---

[87] Since the 1980s though, there has been a growing number of "return" visits from overseas Hmong to Thailand, Laos and China to rediscover the imaginary homeland (Tapp 2002a: 16).

original culture. This is why we like to watch Chinese movies." (Source: field interview, H-PS 13) As Nplaj Thoj, the renowned forty-seven-year-old leader of the Xiong clan in Mae Sa Mai and an important ritual expert stated:

"China is real and very important. The Hmong in China possess the true, complete Hmong culture. The Hmong in Thailand have already adapted and lost some of our traditions. It is good that Hmong people from China visit us from time to time to discuss Hmong culture. As far as I can remember, Chinese Hmong have been to Mae Sa Mai four or five times already. The Hmong in America also try to maintain their traditions. They have created new settlements in America but they are still Hmong in origin, and they remain close by visiting us, too." (Source: field interview, H-S1 98)

Vaam Yaj (a man who is forty-three years old) from Nong Hoi Mai, a village in the vicinity of Mae Sa Mai, longed for the creation of a Hmong nation and was convinced that a return to the Chinese homeland was impossible:

"I would like to see the Hmong have their own Hmong country someday. [...] It makes me sad that Hmong people are scattered across the world. I miss our Hmong homeland in China but I know that we were driven out and cannot go back. We do not belong there any longer, even though our origins lie in China. It is our burden that we belong to an ethnic group that has had to adapt to many countries and learn many languages. Hmong people learn other languages quickly. But Thai monks and teachers spend ten, twenty, or even thirty years in our villages without speaking one word of Hmong! We have even learned to speak Karen just because the Karen work for us and we buy our rice from them. [...] As a minority, we have to work hard to preserve our culture. This is why we pass along our history orally from generation to generation. The history of our common ancestors in China is as important as our clan system that we can rely on wherever we travel." (Source: field interview, H-S1 26)

According to Nicholas Tapp (2001: 14), this strong sense of belonging to larger Chinese based diaspora community explains the Hmong's fairly successful resistance to the Thai state's assimilationist efforts. Due to the global Hmong network and the "diaspora politics" mainly implemented by Hmong leaders in the United States, the Hmong have now achieved the status of an "ethnic group on a global scale" (Tapp 1989: 189). This sense of belonging to a transnational Hmong diaspora obviously varied greatly among the Hmong inhabitants of my research sites. For example, old women from the remote village of Ban Phui, who have little contact with the outside world, tend to conceive of themselves as members of a Southeast Asian Hmong Mountain community. In contrast, the men in my research sites tended to define the Hmong Mountains in a more expansive fashion to include Southeast Asian Hmong who are socio-economically still largely defined by an agricultural mountain lifestyle, and overseas Hmong who no longer live in mountainous regions but nonetheless are members of the far-flung Hmong community.

As the statements by my Hmong informants suggest, China is important both as an (imagined) homeland and as an important reference point for present day Hmong culture in Thailand (and other countries of the diaspora). In this regard, the Hmong in my research area agreed with the theory of "deteriorating knowledge" (Tapp 2001: 16), believing that Hmong cultural knowledge was gradually being lost as each successive generation failed to pass the totality of its knowledge of the far-away Chinese homeland on to the next generation. In addition, due to lack of interest in Hmong knowledge, the younger generation failed to learn all of what was being made available to them. As a result, the valuable Hmong knowledge was in the process of successive erosion. Elders then had to rely on Hmong from China, who were believed to have preserved their Hmong cultural heritage, in order to fill gaps in their knowledge of ritual texts, songs and shamanic practices.

Summary

This chapter outlines the history of Hmong origins in China while emphasising that a single Hmong culture cannot be said to exist. Instead, the

Hmong constitute only one of four subgroups among the Miao in China. The Hmong subgroup is divided into five additional units, one of which was the ancestral group of the White and Green Hmong in Thailand. The Han Chinese (and the Yi) played an important role in influencing Hmong culture. Hmong cultural practice in Thailand developed from the nineteenth-century Chinese Hmong subgroup. This "traditional background" was transformed and developed in the course of migration and accommodation to the Thai host country. In spite of efforts to maintain "original" and traditional Hmong culture by transmitting specific Hmong cultural knowledge, Hmong culture in Thailand has been transformed due to inside developments, outside influences, and the variety of challenges of present-day life. The most prominent example is the transformation from a semi-sedentary society that practiced pioneer swidden agriculture to a sedentary society involved in regional, national and international markets via an increasingly diversified cultivation of cash crops.

In the following chapters, I will analyse in greater detail the impact of this radical socio-economic change on Hmong culture overall and on Hmong cultural spatiality in particular. As I have already demonstrated in the current chapter, Hmong in Thailand increasingly define themselves as members of a global Hmong community. This identification is in part "promoted" by cultural entrepreneurs and male Hmong visitors from China and abroad, and in part promoted by Hmong videos.[88] Images of China founded largely on nostalgic images of the late imperial era continue to constitute the basis of the perception of a lost 'homeland', which functions as symbolic anchor and unifying symbol for the Hmong in Thailand and in the diaspora abroad. As is typical for many diaspora groups, the Hmong are also aware that they will not be able to return to this "mythical homeland" (cf. Michaud 2004: 6). Instead, the Hmong in Thailand will need to come to terms with their current

---

[88] Hauke Dorsch (2004: 107) also underscores the importance of video-clips and music, which transmit ideas of cultural connectedness of the African-American diaspora to the homeland in Africa.

status as one of the sedentarised mountain minorities via processes of place making that is deeply rooted in ancestral China.

Despite the fact that Hmong people have been forced to settle permanently, migration and movement are still integral parts of their culture, both within their remembered experiences of dispersion from China and within ongoing migration movements in Thailand. The memories of the ancestral homeland in China are preserved in rituals and in stories about many places in Thailand and other nations where their ancestors lived. The Hmong visit the graves of their most important lineage ancestors once a year, which is one of their religious practices that link the past to the present, and the regions of former migration with the stable settlements of the present day. This history of migration and the commemoration of their ancestors constitute an important element of Hmong spatiality in Thailand. Indeed, Hmong spatiality in Thailand extends far beyond their current village sites to include many reference points in their mental model of the Hmong Mountains.

As Mbua Yim's father, who lived in Ban Phui, explained regarding the Hmong Mountains:

> "I've seen Thai maps but I don't understand them because I can't read. But I've travelled to many places and they all are still inside my mind, I can remember them all. That is why I can find my way in the Hmong Mountains. Hmong live everywhere in the mountains. But now they also live in other places, so they should actually be called by the place where they live. But we still see that they belong to the mountains. When I go to town and people ask me where I am from, I say 'from the Hmong Mountains'. I can't explain exactly what or which areas belong to the mountains. It's simple, mountain means mountain."
> (Source: field interview, H-S2 13)

6 HMONG COSMOLOGICAL SPACES AND RELIGIOUS PRACTICES

The objective of this chapter is to explain Hmong cosmology and to show how the Hmong are spiritually anchored in space by their beliefs and ritual practices. A discussion of the main characteristics of Hmong cosmology, and of the Hmong belief in supernatural agents and reincarnation, sheds light on the fact that the Hmong conceptualise life as one part of the cycle of birth, life, death, passage to the "Otherworld" and rebirth. Hmong cultural spatiality is strongly influenced by these religious conceptualisations and ritual practices, particularly as they do not bind the people to a single place and time. Religion – as one of the core aspects of Hmong culture – provides the Hmong with a total view of how the world operates and of their place in history and the cosmos.

At the start of my fieldwork, one of my neighbours and key informants, Vaam Zeej, a forty-eight-year-old member of the Xiong clan in Mae Sa Mai, visited me and told me the following:

> "Hmong culture has two central aspects, religion and kinship, which cannot be changed and which need to be handed down unchanged from one generation to the other. Our economic system can be changed at any time. It is our strength that we can adapt to new economic situations so easily. So if you want to understand Hmong culture, you need to learn about Hmong religion and our kinship system first. I can teach you and introduce you to the Hmong manner of rituals connected to dead people. Once you have learned more about these rituals, you will understand the most important foundation of Hmong culture." (Source: field interview, H-R1 22)

Vaam Zeej Xyooj offered to act as my teacher to help me learn Hmong core values, beliefs, and practices as quickly and thoroughly as possible. It is customary that knowledgeable elders teach younger Hmong men elements of Hmong knowledge. Many of the village elders believed it was important that I be formally instructed in key features of Hmong religion so I would learn enough about their complex culture within my year's stay and not only learn about less important "female knowledge".

As Vaam Zeej noted, religion and kinship form the pillars of Hmong society. They are not distinct spheres but rather are highly interwoven. For example, kinship identities are reproduced in the "cultural arena" of religious ceremonies because most "rituals are aimed at underlining the nexus between dead parents or ancestors and descendants" (Leepreecha 2001: 81). In other words, religious beliefs and kinship structures are closely linked cultural domains that reproduce and reinforce one another through socio-cultural practices. As Nicholas Tapp emphasises, "[k]inship, burial, and geomantic practices all form part of a *single conceptual* system, characterised by powerfully 'Chinese' overtones" (1989: 179, italics in original). While Hmong attempt to pass along religious and kinship structures in their most "traditional" and "original" form to the next generation, the Hmong economy is very adaptable, which increases their ability to adjust to new challenges. Yeeb Yaj who is thirty-four years old, married, has four children and was another of my key informants in Mae Sa Mai, said that the Hmong are very "sensitive" in some ways but adaptable in others:

"Sensitive describes the words and the knowledge we have when we deal with aspects other than farming. We can adjust fast, change fast. But change deep inside takes a long time. The world has opened up a lot, and is changing a lot. The old men want to hang on to the old tradition, but we have to adapt our own culture, not change it but adapt it to these new circumstances. The whole world is changing!" (Source: field interview, H-S1 34)

Despite the fact that the Hmong attempt to consciously adhere to central religious beliefs and kinship practices, a number of my Hmong informants stated with regret that most of the former diversity of "Hmong tradition" has been lost, apart from religious knowledge centring around the ancestor cult, shamanic rituals, marriages and mortuary rites. "Many aspects of Hmong culture are lost already, especially knowledge of songs, *feng shui* and the order of the world", Win Huj told me during one of the many mortuary rites we attended together. Win Huj's belief corroborates the notion of "deteriorating knowledge" mentioned above, and underscores that the Hmong people have not been able to limit change and adaptation solely to their economic practice. Despite their attempt to adhere to central religious beliefs and kinship practices, these cultural domains are also affected by "inside" developments and influences from outside, and cannot be totally shielded from loss of knowledge and adaptation (cf. Michaud 2004: 7-8; see Ellen and Harris 2000: 5).

Annual ritual at the ancestor's grave (*hawm ntxaas*)

In spite of these changes, religious and kinship structures continue to greatly influence daily life and constitute a central aspect of Hmong culture and identity. Hmong rituals are rich, complex, and varied and can occur at any time, in any place. Ritual practices profoundly anchor the Hmong in their own cosmological spaces. In addition to various rituals (see below) that can take place daily and can even be performed simultaneously in a single household, the Hmong also have many "ritually charged times" (Tapp 2001: 12) that span several days or even weeks. These include the rituals for illness or death, which can span several days, and the rituals on the occasion of the Hmong New Year.

The extent to which Hmong daily life is influenced by religious practices became particularly evident when my assistant's father, Txwj Xaab (who was sixty-six years old at the time of my research), fell ill with kidney disease. Day and night, Txwj Xaab was visited by (mostly male) villagers and lineage members of neighbouring villages. Shortly before his death, numerous lineage kin from other northern Thai provinces visited for several days. They came to pay respect to Txwj Xaab and show their affection, and also to conduct small rituals on his behalf. These were performed in addition to the Hmong shamanic healing rituals, the ancestor ritual (*nju dab*), diverse healing rituals carried out by ritual experts, shamanic rituals by a female Thai shaman in Chom Thong, visits to the hospital in Chiang Mai for dialysis and treatment with Western medicine, treatment with Chinese herbal medicine, and visits by the Chiang Mai-based Catholic priest. Txwj Xaab's family had "partially" converted to Catholicism in 1998. The Yang clan shaman and Win Huj's father himself believed that the disease was not only a malfunction of the kidneys, but suspected that its causes were also linked to the realm of the supernatural. Generally, Hmong concepts of illness and health are also closely connected to the religious sphere.

The religious system of the Hmong is, in fact, a total view of how the world operates – it is their (therapeutic) science, mythology, genealogy, history, and penal code. If they lose their knowledge of these systems of belief and explanation, the Hmong would lose an important source of information about themselves and their place in history and in the world (Yang Dao 1992: 279).

Hmong cosmology: View of the world

Because most Hmong religious knowledge is passed on orally from one generation to the next, a number of different versions of religious tenets coexist. For example, informants and scholars tend to agree on some elements of the origin myth but disagree on others. The god *Yawm Saub*, or the "Lord of the Sky", is commonly believed to have advised a sister and brother to bear children because they were the only human beings left on earth after a great flood. At first, the sister did not want to violate the incest taboo. She finally gave in after her brother tricked her by "proving" that supernatural beings were in favour of the plan. The remainder of the myth also varies according to the way it was handed down: After being persuaded by her brother, the sister gave birth to a strange thing reported to have been a pumpkin, a shapeless lump of flesh, green essence, clay, or an egg. The object was divided or carved into twelve pieces by the sibling couple; the pieces became human, and the founders of the Hmong clans (for different versions of this myth see Cha 2001: 5-9; Lee 1996: 6-7; Mischung 1990: 284; Tapp 1989a: 60, Bender 1988: 124-125).[89] Some of my informants in Mae Sa Mai and Ban Phui recounted that the pieces were scattered around by the sibling couple and grew into mountains overnight. These were the foundation of the Hmong Mountains, onto which people of different clans were born until the earth was "full of people".

Cosmology entails more than a community's worldview; it also is a people's spatial model of the immediate and physical world (Levinson 1992: 33; cf. Ingold 2000: 15). The sense of belonging in and to particular places and spaces is reinforced by the belief that deities, spirits and other supernatural beings are also, in a sense, localised. In many cosmologies and mental models of the universe, deities, spirits, ancestors or unborn souls are conceived as located within a large three-dimensional scheme, just like terrestrial and celestial phenomena. The Hmong of the two research sites also divide the world into three spheres: the sphere *above* the sky (*ngaum ntuj*, literally: above the sky), the earth (*yaj ceeb*, literally: human place) and the sphere underneath the earth (*yeeb ceeb*, literally: spirit or non-human

---

[89] According to the Chinese system of calculation, the course of the day (as well as the year) is connected to twelve animals: the rabbit, dragon, snake, horse, goat, monkey, chicken, dog, pig, rat, cow, and tiger. Each animal is connected to an hour of the day, as well as to a day and a year. The day starts at 6 a.m. and ends at 6 p.m. The night is connected to twelve animals as well (the same as in the day). The Hmong name for this system of calculation is *ntham xwg* (literally: calculate with fingers).

place).[90] All three spheres are believed to be populated by a variety of supernatural spiritual forces.

Hmong scholars like Jean Mottin (1982: 28) and Guy Moréchand (1968: 173) have recorded Hmong myths of origin that describe how the *ntuj* (the sky) existed prior to the rest of the world. According to these myths, the *ntuj* created the earth and is a superior, indistinct phenomenon reigning above while remaining immaterial and not concrete (see Symonds 2004: 11; Tapp 1989a: 59; Mottin 1980: 114-117; Moréchand 1968: 176-177). The subterrestrial sphere is more immanent for the Hmong. It is regarded as the land of the spirits and also referred to as "the land of darkness" or the "Otherworld". The *yaj ceeb*, in contrast, is referred to as "the land of light", or the land of the living and spirits. In the related Chinese belief system, the world of all people, material objects and nature is called *yang*, while the land of darkness or the Otherworld that parallels the dark world of the spirits is called *yin* (Lemoine 1996: 155; Tapp 1989a: 59; Lyman 1968: 5).

Figure 1: Cosmos depicted as a mouth

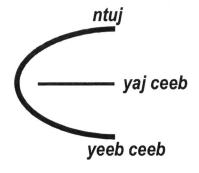

Source: Drawing by Ntxhoo Yaj, Mae Sa Mai, 3 March 2003

One female shaman I met in Mae Sa Mai described the world to me as a "mouth". She conceived of the places and supernatural beings above the sky and underneath the earth as spiritually stronger than "the human place" and its people, who can be easily "eaten" by the powerful "supernatural mouth".

---

[90] In my research sites, *yeeb ceeb* is clearly conceptualised as a mountainous sphere located *underneath* the earth.

The figure below depicts a synthesis of Hmong cosmology based on a figure by Christian Culas (2004: 110). Culas divides the Hmong world into the supernatural and celestial world; the world of humans belongs to the supernatural world because humans are bound to the world of spirits.

Figure 2: Synthesis of Hmong Cosmology

[Figure: Diagram showing supernatural world (terrestial world of humans, world of spirits) and celestial world (heaven of souls of the deceased, heaven of the divinities), with separations between humans and spirits, between sphere of spirits and the deceased, and a vague border between the deceased and the divinities.]

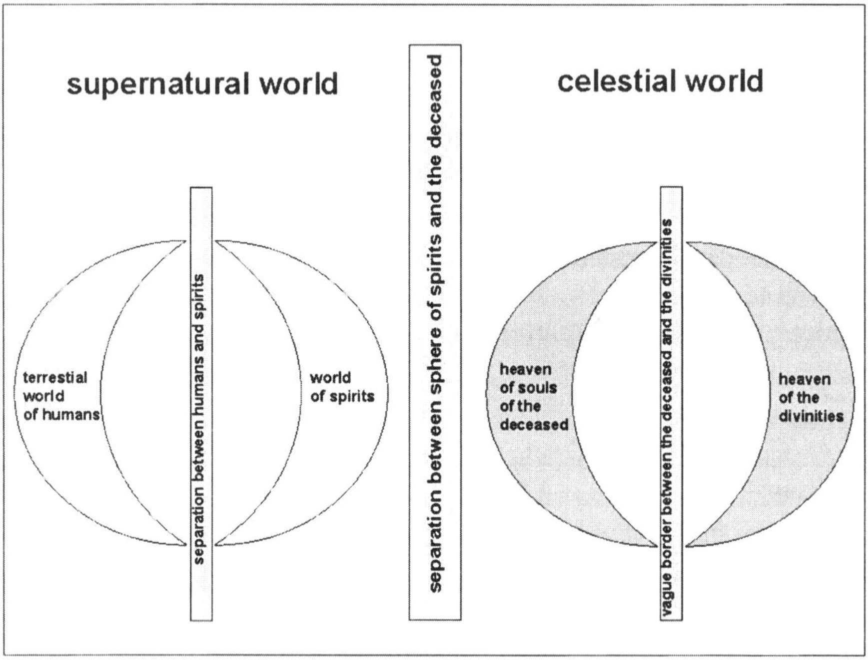

Source: Culas (2002: 100), own alterations

In my research sites, the superior sphere above the sky, with its undefined powers, is believed to be hierarchically structured and divided into twelve floors or twelve great mountains linked by stairs. Godlike creatures, *Yawm Saub* and his wife, *Puj*, rule *ntuj*. The deity couple, who are also referred to as the "Queen and King of Heaven", is responsible for fertility and reproduction but rarely interact with humans. It is believed that they live in the far realms of *ntuj*. A half-god and half-man creature, *Siv Yis*, is believed to be the master shaman who acts as an intermediary between the deity couple and humans on earth. *Siv Yis* is characterised by benevolence, profound knowledge, and strong healing powers. When humans are sick, *Siv Yis* – as the premier shaman – performs shamanistic curing rituals to obtain forgiveness for all the wrongs ever committed by the sick person. The shaman's altar, which is located on the wall of the shaman's house opposite the main door, is believed to represent *Siv Yis'* grotto near the top of one of the supernatural mountains of *ntuj*.

In addition, the sphere above the sky is also believed to be the home of the founder couple *nkauj ntsuab nraum naas* (mother and father) of the origin myth, diverse spirits called *dab* (in Green Hmong: *dlaab*), and the giant dragon called *Zaj* (in Green Hmong: *Zaaj*). There exists a larger *dab ntuj*, as well as *dab* for all "corners" of the sky: *dab paab npeg* (side above all = north), *dab paab ntsaa* (down side = south), *dab hnub tuaj* (sunrise = east) and *dab hnub npoob* (sunset = west). Each clan believes in different *dab*; there appear to be more malevolent *dab* (*dab qus*) than benevolent ones.

Numerous informants told me that the giant and evil dragon *Zaj* is the owner of the water, rivers, ponds and other natural features but also lives in the sphere above the sky.[91] The topography of the land is believed to represent the dragon's body, and its contours and veins are the mountain ridges and watercourses. As my Ban Phui informants emphasised, most Hmong people are afraid of malevolent spirits and *dab* and especially of this giant dragon, which according to Chinese folk narratives symbolises imperial power. A sixty-seven-year-old man from Ban Phui emphasised:

> "Most people are afraid of *Zaj* because of his bad manners. It is very easy to anger him, and he eats humans. His evil sign is the rainbow. When Hmong see a rainbow, we believe that this is *Zaj*. A rainbow is nothing good. If *Zaj* has touched a person who has not respected his rules around water, the shaman must perform a ritual to heal the

---

[91] Nicholas Tapp (1989a: 61) recounts that *Zaj* resides in a palace at the bottom of the sea that is part of the sphere underneath the earth (*yeeb ceeb*) (see also Lemoine 1996: 165).

person. But normally, no things are offered to *Zaj*." (Source: field interview, H-R2 69)

As an extension of the belief that *Zaj* is the owner of all water, Hmong believe that water sources and rivers must be protected so that the evil and powerful dragon is not disturbed or angered. For example, when a water source ran dry in Mae Sa Mai, a sacrificial ritual was held to appease *Zaj* for the overuse of water, and the land around the source was turned into a protection zone.

In Hmong belief, the earth is populated by humans and animals as well as a variety of *dab* and other supernatural spiritual forces, including ancestor spirits called *puj yawm txwv txoob* and *ib tug dab*. These spiritual forces animate objects and thus surround humans everywhere and at all times (cf. Lue Vang and Lewis 1990: 3; Tapp 1989a: 59). Spirits are not evil or malevolent by nature, but can attack a body's vitality (*plig*) when they feel disturbed and disrespected. *Plig*, conceived as a distinctive set of "souls" tend to wander around and thus can easily be attacked by spirits. The actual number of *plig* is difficult to determine; both the Hmong in my research sites as well as the Hmong in other anthropological studies have given widely varying answers to questions about the number of *plig*. At different times, Hmong have stated that there exist one, two, three, five, seven, twelve, or thirty-two *plig* (Holly Peters-Golden 2002: 84; Lemoine 1996: 146-148; Yang Dao 1992: 273-274; Symonds 1991: 44; Tapp 1989a: 75, 87; Lyman 1968: 6). According to shamanic tradition, people have three main souls (or life essences). At death, one soul remains with the grave, one returns to the ancestors, and the third is reborn (Tapp 1989a: 87). In my two research sites, most Hmong spoke of only one *plig*, located in the centre of the head. Although the number of souls appears to vary, the Hmong concept of soul and loss of the soul appears very similar everywhere.

The belief in spirits transcends all aspects of life, including spatial boundaries. Spirits are believed to exist everywhere on earth, above the sky, and underneath the earth. I went on a tour to the mountains surrounding Mae

Sa Mai together with Win Huj, his brother Ntsum Nraiv (thirty-two years, married, four children), and their lineage "brother" Yeeb. We offered the first part of our lunch to the "owner spirit" of the place (*xeeb teb*) where we sat in the forest. When Hmong eat outdoors or outside the village, they first are expected to offer part of the meal to the "owner spirit" of the place, regardless of whether they are in a forest near the village, in Bangkok, or in San Francisco. As Chaiv Yas Yaj, a seventy-one-year-old blacksmith and ritual expert from Mae Sa Mai, explained:

> "Every place has a leader of spirits, whom we call *xeeb teb xeeb chaws* - the leader of the place, or the village, water source, mountains, or the fields. When people eat outdoors, the leader is invited to eat with the people and to protect them from bad spirits. For example, the *xeeb teb* of Mae Sa Mai lives in the sacred tree, the *ntoo xeeb*. [...] We always have to respect and honour these different *dab*."
> (Source: field interview, H-R1 55)

Win' Hujs brother, Ntsum Nraiv, says that Hmong always feel these spirits; in some way they are always there, no matter where one is. They always must be respected and feared, which was one of the reasons for his family's' "partial" conversion to Catholicism. Ntsum Nraiv no longer wanted to fear and pay attention to the spirits in the house, the village, the forests and the fields that can bring bad luck at any time when they have been angered by disrespectful behaviour or actions. Yeeb Yaj still believes in the traditional Hmong religion. He explained:

> "There are *dab* everywhere. All rivers, mountains, forests and other places have *dab*. We have to sacrifice to them when we eat outside our house, or in far away places. Then the *dab* protect you and do not harm you. The *dab ntuj* are the most powerful *dab* because they can see everything from above. People say that the good *dab* are inside the house, but there are also some good *dab* in the place underneath the earth, they work as police there. Outside the house, there are mostly bad *dab* – in the trees, rivers, mountains, simply everywhere. These spirits protect humans when they are asked and when they receive

offerings. If they do not receive offerings, they can bring harm. There is also a dragon at the river who can punish women when they touch the water during their menstrual bleeding." (Source: field interview, H-R1 88-89)

Yeeb's statement emphasises the distinction between the good and safe "inside" sphere of the house and the village (the earth place), and the wild and untamed sphere of potentially dangerous supernatural agents. In the Hmong worldview, all spiritual beings are ambivalent and powerful. They sustain life and give strength, but may also bring harm and disease. In Hmong imagery, there is often a "metaphysical battle" between humans and spiritual beings, which results in illness or misfortune if humans succumb (Conquergood 1989: 45-46). A food sacrifice offered to the spirit of a place can be described as a propitious act, a mystical way to minimise the risk of angering the spirits and incurring harm. Hmong generally strive for equilibrium with the spiritual beings because *dab* (including ancestor spirits) are woven into all their activities: before rebirth in the Otherworld, during their lifetime, and also in the afterlife when awaiting reincarnation. The Hmong belief system also extends to all *places*, even to those unknown and outside Hmong territory. All areas can potentially be "Hmong space".

The Otherworld, or *yeeb ceeb*, is pictured as a mountainous territory. The Hmong way to communicate with the Otherworld is through shamanism and spirit propitiation, both features still affecting much of everyday life in the Hmong villages studied. The Otherworld or land of darkness is also thought to be populated by *dab* and by ancestor spirits, all ruled by the important deity, *Ntxwj Nyug*, and his wife, *Nyuj Vaj*. *Ntxwj Nyug* is responsible for life and death. He issues life licenses in "registration books", called *ntawv pe nyaj vaab tuam teem* (literally: our register book of god's sight), which determines an individual's lifespan. At the moment of death, when the registration book expires, the deity takes the book, evaluates the deceased's life, determines whether all rituals have been performed correctly, and decides whether and in what form the soul of the deceased shall be reborn –

as man, woman or animal (Symonds 1991: 52; Tapp 1989: 82). This means that the moment of death is already predetermined at birth. A shaman can diagnose that a patient's lifespan license is about to expire. Then the shaman enters the Otherworld in a trance and asks the deity to extend the license. In some cases, an old person wishes to die but is prevented from doing so because his or her lifespan has not yet expired.

In summary, Hmong must respect and follow the rules of the supernatural beings, including the giant dragon, the ancestor spirits, and *dab*, lest they be punished with misfortune or sickness. The supernatural sphere above the sky, the earth, and the sphere beneath the earth are characterised by a few benevolent forces and a large number of demonic forces, which must be appeased to avoid punishment and misfortune (cf. Tapp 1989: 81). The supernatural agents are both a supernatural power and an invisible link that unite the Hmong into a tightly organised community.

Religious spatiality: Geomancy

As this description shows, the Hmong include all spaces – known as well as unknown, potential as well as spiritual, on the earth, above the sky and underneath the earth – into the sphere where Hmong, their souls, or their ancestor spirits can be found. The practice of geomancy, called *saib chaw nyob* (literally: look place live), helps to anchor the Hmong in a specific locality and provide instructions about proper comportment in a (possibly unknown) place. This place may be anywhere in the world. Merely by examining the mountain landscape – the Hmong always imagine themselves in the mountains – a Hmong would immediately know where to erect a village and where to bury the dead (cf. Corlin 2004: 307-308; Tapp 2001: 15). Nicholas Tapp (1989: 173) hypothesises that Hmong forms of geomancy, and also their burial and patrilineal naming systems, are derived from complex historical processes of integration, incorporation, and assimilation with the Han Chinese in Southern China. The Chinese geomantic system called *feng shui* is believed to be the basis for Hmong geomancy (Tapp 1996: 83; see Feuchtwang 1974: 243).

Geomancy is especially important for the siting of a new village, houses and graves. The principles behind the siting of villages and houses are nearly the same, while the siting of burial places is more complex. Villagers can be affected by their village's or house's location in relation to the "veins" (*looj mem*) of the giant dragon, *Zaj*. Humans can also be affected by an incorrect siting of an ancestor's grave (Tapp 1988: 230; Tapp 1986: 50). The *looj mem* are lines of natural energy that are believed to run through the landscape, especially near mountains and watercourses, and to determine the sites favourable to the establishment of a village or burial place. In practice, a good location for a village is a location where the mountains are "behind and around" the village. The villages is then "nestled" inside the mountains and protected from "enemies, storms and other dangerous things from the outside", as informant Ntxhoov Neeb Yaj, a sixty-five-year-old expert on Hmong geomancy from Pang Hin Fon near Ban Phui explained. He further stated:

"For locating a village, the directions of the sky are not important, only the position of mountains and water. Hmong call this *roob puav zos* [literally: mountains surrounding the village]. Two mountains should come together. If the mountains come from both sides and the back, that is very good. The more mountains there are, the better. The right side of the mountains is the female side, which is like a tiger. The left side is the male side, which is like a dragon. The rear side of a village should look like a turtle. The fields are down there, or at the side of the mountain. For example, Ban Pui has a good location: There are high mountains behind and at the sides of the village and further away in front there are also mountains. In the area behind the village, no people should be buried. That would bring bad luck and a heavy burden from behind. But the *ntoo xeeb* should be in the top mountain behind or beside the village. It is important for the sacred tree to be above the village to protect the people in the village." (Source: field interview, H-R2 46-47)

Figure 3: Geomantically correct siting of a Hmong village

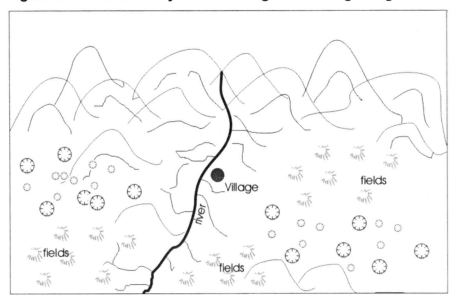

Source: Drawing by Ntxhoov Neeb Yaj, Pang Hin Fon, 10 March 2002

In terms of house construction, geomantic law requires that two houses stand parallel to one another. All main doors should face the downward slope. Directly opposing house doors should be avoided (Tapp 1988: 231). When a new construction site is chosen, a ceremony is performed to ascertain its spiritual suitability. Sometimes some rice is left overnight at the spot to see if it is still there the next morning. If the rice is untouched, the *dab* have approved the site. Another option is to throw the divination horns (*ntaus kuam*), made of two half-pieces of buffalo horn, and ask the oracle if the site is spiritually acceptable. Like many other Hmong rites, this ritual is Taoist in origin. The pattern of the horns as they fall determines whether the supernatural spirits have accepted the sacrifices and whether the ritual is successful. Throwing the divination horns is an easy way to communicate directly with the spirits, and most Hmong men are versed in the practice (see Tapp 1989a: 70; Chindarsi 1976: 48-52). Once the household spirit has "given" its approval for construction, the house can be built. Once it is completed, an altar (*taaj*) made of stamped paper is erected for the spirit on the wall opposite the main door. At the beginning of each Hmong year (according to the Chinese lunar calendar), a chicken or pig is sacrificed to the spirit on behalf of the general health and welfare of all the household members.

The correct location of graves is also extremely important. A correct burial site is important to the soul of the deceased and for his descendants: "[...] *it is upon the welfare of ancestors that the fortunes of their descendants depend* [...]." (Tapp 1989: 137, italics in original) An ancestor buried in a perfect geomantic location becomes a "king in heaven", which makes the son a "king on earth". According to some Hmong, there is no ideal burial site in Thailand. This explains why the Hmong have no king and continue to suffer comparative poverty and lack of political influence (Tapp 1988: 233). In Mae Sa Mai and Ban Phui, some mountain areas are geomantically approved burial sites, but have been "full" for a number of years. According to traditional belief, only one grave can be located in each geomantically appropriate site. Consequently, the dead in Mae Sa Mai, Ban Phui as well as in other Hmong villages have to be buried in the family's cash crop fields where the old geomantic rules can only be followed to some extent.

The unwritten system of geomancy, which is difficult to schematise unless a Hmong explains the geomantic principles "on site" by way of examples from the landscape, was first described by anthropologist Jacques Lemoine (1972: 99). Geomantic knowledge is no longer widespread among the Hmong in my subject villages. In my search for Hmong who could explain the system in greater detail, I was often referred to Chinese books on *feng shui* or sent to older, more knowledgeable Hmong men in other villages. Thus knowledge of one of the major systems of Hmong religion that ensures well-being and explains misfortune on a supernatural level is beginning to successively disappear.

Two reasons account for this gradual disappearance. First, geomantic knowledge cannot often be applied today since villages are permanent and land scarcity has led to the location of burial sites in cash crop fields. Suitably shaped and sized mountains are also scarce. Second, during periods of migration to new settlement areas, geomancy was important for the allocation of land among competing villagers (Tapp 1988: 237). In northern Thailand, where land is now under state jurisdiction and has been turned into conservation sites, competition over land now takes place between the Hmong, state departments, lowlanders and other ethnic groups. Competition over land thus no longer takes place on the supernatural level, but on the level of administration and concrete inter-group conflicts. The system of geomancy is slowly becoming obsolete even though many Hmong still believe that a correct burial site is essential for both ancestors and descendants (see also Tapp 1989: 158).

Shamans and other religious experts

Hmong religion includes several kinds of ritual practitioners, who all have dissimilar tasks and fields of practice: shamans who fall into trance; shamans who acquire shamanic knowledge by learning; ritual experts (sometimes called priests) who perform rituals for the household and the well-being of the people; and magical practitioners who specialise in herbal knowledge and medicinal spirits.

Hmong differentiate between *ua neeb* (shamanism), a special vocation aimed at healing, and *ua dab* (spirit rituals), aimed at propitiating ordinary spirits, assuring the peace and prosperity of a household. *Ua neeb* is aimed at helping people suffering grave illness by entering a shamanic trance, while *ua dab* is performed for one's own benefit. Shamanism cures by calling upon the spiritual sphere, while herbal and Western medicine cures in the physical sphere. *Ua dab* propitiates ordinary spirits and is a ritual practice that normally can be carried out by all male household members who have the necessary knowledge. Rites are usually intended to promote the physical and spiritual well-being of household and lineage members. They are usually performed inside the house at the altar, in the case of the house spirit, or outside the house and in the fields. These rituals by household members are performed in cases of mild sickness, misfortune, to ask for wealth and the protection of children and of people who are going on a journey or returning from one. Most Hmong are familiar with some aspects of *ua dab*, while only a few persons are familiar with *ua neeb* (Tapp 1989a: 65). Both *ua dab* and *ua neeb* "create a rhythm and a tempo of their own: properly speaking, they take place outside time, in a changeless world" (Tapp 1989a: 66). The belief in supernatural agencies populating all spheres of the world and the two ways of communicating with the Otherworld allow Hmong spatiality to stretch beyond the topographical settlement area in space *and* time.

The shaman (*txiv neeb*)

Hmong shamanism is, strictly speaking, not a "proper" religious domain but rather a form of healing. Its main objective is restoring the patient's body image (Lemoine 1986: 339; see also Eliade 1968: 36-37). The shamanic metaphor provides two basic sets of explanation for illness: first, illness results when a supernatural agent attacks the vital essence *plig* of the patience's body; second, illness results when a patient's *plig* is lost due to the intervention of spirits (Lemoine 1996: 148). Suffering and illness are believed to be the result of external aggression by supernatural agents of disease, the result of ancestral spirits who blame their descendants for not having found their way to the land of the ancestors, of improper mortuary rites, or of an unstable and wandering *plig* that was captured by *dab*.

A shaman's trance aims at obtaining information about three aspects: the patient's own vital mechanisms; the spiritual third parties who may have directly or indirectly caused the illness; and the shaman's power to identify and master the patient's condition (Lemoine 1996: 144).[92] A shaman's trance is divided into the diagnosis performance, where the patient does not play any active role, and the curing performance, where the patient and his or her family participate.

As mentioned above, there are two kinds of shamanism: the shamanism that entails trance (*ua neeb muag dub*) and the shamanism that does not entail trance (*ua neeb muag dawb*). The first kind of shamanism cannot be learned but is "imposed" on the shaman by the supernatural beings. The second kind of shamanism does not involve trance. Men who specialise in ways to communicate with the spiritual world learn it over a course of years. Their aim is to help people with protective rituals in cases of protracted misfortune or in instances where the individual fears serious supernatural affliction.

Male and female shamans interviewed in both Mae Sa Mai and Ban Phui all confirmed that shaman spirits are usually passed on from one generation to the next.[93] Usually the spirits first cause the person to become seriously ill before he or she consents to become a shaman and "serve" the tutelary spirits. The six shamans I spoke with in my research sites all claimed that they had not wanted to become a shaman, but were forced to cooperate with the spirits to cure a grave illness and elude death (Fadiman 1997: 21; see also Chindarsi 1983: 187-188). The belief that shamans are "initiated" into their profession by a serious illness or a "*maladie-vocation*" (French term used by Eliade 1968: 44) is familiar wherever shamanistic forms occur.

---

[92] Shamans are not possessed by the *neeb* but instead control the tutelary spirits for diagnosis and cure (Tapp 1989a: 72). For good descriptions of the sequence of events of a Hmong shamanistic trance see, for example, Lemoine and Eisenbruch 1997: 72-80; Lemoine 1996: 150-159.

[93] Four male shamans and one female shaman, who is not as often requested as her male counterparts, are active in Mae Sa Mai. Ban Phui has only two female shamans who are believed to know enough to carry out the standard rituals. When a special shaman is needed for a difficult illness, a male shaman from the Hmong village Khun Wang is either visited or brought to the village. Male shamans appear to generally have a higher reputation (see also Lemoine 1996: 143). Female shamans are not allowed to participate in rituals concerning the patriline of their husbands, such as calling in the *plig* of newborn babies or guiding the soul of the dead back to the Otherworld (Symonds 2004: xxvii).

Shamanism is a difficult role, replete with responsibilities towards the human and spiritual sphere. It is a particularly great burden on female shamans, who must also fulfil their roles as wives, mothers, and respectable women – roles that are not always congruent with that of a shaman. The trance is physically strenuous since the shaman must sometimes sit for many hours on the "shaman's horse", his or her entire body trembling while it is possessed by the spirits that "negotiate and fight" with the malevolent spirits responsible for a patient's suffering. During trance, the shaman, who is called *txiv neeb* (literally: father of the shaman spirits), often addresses the tutelary spirits, the *neeb*, in Mandarin.

Shamans are crucial to Hmong culture, particularly those who undergo shamanic trance. Through the shamans, deeply held beliefs within Hmong culture become apparent.

> "Through his or her healing trances, core tenets of the culture are performed and reinforced. The shamanic spirits, *dab neeb*, select their own representatives among the Hmong; it is not a matter of human choice." (Peters-Golden 2002: 84, italics inserted by M.T.)

When a shaman dies, his/her tutelary spirits, *dab neeb*, search for a new person to function as intermediary between the human and supernatural sphere and to receive the offerings. Even after a person is chosen, he or she must study for several years under a "parent-shaman" to learn about the different *dab*, the chants, the rituals, the trembling on the bench or "horse" (*nees huab cua*) in the trance during which the shaman fights with spirits or captures the wandering souls (*plig*) of the seriously ill. The shaman's shaking and trembling during the trance is an essential component of the healing ritual. For the shaman, it is exhausting and dangerous, because the shaman's own *plig* risks capture. Most shamans with whom I spoke to were reluctant to recount their experiences of trances in detail because they were afraid the spirits might punish them for disclosing the secrets of the Otherworld. However, the forty-seven-year-old female shaman from Ban

Phui (Piav Tsaab, married, four children), was more willing to speak than her male colleagues in Mae Sa Mai:

"When the spirit drives into my body, it feels like something stings me and then it prickles inside. [...] My shaman spirits come from my own ancestors. Other shamans have the shaman spirits of their ancestors. That means that each shaman has his or her own shaman spirits. When I became a shaman, I had already learned a lot on my own. But I still needed someone to guide me. First my mother, who was also a shaman, guided me, but then she died. Then my mother's brother in Mae Tho was my *xib hwb* (master shaman) who guided me. Actually I don't like being a shaman but I have no choice. The shaman spirits chose me. I don't think that I got the shaman spirits from my mother because they came to me before she died. They came from my ancestors. [...] I don't like being a shaman because Hmong women are not supposed to behave this way. But when the spirits come to me during a session I cannot control myself. To be a woman shaman is very difficult. I have to work in the house and in the fields for my family. It is really difficult when I am pregnant. [...] I usually do a shamanic ritual about three or four times per month, but when people ask for more, I have to do more. I share the work with the other woman shaman in the village. During a session, I always sing the same songs to communicate with the spirits. Each shaman has different words to speak with the spirits. I only change the words when I have to communicate with special spirits. Normal people cannot communicate with the spirits, they need shamans. I speak with the spirits for the villagers and then the spirits tell me what to tell to the villagers. The shaman spirits always comes to me, whether or not I wear the black cloth over my eyes. I wear it because, over the generations, the elders have asked us to wear the black cloth. [...] I cannot say how many spirits there are. I cannot see them with my eyes. I can only see them with my heart and my *plig*. The spirits above and underneath the earth look and behave just like normal people. The land of the spirits is full of mountains, and you need stairs to go from one level to the next. It is funny to go travelling in these lands because the spirits are funny and always interesting to look at. When the session is over, I forget everything. Actually I cannot tell you anything about the spirits right now. I only know everything when the spirits come to me during a session." (Source: field interview, H-R2 33-35)

At the end of a trance, the shaman determines what the ancestors or spirits demand as sacrifice for appeaseal, usually a chicken, pig, or sometimes even an ox. This sacrifice will allow the *plig* to return to the patient's body. Shamans are paid about 400 baht per ritual and also receive parts of the sacrificial animal (for example, the pig's head). The assistants in the shaman's ritual (who are usually shamans of the "second kind") are paid somewhat less, and also receive rice and parts of the sacrificial animal. Shamanistic séances are performed at least once per week (see also Ovesen 2004: 463). Since shamans are the mediators between humans and supernatural beings, they give ordinary people a vision of the cosmos during their "performances" when they are in trance. The knowledge of the world "above" and "below" is acquired during trances and direct spiritual access to the Otherworld. For the shaman, there is no place beyond his or her reach; during trance he or she can "go" anywhere. The "metaphorical space of the Beyond", as Jacques Lemoine (1996: 150) terms it, is also a space that opens the path to death and reincarnation. The shaman can enter this space to help humans by providing information about the supernatural. The actual ritual site of the shamanic trance is restricted to the altar, the shaman's bench, and the assistants who work between the altar and the main door of the house. The shaman's altar is usually a hanging or standing wooden altar with two to three tiers, depending on the status of the shaman. This altar, along with its sacrificial items, is believed to represent the grotto of the founder shaman *Siv Yis*, who lives near the top of a supernatural mountain. From this shaman's altar, several cotton threads are spun towards the main door to assist the *neeb*, the shaman's tutelary spirits, in travelling from the altar to the outside world and vice versa (Lemoine 1996: 164-165; Tapp 1989a: 63; Lemoine 1986: 340-342; see also Lemoine and Eisenbruch 1997: 76).

Ritual experts (*txiv plig* or *txiv dab*)

Ritual experts called either *txiv plig* (father of the soul), or *txiv dab* (father of the spirits), can carry out rituals that involve minor illnesses, household matters, mortuary rites, marriages, and white magic ("all the secret words" as one Hmong man said). These ritual experts have learned specific facts about important religious issues, may assist shamans, and may conduct small ceremonies on their own. Most of them specialise in specific certain rituals or events. For example, one ritual expert may be known for his knowledge of mortuary and household rites, while another may be particularly versed in ritual matters of marriage. Txaj Njua, a fifty-two-year-old male member of the Thao clan from Mae Sa Mai (works also for IMPECT), is a *txiv dab*. He describes his work as follows:

> "A *txiv dab* takes care of the spirits of the house and communicates with the spirits outside the house through songs and traditional poems. I became a priest twenty-five years ago when my father died because I wanted to carry on my father's knowledge. My father taught me everything he knew while he was alive. I can do rituals for the dead, weddings, the welcome back ceremony, *hu plig*, and assist the shaman. I am not a priest with 100 percent knowledge, like Nplaj Thoj from the Xiong clan, who can also do the ritual at the sacred tree and at the bridge to ask the god couple to give fertility to parents without children. It is a priest's job to worship the spirits inside the house in a positive way to obtain good health and a good economy. We worship the spirits through sacrifices: paper, incense sticks, tea, whiskey, chicken and animal blood. These things are given to the spirits in a positive way to ask for protection. If something is wrong with the spirits and people fall ill, then we have to call the shaman. The shaman is for the negative things and the things that go wrong." (Source: field interview, H-R1 101-102)

Most Hmong men beyond a certain age have acquired some ritual knowledge from older male relatives in order to carry out sacrificial rituals for ancestor spirits and household spirits. Men, who acquire additional, specialised ritual knowledge about specific areas like mortuary rites and weddings attain the status of a *txiv dab* or *txiv plig*. Women cannot become ritual experts because they are not permitted to conduct the rituals for the ancestors of the patriline. However, some women, called *khawv koob* (magical practitioners), are versed in medicinal herbs and are able to heal the sick by calling forth the spirits of medicine. Some households have an altar for sacrifices to the medicine spirits, *dab ntsuaj*. This hangs to the right of the altar for the household spirits, *dab xwm kab*, which always hangs on the wall opposite the front door. In a shaman's house, it also hangs to the right of the shaman's altar. The altars for the house spirits and the spirit of herbs and medicine are usually pieces of stamped rice paper covered with chicken blood, feathers and gold leaf, often obtained after rituals.[94]

Vaas Poj from the Yang clan, a ritual expert (*txiv plig*) from Mae Sa Mai, explained that Hmong believe in different causes for illnesses:

> "First, a person can become ill when the body is not well and is dirty inside. Then it has to be cleansed with herbs. Second, a person can become ill when the *plig* has left the body. Then the *txiv plig* has to call and fetch back the *plig* and convince it to return to the body. Third, a person can also become very ill when he or she is possessed by bad spirits that have aroused something negative inside the body. Sometimes this has also to do with black magic, which is not done by spirits but by other people. In this case, the shaman has to contact the spirits so that he can see what kind of sacrifices they demand to stop disturbing the ill person. You see, unlike in Western medicine, we believe that illness, worries and misfortune can have many reasons, not just medical!" (Source: field interview, H-R1 66)

In fact, during my fieldwork among the Hmong I witnessed ritual practices by shamans (of both types), ritual experts and magical practitioners, and was also directly confronted with rumours of black magic.[95] Win Huj's father

---

[94] For a good drawing of a shaman's altar, see Patricia Symonds 2004: 15.
[95] Nicolas Tapp (1989a: 66) has been told by Hmong people of his research site that the Hmong have learned the words of magic rites by the Chinese, the Thai, and their Karen neighbours. See also Roland Mischung (2004) for an essay on Karen techniques of magic and its limitations.

Txwj Xaab and his lineage did everything to find the cause and cure for his kidney disease, which they believed was not solely physical in cause. In spite of their partial conversion to Catholicism, they performed all the usual Hmong rituals for serious illness, including the shamanic ritual *hu plig*, the *xaa dab* (send the bad spirit away), and the costly ox ritual (*nju dab*), which is supposed to appease the parental ancestor couple, who may have caused the illness. When Txwj Xaab's condition worsened in spite of the rituals, numerous visits to the hospital, and a visit to a famous female Thai shaman, rumours began to circulate in the village that Txwj Xaab had been possessed by a malicious spirit that might bring misfortune to the entire village. As a result, Win Huj finally moved his parents and family to his older brother's house in the town of Mae Rim for several of weeks, hoping to spare his parents the negative rumours and keep his family from actually affected by "black magic". My assistant suspected that the rumours were being spread by villagers involved in the drug trade who were losing income as a result of the anti-drug policy he had launched as headman. Txwj Xaab and the rest of the household did not return to Mae Sa Mai until after the majority of villagers expressed open support for Win Huj's actions against illegal drug traffic in the village. Txwj Xaab died of kidney failure several weeks after the return to the village. As this incident shows, the belief in "black magic" can be used by Hmong to control "deviant" behaviour or behaviour that is contrary to an individual's interests. It also can be used in a search for scapegoats upon whom to blame difficulties. This belief can test a village and its cohesion to a point that villagers are forced to decide whether to support the person believed involved with black magic or to allow that person and the entire family to permanently leave the village.

Religious practices: Hmong rituals

Even though I witnessed, documented and analysed a great number of different rituals, I will not explain the rites in detail since they are not directly relevant to my topic. Instead, the most important elements within the

Hmong cycle of "ritual protocols" (Culas 2004: 120) are outlined to illustrate the manner in which the Hmong constitute religious spatiality in practice.[96]

Emile Durkheim showed that the function of religion is to create solidarity and to integrate people by way of rituals. Durkheim's most famous argument ([1915] 1994: 19) is that religion, at its most profound level, entails a society's worship of itself. Durkheim ([1915] 1994: 28, 36-42) argues that religion is an important social phenomenon necessary to preserve a society's order and values. Rituals may be understood as a synthesis of several important levels of social reality, including the symbolic and the social as well as the individual and the collective. Rituals dramatise the abstract principles of religion, render its contents concrete and recognisable, link it to experience, legitimise social and political power and, last but not least, divide the world into the profane and the sacred sphere (Durkheim [1915] 1994: 19-28; 61-68). Rituals must thus be understood as important vehicles of ideology that provide believers with strong emotional experiences. In addition, rituals help to elucidate and resolve, at a symbolic level, contradictions in society. Rituals communicate between the social and cosmic order to constantly reaffirm a society's value system. According to Comaroff (1985: 196), rituals provide an appropriate medium through which the values and structures of a contradictory world may be addressed and manipulated.

Edmund Leach (1954: 12) also claims that rituals – which consist primarily of private and public sacrifice – are indirect and oblique ways of conversing about society. Of course, a ritual is not simply a reflection of the institutional conventions of quotidian life. Rather, it is a creative representation of these conventions, which is constantly built up and

---

[96] During fieldwork, I was unable to attend rituals involved in the birth process because they are considered extremely private in Hmong culture. Because it would be considered "immoral" for a woman to attend marriage rites in my research sites, I also did not have the opportunity to participate in these ceremonies. For this reason, both birth and marriage rituals receive only parenthetical mention in this thesis in spite of their importance within the Hmong ritual cycle. Birth and marriage rituals include elements such as the soul-calling ritual, which also exist in other rituals. These are described in detail by Patricia Symonds 1991: 162-197, 136-149 and Christian Postert 2003: 207-261.

dissolved. Richard Schechner (2002: 622) compares the functions of theatre, including entertainment, celebration, commemoration of the past, enhancement of social solidarity, education, and healing, with the functions of religious rituals. Religious rituals are instrumental and efficient in their ability to maintain cosmic order and propitiate the supernatural. They also contain elements of performance and elements of fun, as Tim Ingold (2002: 342-43) correctly emphasises.

Hmong rituals have been described in great detail elsewhere (see e.g. Symonds 2004; Lemoine 1983; Chindarsi 1976). In my analysis, I shall focus only on the characteristics of ritual practices that affect Hmong cultural spatiality. In Hmong culture, rituals are very important, many of them are performed on a regular basis, and are connected to many sorts of offerings. Rituals are costly, and they keep people away from agriculture and other forms of occupation. When fields cannot be attended, or work is missed and income is lost, ritual attendance becomes even more costly. However, this burden is accepted, even expected, within a society that otherwise strives for wealth and prosperity. The Hmong rituals are thus extremely important, and without them it is impossible to maintain the cosmic order or to keep the ancestors and other spirits from harming the living. This danger takes precedence over personal material gain. Moreover, it is by way of sacrificial rituals that spirits are asked for wealth that cannot be obtained and maintained without this supernatural sphere, but only *in accordance* with it.

Most Hmong rituals contain a number of similar aspects: communication with the *dab* and the supernatural to drive away bad spirits and to ask good *dab* for protection and fortune; the worship of ancestor spirits; and the search for reasons for misfortune an illness (see also Lyman 1968: 7). Hmong rituals usually take place in houses, or else outdoors, in or beyond the village. In other words, ritual practice does not require a special, sacred building such as a church or temple. A ritual can be held anywhere at any time. Certain rituals are socially expected. For example, if a family member is seriously ill, the ancestor ritual (see below) must be performed. It is also expected that many people will be invited to join the feast after the rite. When socially expected rituals are not held, rumours can spread quickly that the family is failing to observe religious norms and is behaving in a manner disrespectful to Hmong society. This deviant behaviour can be "punished" by the community, which can refuse to invite the family to rituals, or which can refuse to attend those rituals which the family does organise. Mortuary rituals, for example, are fairly similar in procedure but may nonetheless express the status of the deceased. Old men and women who died a natural death are particularly revered. Their mortuary rites can take as long as six days and nights and be attended by more than 1,000 people. However, full mortuary rites are not performed for everyone. Mortuary rites for small children are less extensive. People who died in accidents, by drug overdose, or by suicide are buried as quickly as possible because the Hmong believe they assume the form of hungry and evil spirits. For an ordinary mortuary rite, the presence of many respectful mourners is believed to assure the dead of a safe and undisturbed passage to the land of the ancestors. The spirit of an ancestor who does not safely pass over to the Otherworld roams the earth restlessly and can pose problems for descendants. Thus the present-day fortunes of the descendants depend on the welfare of the ancestors. Individual moral behaviour immediately reflects on and involves the wider social network, especially people from the same household and lineage (see also Tapp 2002: 103). When a mortuary rite is sparsely attended because of the deceased's deviant behaviour, the deceased and his or her family are punished for not ensuring the observation of Hmong norms.

For other important rituals, the social expectation is also that it will be attended by large numbers of people who wish to pay respect to lineage and clan members. During the weeks of Win Huj's father grave illness, twenty to thirty persons were present in the house day and night. Rituals such as shamanic healing rituals, marriages, mortuary rites and New Year celebrations are important events that maintain and renew the ties that bind individuals to their household, lineage and (sub-)clan group. These rites also help to link diverse social units such as lineages, clans, and villages (cf. Yang Dao 1992: 274).

Most of the Hmong rituals that do not entail trance are quite similar in sequence, content, and sacrifices. The rites make visible the belief and respect accorded to the supernatural beings that surround Hmong at all times and which can do both good and harm. Rituals attempt to influence supernatural beings and so positively influence Hmong fate. Many rituals open with the preparation of the sacrifice, for example stamping white paper symbolising ancient money and setting up a small offering table with cups of whiskey, tea, rice, an egg, and incense. Then the *dab ntuj* (spirits of the sky) of all four directions (*plaub tus dab*, four spirits) and the *dab nteb* (spirits of the earth) or the ancestor spirits are called to accept the offerings. Finally the paper or "spirit money" and the incense are burned and divination horns are thrown by the shaman or the ritual expert to determine whether the sacrifices have been accepted.

During most Hmong rituals, malevolent spirits are "thrown out" of the house. This can be done, for example, by throwing corn into the room and then out of the house, or by spitting water into a room, as the shaman's assistants may do during a trance. The water spit by the assistant shaman is believed to distribute energy against the bad spirits and cleanse the house's interior of bad energies. Water also arouses and refreshes the good spirits. The bad spirits can also be banned onto a material object which is then either destroyed or placed outside the village, as is done in the *xaa dab* ritual. In this rite, a ritual expert bans bad spirits and all bad things of a sick person on to a banana basket. Clay figures inside the basket represent the bad *dab*, which are then "thrown out" of the house and the village. The spirits are attracted to the basket by offerings such as chicken and burning incense. In the ox ritual, the *ua ncuj dab*, an ox is offered to an ancestor who appears not to have found his way back to the ancestors in China and is now disturbing the living. In this ritual, bad spirits are banned on to a small bamboo bridge (*chais kauj*). The bamboo structure is covered with chicken blood offered to the spirits, who are summoned as follows: "You can come today for the ritual but afterwards you should not come again."

During the course of any ritual, the ritual practitioners must ensure that bad spirits are not attracted by the sacrifices offered to the ancestor or other spirits. Bad spirits are either thrown from the house or are tricked. In the ox ritual, for example, a fake house is built next to the actual "ritual house" (*ntev rwm xaav*) for the offering to placate the ancestor spirit. The bad spirits are first lured to the fake house, which is then destroyed. After the ox is slaughtered and carefully divided, it is also necessary to get rid of the ancestor spirit that is disturbing the descendants and causing illness. In the *tso dab* (free the spirit) ceremony, small sections of the ox are offered by the ill descendant to the ancestor spirit in the ritual house: "Please eat up, leave, do not bargain with me, please be reborn again and do not bother me again."

A shaman can also determine that a *ncaiv* (taboo or "prohibition" day) is necessary for his or her clan to protect its members from the recurrence of an earlier misfortune. On this day, the clan members must remain at home, may not work, and are not permitted to use sharp tools or speak bad words. This is done to appease the bad spirits and keep them away. People from other clans should not visit on *ncaiv* days. The "taboo houses" are marked by a bamboo star decorated with fresh leaves, which hangs in front of the main door of the house (cf. Culas 1994: 16). This kind of taboo was held five times for the Xiong clan and twice for the Yang clan during my stay in Mae Sa Mai, and once for the Yang clan in Ban Phui.

Negative or bad elements are also banned passively by gates that protect the village or "strong protective items" such as wooden knives, goat feet or curiously formed tree branches hung over a house's door (see also Chindarsi 1976: 133-134). Protective items such as silver necklaces and small bags containing herbs are also hung around children's necks to safeguard them from the malicious actions of bad spirits, which are believed to be able to easily capture the *plig* of a child.

In addition to combating bad spirits, the rituals attempt to influence the good spirits and gain their protection. The offerings include paper money, gold bars made from cardboard, incense, whiskey, rice, animal parts, and animal blood. In religious rituals, symbols of wealth in the form of paper money or cardboard gold bars play an important role as offerings for the ancestors and other supernatural agencies. Since striving for surplus and wealth is an important value in Hmong society, the rituals are supposed to extend the wealth of the ancestors to the descendants. Chinese paper money with the inscription "Hell Bank Note" or gold coloured papers, purchased in Chinese shops in Chiang Mai, are also offered as symbols of wealth. In addition to wishes for good health and a secure future for children, prayers to ancestors often include a wish for a lotto win. By burning the paper money, the money is turned into spirit money and the spirits are able to receive it. Incense sticks are burned because they symbolise energy and their odour is supposed to appeal the *dab*. Eggs are thought to keep bad spirits away. When eggs are thrown, the egg-yolk "illuminates" the bad spirits and makes them visible. Eggs are also offered for the spirit's children to play with. Whiskey is offered because spirits are attracted by odour. When the spirits are drunk, it is said that they "listen easily and go when they are asked to go", as many Hmong informed me to explain the purpose of this offering (Source: field interview, H-R2 51). Whiskey is also a favourite "mediate substance" consumed by Hmong men during rituals to enhance social cohesion, pay respect to each other, and enhance enjoyment.

Food is usually offered to the spirits only in small quantities ("spirits can be deceived in this regard"), whereas paper money and incense sticks are often burned in large quantities to gain the spirits' goodwill. The rituals accept, re-enact and reinforce the superiority of the *dab* and the ancestor spirits. "Ancestors eat first" as I was often told during rituals when the first parts of the meal were offered to the ancestor spirits of the house.

During rituals and offerings, the Hmong also attempt to make agreements with certain spirits. The *fiv yeem* (the promise made to spirits of all four directions) and *pauj yeem* (payment of agreed sacrifices) are a two-step ritual in which all the *dab* of *ntuj*, the earth and the house, are asked to protect the people. Before a field is planted, for example, an offering is made to the field spirit to ask it to protect the fields and help obtain a good harvest. The promise is made that the spirit will be offered more after it fulfils its part of the agreement with a good harvest. In that case, the farmer needs to conduct the *pauj yeem* ritual and offer the promised sacrificial items to the field spirit. If the second ritual is not held, bad luck may visit the people who did not keep their side of the agreement. This combined ritual can also be held to call upon the ancestors to reward the descendants with protection, health and wealth.

The ancestral cult

The ancestral cult entails offerings from the male head of the household to the spirits of the dead relatives. In special cases, this requires the sacrifice of domestic animals. Approximately twice a month, the head of the household sits down, usually unobserved by other household members, to "feed" (*laig dab*) the immediate ancestors rice and pork. The first part of every harvest, regardless of the crop, is always offered to the ancestors. On the final day of the old year, before the New Year celebrations begin, sacrifices are again made to the ancestors. Close observation of ancestor worship is compulsory to ensure the well-being of the family and even the whole lineage. Nyaj Sua, who is forty years old and a leader of the Yang lineage in Mae Sa Mai, commented as follows:

> "They protect us and they can see what we are doing. When our ancestors need something from us, they make us sick and then we sacrifice to them and take care of them. If you offer them money, clothes or food, they receive it and one day, they give it back to you."
> (Source: field interview, H-C-MSM 5)

The ancestral cult unites the living and establishes mutual dependence between the dead and the living across generations. The ancestors are placed on a supernatural level, while ceremonies honouring the dead preserve the power structure and gender relationships of the living. Hmong people thus might be said to worship their own images, or, more precisely, the images represented by the male line of descent. Through relatively unchanging ancestral rituals, lineage members are encouraged to act according to group norms, such as providing help to lineage members if needed. Ancestor spirits are to be remembered, respected and fed with food and paper money in sacrificial rituals. The practice of feeding the ancestral spirits is called *laig dab*. In return for *laig dab*, ancestors protect the living from misfortune but bring illness and harm upon descendants when norms are disregarded and ancestors neglected. In the relationship between the ancestors and the living, a direct connection between the religious and the social domains of Hmong society is created:

> "Ancestral rites are the symbols which express, regulate, maintain and transmit this association from one generation to another, thereby enforcing lineage solidarity and inspiring members to carry out their duties to the living, the dead and those yet to be born. [...] These worship activities clearly define the position of each Hmong, male and female, within a social system in such a way that both the religious observation and the social mutually reinforce and justify each other's existence." (Lee no year: 5-7)

When descendants fall seriously ill or a family suffers from misfortune, the shaman performs a ritual. The shaman's tutelary spirits, for example, may show him or her that the ancestors have come to "knock on the door" of their descendants to request special sacrifices. When the "ancestors knock on the door", there is a traditional order of animal sacrifice: at the first 'knock' (the first serious illness of a direct successor) the first pig (*npuas rooj*) must be sacrificed, at the second knock the second pig (*npuas dab*) is offered, and at the third knock an ox (*ua ncuj dab*) is sacrificed. In some families or lineages, the ancestors may never request a sacrifice of this sort, while another family may find that these sacrifices are demanded of within a span of only a few years. But as is the case with all ritual practices linked to ancestor worship, it is important to observe the ritual exactly as demanded.

The ancestors "show the way", as one informant explained. The shaman and elders are their intermediaries, and the younger descendants must listen and obey. The respect paid to ancestors thus has a politically legitimating and socially stabilising effect.

Only men may make offerings to the ancestors because only men are permitted to formally acquire this complex religious knowledge. Only men are permitted to sit down to eat the ritual meal, to ritually drink whiskey, and to strengthen social cohesion through formal speeches. During mortuary rites, only men may perform the various rituals, including playing the reed pipe and drum, officially communicating with the dead, and sending the soul on its way to China.[97] On the last night of the mortuary rites, men take turns being the intermediary for the deceased, who addresses the family for the last time in a speech or song that can last for hours. Women play only minor roles in rituals. They serve the men from the back, cook the rice during mortuary rites (other food and everything else is prepared by the men), and usually are not even present at rituals like the lineage-centred *lwm tauj* (clean the house with a broom) ritual on the so-called "tofu day". Women are also not present at the *ntoo xeeb* ceremony, when one representative of each household offers incense sticks to the sacred tree in the forest above the village. While women are not forbidden to join these rituals, only a few do so because "we are the minority there and we have to sit in the back which is boring", as my neighbour, Zuam, Vaam Zeej's wife, explained. Women are aware of the rituals, but are not permitted to carry them out, with the exception of the female shamans who have been "chosen" as intermediaries by the shaman spirits.

---

[97] Among the Hmong, death is conceptualised as a "journey to the land of darkness" (Symonds 2004: 110). It is accompanied by a cycle of rituals that the Hmong call "the way of illness and death" (*kev mob kev tuag*), which include complex funerary rites immediately after death that last for a number of days, as well as rituals that are performed some time (thirteen days to several years) after the burial. This second part of the mortuary rituals is not a second burial but is aimed at "setting the soul free" (*tso plig*) to permit the rebirth of the deceased. For a detailed description of these rituals, see Symonds 1991: 214-262; Lemoine 1983.

In summary, by way of their ritual practice, Hmong accept the superiority of supernatural agencies in cosmological space. These entities demand respect and can harm humans when they are not honoured, but may also act favourably toward people who offer sacrifices (see also Culas 2004: 111). Spirits are omnipotent, occupying every place on earth as well as the two spheres of the Otherworld, which every Hmong will join as an ancestor spirit after death and before reincarnation. In this regard, Durkheim's theory that society only worships itself during rituals and by means of other religious practice is confirmed. By worshipping the ancestor spirits of the patriline, the kinship system and male hierarchy are maintained. Hmong society also maintains and reinforces the social order through its ritual practice. Rituals strengthen the bonds between the ancestors and the living as well as between individuals, households, lineages, clans and the Hmong people as a whole.

Conversion to other religions

Christianity was first introduced in the 1920s by missionaries to the Hmong in Thailand. As the list of villages and their populations' religious affiliation in the appendix demonstrates, the majority of Hmong have chosen to preserve their traditional beliefs, which play an essential role in the survival of their culture and identity.[98] No definite figures exist on the total number of Hmong Christians in Thailand. Lue Vang (1998: 292; Lue Vang and Lewis 1990: 3) has estimated the number of Christians to be between five and ten percent of the Hmong population. In the twenty Hmong villages I visited, a mean of 25.5 percent of the villagers had converted to Christianity. This includes some villages with a proportion of converts of three to five percent, and two villages in which ninety-two percent and 100 percent of inhabitants have converted to other religions (see also Leepreecha 2001: 188).

---

[98] It is known of the 2.000 Hmong people living in Australia, for example, that ninety-three percent of them also have retained traditional Hmong religious beliefs (Yang, Kou 2003: 279).

The number of converts to Buddhism is even lower. In both villages in my study, no one formally observed the Buddhist religion. Nicholas Tapp (1989: 88) suggests that the Hmong have not adopted Buddhism because it is so closely associated with the fundamental values and beliefs of Thai society. Young Hmong boys usually attend Thai temple schools for largely pragmatic reasons, and remove the rope as soon as they have completed their education. Hmong people do not want to submit to the Thai system even though they do feel a certain sense of belonging. However, the Hmong act out this belonging on their own terms, if at all (see also Leepreecha 2001: 188).

Catholics, Protestants and Seventh Day Adventists apply different strategies in their work among ethnic mountain groups in Thailand. Catholics try to win converts by working *with* rather than *against* the "traditional" beliefs of the people. Protestants and Seventh Day Adventists employ culturally radical techniques that interdict certain aspects of Hmong culture and encourage "the burning of altars and shamanic equipment" (Tapp 1989: 99). In other words, Protestants and Seventh Day Adventists display radical intolerance of everything that is not related to their own religious belief. The Catholics, on the other hand, agree that some aspects of "traditional" Hmong religion may still be performed, including the major mortuary ritual *qhuab ke* (the opening of the way for the reincarnating soul of the deceased). Catholic Hmong are permitted to consume alcohol, smoke, eat pork, and perform almost all the ancestral rituals, including the mortuary rites. Protestants do not permit adherents to consume alcohol. The Seventh Day Adventists are the strictest, and forbid smoking as well as the consumption of alcohol and pork. This poses a great threat to Hmong identity and culture because many Hmong rituals contain offerings of pig and are followed by joint meals of a special Hmong pork dish, which Seventh Day Adventists are then not permitted to eat. Conversion to Christianity also causes problems for the kinship system because descent lines are maintained and reinforced by certain rites.

The Christian churches invest a considerable amount of financial and human resources to bring their religion to the Hmong and other mountain groups. "Teachers of God" and priests travel to the villages to find new converts, and Christian boarding schools in the lowlands provide free education as an incentive for parents to convert with their children. The Hmong Catholic Centre in Chiang Mai serves as a hostel, a Bible school, a religious centre, and a publishing house for Christian literature in Hmong. Since 1970, a Protestant radio station transmitted worldwide by the Far East Broadcasting Company (FEBC) in Manila, has broadcasted Bible instruction and preaching in the Hmong language (mtw-frequency 15095.0). Another radio station that transmits religious radio programs in Hmong is also broadcasted from the Philippines; it is called "Veritas Asia" (mtw-frequency 9615.0). Approximately 100,000 Hmong have been converted by these programs worldwide (cf. Tanabe and Keyes 2002: 14; Vang 1998: 76). The Protestant Church in Thailand receives significant backing by Taiwanese believers who support the church financially and send missionaries to travel to the Thai mountain areas.

Sau Mim Yaj, a former deputy (*Phu Chuey*) of the village headman in Mae Sa Mai and a gifted silversmith who is forty-two years old, told the following story about his conversion to Protestantism:

"My parents became Protestant in 1989 because they were both very sick. They suffered spiritually but traditional shamanic rituals did not help. So as a last resort they converted and then they got slowly better. I converted along with my parents because this is the custom. If Hmong do something wrong to the spirits, the sickness and the punishment comes to us. Then you have to pay and donate a chicken; you have to pay the spirits all the time. If you are sick or if you have bad luck, the shaman shows that the spirits are bad and aggressive. People have to pay and that is very difficult to follow, especially in the twenty-first century. In Christ you feel free. However, the different religions sometimes oppose each other as though in a war. Conflicts arise between Christians and people who believe in *dab* because we do not help each other in rituals; people blame each other for not helping each other even though they are lineage brothers. [...] But we still think that the new belief is more comfortable and offers more freedom. People learn more about the future. But actually I don't know much about Protestant religion because I never went to a Protestant school. I just converted along with my parents and then believed in the one God. When my parents converted, they asked the former headman of Mae Sa Mai, who is the Protestant priest, to come to the house. He took the five spirits out of our house and burned them in the name of God. This way we became Protestants. Now we do not worry anymore when we go outside the house. We only think of God, we do not have to worry about the ancestors or spirits anymore." (Source: field interview, H-R2 2-3)

Sau Mim's story demonstrates the pragmatism of many people in their adherence to religion (see Lewis 2002: 569). People may decide quite pragmatically which belief suits them best, in which form and at what time. For example, Win Huj's father, Txwj Xaab, was a ritual expert before he became Protestant in 1987. In 1998, he became Catholic because, he explained, the Catholic religion allows more room for Hmong religion, and for ancestral cult and shamanic practices. When he felt disappointed by Protestantism, Txwj Xaab did not convert fully back to the Hmong religion because he did not want to "be under pressure by all the different good and bad *dab* that are everywhere. The more we know about *dab*, the more we have to be afraid of them." He continued:

"The Catholic religion is good because we only have to believe in one God but can still follow our traditional customs like the ancestral and shamanic rituals. For Hmong, it is easy to convert to Christianity since the Christian cosmos and the Hmong cosmos are quite similar. To believe half and half is the best way." (Source: field interview, H-R1 17)

In his own research, Nicholas Tapp (1989: 101) also reported that most informants who converted "half believed" in the Christian teachings, while Prasit Leepreecha (2001: 235) speaks of a "trend of accommodating

Christian beliefs and rules to Hmong traditions". Anne Fadiman (1997: 35) agrees, noting, "to my knowledge, at least – no Hmong is ever fully converted." Most converts do so for social and economic reasons, for example because they want to save money by avoiding expensive and time consuming rituals, and hope to send their children to missionary boarding schools in the lowlands. However, most Hmong who convert also explain that their conversion should be understood as a strategy to circumvent the omnipotent influence and presence of the supernatural. The adherence to the spirits' rules and norms seem to be a heavy burden for some Hmong.

Nicholas Tapp (1989: 85) also regards conversion to Christianity as an alternative to Thai identity and the state religion. By converting to a Christian religion, Hmong belong to a "dual" minority because of their different ethnic and formal religious affiliation. Christianity offers an alternative way to remain Hmong without being overly assimilated into the Thai state, as would be the case in converting to Buddhism. Being Christian provides converts with a religion and identity that is distinct from the Thai system and avoids the need for a decision between clearly maintaining Hmong ethnic minority status and becoming more assimilated into the majority society.

In Ban Phui, I also discovered a further reason for conversion to Protestantism. Because Hmong women in Ban Phui are more tied to their "traditional" roles as wives and "servants" of their husbands (see chapter seven), some seek to circumvent gender inequality and to gain more power (at least unofficially) within the religious field. At least ten women claimed that they were Protestant even though their husbands still believed in the traditional Hmong religion. Normally all household members must belong to the same faith as the male household head. Some women in Ban Phui, however, have "unofficially" converted to Protestantism and visit the church on Sundays where they can actively engage in rituals, personally influence their own fate independently of their husbands and other male kin, and acquire some positions of power normally withheld from women in patriarchal Hmong society. Men do not interfere with their wives' religious activities; since the women are not permitted to convert on their own, the men take it as an unquestionable given that their wives are still members of the traditional Hmong religion. I suspect that Hmong women in Mae Sa Mai do not opt for this strategy of unofficial religious conversion because they usually enjoy more freedom than women in Ban Phui due to the proximity of Chiang Mai and better education opportunities (see chapter seven).

Summary

Hmong religion is characterised by its complexity, its obvious Chinese influence, and its overriding impact on the daily life of its followers. Hmong believe they are everywhere and at all times surrounded by supernatural agencies and ancestor spirits – a category to which the living will also belong one day. People are thus involved in a circle of birth, life, death, passage to the Otherworld, and rebirth. The Hmong I studied thus do not conceive of themselves as bound to a single place and time. Instead, they conceive of life as one of many stations on earth and within the Hmong cosmos. Hmong people "think big", as they themselves claim. Space and time is relative; it is not limited to material existence in a specific geographical area or time, but can extend to other locations on earth as well as to the Otherworld, and can connect the past, the present and the future into a single whole. By means of a continuous flow of material and immaterial resources, the different cosmological spaces of the living and the spirits are interconnected; these socio-cosmic relationships are indispensable to the maintenance of the Hmong social order.

Because of its special ritual practice, forms of behaviour and belief, Hmong religious topography is a cardinal point that extends both into the horizontal and the vertical level (cf. Hauser-Schäublin 2003: 48). Relationships to the supernatural (under and above the earth) are constantly represented and manifested in the range of rituals that the Hmong perform almost every day. During a ceremony, a fusion takes place in relation to space (horizontal and vertical) and time. Past, present and future are interconnected through the ancestors, the living descendants, and the belief in reincarnation. The ancestors thus play a vital role in daily life and exert power over the living, demanding that they behave according to traditional Hmong norms (cf. Symonds 2004: 4). The equilibrium between ancestor spirits and the living descendants is an important aspect of Hmong socio-ritual structure. In the past, Hmong life was characterised by patterns of migrations and frequent resettlements. Under these conditions, Hmong belief and ritual served to anchor them in the Hmong cosmos. Geomancy provided guidance for behaviour in any mountainous environment, the Hmong's natural habitat. Mountainous landscapes anywhere on earth are conceptualised as belonging to the Hmong lifeworld, which is, applying Durkheim's theory, mirrored in Hmong conceptions of the mountainous Otherworld.

However, knowledge of the Hmong Otherworld and the ability to communicate with it varies greatly within Hmong society. Apart from female shamans, women, officially at least, are the least well informed about the Hmong cosmos, the omnipotent *dab*, and the rituals for interacting with the supernatural agencies. During their lifetime, most Hmong men acquire sufficient general religious knowledge to perform household rituals and offerings to ancestral spirits. Some men invest more time in learning religious knowledge to become specialised ritual experts (*txiv dab*) or assistant shamans. This allows them to perform specific rituals and acquire status in Hmong society. Although women are not permitted to perform rituals relating to the patrilineal ancestors, women who have acquired knowledge of medicinal herbs and the metaphysical cleaning of the body may perform certain healing rituals. Regardless whether they have specialised knowledge, all Hmong are socially expected to participate in great numbers in important rituals inside and outside the community. Bonds between Hmong, especially between kin, are strengthened and reinforced through religious practice. Rituals such as mortuary rites or New Year's celebrations interconnect people on a large scale throughout the Hmong Mountains.

Ritual experts know ways to communicate with supernatural agencies. Only the shaman, male or female, has direct spiritual "access" to the Otherworld and can travel in a trance to the land above and below the earth. The shaman is the intermediary between the supernatural world and the world of the living; he or she has the power to "travel symbolically" (Culas 2004: 102. He or she serves his/her tutelary spirits (*neeb*) when they possess him/her, but also controls them to perform a diagnosis and cure. Through the shaman, supernatural agencies communicate with the living, control them, punish them for misconduct, and thus secure adherence to traditional norms and practices. The system of hierarchy that demands respect for the ancestors from the descendants has its equivalent among the living who must respect the elders and those with special knowledge. These latter ensure the continued adherence to religious norms and values and emphasise the transmission of the complex knowledge of the Hmong cosmos.

Hmong beliefs are closely interwoven with Hmong everyday life. Hmong who fail to observe religious principles are thought to have strayed from the path of life, and will probably fail to accomplish their goals. Only by adhering to traditional religious norms and beliefs, the Hmong believe, is it possible to achieve anything in life and improve one's situation. Investing in rituals is not an irrational use of money, but an investment in one's own fate and future.

To date, comparatively few Hmong have converted to other religions because Hmong religious belief is closely tied with the Hmong kinship system, healing practices, and identity. Many Hmong who convert continue to pragmatically adhere to the ancestral cult and shamanic practices. Others, like the Protestants and Seventh Day Adventists, are not permitted to observe synchretic religious forms, are confronted with conflicts with the Hmong majority who strive to maintain the traditional forms of belief as one of the core tenets of Hmong culture.

7 HMONG SOCIAL ORGANISATION: THE SIMULTANEITY OF SOCIAL PROXIMITY AND SOCIO-SPATIAL EXTENSION

This chapter sketches the most important kinship and other social structuring principles of the two villages researched.[99] In addition to the principle of religious domain, these principles are at the root of Hmong cultural spatiality. They provide for social proximity among group members and an immense socio-spatial extension of the Hmong and their clans throughout the world. The Hmong social system also consists, as I suggested above, of a complex web of social obligations and moral norms that must be observed in daily life. Kinship structures maintain and strengthen social cohesion while assigning each member to a specific position within the geographically dispersed social system. Lineages, sub-clans, and clans form the most important conceptual framework within Hmong society. Without them, Hmong social existence is inconceivable. Other important categories include the household, which is probably the smallest and strongest affiliation, and the village community, which is probably the weakest social unit in Hmong society. I thus also discuss Hmong kinship structures like the household, the lineage, the (sub-) clan, and the village community. These are the foundation for the "endosocial" Hmong network structure, which is marked by the closeness and social proximity of group members and the simultaneous

---

[99] The Hmong kinship system is, apart from the Hmong economy, the most thoroughly researched aspect of Hmong culture. Here I sketch only its most important facets. Authors like as Yih-Fu Ruey (1960), Jaques Lemoine (1972), William Geddes (1976) and Nicholas Tapp (2001) have, for example, devoted large parts of their publications to this topic. Hmong scholars Gary Yia Lee (1986) and Prasit Leepreecha (2001) describe most of the Hmong kin terms. Leepreecha's publication is a comprehensive account, based on fieldwork in Mae Sa Mai, of the dynamics of the Hmong kinship system and culturally reshaped kinship identities among the Hmong in contemporary Thailand.

socio-spatial dispersal of the people. Jonathan Friedman (1997: 287) uses the term "endosociality" to describe group exclusive social networks and relationships of native Hawaiians on the Big Island. As my discussion of Hmong social networks will demonstrate, the term is also applicable to the Hmong. To provide a better understanding of the constitution of Hmong cultural spatiality, I will outline the social and geographical dispersal of social relations among the Hmong villagers of my study, and examine who is potentially and actually included in their networks.

Hmong society is seen to be composed of interrelated groups, not of individuals. Rather, Hmong individuals are tied up in complex family, lineage, and clan obligations. These determine the Hmong's everyday life to a great extent and diminish individual freedom of choice while simultaneously providing each member a support network of social relations (Yang Dao 1992: 280; cf. Giddens 1990: 101). The Hmong social system is characterised by interdependence as it is expected that especially relatives should always assist each other (Hall 1990: 28). Loyalty and commitment towards kin generally decrease, however, with growing genealogical distance (from the extended family to the lineage, from the lineage to the sub-clan, from the sub-clan to the patrilineal clan, and then to other Hmong clans). But loyalties are not absolutely compelling and can change according to context, circumstances and personal preferences. This fact complicates general statements about Hmong priorities of commitment, trust and loyalty towards the different forms of social organisation.

Furthermore, lineages, sub-clans and clans do not exist as permanently organised and localised units, but rather as a kind of "social infrastructure" (Mischung 1990: 284). This social infrastructure includes potential solidarity and cooperation on which the Hmong can rely in locations where other Hmong live, whether in the neighbouring village, a Hmong settlement near the Laotian border, Bangkok or a city in France. As Jan Ovesen aptly notes:

"The sociality of the Hmong is predominantly focused on the spatial proximity of relatives. A Hmong can only be really happy when he [or she, M.T.] is together with his [or her, M.T.] relatives, since such close contact represents emotional assurance, social support, spiritual comfort as well as the greatest possible economic security. The spiritual aspect of being together with relatives is quite literal, and its practical implications should not be underestimated." (2004: 463)

Thus the ancestors are an equally important component of the Hmong social system. They affect daily life and are as much part of the complex web of social relations and obligations as the living.

"[...] Hmong kinship identities thus give one a place in society and provide guidelines on how to relate to others. They mark the way in which one is the same as others who share the same kin category, and the way in which one is different from those who do not." (Leepreecha 2001: 64)

Hmong society is both patrilineal and hierarchical in structure, although as chapter four showed, hierarchical positions are not connected to strong formal positions of political power. Husbands dominate over their wives and children, ancestors and household heads over household members, lineage heads over lineage members, clan elders over clan members, and the elders' council over villagers. The young have to respect, honour and obey the old. During Hmong New Year, large groups of unmarried Hmong visit the households of every older villager to show their respect by offering food and whiskey to the elders. This is a socio-religious practice that underscores the importance of hierarchical structure while ritually interconnecting the old with the young.

Concepts of age are closely related to authority and hierarchical structure in general and acquisition of knowledge and status in particular. Until Hmong girls and boys marry, around the age of seventeen for girls and twenty-one for boys, they are viewed as children; only after marriage are they seen as "adolescents".[100] People between the ages of thirty and fifty are considered adults, while only people of fifty and above are viewed as *old* adults, or elders in the case of men.[101] A man around thirty-five to forty who has had one or more sons and acquired the status of a respectable, knowledgeable man (knowledgeable especially regarding ritual practice) can ask his parents-in-law to give him, through a "mature naming ceremony", an additional first name. This name symbolises the status of an "adult, respectable family man" (cf. Lee 1996: 16). Gender and age thus represent criteria for authority and status closely linked to (religious) knowledge and to some degree also to economic success.

"One-house people" (ib yim neeg)

People living in the same household are called "one-house people" (*ib yim neeg*) and form the smallest recognised and strongest social unit in Hmong society (Cooper 1978: 309). As part of the kinship system, the household is a structural category and model of thought. Households form residential units and real settlement groups. In contrast, formal residence rules cannot always be followed, as the location of partly scattered lineage and clan houses in Mae Sa Mai clearly demonstrates. Residential units are composed according to specific kinship criteria; thus the spatial arrangement of households disclose a certain, analysable morphology.

Households consist of either nuclear or patrilocal extended families: Daughters, often referred to as "other people's women", live with their parents only until they marry and move out to live with their husband's

---

[100] This is not to suggest that all Hmong marry between the age of seventeen and twenty-one, but rather demonstrates general tendencies. In the two villages researched, men generally marry between seventeen and twenty-one; women marry earlier, between fifteen and eighteen. One young man interviewed, who had married at the age of twenty-two, claimed that he was the last one to marry within his age group (see also Ovesen 1995: 20-21; Lee 1988: 167).

[101] For an even more diversified perspective on age categories and their terms of reference, see Patricia Symonds 2004: 39-41.

family. Sons bring their wives into their households.[102] This means that most households are composed of several families (mostly between two to three), as well as several generations. The patriarchal household head is the religious leader of the household. He also owns all items belonging to the residential unit and money generated through common work in the fields, unless he has already officially willed parts of the land to his married sons (cf. Lee 1986a: 57). In that case, the sons and their wives cultivate their land on their own terms and only contribute one part of their income to the larger household economy. As the household head exerts power over all household members and makes the most important decisions for them, interests of nuclear families are of only secondary importance within a residential unit.

Each member is both socially and ritually connected to the household through ancestor worship and the five common household spirits.[103] In addition, the Hmong typically bury the placenta of a boy at the main post of the house to honour the main house spirit. The placenta of a girl is buried underneath the parent's bed to honour her parents. During the mortuary rites, the soul of the dead is guided back, via the stations of their life geography, to retrieve their placenta on the path full of dangers to rejoin the ancestors in China. The Hmong term for placenta means "jacket" and is considered one's first and finest garment. If the soul of the deceased cannot find its placental jacket, it is condemned to wander naked and alone for an eternity (Fadiman 1997: 5). Nowadays, the majority of children are born in lowland hospitals, and their placentas can no longer be buried inside the house. However, people interviewed found this of little importance because, after birth, a ritual expert can ask the spirits of the house to protect the newborn and "attach" their spirit to the house, which is seen as equivalent to actually burying the placenta.

---

[102] Patrivirilocality is the preferred post-marital residence because it permits the continuance of the lineage under the guidance of the kin group. Robert Cooper (1979: 178) claims that, besides the normative practice, several forms of patriuxorilocality can also be found among some Hmong. However, I did not encounter these at my research sites.

[103] For more details on these spirits, see chapter eleven.

William Geddes' (1976: 37) survey shows that in the 1970s, the average household contained 6.9 people and average number of households per village totalled twenty-one. The largest household I encountered was located in Hmong village in the North of Mae Hong Son Province. It belonged to a sixty-year-old man, married to four wives with a total of twenty-two children. He was proud that he could set up two soccer teams with his children alone. Twenty-nine households in Mae Sa Mai and twenty in Ban Phui were surveyed to gather socio-economic census data. At the time of the appraisal in 2001/2002, the largest household had eighteen (MSM) and forty (BP) members, the smallest, two (MSM) and four (BP) people respectively. In Mae Sa Mai, the average number per household totalled 8.3 people, in Ban Phui 11.1. A mean of 1.34 (MSM) and 2.3 couples (BP), and 4.93 (MSM) and 6.25 children (BP) live in each residential unit. In Mae Sa Mai, a maximum of twelve and in Ban Phui a maximum of twenty children could be found in one household. At the time of the survey, a mean of 0.28 adults and 1.31 children per household were living outside Mae Sa Mai for most of the year, while in Ban Phui no adults and a mean of 0.5 children lived in the lowlands. Direct comparison of both villages shows that Ban Phui is characterised by more traditional structures with typically larger households including more nuclear families and children per social unit.[104] In Mae Sa Mai, households are on the average smaller, include fewer nuclear families and children, while more adults and children spend large parts of the year outside the village. These adults and children are included in the household numbers above because, despite their absence, they are considered part of the residential unit in socio-economic and religious terms.

Among the Green Hmong, it is common for married sons and their families to stay in their parents' household until the parents have died. Among the White Hmong, the eldest son can move out of his parents' household a few years after marriage (Leepreecha 2001: 49). I have

---

[104] See also Peter Kunstadter's comparative paper (1984) on the typical household composition of several ethnic mountain groups, including the Hmong (pages 315-317).

encountered many cases in Mae Sa Mai and Ban Phui where married sons at the age of around forty still lived in their parents' house and said they were not allowed to move out as long as their father was alive. When the household head has passed away and only the mother is still alive, older sons can set up their own households. The youngest son continues to form a household with his mother and his own family. According to patrilineal descent, men inherit the household spirits of their parents when they move into their own houses. In Ban Phui, I came across two men who, with their parents' consent, had moved into their own houses next-door about four years earlier. Spiritually, and therefore also socially, they still belonged to the households of their parents because the patrilineal heads had not yet "divided" the household spirits and transferred them to the new homes. These houses thus still lacked altars for the house spirits. This example demonstrates that the Hmong can spatially relocate while spiritually and socially still belonging to their unit of origin.

Another example concerns the household that had ritually adopted me. At the time of my research, my Hmong assistant Win Huj, his younger brother Ntsum Nraiv and his younger sister Vaab (twenty-four years, unmarried, one son) were asked by their parents to continue living with them in their household. Consequently, fourteen people lived in one house with little space available for each person. The house next door, which belonged to Win Huj's older brother Vaas Naaj (who lived with his family in a Hmong community in Mae Rim) was empty for me to move in. Win Huj's own house, which he had built years ago on the outskirts of the village, was also uninhabited. Only a year after his father's death in October 2001, could Win Huj move with his family to yet another small house located near his older brother in Mae Rim. He then became the head of his own household. In the meantime, his mother, younger brother and sister still live in the old house in Mae Sa Mai.

Win Huj's family moved to Mae Rim because one of the daughters had finished the primary school in the village. If she wished to continue her school education, she had to visit a school in the lowlands. Win Huj's other two children still visit the primary school in Mae Sa Mai and stay for the large part of the week with their grandmother and other lineage relatives in the village. The lack of opportunities to educate children above the age of ten in the village school or anywhere near the village, forces Hmong parents, like their counterparts from other ethnic mountain groups, to send their children to lowland schools. The geographical distances and inadequate transportation always imply children's separation from their families. Parents who cannot afford to finance a room in a rented house in the city must send their children either to free temple schools or boarding schools run by Christian missionaries or the Social Welfare Department, which are usually far away. At an early age, these children thus become used to separation from their families and lineage members for most of the year, returning to their villages only during school holidays. Despite long periods of absence, these children are, like Hmong people who work and live in the lowlands for most of the year, an integral part of the household. They must be present for the performance of certain household rituals, like the door spirit ritual (*dab roog*). Because of outside influences, young children are already forced to physically separate from their kin and village and relocate to places belonging to Thai lowland or Western societies. At the same time, they remain cognitively attached to their original households and Hmong kinship network. In a way, aspects of migration culture ingrained into Hmong culture in the past are continued here.

"Brothers from one family" (ib cuab kwv tij)

Besides the household, the lineage group represents another fundamental pillar of Hmong society. A lineage consists of a group of male relatives and their families united around an agnatic core. The men can indicate, by stating all the intermediate links, common descent from a shared procreator. Yet, members are not only recruited through partilineal descent but through marriage and sometimes even adoption (Mischung 1990: 290-292; Geddes

1976: 61-62).[105] One other distinguishing feature of Hmong lineages is that members can die in each other's houses and receive proper mortuary rites from their close kin. This is not possible for members of the same sub-clan or clan because they do not belong to the "immediate" family. Spatially, lineages are not necessarily confined to one village but can be scattered over great distances throughout northern Thailand or even other countries. Unlike lineages among other groups of the region, such as the Kachin of Burma (Leach 1954:131), Hmong lineages are not ranked.

All lineage members are socially bound to each other through close ties between "brothers from one family" (*ib cuab kwv tij*). In contrast, members of the overall clan are called "distanced brothers" (*kwv tij kub*). It is these clan segments or lineages that Hmong depend on for immediate economic help and daily assistance.[106] Jan Ovesen (1995: 23) points out that lineages actually function like large extended families in which people act like members of one household towards each other (see also Geddes 1976: 54). Chapter eleven also provides a description of this. The social, emotional, and spiritual value of lineage connections typically matters more than any material assistance. This explains why large wealth differences can exist between lineage members of one village neighbourhood, despite relationships of mutual aid (cf. Petersen-Golden 2002: 81). Jan Ovensen underlines this point:

> "The sociality of the Hmong is predominantly focused on the spatial proximity of relatives. A Hmong can only be really happy when he is together with his relatives, since such close contact represents emotional assurance, social support, spiritual comfort as well as the greatest possible economic security." (1995: 23)

---

[105] Sometimes parents who cannot give birth to a son adopt boys from relatives or even other ethnic groups. In Ban Phui, one of my main informants was a man with biological Karen parents who had been adopted into the Yang clan by his social Hmong parents at the age of four. *Chuv Tuam Yaj* speaks Karen and Hmong (and Thai) fluently, is well acquainted with both cultures, but is considered to be "100 percent" Hmong.

[106] Roland Mischung (1990: 290-291) emphasises that Hmong lineages are not lineages in the classical sense of the term because they also include, in addition to close blood relatives, the women married to lineage members.

If possible, lineage members usually remain in close proximity to each other within the Hmong settlements. However, as Roland Mischung (1990: 302-304) has shown for the Hmong village he studied in Doi Inthanon National Park, lineage connections are only *one* of several spatial ordering principles. Villagers in his research area tended to settle more according to personal preferences and other kinds of alliances. Nonetheless, social and ritual closeness to lineage members is vital for most Hmong. This explains why the Hmong have tended to migrate in patrilineal descent groups as well as in affinal groups, and why they established Hmong neighbourhoods when they settle in lowland cities like Mae Rim and Chiang Mai. The Karen people, for example, who live in Chiang Mai in greater numbers than the Hmong have not settled together in specific areas but are spread throughout the city (personal communication with the Karen scholar Prasert Trakarnsuphakorn, 10.05.2001, Chiang Mai).

Lineages are both kinship groups and cult groups because their members are ritually connected through common ancestor spirits (*ib tug dab*). For an outsider, the minor differences between the ritual practices of the lineages, as well as of the clans, are difficult to detect without a thorough knowledge of Hmong rituals. In addition, lineages do not have any specific names that clearly indicate the group. Most lineages and clans maintain dietary prohibitions. For example, members of the Yang clan are prohibited from eating heart, a taboo strictly followed.

The most knowledgeable man, who has the greatest authority to keep the lineage united and can care for the lineage's spiritual life, assumes the function of lineage head. The lineage head is instructed by his predecessor and must pass on his own knowledge to a successor during his lifetime. The leader and other knowledgeable members of the lineage are not always allowed to act as ritual practitioners for households of their lineage. For example, during mortuary rites in one of the lineage's households, lineage members host (*tswv cuab*) guests together, which compels them to hand over ritual responsibilities to practitioners from other lineages, regardless of their clan affiliation (Leepreecha 2001: 64).

From an early age, the Hmong teach their children to use the kinship terms. Children are scolded if, for example, they do not call their father's older brother "older father" but by their first names instead. It is extremely impolite to use the proper name when addressing kin. Instead, Hmong are expected to employ the appropriate classificatory kin term. For instance, men of the same generation call themselves *kwv* (younger brother) or *tij* (older brother), while their children refer to them as *txiv* (father), *txiv hlob* (older father), or *txiv ntxaum* (younger father).[107] Only spouses are allowed to call each other by their first names, even though they mostly address each other as if they were speaking through their children, for example a husband calls his wife "your mother". Because of the patrilineal system, most Hmong who explained the kinship system to me acknowledged only male kin in their genealogies. Xaiv Lawm, a fifty-three-year old man from the Thao clan in Mae Sa Mai commented:

"The usage of kinship terms creates a sense of closeness while the usage of first names creates distance. It is almost like an offence when a Hmong addresses another Hmong by the real name because then warmth and closeness is not allowed to develop between these people. If the real name is used, one cannot speak about everything. Only the usage of kin terms permits respect and confidence." (Source: field interview, H-C-MSM 19)

Prasit Leepreecha thus astutely observes "[t]he use of kinship terms instead of proper names to refer to one another in Hmong society is a method of locating an individual in the kin-based social space. It is a strategy for creating a sentiment of close relations between individuals within the group" (2001: 72). In other words, kin terms assign social roles and status, store information, and, last but not least, guide social action. The spatiality of the lineage group is reproduced and constituted through everyday practices like the daily use of kinship terms, mutual socio-economic assistance, common

---

[107] See Leepreecha 2001: 297-298 for further classificatory terms and kinship charts of Hmong Daw and Hmong Njua.

ceremonial and ritual practices, as well as passing on stories about common ancestors and legends of the Chinese homeland. In chapter eleven, I discuss the daily practices of lineage groups in relation to the example of the neighbourhood square setting.

Patrilineal clans and subclans

Neeg no, yog tsis muaj xeem, ces tsis yog neeg.
(A human being without a clan name would not be one.)[108]

Within Hmong society, patrilineal clans form the primary basis for social interaction because individuals are categorised according to their clan membership. Here, I understand Hmong clans as social phenomena that recruit members through unilinear descent and in-marriage. Another characteristic of the "classic" anthropological definition of clans, a common territory, is not a given because of the Hmong's diasporic background. The genealogical structure of clans is rarely known in great depth, although clan members assume shared descent from a common ancestor (Mischung 1990: 292-293; Geddes 1976: 55; Lemoine 1972: 197). The popular and much-narrated legend of the common origin of Hmong clans, recounted in chapter six, plays an important role in Hmong oral history. It creates a "sentiment of shared descent" (Leepreecha 2001: 54) that unites the people of different clan into a single social entity.

Children are members of their father's clan and take on his clan name at birth. The clan consists of a male ancestor, his sons and unmarried daughters, the children of his sons, and so forth, presumably stretching back 160 generations or more (Yang Dao 1992: 288). The Hmong myth of origin shows that clans sprung from the union of a brother and sister. Hmong marriages are clan exogamous. Since people belonging to the same clan are considered brothers and sisters, the incest taboo forbids them from marrying each other. Often, married women comprise an important link between their

---
[108] Hmong proverb quoted in Kao-Ly Yang (2004: 179).

natal clans and clans of their husbands. Inter-clan marriages thus play an important part in strengthening the harmony and unity of the Hmong beyond clan boundaries and village communities. They create a broad network covering the whole of northern Thailand, as well as other countries where Hmong reside.

Polygyny is still permitted, but less practised than in the past. The levirate, connected to the customary practice in which widows would marry the younger brothers of their deceased husbands (see Tapp 1989: 19), also occurs less frequently today. In Mae Sa Mai, there is one polygynous marriage, while in Ban Phui four men have more than one wife. One of these men is married to one Hmong woman and to two Karen wives who live with their children in different Karen villages in the vicinity of Ban Phui. The Hmong husband visits each of these wives. In Ban Phui, he, his Hmong wife and children form part of his parents' household.

Hmong still prefer cross-cousin and maternal parallel-cousin marriage. When parents from both sides are more closely connected, they can handle problems of the couple more easily. There is also a general preference for exchanging marriage partners between clans on a reciprocal basis. However, young people, especially those who attend lowland schools or colleges, do not choose their marriage partners along these lines. Rather, they give priority to emotional attachment, although falling in love with a member of the same clan is a deeply rooted taboo among the Hmong. Most unmarried boys and girls I have spoken with stressed that their parents' influence in choosing a marriage partner has diminished while their own freedom of choice increased (see also Lee 1988: 169).[109] This became particularly apparent during Mae Sa Mai's big Hmong New Year celebrations in 2001. Girls and boys flirted openly with each other while touring households to pay respect to the elders. Moreover, in the evenings, girls danced and sang

---

[109] In the past, it was also customary that the groom "abducted" the bride to enforce marriage, either with or without the prior consent of the women. In my research sites, this tradition is no longer observed because it is now considered disrespectful to the bride and her parents (cf. Kunstadter 2004: 377; Cooper 2004: 428).

Hmong and Thai pop songs on an open-air stage set up in the school yard while boys courted them with flowers or other small gifts (see also Leepreecha 2001: 79). Many people assemble in the villages for the New Year's Celebrations, also in search of marriage partners. Because partners must be chosen clan exogamously, their clan affiliation must always be known.

The Hmong term for clan is *xeem* (pronounced seng) which is modelled on the Chinese surname group "shing" or "xing" (Leepreecha 2001: 50; Cooper 1984: 50; Cooper 1979: 173). *Xeem* is a reference term put before the clan name, typically used when dealing with non-Hmong. A Hmong from the Thao clan would therefore introduce him- or herself to a non-Hmong person as *Xeem Thoj* and to an unknown Hmong as *Hmoob Thoj*. *Hmoob* (meaning people) is the general ethnonym for the Hmong. It is also a term classifying the sub-category "clan", which divides the group of the Hmong into *Hmoob Yaj, Hmoob Thoj, Hmoob Xioov*, etc.[110] A *Hmoob Yaj* might feel closer to the *Hmoob Yaj* group than the *Hmoob* in general, whereas obligations towards members of the same lineage can take precedence over general clan obligations (Mischung 1990: 286). Generalisations concerning priorities within the Hmong kinship system are, however, difficult to make. Each member of the society is involved in a range of possible relationships of different types while degrees of importance are principally determined according to people's personal situations and interests (see also Geddes 1976: 69). That is to say, principles of clan solidarity remain rather vague and non-binding as long as closer ties like common sub-clan or lineage membership have been ascertained and, like other identity affiliations, situationally evoked. Clans are not permanently organised units located in a single terrain. Rather they are associations that can temporarily, in case of face-to-face encounters by their members, be

---

[110] The Green Hmong also use the Hmong term *qhua* (ritual) interchangeably with *xeem* and *hmoob* to designate clans, since they also differ slightly from each other in terms of ritual practice. This habit is unknown among the White Hmong and is one reason for the confusion about the exact number of Hmong clans.

Hmong Social Organisation

relevant for mutual aid and assistance. Roland Mischung (1990: 289) understands clans as a potential. They can be mobilised when their interests do not diverge from other, maybe more important, units like households or lineages. William Geddes (1976: 64) supports Mischung's argument, highlighting an important aspect of the Hmong mental model I call the Hmong Mountains: "The wide scatter of clansmen provides staging posts over much of the countryside."

In other words, Hmong people can rely on a clan network that provides them with social structures even in an unknown environment such as Bangkok, Koh Samui, or New York. The kinship system in general and the widespread clan network in particular are a potential for Hmong people. They can draw on them for processes of place making within Thai society and the wider world, to learn and understand more about these spheres, overcome impediments and choose from various opportunities.

Informants in Mae Sa Mai and Ban Phui generally said that twelve different clans can be found in Thailand, the number twelve being spiritually significant because of the myth of origin. The overall number of clans in Southeast Asia is estimated by scholars to lie between fifteen and twenty clan divisions (Leepreecha 2001: 56-60; Ovesen 1995: 19; Yang Dao 1993: 23; Mischung 1990: 284; Tapp 1989: 169; Lyman 1968: 3). However, as Prasit Leepreecha (2001: 60) stresses, it is next to impossible to obtain an accurate total for the number of clans since clan boundaries, just like ethnic boundaries, are permeable and malleable. New clan names have been, for example, added to the Hmong clan system through the intermarriage of Chinese men and Hmong women in Thailand and Laos.

Members of the same clan often refer to each other as *kwv tij* (brothers) while affinal relatives and blood relatives of other clans are generally classified as *neej tsa*. At the time of marriage, women are "adopted" into the husband's clan. For women, members of the new clan become *kwv tij*, while members of their own natal clan become *neej tsa* (Mischung 1990: 285). More generally, the term *neej tsa* can be used to refer to any Hmong person of another clan, since the clans are all interlinked in one way or another through marriage. Married women who share the same natal clan and are on friendly terms refer to each other as *viv ncaus* (sisters). In-laws within the Hmong kinship system differ from in-laws in Western kinship systems because Hmong women are incorporated into the husband's clan upon marriage. They are not in-laws, but regarded as "sisters" by the husband's brothers. To sum up, *kwv tij* and *neej tsa* are two important, opposing categories. They generally class Hmong people into closely related people one can rely on for consultation and assistance (*kwv tij*) and more distant people (*neej tsa*) from whom only minor aid is available, but who form an important part of the broad, de-localised Hmong network (see also Cooper 1978: 307; Geddes 1976: 64).

The marginal differences found between lineages also exist within clans. Due to these dissimilarities, clans are also divided into sub-clans that are "spiritual association[s] symbolised by the same ritual practices and the same mythology" (Geddes 1976: 65). Green Hmong people refer to sub-clans with the interchangeable terms *cum* (group) or *ib tug dab tug qhuas* (those whoe revere one spirit). They assume members of a sub-clan share a common ancestor who, as in the case of clans, cannot be traced back to any known predecessor. The distinctive markers of sub-clans are different ritual practices, such as the diverse combination of big and small bowls (*txim*) used for sacrificial items and varying numbers of small piles (*ntsau*) of sacrificial items like pork meat. Hmong can only ascertain a common sub-clan membership by exchanging detailed information on how ceremonial practices are conducted, such as the door spirit ritual (*dab roog*), the ox spirit ritual (*nyuj dab*), the funeral ritual (*kev pam tuag*), the type of grave construction (*toj ntxa*) as well as the clan taboos (Leepreecha 2001: 61). William Geddes (1976: 66) underscores that these sub-clans are most important on a local scale at the village level, providing members with mutual aid and "cooperating bodies in ritual".

"*Koj yog xeem dlab tsi?*" – What is your clan name? This question is instantly asked when two unknown Hmong meet each other. They then inquire about the names of each other's parents in order to learn about the other person's background and possible common ancestors. Gender, generation, and age also play crucial roles in finding the appropriate kin terms to use. The common affiliation to a sub-clan is established through questions about how one's sub-clan constructs graves. When common sub-clan membership is given, questions go into further detail about ancestors to see if one belongs to the same lineage. Even though lineages and sub-clans do not have any specific Hmong names, Hmong establish affiliation to the same sub-clans and lineages through this kind of "greeting ritual". Through the kinship reckoning system, Hmong seek kin on either the side of the patrilineal or affinal clan (to which each Hmong is connected through e.g. the mother or wife), as well as a possible shared membership in one sub-clan or lineage (Lee no year: 4). Importantly though, women cannot interrogate an unknown Hmong man about his kinship background. The Hmong view such behaviour as highly disrespectful and impolite. Men must address women first, thus signalling their willingness to find out more about the nature of their relationship to each other. Generally, the credibility of a person is determined by his or her extended family's reputation, which rests on a generations-long process. If even one (male) family member has ruined this reputation – through theft, sexual harassment, or drug trafficking or addiction for example – it can be difficult to restore (cf. Cooper 2004: 421; Michaud 1996: 278; see also Lyman 2004: 172).

> "What is of interest here is how individual moral behaviour is not seen as only individual, but immediately reflects on and involves the wider social grouping, and particularly the immediate family and lineage segment; the notion of *koob meej* [reputation] is thus importantly related to the notion of *ua tsim txiaj neeg* or the "man of worth" who [...] helps others as well as his own family, and importantly assures his position through the performance of appropriate ritual, etiquette, and courtesy to strangers and visitors." (Tapp 2002: 103, italics in original)

As in most patrilineal societies, the Hmong commitment to the lineage and clan of the male head of the household is, in most situations, stronger than their sense of obligation towards the mother's lineage and clan. However, through clan commitments and connections, the matrilineal kin plays also an important role. A common Hmong proverb refers to the importance of interclan relationships in the following way (cited in Yang Dao 1992: 289): *Koj qaib pw kuv cooj. Kuv os pw koj nkuaj*, which can be translated as "Your chicken sleeps in my coop. My duck sleeps in your stable."[111] The maxim expresses the fact that families, and therefore clans, are interlinked by marriage. The general sense of patrilineal and affinal clanship enlarges the socio-spatial horizon of the Hmong group as clans are closely interlinked through marital relations (Lee 1986: 26; Geddes 1976: 64).

The Hmong initiate or strengthen alliances between two clans through a process that includes exchanges between wife-givers and wife-takers, such as the bridewealth. Often mistaken for a "bride-price" or a "commodification" of women, the bridewealth has many levels of meaning. Bridewealth is paid to compensate the parents of the bride for the costs and labour they have invested in raising the daughter. As one thirty-year-old male villager from Ban Phui remarked:

"When I am asked how many children I have, I always answer: two sons. I do not name my three daughters because I know that I only raise them until marriage. Then they change over to another clan. My sons stay with me forever. But daughters are also important because they connect our clan to another clan forever, and this kind of alliance cannot be made in any other way." (Source: field interview, H-C-BP 17)

Marriage alliances thus have an important function within Hmong kinship relations; they can be as important as clan or even lineage affiliations on the local scale because they widen the Hmong network and join households and clans. These important affinal interconnections are, for example, symbolised

---

[111] See also Thomas Amis Lyman (2004) for a discussion of additional Green Hmong proverbs.

through a respectful rite performed by the groom in the bride's parent's house that unites both clans involved (see Leepreecha 2001: 65). Wives maintain close ties with their natal clans by visiting of their parents' homes. In the event that a woman's natal village is far away from her new village of residence, her nuclear family accompanies her on yearly visits to her parents' village. Some husbands in Mae Sa Mai even "allow" their wives to travel alone to visit natal kin, although women from Ban Phui have less freedom of movement.

During interviews on the Hmong kinship system, informants and interviews repeatedly stressed the importance and meaning of inter-relationships with in-law clans. Despite clear notions about relative genealogical distance, networks of reciprocal obligation *within* clans as well as *between* different clans are fundamental to Hmong social unity (cf. Yang Dao 1992: 280).

While the importance of intra-clan ties is often emphasised, conflicts also arise between clans. As already mentioned, in Mae Sa Mai the three minority Hmong clans criticised the majority Xiong clan for having too much power before the village's partition. In addition, conflict has existed between the Thao and Xiong clans across generations, but the actual reasons for the tensions are long forgotten. Nevertheless, one night during my research in Mae Sa Mai, young men from the two clans fought each other. Those involved pointed to the gap between the clans in the village as the main reason for the fight. Elders of both clans had to convene to settle the reinvigorated conflict.

I was also told about past tensions between Hmong clans throughout northern Thailand that arose especially over bridewealth. Some families had asked for high prices, others were only willing to pay low sums. Clan representatives from different provinces decided that a total of 12.000 baht should be generally paid for bridewealth. Lower sums might be offered for divorced women or widows. To strengthen clan and kinship ties among Hmong in northern Thailand, representatives from diverse clans in the nine Thai provinces (Chiang Mai, Chiang Rai, Mae Hong Son, Phayao, Nan,

Petchabun, Lampang, Lamphun, Phrae) that harbour Hmong settlements meet yearly to discuss Hmong affairs. The Hmong Association in Chiang Mai facilitates such meetings. This conscious strengthening of clan and kinship ties through interregional clan meetings helps solve inter-clan disputes and strengthen Hmong identity. It also counters efforts by Thai society to integrate, acculturate and ultimately weaken Hmong culture and its clan structures (see also Leepreecha 2001: 239).

The village community

Compared with those of other ethnic groups, Hmong villages are characterised by a relative lack of cohesion. The focus is directed more towards socio-economically autonomous households and lineages living mostly together in neighbourhoods within villages. These units support each other on a daily basis and are the centres of interaction (cf. Ovesen 1995: 24). The fact that Hmong do not name their villages, unlike the Karen for example, also brings out this point. Instead Hmong people employ the names given by Thai authorities that relate to characteristics of the villages. For instance, near Mae Hong Son, one Hmong village is called "Ban Microwave" (Village Microwave) because Thai TV channels have placed their transmitters in the middle of this small mountaintop village that lacks electricity.

Walking through a Hmong village, especially a large one such as Mae Sa Mai, one can sense that the settlement is less a strong unit than conglomerate of clan's people who have other, more important support networks. People do not necessarily greet each other unless they live in the same section or neighbourhood or meet a person of high status. However, for special occasions like the discussion of village-related matters, mortuary rites, wedding or New Year, villagers (mostly the men) join in social gatherings and visit each other to reinforce village cohesion.

Fairly weak village unity may be related to former types of agriculture and migration, since swidden agriculture demanded mobility and resulted in a frequent abandonment or separation of villages. Most Hmong tried to set up large villages for reasons of security and enjoyment. However, settlements were less important than kin units that relocated together and followed each other in the search for new, fertile land. In his comparison of seven mountain groups and their average village sizes, Roland Mischung (1990: 268) shows that already in the 1960s and 1970s, Hmong people had exceptionally large settlements of about forty households or 350 people.[112] My twenty Hmong village survey, found in the appendix, confirms his findings, showing that the average size of a Hmong village today is eighty households or 700 people.

Through his bird's flock analogy, William Geddes suggests that main reasons for Hmong migrations were the search for new primary forest and land. Peter Kunstadter (2000: 173-174) supports this assumption in his survey of Hmong villagers' reasons for past movement. According to this study, the search for land and other natural resources, such as fertile soil or water, clearly comprised the major reason for migration. However, I would agree with Roland Mischung's (1990: 281) argument that Hmong have also had social motives for moving to large settlements and communities: A large population guaranteed a varied social life and ritual multiplicity. It also offered social support and security, in contrast to Thai lowland society or other ethnic groups. I would argue that social cohesion within Hmong villages has even intensified in present times because residents are sedentarised, more involved in communal, village-wide projects and political structures have changed in mountain settlements. Today, the elected village headman and his deputy represent residents collectively. These work in cooperation with the elders' council on village matters and the cohesion of the community. Joint projects, such as the redefinition of the sacred tree ritual and communal conservation of areas declared "protected community forests" (see chapter ten), to some extent ensure the continuance of the

---

[112] Authors like the French missionary François Marie Savina ([1924] 1930: 182), writing about the Hmong in Laos, or Hugo Bernatzik (1947: 102, 262), writing about the Hmong in Thailand, were convinced that the Hmong had a preference for small settlements.

village community, as well as the maintenance of ethnic boundaries. In Mae Sa Mai, village representatives have worked hard for years to solve inner-village conflict. Only as a last resort has the settlement been divided into two administrative units to avoid further problems.

Hmong people generally seek the presence of a large number of Hmong commoners – belonging to the same clan as well as to others – because a large group of Hmong still implies security and social support within societies largely dominated by others. As mentioned above, Hmong villagers who have built houses in Mae Rim or Chiang Mai have only done so in neighbourhoods where other Hmong live already. Or, to give another example, Hmong refugees who had been settled in U.S. states such as Kansas, Iowa, Colorado or Texas moved – in a wave of "secondary migration" – to places in California, Minnesota and Wisconsin where large Hmong communities and the traditional group support already existed.[113] The move was aimed at retaining Hmong culture in a foreign environment by assembling social support in one locality and consolidating the group's power (Bulk 1996: 13-24; Chan 1994: 59-60; Yang Dao 1990: 6). The Hmong in Australia also settle communally in the same areas so they can interact with members of their own ethnic group (Lee 1986a: 55). In the case of the Hmong in France and French-Guyana, Hmong families move in a "two-way-migration", (Yang, Kou 2003: 280) back and forth between the two countries to interconnect families and their ways of life. The Hmong in French-Guyana are said to have adapted well to the country's mountainous areas, which allow them to successfully pursue Hmong life and agricultural work. In France, Hmong men are either self-employed as taxi-drivers, entrepreneurs in the cities of Paris, Lyons or Nice, or engage in agriculture in the rural areas (Yang, Kou 2003: 280). In general, there is a trend towards Hmong migration from the smaller communities to larger Hmong

---

[113] In a "third migration" in the 1990s, Hmong Americans moved out of California, especially Fresno, to Minnesota and other mid-western states in order to find better economic opportunities and social environments for their children (Yang, Kou 2003: 286).

concentrations, and from other countries to the United States (Yang, Kou 2003: 297).

To sum up, villages or Hmong settlements have an ambiguous position within Hmong society: They do not have any formal traditional leaders and lack strong social cohesion. Household, lineage and clan interests typically take precedence over village matters. Daily interaction concentrates largely in the neighbourhoods of the lineages, whereas gatherings of the whole village occur only on special occasions. The entirety of Hmong villagers thus assembles very seldom and acts as a social unit only rarely. For example, this is the case on the last day of New Year when representatives of each household, mostly Hmong men and boys, walk up to the sacred tree together to honour the most important spirit of the place (see chapter ten). Hmong villages lack cohesion and are of only secondary importance in everyday interactions. However, the Hmong place strong emphasis on large rural villages or strong inter-clan Hmong communities within cities because they provide security and support in settings largely dominated by Thai, Laotian, U.S. American, or French majority societies. The spatial proximity of a large number of Hmong people in settlement areas – whether in Mae Sa Mai, Bangkok, Fresno (California, U.S.A.) or Gammerdingen near Stuttgart (Germany) – is one means of "place making" and constituting a Hmong spatiality. It provides the Hmong with alternative support networks suited to their socio-cultural needs in otherwise culturally foreign environments.

"Maleness is Hmong and Hmong is maleness": Gender differences

One of the Hmong attributes that struck me most at the beginning of my fieldwork was the strong separation of male and female domains and influence of this separation on every aspect of Hmong society. These initial experiences reminded me of the Hmong saying: "Maleness is Hmong and Hmong is maleness" (quoted in Symonds 1991: 31). Hmong cultural spatiality is importantly influenced by the gender differences that are integral to Hmong society and culture. My "neutral gender" status as a female anthropologist, as I mentioned above, made it possible for me to participate in both female and male dominated settings and thus learn about both cultural domains.

Cosmological complementarity of the sexes

Generally, the position of women among the Hmong is less one of inferiority than a reflection of fundamental social differences and principle of complementarity between the sexes (Ovesen 1995: 73). As seen above in the chapter on Hmong religion, Hmong cosmological thought is characterised by oppositions, especially those organised around gender. Men are, in accordance with the Chinese medical system, associated with a hot life force (*yang*) and females are associated with a cold life force (*ying*) (cf. Symonds 1991: 47). The Hmong also describe aspects of topography and directions according to concepts of gendered pairs. Mountains on the left side of a river are associated with tigers and are male, while the right side is associated with dragons and females (Symonds 2004: 7; Tapp 1989: 151; see also citation above). In addition, the Hmong view the earth and sun as female, the sky and moon as male. As common in many Southeast Asian societies, Hmong men are believed to represent the "bones" of a body and seen as the "skeleton" of Hmong society. Women are associated with the "flesh", without which a skeleton would not constitute a human being (cf. Lévi-Strauss 1969). Or, in another metaphor, the Hmong compare men to the everlasting trunks and branches of trees and view women as the perishable leaves and flowers (Hang 1986: 34).

Cosmological concepts of binary gender pairs are also closely related to the needs of the exogamous clans. The clans require the in-marriage of women and their fertility in order to secure the continuity of their own and the lineage's genealogical line. Thus, although men exert control over women within the patrilineal system, motherhood and reproduction endow women with two roles highly valued by Hmong society (Symonds 1991: 35).

Furthermore, the trans-generational and cosmological perspective shed a different light on gender relations within Hmong society because the Hmong believe that the soul of a deceased person is not a gendered but "neutral" phenomenon. A soul or spiritual being can be reborn in a female or male body. Potentially at least, this means women are not completely excluded from the patriline, but have the opportunity to be reborn in the body of a male upon their next reincarnation (Symonds 1991: 272). This implies, of course, that men can also be reborn as women, animals or even vegetables. One male informant told me jokingly that men will be reborn as women or even insects if they do not behave according to moral norms and the ancestors' demands during their lifetime on earth. This should be avoided at all costs because "Who wants to be reborn as a woman?" the man asked with a smile on his face. In short, cosmologically, gender is a central organising principal dividing women and men into binary and dichotomous, yet complementary entities.

Hmong ideology constructs men as the appropriate leaders of society. Educated men in particular play a vital role in the moral leadership and ideological formation of society. Their knowledge of morality and social relations extends to the spiritual realm. Male power stems especially from the area of spirituality. Male agnates are allowed to perform the ancestral worship rituals, which remembers and perpetuates the lineage. For example, during mortuary rites, women can only act in the background as "unofficial" hosts. Male lineage members are the official hosts of guests, marked by white scarves around their head. Men are the ones who prostrate themselves three times in front of arriving guests, placing head and knuckles on the ground. They are usually responsible for the provision of food and drink, while female lineage members have to perform the deathwatch. Women maintain asymmetrical religious power since they are connected to the patrilineal family either through their fathers or their husbands, but have no own obvious or official power in this sphere (Leepreecha 2001: 14; Symonds 1991: 267). In other words, "[...] women are excluded from the most sacred and highly valued aspects of rituals concerning the patriline" (Symonds 2004: xxvii).

Gender relations in practice

In practice, women are responsible for the physical substance of life, matters connected to the organisation of the household and the assistance of their husbands. Men are clearly connected to the political, economic and ritual spheres. A young woman's marriage is usually linked to great, sometimes disturbing changes in her life. At marriage, a woman is adopted into her husband's family. She must not only change clan membership, but more often than not also move from her natal village (and district or province) to that of her husband. She must adjust to totally new surroundings and integrate herself into a new household by proving herself "worthy" to her parents-in-law. Women who already have grown-up children and daughter-in-laws can obtain a certain status within Hmong society. Should a woman be widowed or divorced, she can return to her consanguineous relatives. However, she must live in a separate house because she no longer shares the same ritual system as her birth parents.[114]

In times of poppy cultivation, actual gender relationships resembled those of male employer and female employee, as Robert Cooper (1983: 173) asserts, that of "master" and "servant". For the most part, women still have a greater workload than men, since they have to help their men with agricultural tasks, as well as rear the children and do housework (see also Cooper 1983: 176-177). In practice, this means that women have to get up before everyone else to cook breakfast. Afterwards, women typically accompany their husbands to the fields (unless they have just given birth) around six to seven o'clock in the morning and return only about ten hours later to do housework, prepare dinner and take care of the children. Women are expected to be diligent, display subdued behaviour to males and respect

---

[114] For more information on Hmong divorce patterns, see Peter Kunstadter 2004: 379-380.

Hmong society's moral norms (Symonds 2004: xlvii). One example illustrates this: Maiv Las, Win Huj's wife, is picked up every day around three p.m. to accompany other women to the Night Market in Chiang Mai where they sell souvenirs. The men, who do not like this kind of work, seldom accompany them. Maiv Las only returns home to the village around one o'clock in the morning but along with her sister-in-law Ntxais, is the first one to get up to cook breakfast for the other household members at about five o'clock. Only after the family has eaten and left for the fields or school can Maiv Las rest before cooking lunch and driving to the Night Market again. Even if Maiv Las wanted to sleep in the mornings and her husband Win Huj would allow her to do so, she could not display such behaviour. This would contradict customary expectations of women. Other family and lineage members, who pass through the house frequently, would notice such non-conformist conduct, and this would shed a negative light on both her and her household.

Women are socially expected to show bashful behaviour towards men of their age and older. They are only allowed to display more open ways of conduct towards close, male lineage members. This moral norm creates a general spatial separation of males and females, especially at informal and formal gatherings, as the description of the setting of mortuary rites in chapter eleven illustrates more clearly. At social gatherings, men and women sit and eat separately and participate in different activities. Men are concerned with ritual practices or political discussions, while women lack "official" tasks. Instead, they exchange information about personal matters and provide food and drink for the men. When families help each other in the fields and work together in larger groups, women and men mostly work and sit in separate units. If a married man has already inherited fields from his father, he pays daily wages to all helpers, even for his close lineage members and household members not belonging to his nuclear family. Because women generally perform the work requiring the least physical strength, they receive the lowest salaries, about sixty to eighty baht. Men earn between eighty to 120 baht per day from their kin.

In both Mae Sa Mai and Ban Phui, the Hmong women I interviewed about their tasks and position within Hmong society said that their main duty is to serve the husband, take care of the household and children, work in the fields and embroider clothes. All women spend some of their day embroidering clothes, an important female skill that reveals such facets of women's character as patience, diligence, quietness, and creativity. Women take pride in doing "flower cloth" (*paj ntaub*) and attain social status by producing good handwork (Symonds 2004: xlv). Women's status, however, also very much depends on the people surrounding her. Ntxhum Yaj, a forty-eight-year-old woman from Ban Phui expressed the opinion of many other women interviewed:

"Women have to show that they work a lot and follow the rules of their husbands. A woman's position depends on the position of her husband. If the husband is important, his wife is important. But her position also depends on her kin surrounding her. If they say that a woman is a good person, then she is important. If other people say that she is bad, her position is very low and she cannot do much to change that." (Source: field interview, H-C-BP 3)

A woman's position within Hmong society thus depends on her husband's status and reputation, as well as the status assigned to her by her lineage relatives. Men interviewed about women's roles and positions within Hmong society mostly underlined women's special knowledge about child rearing, housekeeping, agriculture, making clothes, and collecting medicinal herbs. However, they also emphasised that men had the more complex and detailed knowledge, especially regarding rituals and genealogies. According to the men, women have to subordinate themselves to male authority and display respectful behaviour towards men. In other words, an ideology of male supremacy characterises Hmong society that gives men certain forms of control over women. Men and women are hierarchically related to each other and women clearly assume the structurally subordinate position (see also Donnelly 1994: 29).

Women are socialised to publicly exhibit respectful, bashful, shy and deferential behaviour towards male authority (see also Symonds 1991: 133). However, as in many other societies, there is a discrepancy between an appearance of powerlessness and reality. Women at my research sites, especially in Mae Sa Mai, seem to exert more power than allowed for by explicit norms. Ultimately, the subordination of women cannot be assumed *a priori*, since people do not always act according to social norms. The male-dominated Hmong culture contains a few arenas in which women exert limited power, such as within the household, where they exert a "background power" that influences important decisions of their husbands. Women also have certain forms of authority in the domain of healing if they possess special knowledge about medicinal herbs. Similarly, they exert certain forms of power as female shamans or in the souvenir business, where they seem to be more apt than men to learn English phrases for dealing with Western tourists. Some women in Ban Phui, where alternatives are more limited, choose Christian religion to gain certain forms of power.

A number of men interviewed even "confessed" that they always consult their wives before making important socio-economic decisions. These men claimed that women generally have a so-called "bedroom-power". Usually couples share small bedrooms with their children divided off from the main large room either by curtains or wooden planks in the rectangular Hmong houses. These makeshift bedrooms are the only private space a couple has to discuss personal issues and make important decisions. For the most part, men cannot "publicly" ask their wives for advice in front of other household or lineage members because of his expected superiority. But in the private bedroom, women are certainly asked for their opinions and advice.

At least in Mae Sa Mai, some men have started to criticise gender inequality in Hmong society. In particular, men complained that Hmong girls had to marry too young, that women suffered from giving birth to too many children, had too little official power in Hmong society and should be given more respect by men. But they also emphasised the general complexity of changing Hmong norms and customary practices. As shown above, gender differences are closely connected to the Hmong worldview and religious beliefs, strongholds of Hmong culture that can only be changed slowly, especially since the elders try to preserve them as best as possible.

Nonetheless, women's status and roles in Hmong society do change. Especially due to transformations in resource use systems and an ever-growing interaction with Thai and Western society, traditional Hmong codes of conduct have slowly weakened. For example, polygynous marriages used to be important symbols of wealth, signifying family affluence if men could afford the bridewealth for more than one wife. The bridewealth was seen as an investment in family prosperity since women and their offspring added to the labour force of the family. In times of subsistence farming and laborious poppy cultivation, this was of major importance (Michaud 1997: 222). Further symbols of wealth were silver bars and silver jewellery used to pay for the bridewealth, which showed the prosperity of a lineage and attracted potential marriage partners (Michaud 1997: 223). However, due to changed moral codes, more emancipated women, and less labour-intensive nature of commercial agriculture, the Hmong do not value polygynous marriages to the same degree today. Nowadays, a man usually takes a second wife only when the first wife does not give birth to a son, who is essential for continuing the lineage-line.

The women I interviewed in Mae Sa Mai no longer tolerate the practice of polygyny and claim they would put their husbands under pressure if they decided to follow this "outdated practice".[115] Indeed, in Mae Sa Mai, there are no known cases of polygyny, whereas five still exist in Ban Phui. Roland Mischung (personal communication 16.06.2004) stresses that polygyny had already declined among the Hmong in Thailand during the 1960s because day labourers like the Karen or Shan could by hired to do the weeding in poppy fields. Households could hire people for work peaks on a day-to-day basis instead of being forced to provide their own large labour force. This

---

[115] In contrast, Peter Kunstadter (2004: 395) claims that polygyny among the Hmong in Thailand has increased rather than decreased, especially in more "remote" areas and among Hmong Christians.

rendered one of the main causes of polygyny obsolete and changed the status of women to a certain extent.

To sum up, intensified contacts to Thai and Western societies, intensified integration in lowland and world markets, as well as changing Hmong cultural traditions have brought women more freedom and equality (see also Tapp 2002: 105). This freedom and equality are clearly connected to the increased spatial mobility of women from Mae Sa Mai. The next section discusses social networks and the mobility of women in more detail.

Spatial dimension of social networks and Hmong endo-sociality

Actors and their relations define social networks. This section explores how Hmong villagers act and organise their daily lives within their personal cultural contexts and provides an idea of the social context in which most people spend the majority of their lives, "living and interacting with the small groups that make up the world around them" (Trotter 1999: 7). Through the discussion of network data, I shed light on the composition of relationships and identify the actors and their patterns of interaction, including kinship and non-kin relationships as well as interethnic contacts, and outline the endosocial structure of Hmong networks.

Network analysis helps define the (spatial) boundaries of a social group's network and illuminates core participants and cross-group differences. To grasp the constitution of Hmong cultural spatiality, it is important to identify key actors, sub-groups, and differences, as well as any socio-spatial boundaries created by the actors themselves. How far does the Hmong villagers' network actually extend, socially and geographically? In the villages studied, who is (potentially) included in the network in a real sense and who is not?

Generally, the field of network analysis assesses either ego-centred personal networks or total networks including all actors. Network data is then considered according to the size, density, closeness, multiplexity, extent of centrality, and typical patterns of social relationships (Schweizer 1996: 37; see also Schnegg and Lang 2002). However, my approach towards the social and spatial dimensions of Hmong networks and relations does not rely on the highly technical quantitative models derived from graph theory and matrix algebra although these can, without doubt, provide valuable insights into human relations.

I apply ethnographic network mapping as my method here, including interviews and observation of people's behaviour, rather than personal or full relational network research. Nevertheless, I have documented personal networks to furnish insight into typical network profiles (see Trotter 1999: 5). For a village as large as Mae Sa Mai, or even as small as Ban Phui, it would not have been possible to explore, in addition to the many other aspects of the research, key relationships between *all* members of the social networks of the villages. Due to obvious time and financial constraints, I was unable to assess the total network of both villages. I also did not opt to assess typical networks, so-called "quasi-relational", "substitute" networks (see Schweizer 1996: 170).

Instead, I tried to gain a representative insight into the network relations of villagers, young and old, female and male, poor and wealthy, through participant observation and in-depth interviews according to a questionnaire. I wished to learn not only about relations within the villages, but also outside them in order to get an idea of the Hmong network's boundaries within Thailand. I therefore included questions about places frequently visited for work, leisure, attendance of ceremonies, and maintenance of kinship relations. In Mae Sa Mai, twenty-eight people were interviewed, in Ban Phui thirty people. At the beginning of the questionnaire, the person's basic personal network data was recorded in order to understand the Hmong network's connectedness from the perspective of the informant. For example, I asked the respondents who they view as important people, with whom they spend most of their time, who they visit, who visits them frequently, and who they consider to be friends. The questions were designed to provide insight into reciprocal actions, kinds of relationships,

Hmong Social Organisation 223

actual and potential connections between people in the network, sub-groups and social roles, as well as positions within the village network.

Before presenting data from the interviews and observations, I want to draw attention to an important point. According to Hmong belief and cosmology, Hmong networks and relations also include the supernatural agencies, especially the ancestors. The living take the ancestors' existence into account in patterning their actions, and they are thus as much a part of the community as those who spend most of the year outside the village. The "religious topography" (Hauser-Schäublin 2003: 48), with its interlinked actions, forms of behaviour and perceptions, is a cardinal point because it includes, besides the horizontal level, the vertical level. Hmong patterns of social order incorporate the existence of strong relationships to the supernatural in the Otherworld. Hmong believe that the ancestors have an especially vigorous impact. They can bring misfortune if unsatisfied with the relationships between them and the living. During fieldwork, I often heard the sentence, most often uttered by older Hmong men, "Throughout my whole life I have always honoured the ancestors and performed all the rituals, but I am still poor. Why?" This query suggests that in Hmong belief, the supernatural and living are closely related and affect each other. The horizontal and vertical spaces are fused (cf. Hauser-Schäublin 2003: 56). This level of relationship must be kept in mind when looking at social relations among the people.

Social relations among the Hmong of Mae Sa Mai and Ban Phui

When asked to name the people most important to them, most informants first gave either their parents' names, their parents-in-law's names in the case of married women and their husbands' names when the wife's parents-in-law had died already. Only two male villagers named their wives as the most important people, and three saw their wives as occupying third place. Most married men named their parents if they were still alive or their classificatory younger or older father, in other words people of respect. Both married men and women also saw their lineage elders as having personal importance to them, while in Ban Phui eight people also gave the name of the village headman.

Young (unmarried girls and boys of fifteen to twenty years) and married people still living in their parents' home spend most of their everyday time with their parents, as well their wives/ husbands and children when married. Even when a married son and his wife have moved into their own house, they still spend a large part of their time in the husband's parents' household. Three of the women interviewed were widowed and lived in their sons' households. They spend most of their time with their children and grandchildren, as well as with women who share a similar fate. Women who cannot work in the fields because they are weaning or caring for children also named their neighbours and female lineage members as people with whom they spend much of a day's time. Strong relationships are characterised by large time investments in them, as well as emotionally intensive and reciprocal expectations.

Hmong Social Organisation

Figure 4: Chart including categories of important reference persons

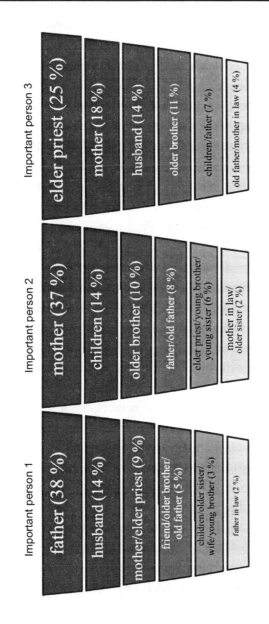

Source: own survey, N=58 (MSM, BP)

In my chapter on settings further below, I show that visiting other village households can be formalised, at times even for lineage members. Therefore, it is important to ascertain which people visit each other. Because the Hmong can view early evening or morning calls on neighbours, relatives, or friends as conscious efforts to maintain good (reciprocal) relations, the answers to this interview question were of particular importance. Interestingly enough, responses usually did not correspond with the people mentioned in the questions above. Here, respondents gave the names of people viewed as "friends", even though people visiting the informant frequently did not correspond with the people the informant visited. Girls and boys in both Mae Sa Mai and Ban Phui named their Hmong friends within the villages. These friends are of the same sex and typically live in the informants' vicinity. They do not all belong to the same clan but are connected to each other through joint settlement, membership in the same age group and their attendance of village or lowland schools together. Married men stay in close personal contact with their "younger" and "older" brothers, but also have male Hmong friends belonging to other lineages or clans. It was striking to learn that all of these non-kin relationships had existed for lengthy periods of more than eight to ten years. They had developed over time because the men were neighbours or their fields were located next to each other.

Some men also have close relationships with Hmong men in other villages to whom they are either related or connected through long-term friendships. If male relatives of the same age get along well and spend significant time together, they might have emotional feelings of friendship towards each other. However, it is considered awkward when they call each other "friends" instead of by their classificatory kinship terms. Two married men can become "brothers" or friends (*npawg*), while two married women can become "sisters" or friends (*viv ncaus*). These terms, however, are only applicable when the two men or women do not have a third person in common to assign them their places within the kinship system and require the use of the specific kin terms.

Married women, especially in Ban Phui, named fewer people to whom they are simply connected through friendship. Women stay in close contact with female lineage members or women belonging to their natal clan to whom they have some kind of connection. The personal network of married women thus seems more restricted to kinship and neighbourhood relations within the village than for men. Robert Cooper (1984: 53) finds that the Hmong have a strong tendency to limit social visits within their villages to their own relatives. My data suggests that this finding holds especially true for married women. One fifty-five-year old woman from Ban Phui explained:

> "I do not want to visit anyone. My neighbours and I, we live close together, so we visit each other. But if someone lives a bit further away in the village, we do not go anymore." (Source: field interview, H-SNI-BP 14)

Hmong women need to follow strict moral norms, displaying subdued and honourable behaviour that does not bring shame to either her natal or husband's family clan. Hence, it would be inappropriate for a woman of Ban Phui to go from one end of the village to the other without a special purpose or in the company of her husband, other women or children (cf. Symonds 2004: xlviii). In Mae Sa Mai, women enjoy more freedom of movement inside and outside the village. However, in practice, most women also stay in their neighbourhoods when they are not in their fields or at the markets. The mobility of women is largely connected to that of their husbands and sons. It is relatively restricted because they must observe norms, have more household chores and, with a few exceptions in Mae Sa Mai, cannot drive cars or motorbikes themselves. Further below, I compare the mobility of women and men outside the villages.

If women have moved away from their natal clan to join their husbands in Mae Sa Mai or Ban Phui, clan's people from their own village remain important to them, even when they see them once a year or less often. Women regard their blood sisters as their best and most intimate friends.

During interviews with these women, I could sense a longing for the natal lineage group and its female members, expressed for example in the comments below. A thirty-year-old woman from Ban Phui also stresses restrictions on the spatial mobility of women:

> "When I came here from my own village, I did not own anything. That was hard. I had to start a new life here with a new family, in a new house and a new clan. We are moving people so I do not mind. But I miss my own parents and my sisters, who are in other villages now. My mother taught us to get used to this idea of moving away to a new life when we were young. We had to submit to our fate as women. I have also prepared my heart to stay at home and be a good wife. I mostly stay here in the neighbourhood or go to the fields with my husband. When I go to Mae Chaem or Chom Thong, I always go with my husband. Who can I go with? It is the traditional role of the women to stay at home. If women socialise too much, that is a reason for divorce. If I would start to travel and see the world, I would miss it and soon be unhappy. The way it is now, is okay." (Source: field interview, H-C-BP 7)

Women from other villages married to men in Mae Sa Mai or Ban Phui come from many different districts and as many as five different provinces, the farthest about 500 kilometres away. Roland Mischung (1990: 306) has already drawn attention to the higher percentage of long-distance marriages among the Hmong than among the Karen, who mostly marry partners within a thirty-kilometre radius of the village. Hmong marriage networks are quite expansive and maintained by wives and their husbands, who try to visit the parents from the natal village at least once a year (see also Cooper 1984: 64-66). In their search for potential wives from other clans, adolescent boys travel together to New Year's celebrations in other districts or even provinces. In doing so, they also contribute to the continuation of a broad Hmong network.

During my network interviews, I asked respondents to rank the categories "friend", "extended family", "clan", and "the Hmong people" (in that order).

Typically the informants named "friends" as the least important category, but kept the sequence of the other categories the same. Only unmarried girls and boys saw their friends as more important than the Hmong people. By placing friends, who are mostly "outsiders" either belonging to other clans or even other ethnic groups, behind the other categories, most people were adhering to Hmong moral norms. These norms stress that individuals must subordinate their personal interests to those of their lineage and clan in order to retain the 'inside' Hmong group. For example, according to the traditional social system, it would be intolerable for Hmong to ask an outsider for help before approaching members of their own lineages or clans (Hall 1990: 37).

A thirty-six-year-old male villager from Ban Phui, Ruam Tsaab, described the results of his own ranking in the statement below. It furnishes a useful explanation for the overall outcome among respondents:

> "The family is most important because it belongs to you. You have no choice because you are born into it. You stick to the clan for your lifetime, which is not always easy but the clan also supports you. When you have friends that is good, but for your life that is not enough. Only your clan and your own Hmong people will always support you, no matter what happens. In that regard we are different from other peoples." (Source: field interview, H-SNI-BP 13)

Interethnic relations

Most Hmong villagers differentiate between relations to kin and Hmong friends and their connections to people from other groups. This is a general tendency in social relations among Hmong people. During his fieldwork among White Hmong in northern Thailand in the 1980s, Nicholas Tapp (1989: 6) was surprised to find that the Hmong of his research area maintained more "extensive contacts with the outside world than originally anticipated" (Tapp 1989:6). In contrast, I was surprised to discover that although Hmong villagers indeed have many contacts to the outside world through their crop marketing and trade, most of these contacts remain superficial or restricted to work relations.

During the network interviews, only adolescent girls and boys and a few married Hmong men stated that they have close friends belonging to another ethnic group. When Hmong students attend lowland schools, they have Thai, Karen, Akha or Lisu friends, for example. However, they cannot or do not continue most of these relationships when school ends and the children return to home villages scattered throughout northern Thailand. For girls and boys from Mae Sa Mai, it is easier to maintain friendships with young Thai from nearby Mae Rim or Chiang Mai than for adolescents from the more remote Ban Phui. In most cases, the Hmong students visit their Thai friends in the lowlands and not vice versa. For the young Hmong, it is easier to integrate into a Thai setting than the other way around. Some married men also claimed to have Thai or Karen friends, but the majority do not. Married women hardly have any deeper interethnic contact extending beyond work relationships. Instead, they named their husbands' Karen or Thai friends if these frequently visited their husbands at home.

Figure 5: Social relations with other ethnic groups

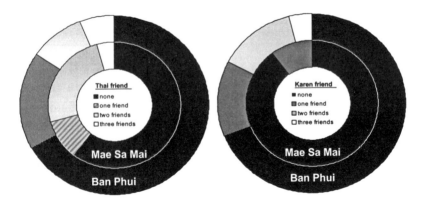

Source: own survey

Despite the interethnic friendships with Karen and Thai people that young Hmong and some married men maintain, most relationships between Hmong villagers and other groups are seen as mere work acquaintances. Ban Phui is surrounded by many Karen villages. In general, the Hmong there feel friendly towards the Karen and even speak their language. Yet few informants claimed to have closer contact to their neighbours. Social relations among the Hmong people are thus largely marked by an endosociality, a term Jonathan Friedman (1997: 287) uses to describe the group-exclusive social networks that characterise relationships of the Big Island's native Hawaiians. Endosociality can be seen as an important strategy of social survival for groups whose main resource is social capital.

Spatial boundaries and contact with the outside world

Roland Mischung (1990: 310) contends that Hmong networks have decreased due to processes of sedentarisation while, simultaneously gaining a new dimension through the improvement of northern Thai infrastructure and rapidly increasing motorisation of Hmong society (see also Rigg 1997: 169). In fact, in Mae Sa Mai, of the twenty-nine households interviewed in the survey, sixteen had one car and two each owned two cars. Seventeen additional households owned one motorcycle each and four households had two. People in Ban Phui have more vehicles: eight households have one car, seven have two, one has three and another one even has four cars. Ten families are in the possession of one motorbike and three have two motorcycles. As shown in the chapter on the economy of both villages, Ban Phui's households are generally wealthier than those in Mae Sa Mai, which have less land at their disposal. Even Hmong people who do not own a vehicle are more mobile than in the past, since pick-up truck owners transport other villagers and their commodities to the marketplaces or take them along to mortuary rites in far away places. Mobile phone ownership has also given Hmong social networks a new dimension, facilitating the maintenance of widespread networks. Dates of important lineage or clan rituals can now be easily disseminated to summon a great number of people, including kin living overseas.

In order to gain a better understanding of villagers' actual mobility, the network interviews analysed how frequently the Hmong go to other places. From prior conversations and participant observation, I knew that the villagers generally differentiate between two kinds of travel: trips to the lowlands for business, administrative, shopping or other purposes, and travels to other Hmong villages to attend religious ceremonies. Generally, they employed the Thai word *pai thiao* (literally: go have fun) to describe the latter type of travel, even when it entailed attending mortuary rites in another village.

Residents from Mae Sa Mai mainly visit their nearby towns of Pong Yaeng (eight kilometres or a fifteen minute drive on dirt road), Mae Rim (twenty kilometres or a thirty minute drive) and Chiang Mai (thirty-seven kilometres or a forty-five minute drive). People from Ban Phui frequently drive to the nearby town of Mae Chaem (twenty kilometres or a forty minute drive on dirt road), Chom Thong (seventy kilometres or a 100 minute drive), Mae La Noi (fifty kilometres or a two hour drive on dirt road) and Chiang Mai (110 kilometres or a two hour and forty minute drive).

The table below shows how frequently men and women drive to these destinations. When looking at the data, it is important to keep in mind that some women from Ban Phui may go to Mae Chaem, for example, quite frequently to market their products and sell them to Thai traders. However, these women are always in the company of their husbands or other male relatives. Women from Mae Sa Mai who go to Chiang Mai daily typically go in groups of women and then sell souvenirs at their Night Market stalls by themselves. During the week, some young students also go to either Mae Rim (from Mae Sa Mai) or Mae Chaem (from Ban Phui) every day in order to attend high schools there. Some students only return to their villages on weekends or for holidays if they can stay in boarding schools or with closely related kin living in the lowland towns.

Figure 6: Trips to other cities (Mae Sa Mai and Ban Phui)

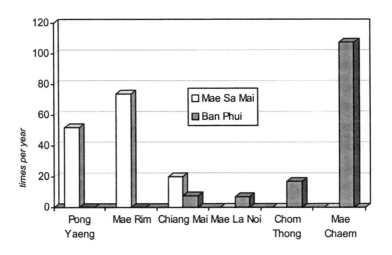

Source: own survey, N=58 (MSM, BP)

Figure 7: Trips to other cities, separated by gender (Mae Sa Mai and Ban Phui)

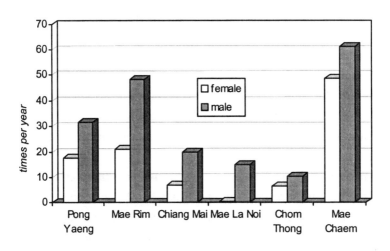

Source: own survey, N=58 (MSM, BP)

The majority of people from Mae Sa Mai goes to Pong Yaeng once per week. This town is located on the way to the district town of Mae Rim, which offers a larger variety of items for purchase and contains the administration office, hospitals and a daily market. Most villagers drive to Mae Rim once to twice per week. Trips to Chiang Mai are less frequent, typically twice per year, although some respondents said they go once per month or even more often to market their products. The majority of Ban Phui inhabitants visit Mae Chaem twice a week. This town is only twenty kilometres from the village, and contains a market and administration office. Other cities like Chom Thong, Chiang Mai, and Mae La Noi are visited less frequently for marketing purposes than Mae Chaem.

As the data presented above implies, women move around less than men. Significant age differences also exist. Some older women hardly leave the village, whereas young men might drive to Mae Chaem (BP) or Mae Rim (MSM) on a daily basis. However, it should be kept in mind that my data is based on respondents' estimates of their trips to these towns. In some cases these estimates seemed too low compared to my own observations of the villagers' movements.

Ban Phui was not involved in the "souvenir fever" of the 1980s (see chapter nine) and villagers did not go to Bangkok to sell commodities at the weekend market there. As a result, fewer people from Ban Phui have ever been to Bangkok or other places in southern Thailand. Many of the people from Mae Sa Mai have already been to Bangkok and worked there, even youth under twenty. In other words, the spatial mobility of villagers from Mae Sa Mai to far away places is generally greater than that of Ban Phui residents.

A second kind of travel is connected to visits of rituals in other Hmong villages, in most cases located within Chiang Mai Province or not more than three to four hours drive from the home village. Many women claimed they cannot attend outside rituals other than mortuary rites or New Year Ceremonies since they play no role in ritual performances. For example, they rarely attend weddings or rituals conducted for sick people. Married men mostly travel in male groups to outside ceremonies in order to bolster clan relations. If they are trained ritual experts, they also travel to help with the performance of rituals. Young male adolescents prefer to visit New Year Festivals in their search for potential marriage partners. Among the Hmong, this "explorative journey" (Culas 2000: 42) has always been the most common way to reach other Hmong in distant villages. Young, unmarried women also visit New Year Celebrations in villages other than their own, yet only together with their parents, claiming they are "too young and too shy" to travel by themselves. Interestingly enough, numerous villagers from Ban Phui stated that they visit rituals in other Hmong villages, but are too timid to attend them in Mae Sa Mai or nearby Doi Pui. They explained that they would be ashamed of their backwardness in these two "modern", developed villages.

Figure 8: Trips to rituals in other Hmong villages

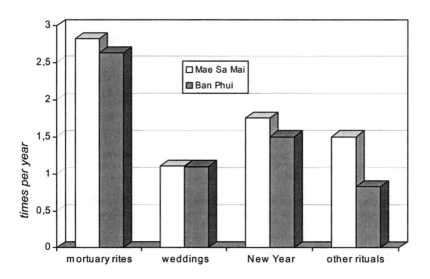

Source: own survey, N=58 (MSM, BP)

In my opinion, one can speak of an extensive Hmong network because of both the frequent face-to-face interactions between Hmong of different areas and "oral networks". These oral networks interconnect the Hmong people not only within Thailand but the whole diaspora. Through them, information is exchanged about other clan's people and Hmong dispersed across different villages creating "mental networks" for the Hmong. Oral and kin networks contribute to a compression of geographical space and (transnational) extension of Hmong spatiality.

To sum up, social networks are primarily maintained by men, within and outside the villages. Social contacts of women are largely restricted to lineage members, people from the neighbourhood and the natal clans. Moral codes of conduct do not allow women to move around freely and without "official" purpose, such as the visit to a mortuary rite. They also compel women to travel in the company of their husbands, male relatives or other women. In Mae Sa Mai, this norm has been pragmatically adapted to new situations in which women travel by themselves to Chiang Mai to sell souvenirs at the Night Market. Young Hmong, girls and boys alike, have more and deeper interethnic contacts than the older generations. In contrast to women, men are free to travel extensively – or more precisely, men are socially expected to maintain the extensive network of the Hmong Mountains through their visits of relatives and rites in other Hmong settlements.

Summary

In conclusion, I wish to reiterate that the socio-cultural strength of Hmong society depends on three main pillars, namely the household, the lineage and the clan, as well as on inter-clan alliances built through exogamous marriages. The kinship system provides for social proximity of its members despite a socio-spatial dispersal of the Hmong. Religious beliefs – above all ancestor and spirit worship – help to uphold the lineages and solidify links between kin and non-kin alike. Classificatory kinship terms strengthen social

Hmong Social Organisation 237

cohesion within the lineage, as well as within and among the clans. Clans and sub-clans are based on cultural or ritual ties, whereas lineage members are connected through common blood ties. The clan system is an ontological structure, idea as well as value system. The clan implies hierarchy, affiliation, social security and religious entity. Clans are an important part of the religious-social order and, as such, of Hmong cultural spatiality. This spatiality is marked by widespread (orally and practically enacted) endo-social networks, as well as by an integration of the living, the ancestors, and the supernatural agents into one cosmological order.

In terms of the spatial boundedness of the three main pillars of Hmong society, households are located in sedentarised villages. Lineages are partly located in one village, but can extend to other villages as well. They form important units of daily interaction within the villages. Sub-clans and clans are not territorially bounded but are instead spread over the northern Thai provinces, other Asian countries, as well as other parts of the world overseas. In other words, households tie the Hmong to certain territories or villages that have become stable, localised units in the course of sedentarisation. Lineages mediate between localised units in a village and dispersed units elsewhere. (Sub-)clans are scattered over large areas and countries, contributing to the spatial flexibility and extension of the Hmong. Through greeting rituals, the clan structure helps situate unknown people within the Hmong social system no matter where they meet in the world. It also provides a reliable reference point for trust and help.

Today, kinship organisation constitutes a spatiality in which Hmong are both linked to permanently localised households (and in part lineages) while simultaneously forming part of a spatially widespread social system independent of any particular location. Religious and social systems enable the Hmong to spatially relocate, whether to the nearby town of Mae Rim or far away Bangkok, while still belonging spiritually and socially to their households, Hmong lineages and (sub)clans. Relationships of mutual aid enhance the relative mobility of Hmong because they can potentially rely on a clan network beyond local boundaries. This provides them with social structures even in unknown places. Hmong can draw on the kinship system and widespread clan network to situate themselves in Thai society or other parts of the world, where they can create alternative spaces of their own. Both the kinship system and, more specifically, the widespread clan network, can be drawn upon to situate themselves in Thai society and elsewhere, and to fashion an alternative Hmong space. Improved infrastructure, motorisation and communication systems have strengthened clan networks within the Hmong Mountains, despite processes of sedentarisation that bind the Hmong more to their villages than in the past. Men are primarily responsible for continuing kinship relations beyond the borders of the villages. The women carry out most of the household chores and, through their daily interactions, remain socially anchored within the neighbourhood and lineage group of their husbands.

Hmong society is still strictly gender-stratified. However, women can obtain power and freedom from male domination in several spheres, including the domain of healing or, to a certain extent, in the household. Hmong women from Mae Sa Mai profit from their proximity to Chiang Mai; they are free to move around and even go about their business by themselves. Some women from Ban Phui strive to gain more control over their lives by unofficially converting to Protestantism and attending largely female-dominated church services.

In the following chapter, Hmong ethnic identity and interethnic contacts are analysed to explore how the Hmong position themselves in the context of Thai society and in opposition to other ethnic mountain groups. As I mentioned above, Hmong social relations are largely marked by endo-sociality, which serves as an important strategy of socio-cultural survival in a dominant Thai environment. To comprehend cultural spatiality, it is necessary to understand how a group draws boundaries between "us" and "them" and between "inner" cultural spheres and "outer" spheres believed to be dominated by other peoples. In this regard, it is also important to more closely examine Hmong youth, since they interact with Thai lowland society on a regular basis and are introduced to many aspects of Thai culture at school. I thus explore how young Hmong maintain their Hmong identity and culture in the face of increased interaction with Thai lowland society, an interaction, which their parents did not experience to a similar degree. This Hmong self-definition and the boundaries drawn between Hmong and non-Hmong document their socio-spatial scope and the delimitation of Hmong culture, making it an important aspect of Hmong cultural spatiality.

8 POSITIONING OF THE HMONG: ETHNIC IDENTITY, INTERETHNIC CONTACTS, AND PROSPECTS OF THE HMONG YOUTH

In conversations about ethnic identity, most of my Hmong informants stressed that markers such as language or dress constituted less significant identity markers than phenotype, clan membership, ancestor worship, and most important, the "Hmong way of walking."[116] They stressed that although the traditional dress is important to the people, it does not comprise a central indicator of Hmong identity. People who work for Hmong villagers such as the Karen or the Shan also dress, at times, in Hmong clothes. Even tourists occasionally wear components of the attractively embroidered costume. Language is not one of the most important markers of identity either, and Hmong villagers explained that languages like Yao are quite similar to Hmong.

This is different for the phenotype and manner of walking. Supposedly, Hmong people have a special way of walking, which is typical for the group and clearly differentiates it from others. Since I had not noticed this phenomenon myself before I was informed about it, I asked people to describe typical Hmong movements in greater detail. The answer given (and physically demonstrated) was that the Hmong walk in a very upright, deliberate but self-conscious manner that apparently distinguishes them instantly from the members of any other group. For example, when Hmong people walk through the city of Chiang Mai, my informants say that they

---

[116] The survey interviews in the twenty-nine (MSM) and twenty (BP) households also included questions about the ways the Hmong are different from other groups and about important markers and aspects of Hmong identity. The section on youth perspectives is mainly based on thirty interviews with unmarried girls and boys both in Mae Sa Mai and Ban Phui about their perspectives of and wishes for the future.

take the phenotype and way of walking as a reliable indicator for distinctive "Hmongness". A thirty-four-year-old woman from Mae Sa Mai, Zuam Yaj, explained during an interview:

> "The Hmong have a very special way of moving, that is a Hmong habit. I always know when a person is Hmong or not Hmong. Even with people from America I know who is Hmong and who is not Hmong. Hmong people can wear any clothes, they are always Hmong. Nowadays, Hmong women prefer to wear trousers because the Hmong skirts are too cold to wear and it also takes too long to make them. It is easier to buy clothes in the towns but we are still Hmong even when we wear Thai clothes. We have our own blood and our own way of walking." (Source: field interview, H-SNI-MSM 8)

Hmong people say that important Hmong characteristics such as their "pride", love of freedom and independence from other peoples is expressed in the typical way of Hmong movement. Of course, markers of cultural difference in inter-ethnic situations are always subjective. As exemplified by the criteria "manner of movement", these are not always visible to outsiders. However, if any particular marker is socially recognised as an indicator of an ethnic contrast, it matters little if "objective cultural differences" are negligible. Ethnic stereotypes also resist taking individual variations into account, which means, of course, that not all Hmong walk in the same way or are similar in appearance. Nevertheless, ethnic stereotypes strengthen group cohesion, boundaries and one's self-perception. In a poly-ethnic society, such as that of Thailand, it is important that people commonly hold stereotypes that implicitly contrast their own group to other ethnic groups. These stereotypes provide an ideological legitimacy for ethnic boundaries and strengthen group cohesion. Along these lines, Nicholas Tapp argues:

> "[...] it is through defining themselves for significant others that the Hmong have established their own specificity." (2001: xix)

However, it is important to note that a pragmatic eclecticism characterises Hmong ethnic identity that is also typical for the cultural identities of diaspora groups. In other words, Hmong cultural identity is not a static and fixed continuum with its roots in the "traditional" Hmong culture of China. Instead, it evolves and adapts to influences from neighbouring peoples such as the Thai or the Karen (cf. Tapp 2001: xx; Boyarin and Boyarin 1993: 721; see also Rehbein and Rüland and Schlehe 2006; Leach 1954: 9). Over time, these outside influences become Hmong in every respect and cannot be distinguished from any "real" Hmong cultural elements. Nicholas Tapp's statement about the changing variables and stable parameters of Hmong identity is relevant within this context:

"While the variables may be changed, the parameters of the system remain constant, and it is through the constancy of these parameters that the Hmong define their own ethnicity." (1989: 187)

Stuart Hall also observes that the process of adaptation and simultaneous maintenance of a particular cultural identity that runs parallel to mainstream society is idiosyncratic for diaspora groups. He understands this process as "translation":

„This describes those identity formations which cut across and intersect natural frontiers, and which are composed of people who have been *dispersed* forever from their homelands. Such people retain strong links with their places of origin and their traditions, but they are without the illusion of a return to the past. They are obliged to come to terms with the new cultures they inhabit, without simply assimilating to them and losing their identities completely. They bear upon them the traces of the particular cultures, traditions, languages and histories by which they were shaped. The difference is that they are not and will never be *unified* in the old sense because they are irrevocably the product of several interlocking histories and cultures, belong at the same time to several 'homes' [...]. People belonging to such *cultures of hybridity* have had to renounce the dream or ambition of rediscovering any kind of 'lost' cultural purity, or ethnic absolutism. They are irrevocably *translated*." (1992: 310, italics in original)

The adaptation and transformation of Hmong identity facilitate the location and fixing of Hmong minority society within a multi-ethnic Thai space. Hmong people have their own hybrid cultural identity, which on the one hand enables them to live within Thai society and, on the other, allows them to remain Hmong despite processes of "translation" and the absence of a genuine Hmong territory. Instead, the Hmong are rooted and fixed by their own cultural spatiality, constituted through spatial structures and socio-cultural practice in Thailand and other parts of the world. This spatiality, which bears diasporic characteristics, allows the Hmong to maintain close networks, typical Hmong settings and a cultural identity that protects them from a too rapid and thorough assimilation into their host cultures (cf. Michaud 2004: 6). Timothy Dunnigan's concluding remarks to his 1986 paper on processes of identity maintenance among the Hmong still hold true:

"[…] Hmong adjustment strategies in the United States replicate approaches followed in Southeast Asia for managing cross-cultural contacts and preserving Hmong ethnic integrity. The process of Hmong culture change appears to be both linear and cyclical. […] The Hmong […] have survived extremely difficult times by changing without suffering identity loss." (1986: 50-51)

"Cultural brokers", for example the elders or representatives of Hmong organisations, consciously help maintain such "strongholds" of Hmong culture and identity as the clan structure or ancestor worship. Another important means of preserving Hmong identity is the transmission of knowledge about the historical continuity of the group. Appeals to notions of a shared oral tradition and history underscore that the Hmong have enjoyed a cultural continuity over a long period of time and offer members a feeling of cultural belonging and security. By connecting "roots and routes" (Clifford 1997: 308) in the diaspora, the Hmong people can constitute a diaspora consciousness and group solidarity based on a common history of migration from a Chinese homeland that run parallel to identifications in the mainstream societies.

Hmong people have a strong sense of belonging to a far wider, sometimes "imagined" community and "great tradition" connected to – a long-vanished – late imperial China (Tapp 2001: 14-15; cf. McKinnon and Michaud 2000: 6-7). This sense of belonging to a wider community within the Hmong Mountains gives the Hmong self-confidence and explains their largely successful resistance to the Thai state's assimilationist efforts. In both Mae Sa Mai and Ban Phui, people have a clear notion of belonging to a larger transnational community, whereas recollections of life in China are vague and blurred. Some of those interviewed claimed that knowledge of the Hmong's Chinese cultural heritage and clans' presence in a number of countries throughout the world strengthens Hmong identity and "pride in being Hmong". Events where large numbers of Hmong people meet, for example mortuary rites or New Year Festivals, are even celebrated in Western countries and help preserve a sense of being Hmong throughout the diaspora. A transnational Hmong identity has developed that includes Hmong from across the globe, for example Chinese Hmong, Thai Hmong, American Hmong, Canadian Hmong, or French Hmong. Global communication and transportation systems facilitate interaction between these "new Hmong sub-groups" (Yang Dao 1992: 308).

Hmong-Thai identity and relations

Despite the specific cultural identity and sustained diaspora consciousness among the Hmong, the majority of respondents at my research sites understood themselves both as members of a widespread Hmong community *and* the Thai nation-state. Consequently, most Hmong informants defined themselves as "Hmong-Thai" (cf. Jónsson 2000: 227-228, 231-233). The Hmong demand their rights as a distinctive ethnic group *and* as Thai citizens. Hmong identities, as is true for many migrant and diaspora groups, are thus group identities that bear upon a variety of points of references that can all be elements of a lifeworld. The Hmong and Thai societies are only the most important reference-points of the Hmong-Thai identity. Many Hmong also identify with their ancestors' former places of residence, their own place of birth, as well as with their current settlement site. Especially for Hmong over forty years of age, some of whom have migrated with their parents or grandparents, the various locations of former settlements distributed across northern Thailand represent reference points that connect the past with the present.

This multi-local constitution of identity also becomes clear in the encounter of different groups of people. For example, when Western tourists ask Hmong villagers about their place of residence, many Hmong people give the name of the largest Thai city in the vicinity of their mountain village. When the Thai or Karen ask the Hmong about their origins, most answer with "Hmong Mountains". Even Hmong villagers from Ban Phui who live in an area surrounded by numerous Karen villages would give the answer "Hmong Mountains". The term is not merely intended to describe the immediate area of the settlement. It represents a broader concept of origin that encompasses both a widespread area inhabited by the Hmong people of several countries *and* a lifestyle. When Hmong from different villages first meet, the current place of residence is of minor importance and mostly given after other information has been exchanged: People first mention their clan background, then search for common kinship affiliations and talk about the settlement areas of their parents and grandparents. By doing so, they find a common ground rooted in the past and present, in consanguinal or affinal relations. They also situate themselves within the wider Hmong social system. The village of residency remains secondary in importance to individual and family status within the broader Hmong network.

Despite their distinct Hmong-Thai identity, many Hmong people disclosed ambivalent, sometimes conflicting attitudes towards Thai society. On the one hand, Hmong have always had problems with Thai officials and therefore feel resentment towards the majority society. They feel impeded by lowland society and complain about discrimination and the difficulty in acquiring social status (cf. Tapp 2002: 100). On the other hand, many Hmong define themselves as "Hmong-Thai" since they were born and raised in Thailand and are loyal to their country of birth. Beyond this, most Hmong also respect and admire Thai people for their advanced levels of economic development and education. Hmong villagers would like to achieve the economic success of some Thai and thus strive for equal opportunities. In addition, a few Hmong men are also married to Thai women.[117] According to their accounts, these inter-ethnic marriages recombine Hmong and Thai society on a personal level and intensify ambivalent feelings of antipathy and admiration. Yet most Hmong villagers differentiate between their personal relations and sometimes even friendships with individual Thai and relations to the Thai administration and society, which are mostly characterised by negative experiences.

Although Hmong face discrimination, as well as open conflicts with the Thai around resource protection, many of my informants claimed they get along quite well with Thai people. They avoid dealing with Thai who are corrupt and racist and for the most part, do not take negative remarks by Thai seriously. A fifty-five-year-old man in Ban Phui, Ntxawj Xwm Tsaab, explained:

"If Thai people talk badly about us and look down on us, then they are stupid and do not know any better. That does not really bother us. It is sad but we don't see it as a big problem. For us Hmong, a big problem is when someone steals, kills, deals drugs or harasses women. All the small conflicts we have with Thai people are not problems, just everyday trouble. [...] Many Thai people are corrupt and not fair at all. But we can sit down with them over a bottle of Hmong whiskey and solve a large part of our daily troubles about village boundaries, illegal tree-cutting, and applications for Thai identity cards or stalls at the markets. [...] The Thai government is very slow to bring roads,

---

[117] The brother of my assistant, Win Huj, lives in the lowland town of Mae Rim and is married to a Thai woman who speaks the Hmong language fairly well; their children are taught aspects of both Hmong and Thai cultural practices.

electricity and running water to our villages because they think that we are third-class people. When we go to the hospitals in the lowlands we only get the worst treatment, but we don't have the money or insurance to change that. We don't get angry about this any more. In the meantime, we can wait and help ourselves. We have better morale than most Thai people and always support each other." (Source: field interview, H-SNI-BP12)

Many Hmong men have experience and display self-confidence within the inter-ethnic framework of dealing with Thai society. For the most part, Hmong women refrain from direct interactions with unfamiliar Thai people and act reserved. At the markets, Hmong men try to bargain with Thai traders for the best prices. When profits are too low, they sometimes do not vend their crops and take the risk of not selling their commodities at all. They would rather throw them away if they cannot find another buyer. As a matter of pride, Hmong usually prefer to forego transactions than be cheated.

Hmong villagers have also learned to interact according to their own ideas with Thai staff from administration offices, the police, the Royal Forestry Department and the National Park. They invite representatives to their celebrations and rituals and treat them like honoured guests. This incorporates the Thai officials into a network of social obligations, facilitates cooperation on a personal level and impedes discrimination. However, despite attempts at forging harmonious personal relations with the Thai, Hmong villagers do not fear open confrontation with others or among their own people in order to enforce norms, morals and overall group cohesion. For example, Hmong elders even turn over villagers who have committed crimes and are not willing to accept the people's punishment to the Thai police.

To sum up, Hmong people define themselves as an integral part of Thai society. They are Thai citizens who are loyal to the nation, the King and its people. They interact with Thai lowland society economically and personally, but without relinquishing their special Hmong identity and way of life. They adapt their Hmong identity to Thai society; however they preserve its cornerstones and have thus far successively defended their cultural identity against too much outside influence and change. Despite notions of a distinct Hmong-Thai identity and daily inter-ethnic relations, the Hmong still make clear distinctions between "us" and "them", between mountain people and lowlanders, between Hmong and Thai people. Many Hmong view themselves as part of a wider, transnational Hmong community, which, despite its dispersal, remains united by the common historical experience of exodus and migration from China.

Hmong perceptions of and relations with the Karen

In addition to their close inter-ethnic ties with the Thai people, the Hmong at my research sites also maintained relatively close contact with the Karen. Other Hmong or Thai villages surround Mae Sa Mai and contact to Karen exists exclusively on an employer–employee basis. About ten percent of the households from Mae Sa Mai have Karen families employed on their fields. These labourers originally came from other districts within Chiang Mai Province. For the greater part of the year, they live with their families on the Hmong farmers' fields. They receive a minimal salary of sixty to eighty baht per day and portions of rice for daily consumption. These Karen are not typically seen within Mae Sa Mai, but work and live (in field huts or makeshift shelters) on the nearby fields.

Ban Phui is surrounded by numerous Karen villages and inter-ethnic contact to Karen villagers occurs more frequently than to Thai. Karen people also work on the Hmong fields and stay either overnight or return to their own settlements in the evenings. In the area of Ban Phui, Hmong and Karen people have multiple, everyday interactions. Karen villagers work on Hmong fields or visit the Hmong villages to search for work. They patronise the small noodle shops for lunch or dinner, which the poorer Karen settlements tend to lack. Hmong farmers rent fields from their Karen neighbours and visit the Karen villages to buy rice. Despite recurring disputes over land issues, relations between the Hmong and Karen are quite good. Many people know each other because they frequently pass through each other's villages. Many stay informed about news from the neighbouring villages, whether they are Hmong or Karen. Also, both Hmong and Karen inhabit the village of Pang Hin Fon.

Personal relations are generally harmonious. Hmong villagers thus visit large ceremonies, such as Karen marriages or the Karen New Year while Karen people attend Hmong mortuary rites and Hmong New Year celebrations. When Hmong women cannot bear children, especially sons, Karen children are even adopted in some instances. They are incorporated into the Hmong kinship system and "turned into Hmong" (see also Tapp 1989: 169; Lee 1996: 13). In Ban Phui, five men are married to Karen women. One man lives with his first wife, a Hmong woman, and their Hmong children in a house in the village. His two Karen women and their offspring together live in neighbouring Karen villages. Despite these examples however, traditional sanctions against inter-ethnic marriages and adoptions do exist. These sanctions try to prevent a weakening of the autonomous and endogamous Hmong group. Most important, a taboo stigmatises marriages between Hmong women and men of other ethnic groups, since any children from these relationships would be lost for the Hmong patrilineal system (cf. Symonds 2004: 8). Therefore, the Hmong only tolerate marriages between Hmong men and Karen women and families that adopt Karen children because such relationships can be incorporated into and can even strengthen the Hmong kinship system.

Karen and Hmong from the Ban Phui area also cooperate on an official level. In their efforts to prevent the region's incorporation into the Mae Tho National Park, representatives from both the Karen and Hmong villages assist each other and act in unison when negotiating with the Royal Forestry Department and other authorities. Moreover, the Karen and Hmong, as well as other ethnic mountain groups, share a bond each May when tens of thousands of villagers from the northern Thai mountains gather in front of the Chiang Mai City Hall to demonstrate for equal citizenship, land rights, better education and job opportunities.

Over the past decades, strong enough relations have existed between the Hmong and Karen to ensure that many Hmong villagers, especially men, speak Karen fluently. Some people from Mae Sa Mai also speak Karen because they once lived in areas mostly populated by Karen farmers working in large numbers as day labourers on Hmong poppy fields. While Karen"only" speak Karen and Thai, many Hmong from Ban Phui are quite fluent in Karen. They contend that the Karen language is easy to learn and constitutes the "language of the mountains" in Thailand because Karen make up the largest ethnic minority group. Even young children can already speak some Karen in Ban Phui, since Karen children from neighbouring villages also attend the school there. The village's headman, Mbua Yim Yaj, told me in Karen that Hmong and Karen people are *dau puj waij* (brothers and sisters) because both groups live in the mountains and have to assert themselves against the lowland Thai. A sense of a shared experience of discrimination and hardship has forged a solidarity between these two groups, as well as other mountain peoples.

Overall relations between the Hmong and Karen are thus quite strong. However, many prejudices exist against the "others" from both sides (see also Mischung 2004: 343). The Hmong often condemn the Karen morally in order to strengthen their own intra-ethnic ties and draw clear identity boundaries between "them" and "us". Many Hmong villagers feel superior to their Karen neighbours because they employ Karen labourers and are, in most cases, economically more successful than the Karen. Hmong conceptions of the Karen lifestyle include the notion that Karen farmers typically work less than Hmong. The Karen are said to remain content with a subsistence economy that only sustains their own lives.

Hmong villagers claim they work much harder than the Karen because of their dissatisfaction with low economic output and effort to achieve the greatest success possible. This effort leads Hmong villagers to rent fields from their Karen or Thai neighbours. Hmong villagers generally view Karen people as less developed because they do not use their land "in a sensible way", cultivating their fields all year round to reap maximum profits. In both villages studied, it is a common saying that the Hmong, just like the Lisu and the Chinese, resemble Thai people far more than the Karen because they value economic success. In contrast, the Karen people are believed to have more appreciation of social values. The Hmong do not interpret this major difference between themselves and their Karen neighbours in exclusively positive terms. Many feel that the Hmong work far more than the Karen, but earn only slightly better profits. In return, the Hmong have less time to rest and are unable to devote much spare time to their families. Hmong perceive themselves as more ambitious than the Karen, but also believe they lead more stressful lives. On the other hand, they say that Hmong farmers are more innovative and flexible than their Karen neighbours, who mostly change and adapt their land use systems exclusively on the basis of outside input. Hmong villagers also noted that they had a different conception of age than the Karen: They believe they are old when they have an accumulated body of knowledge at around the age of fifty. Karen believe they have reached old-age after thirty, when they cannot work at full capacity any longer. Interestingly, the Karen people at my research sites in the Doi Inthanon area shared even most of the negative conceptions held by many Hmong villagers from Ban Phui and Mae Sa Mai.

All of these subjectively perceived differences between the Hmong and Karen help legitimate the Hmong villagers' claim that the Karen people are culturally too different to allow intermarriage on a large scale. Despite, or even because of frequent contact, cooperation, and personal relations, the Hmong nonetheless consciously maintain and morally justify inter-ethnic boundaries to preclude a softening of group differences, loss of special group identities and weakening of socio-cultural practices. The Hmong continue to see themselves as an in-group called *peb hmoob* (literally: us Hmong) in relation to outsiders, who are perceived as *mab sua* (literally: strangers). *Peb hmoob* is an inclusive concept that stands for a Hmong identity and collective consciousness intentionally maintained by many. Just as the Hmong house represents an "inside" contrasting with an "outside", Hmong perceptions of an "us" and "them" differentiate between an "inside" and "outside" (see also Lee 1996: 24-25).

The Hmong youth: Living in two worlds

Chapter seven has already indicated the differences that exist between (unmarried) young and (married) older Hmong in their direct involvement and daily interaction with Thai society. Older Hmong primarily visit the lowlands to market their products, or go to administration offices or the hospital. Many young Hmong live in more profound contact with Thai lowland society because they visit schools there. They are confronted with the Thai education system, Thai teachers and students – an experience most of their parents did not have because they attended no school. The differing scope of interaction with Thai society and the Thai education system among young versus older Hmong sometimes precipitates inter-generational misunderstandings and conflicting identity models. Younger Hmong may also have perceptions of the future that were unthinkable for older generations.

Differences between old and young people

Many elders of both Mae Sa Mai and Ban Phui complained to me about a lack of interest among young Hmong in traditional Hmong knowledge such as oral history or the correct performance of rituals. One respondent claimed that only ten percent of the young men are still "open and strong enough" to be successfully introduced into the broad scope of Hmong traditional knowledge. While disinterest in Hmong knowledge faces censure, the elders also recognise (a) that they are still relatively poor, despite their profound wisdom and proper performance of rituals, (b) that the old can also learn from the young about environmental protection measures and the cultivation of good relations with the Thai administration, and (c) that young Hmong need lowland education to improve their future job opportunities in the lowlands.

Older people might remember species of plants, animals and crops that used to exist; they might still be able to detect bioindicator plants and good soils for the cultivation of different crops. However, the young are affected by changes in land use and the economic system. They require a degree of integration into lowland society sufficient for acquiring the knowledge and diplomas needed to live outside agriculture and the mountain villages. Nandini Sundar, analysing the construction and destruction of indigenous knowledge in rural India, sums up her findings in a statement that also rings true for the young Hmong today:

"The horizons of 'civilization' now lie in another direction, in the sphere of urban employment rather than what is seen as old-fashioned botanical knowledge, an emphasis which is reinforced by the entire education system which values bookish literacy and certificates alone" (2000: 83-84)

Future perspectives

Due to an increasing land scarcity, diminishing natural resources and a growing incorporation into the Thai education system, many female and male Hmong adolescents from Mae Sa Mai and Ban Phui recognise that their future is linked to employment in the lowlands, not to agricultural activities in the mountains. Their parents, most of whom lacked the opportunity to attend school, invariably support their children's perceptions of the future. Yiv Xyooj, a twenty-year-old mother of three young children and the daughter of one of the shamans in Mae Sa Mai, commented:

"My husband and I have to send our children to school so they can get a job. If they do not have any education, their life is finished. If they have a job they can live in the city and send money back to their parents, to us. We cannot save much money. We only get by day-to-day." (Source: field interview, H-C-MSM 10)

A forty-three-year-old man from Ban Phui, Looj Tsab, also regards education as important, but views migration to the urban centres critically:

"The children's education is more important than anything else. But I fear that our children might lose their Hmong culture when they go to schools in the lowlands and then stay there permanently. It might be that, in one or two generations, Hmong people will still have their Hmong names but have lost everything else." (Source: field interview, H-SNI-BP 20)

Hmong anthropologist Prasit Leepreecha (2001: 122-125, 159-163) indicates that many young Hmong in the cities do not even retain their Hmong names, instead adopting Thai names and kinship terms. Anthony Giddens (1990: 101-102) points out that traditional social relations and use of kin terms are less valid in urban settings than in pre-modern societies. I would argue however, that young Hmong in the cities do not necessarily give up their Hmong identity when they adopt Thai names and kinship terms. Rather, they adjust to new circumstances within the urban context. They struggle to preserve their Hmong cultural identity by meeting in Hmong groups and returning home to the mountain villages whenever they can afford to do so. Hmong diaspora communities in other parts of the world, such as in the United States or France, also illustrate that settlement in urban, "foreign" environments does not necessarily entail the loss of cultural identity. Cultural identity instead undergoes a process of adaptation and reconstitution. Nonetheless, Hmong youth in Chiang Mai often do try to hide their ethnic affiliation, even speaking Thai among themselves in public spaces to avoid being recognised as "backward" Hmong and facing discrimination against them (Tapp 2002: 103; Leepreecha 2001: 164-165).

Many unmarried girls and boys I spoke with in the villages prefer employment in the lowlands over farming, dream of secure salaries and believe their parents will be the last generation to live completely off the fields. Young men who no longer attend school mostly prefer to work, on a day labourer basis, for road construction, fire protection or other companies than fully engage in agricultural activities with their parents. Npugchoj Xyooj, a twenty-year-old father of two sons from Mae Sa Mai emphasises:

> "Working is better than being in the fields. Any job is better as long as it can feed the family. My wish for the future is to have a nice house, a car, and lots of money. I want my family and my parents to live together and not to lead a poor life like this." (Source: field interview, H-JB 33)

Npugchoj Xyooj is head of the Mae Sa Mai Youth Committee, composed of 325 members. Because half of the members work or study in the lowlands, the Committee can only convene during the holidays. Members are unmarried and married men and unmarried women between the ages of fifteen and twenty-five. Hmong moral norms militate against the cooperation of married women with men not related to them and as a result, they cannot participate in the Committee. The group assists in reforestation activities organised by FORRU, meets to learn Hmong and Thai pop songs and organises celebrations for the fourth day of the New Year, when youth pays its respect to the village's old people. The Committee also received special training from the Royal Forestry Department and Royal Project for dealing with environmental protection measures and awareness. Many young men thus strive for "development with nature", as they term sustainable development in Hmong language. They wish to set up forms of international eco-tourism that would secure the villagers' income by combining environmental protection and income-generating activities. They claim that eco-tourism would at once enable them to earn a salary outside of agriculture and remain in the mountain areas (see also Michaud 1996).

Nevertheless, some young men and women in Mae Sa Mai and Ban Phui are quite content with their work as farmers. Most of these people have been married for a few years and have already lived in Chiang Mai, Bangkok or other lowland locations for a while. But they have returned to their home villages and, most significant, to their social networks. These young, married Hmong, all of whom are just above 20, still live in their parents' houses, cultivate their parents' fields together with other household members and are convinced that mountain life still offers a viable alternative to the hectic and strenuous life in the cities. A twenty-six-year-old man, who had earned a Bachelor of Arts degree from the Teacher's College in Chantaburi Province southeast of Bangkok, explained, "[...] to have a field, to have enough to eat, to grow a variety of crops and to be able to save some money is enough for us. It is easier for us to live with our wives and children in the mountains than in the lowlands". He had returned to the village because even with a diploma, he could not find employment in the lowlands. Because he is now married and has a young child, he prefers to live among his kin and raise his child in a Hmong setting. Christian Culas also asserts that "[m]ost young people still seem to prefer to stay in their villages where they are free workers and where solidarity and social pressure still counts" (2000: 42-43).

Identities are negotiated and may change according to situation, people and individual or group interests. This negotiation is especially pronounced among young Hmong students who visit (boarding or temple) schools in the Thai lowlands for most of the year. Many Hmong children spend between one and six or more years in the lowlands, depending on the schools that accept them and their ability to continue on to secondary or high school. The schools of Mae Sa Mai and Ban Phui offer classes only until sixth grade. If children want to continue their education, they need to visit schools in the lowlands, which are either boarding schools run by Christian organisations or the Social Welfare Department. Boys can also opt for one of the lowland Buddhist temple schools. These schools typically offer education and board free of charge. Yet some parents still cannot afford to send their children to such institutions because they are unable to cover the costs of transportation and meals. Furthermore, they would have to sacrifice the labour of their older children, which some households still need.

Despite the fact that many Hmong children spend most of their school year outside their villages and away from their extended families, they are still perceived as belonging to the village community. Their parents require them to live according to Hmong norms and morals. Most children are sent to lowland institutions also visited by other (related) Hmong youth. Even though children might go to school hundreds of kilometres away from their home village, parents always ensure that other Hmong are in attendance to provide mutual support. A special Hmong consciousness is ingrained into the children from an early age on. They know who they are and where they belong, even while far away from home at ages as early as five.

Hmong students enrolled in lowland high schools, colleges or universities also consciously maintain networks among themselves. For example, Hmong students at Chiang Mai University and the Technical College have founded the Hmong Youth Group which meets regularly not only for social activities but also to keep Hmong culture alive in the city (see also Leepreecha 2001: 162). They engage in fundraising and organise joint cultural activities in Chiang Mai. The Youth Group also visited Mae Sa Mai before the big New Year celebrations in 2001 to offer their help with the management of the days-long festivities and receive instruction from village elders about the proper way of conducting New Year's rituals. Some of the students originally come from other provinces and could not return home for the rituals. They opted for support and instruction from Mae Sa Mai's elders instead.

The New Year celebrations provide a chance for urban Hmong youth to reinvigorate their Hmong-ness and cultural knowledge, but also enable village children and adolescents to openly display their own brand of Hmong (-Thai) identity. During the days of the celebrations, they participate in traditional activities, such as tossing a homemade cloth ball between opposite sexes or other courting games and competitions intended to unite potential marriage partners. In particular, parents interested in marrying off their children support these types of games. Hmong youth thus plays a central part during the New Year festivities and wear the traditional Hmong costume with as much pride as older people. Girls and boys alike try to outshine each other with their elaborate silver jewelry and arduously embroidered clothes, which the girls combine with high-heel shoes and make-up, the boys with sunglasses, baseball caps and sneakers. In the evenings, they organise singing and dancing contests on the open-air stage set up in the schoolyard.

While the older Hmong perform sung poetry on stage, the young girls and boys sing modern pop songs, in either the Hmong or Thai language. Unmarried Hmong women also perform modern dances accompanied by techno or hip hop music and wear tight and short Western clothes, which they would not be allowed to wear in public otherwise. For each non-traditional or non-Hmong song and dance performed, the young have to pay two baht to the elders' council to compensate for their non-conformist behaviour. In other words, the young people's behaviour is punished in a sense, but at the same time tolerated because the Hmong youth still act within the Hmong frame of reference. They engage in Hmong endogamous courtship and excite pride when their performances display talent. Furthermore, they always include aspects of traditional Hmong culture and remain controllable to that extent that they act out their "modernity" in public. The young people gain a chance to openly perform their Hmong and Thai identities, which are partly influenced by Western or "global youth culture". If the youth are talented performers, they receive open recognition from the whole community, young and old alike. Some young Hmong people have even started their careers as singers on such New Year's stages and become "pop stars" known throughout the Hmong Mountains.

To sum up, Hmong youth is torn between the rural life of the village, which includes hard farm work, relative poverty and insecurity about the profits from crop yields, and an urban life comprising separation from family and friends, confrontation with discrimination and many expenses that would not exist in the village. The village offers the traditional family support network and chance to live according to traditional Hmong norms and values that remain important to many young Hmong despite their loss of traditional knowledge and increasing incorporation into Thai society. Many young Hmong want to preserve their Hmong culture and identity because most have already been confronted in some form with racism and discrimination, whether at Thai lowland schools or in dealing with the Thai administration. From their own experiences and the accounts of other Hmong people, they know that they will never achieve a full integration into Thai society, even if they speak Thai fluently and without any accent, adopt Thai surnames and receive good degrees from schools, colleges or universities. They struggle to combine their Hmong background and Thai identity, forge new paths between tradition and modernity and find viable ways to earn a living in either the mountain areas or lowlands.

Summary

Concerted efforts to assimilate Hmong into Thai society and replace Hmong identity and cultural attributes with Thai notions of belonging, loyalty and Buddhist belief have not succeeded in minimising Hmong identity. Hmong people from Mae Sa Mai and Ban Phui, like many other minority groups around the world, have a dual identity concept. This concept mixes their "original" Hmong identity with elements from their country of residence and citizenship. Of course, identities are situationally negotiated. They can also embrace notions of belonging to an overall ethnic mountain community that includes other groups such as the Karen or Akha, groups also fighting for civil and land rights. As discussed, the Hmong have cultivated relatively good relations to the Thai and Karen people, as well as friendships with members of these groups. However, such relations seem to have little "meaningful intercourse" (Dessaint and Dessaint 1992: 98) for the Hmong system. Instead, relations to other groups remain located in the "outside" sphere of Hmong society.

The identities of Hmong people can, for example, switch between Hmong trader at lowland markets and respected elder in the mountain village, or between a "backward" *chao khao* ("hill tribe") and an important member of a far-flung Hmong diaspora network, or between a knowledgeable college student in the lowlands and a Hmong youth in the mountain village who must submit to the elders. However, notions of Hmong, Thai and ethnic mountain group identity should not be seen as oppositions, but as concepts united by the Hmong. Even when lowlanders ascribe negative characteristics to the Hmong, this helps shape Hmong identity in Thailand. It prompts self-reflection, the reconstitution of Hmong identity and a conscious maintenance of cultural values throughout the Hmong Mountains.

9 Transformations, Outside Influences, and Socio-Spatial Dimensions of Hmong Economy

In the previous chapters, central aspects of Hmong religious and social structure that play an important role in the constitution of Hmong cultural spatiality have been delineated. In the process, I have worked towards an outline of the cognitive concept of the Hmong Mountains, understood as a representation of the mental model of the Hmong lifeworld among the village inhabitants.

The ways in which humans interact, practically and technically, with environmental resources also shape their perception. In order to analyse Hmong cultural spatiality, it is essential to first analyse the range and meaning of Hmong economic activities: which activities are pursued, which economic potentials are perceived and exploited, and which are ignored. Just as religious and social activities can illuminate aspects of Hmong spatiality, so, too, can economic activities reveal how Hmong constitute, experience, perceive, and shape spaces to serve their aims. In what follows, I analyse which economic activities are pursued, which possible activities are ignored, how social dimensions shape activities and decisions, and how changed resource use systems have influenced religious and social structures and practices.

The chapter will first sketch the traditional Hmong economy and then explain the rapid transformation of Hmong economic activity during the last two decades. Many Hmong informants argue that the Hmong economy is – unlike religious beliefs and the kinship system – a highly adaptable element of Hmong culture. Indeed, Hmong economic activities and structures have proven quite adaptable, as research data from the two communities confirms. This data is based upon participant observation, open interviews, activity protocols, and structured survey interviews of twenty-nine households in

Mae Sa Mai and twenty households in Ban Phui. Survey interviews generally lasted one to two hours (or longer in Mae Sa Mai). The interviews covered the activities of all household members.

Transitions in the Hmong traditional resource use system

Until the introduction of poppy substitution programs in the 1960s and the ban on swidden agriculture, Hmong in northern Thailand practiced pioneer forest swidden agriculture. In the Hmong swiddening method, primary forests were cut with no attempt to preserve trees; this is in contrast to the practice among "established" swiddeners such as the Karen, who leave tree trunks for regeneration. Until the late 1970s, the Hmong cultivated mainly opium poppies (lat. *papaver somniferum*), dry rice and maize on mountain fields located mostly over 1,000 metres above sea level. Subsidiary crops like buckwheat, pumpkin, yam, sorghum, mustard, sugar cane, and a variety of fruit for home consumption were planted along the borders of the swiddens (Yang Dao 1993: 50-51; Tapp 1986: 19-28; Geddes 1976: 138-98; Keen 1966: 18-38; Savina [1924] 1930: 214). Many Hmong also grew hemp for cloth making; however, hemp production was banned by the Thai government in the late 1980s, probably due to the mistaken belief that it was closely related to the narcotic *cannabis* (Kunstadter 2000: 176).

The Hmong method of traditional swidden agriculture entailed periods of cultivation followed by a very "long fallow period" of thirty or more years, according Peter Kunstadter who has studied the Hmong field rotation system (2000: 177). Jan Ovesen, who conducted a case study in a Hmong community in the Laotian Vientiane Province, argued that the Hmong are not culturally "irrational" (1995: 55) in their economic strategies, as is widely believed. Ovesen also questions whether what is perceived as the historical and "traditional" reliance of the Hmong on swidden cultivation is truly "based on some deep-rooted "cultural inclination" for swiddening, for migration, and for living on mountain slopes at high altitudes" (1995: 55). However, the majority of scholars, Thai authorities, and the lowland population believe that pioneer swidden farming system is a "genuine" aspect of Hmong culture that is irrational in the sense that its methods lead to soil depletion and extreme weed growth (Kunstadter and Chapman 1978: 10, 19; Keen 1978: 212, 219). After short cultivation periods for dry rice (approximately three to four years) and long cropping periods for maize and opium poppy (approximately ten to fifteen years), the soil is depleted of nutrients and converts to *imperata* grassland, which makes the natural regeneration of forests nearly impossible (Géraud 1993: 34; Lemoine 1972: 33). When fields were depleted, which could happen in three to four years in the case of unirrigated rice fields, Hmong farmers cut new fields near the village. Eventually, they migrated again to more fertile areas, and again transformed the primary forest into swiddens (Keen 1978: 215). This kind of semi-sedentary swidden agriculture led to a high degree of mobility and a low emotional attachment to specific territory (Geddes 1976: 29). Even though forests and land were key assets in the Hmong traditional economy, agricultural organisation and "faulty technology" resulted in the degradation of these assets and exposed a "lack of intersectoral harmony", as F. G. Keen (1978: 218) argues. Rather than preserving natural resources for future use, Hmong cultivation was a very land-intensive system:

"[...] the economic organization, in spite of its being of an agricultural nature, is based on *people*, not *land*. Implicit in the attitudes of the Hmong is the idea that land is an expendable commodity in the production process, not a focal point around which both living and life are to be conducted." (Keen 1978: 218, italics in text)

Ron Renard goes as far as to argue that this attitude prevails among all the ethnic groups who migrated from China:

"As practiced in the northern Thai hills, the practitioners of pioneer swiddening were mostly migrants from Yunnan who raised opium [sic]. The groups such as Hmong, Mien, Akha, Lahu, and Lisu lacked attachment to local places and people in northern Thailand, aiming primarily to make a living in what seemed like an endless wilderness." (2001: 27)

According to William Geddes:

"They appear to have little attachment to places as such. If they are 'sons of the soil', they are not sons of any particular soil. [...] Land is to be exploited and its local spirits are placated not worshipped. They seek always to maximize their opportunities." (1976: 29)

Marie-Odile Géraud, who has conducted research among the Hmong in French Guyana, believes that in spite of their history of migration, Hmong are nonetheless attached to their territory: "Pourtant, il serait faux de croire que les Hmong se perçoivent comme des 'nomades': ceux de Cacao se souviennent d'avoir été en déplacement permanent, mais n'en étaient pas moins attachés à un territoire." (1993: 35)

Kao-Ly Yang also argues that the Hmong build "psycho-symbolic markers" (2004: 202) and crystallise new attachment to places by the exploitation of resources and the burial of the dead in one territory. Thus the Hmong cannot be said to lack a sense of place. Through their history of migration, they have been attached to more than one place of origin and settlement. In the past, the Hmong already strived to establish themselves as economically successful and remain as long as possible in one settlement area. Despite a long history of migration, Hmong do not have a "cultural urge" for a change of scenery but want to be economically successful in one place (Ovesen 1995: 56; Geddes 1976: 28). Success is closely connected to the accumulation of wealth like silver and opium (in the past) or money (today). Above all, success entails food security and independence from other Hmong and non-Hmong (Mischung 1990: 311; Geddes 1976: 34). This form of success was also facilitated by the mutual obligations of the clan system, which were important functional elements in Hmong swidden agriculture (Cooper 1984: 36). Clan and lineage networks spread information about alternative resource locations and provided the labour force to exploit resources on a large scale. The pattern of temporary settlement and frequent relocation of entire lineages (which in the past usually entailed a village) was adapted to the exploitation of resources in faraway places (Grandstaff 1976: 201).

Opium poppy cultivation

It is commonly but mistakenly believed that opium poppy cultivation always played an important role in traditional Hmong agriculture. Hmong rituals always include an offering of rice, which demonstrates that rice, and not the opium poppy, remains central to Hmong society and culture (see also Grandstaff 1979: 70). Largely in response to Chinese traders after the Chinese-English Opium War in the mid-nineteenth century, Hmong began to cultivate the opium poppy in the limestone-rich mountain areas where they had escaped Han invaders (Tapp 2001: 7, Mischung 1990: 311; Grandstaff 1979: 73). After that point, Hmong in China and later in Vietnam, Laos and Thailand began to focus on poppy cultivation. This was a source of income when the opium was sold to local lowland merchants and Europeans. Opium poppies grow best at high altitudes in a monsoon climate, poppies were particularly suited to the mountain environments where the Hmong had settled (Peters-Golden 2002: 79; Ovesen 1995: 12).

While Hmong dry rice cultivation needs less care and weeding and thus a smaller labour force than opium poppy cultivation, opium poppy grows also on soils of low fertility and opium swiddens can be cultivated two to three times longer than dry rice swiddens. Opium is easy to store, and in the past could be exchanged for silver bars; silver is still highly valued among many Hmong today (Tapp 1986: 21). For most Hmong, silver remains an important sign of wealth, and is used for personal adornment and bridewealth. Another advantage of opium was its high value-to-weight ratio (one kilogram opium often could be exchanged for roughly half a ton of rice), was slow to perish, and could easily be transported during migrations in the mountains (Fadiman 1997: 123; Tapp 1986: 21). Labour intensive poppy cultivation spurred high fertility rates in families, but large families in turn also required increasing amounts of land. The Hmong traditional system of cultivation was thus quite land intensive. The traditional solution for accommodating this system of cultivation was migration, which allowed the Hmong to balance population and land resources while increasing population, productivity, and wealth (Kunstadter 2000: 169).

Opium poppy cultivation and sale enabled the Hmong to migrate within Southeast Asia because it was a commodity that could be easily stored and transported. Opium-financed migrations permitted the establishment of Hmong settlements in new regions (Grandstaff 1979: 75; Geddes 1976: 224). Opium poppy cultivation was officially banned in Thailand in 1959, but continued to be unofficially supported by some corrupt bureaucrats, police and businessmen for a number of years (Tapp 1986: 36). In my research areas, opium poppy cultivation had come to a complete halt by the late 1980s. In other Hmong villages, small plots are still planted with opium poppy for personal (therapeutical) use only (see also Grandstaff 1979: 74).

Hmong scholars like Jean Michaud (1997: 231) and Robert Cooper (1984: 196, 211) believe there is a causal relationship between the Hmong's former cultivation of opium poppy and their current success with intensive agricultural methods. The Hmong appear to have adapted to the change from traditional to commercial agriculture more easily than other mountain groups. In contrast to most of their neighbours, the Hmong have a great deal of experience in marketing and selling crops because of their history of opium cultivation:

> "[T]he cultivation of the poppy and the marketing of the opium set a precedent whose consequences were instrumental in the apparently high capacity of this group to adapt to the present economic situation. Their relatively long term apprenticeship in this form of intensive commercial agriculture, in comparison with many other groups of swiddeners of the eco-region, gave them a precedent from within their traditional economy." (Michaud 1997: 231)

Many of my older Hmong informants (female and male) had very positive memories of the "good old opium days", and regretted their end. For these Hmong, the era of opium cultivation was characterised by relative wealth, independence from other peoples, and freedom of movement in the mountains. In contrast, the years following the end of poppy cultivation are remembered as very harsh and poor years. Informants reported that they had to adapt to the dramatic change, learn new cultivation techniques for unfamiliar crops, and survive lean years while waiting for the first harvest of newly introduced perennial crops like coffee, "western peach", and litchi. One male informant from Mae Sa Mai, Buag Maim who is sixty years old, explained:

> "People were richer with opium and life was much nicer then, but life is better now because litchi is steadier. We stay in one place and know that we will have a harvest." (Source: field interview, H-C-MSM 5)

It was not until the end of the 1980s that improvements in road infrastructure in northern mountain areas permitted better access to markets and traders in the lowlands. This made it possible for Hmong farmers to market their new agricultural products more easily and increase their income. Philip Dearden suggests that the development of the road network in northern Thailand "has probably done more to change the landscape of the North and the mindscape of [its] inhabitants than any other single factor" (1995: 118). Indeed, most economic studies emphasise that road improvements usually integrate isolated and marginal peoples into the larger economic context (Rigg 1997: 173). Roads bring new business opportunities to local peoples, increase consumer choice, improve access to services like schools and health facilities, promote the cultivation of secondary cash crops, improve access to agricultural input such as fertilizer, and ease marketing constraints for produce. They also promote economic and social differentiation (Rigg 1997: 174).

Rice and maize cultivation

Just as it has commonly been believed that the opium poppy is the most important traditional Hmong crop, many also believe that the Hmong did not traditionally engage in wet rice cultivation (Keen 1978: 220). However, as a number of scholars have documented, Hmong have engaged in irrigated rice cultivation in terraces for at least 100 years (Yang Dao 1993: 53; Yang Dao 1975: 76, 79; Lemoine 1972: 54; Savina [1924] 1930: 215; Abadie 1924: 159). Hmong agriculture has always been based on mixed cultivation rather than a single crop, as many authors have claimed. The Hmong economy always adapted to specific local conditions, elevations, and socio-economic circumstances and requirements (Tapp 1989: 45-46). For the Hmong in Thailand, dry and wet rice, self-grown or bought, has been the staple food since the beginning of the last century. Maize continues to be grown mainly as animal fodder. Maize may have been the "emergency food" during precarious economic circumstances in the past; it was undoubtedly an important supplement to the Hmong diet in China (Ovesen 1995: 50; cf. Cooper 1984: 19-22).

Despite its importance to rituals and subsistence agriculture, some Hmong families in Thailand stopped growing dry rice by the 1960s in favour of the most important cash crop, the opium poppy (Keen 1978: 216). Rice was then purchased from neighbouring Karen and Lua' villages. Hmong preferred to locate their settlements near these ethnic groups because they were suppliers of staple crops and cheap labour. In Roland Mischung's former research site in Mae Ya Noi, Hmong villagers devoted more land to poppy than to rice cultivation in the 1960s. By 1982, however, the villagers had resumed cultivation of (wet) rice and were again able to cover most of their subsistence needs. An important reason for this shift was that rice had gained in market value in comparison to opium. Until 1987, poppy and rice were the two major crops grown in that village. Flexibility, profit maximisation, and intensive cultivation methods characterised Hmong economic and agricultural activity (Mischung 1990: 314-315).

In my research areas, traditional species of maize are still grown mainly for animal fodder and, occasionally, served as a snack after meals. On small patches of one-third or one-half of a *rai*, many Hmong villagers in Mae Sa Mai and Ban Phui grow traditional species of dry rice, which is consumed as a special dish at the New Year. These dry rice and maize species are, along with other traditional Hmong crops such as Chinese peach, pumpkin and Hmong "green leaf vegetables", planted along the borders of commercial cash crop fields for home consumption.[118] In the traditional Hmong resource economy, these crops are cultivated for special ritual occasions, to maintain traditional species endangered by newly introduced hybrid species, and to consciously preserve an element of the Hmong "cultural heritage".

Poppy substitution, development projects and international companies

As the main producers of opium poppy in the northern Thai highlands, Hmong farmers were the major target of national and international development projects following the 1958 opium ban (Tapp 1989: 64; Kesmanee 1989: 76). Most of the projects were started between 1961 and 1988. They were located in many Hmong villages and spent large sums in the name of "development" (Kunstadter 2000: 175; Kesmanee 1989: 64-69). The projects introduced substitute crops like litchi, peach, coffee, flowers, and a great variety of vegetables, including beans, cabbage and lettuce.

The main goal of the Thai state and its extension work was increasing state influence in remote mountain areas. The means used to enhance control included a variety of agricultural, educational and health programs, along with army and border patrol police projects and taxation and more restrictive land use policies. The intent was to enhance control over the mountain minorities and to cause them to adapt their way of life to the manner

---

[118] On their migration from China to the mountainous regions across Southeast Asia, the Hmong brought seeds of Chinese peach trees, which bear a small fruit liked by many Hmong. The western peach, which was introduced into Hmong agriculture by development projects, bears bigger but less tasty fruit, according to the Hmong.

approved by the Thai state (Tapp 2001: 11; cf. Bhruksasri 1989: 15-21; see also Rehbein 2004). Government policies and regulations also aimed at "stabilising" Hmong settlements, efforts that struck "directly at underlying principles of "traditional" Hmong economy" (Kunstadter 2000: 169). According to Nicholas Tapp (1989: 39), the underlying aim of assimilation of ethnic groups into the state led to the failure of many development projects, which did not integrate local culture into development projects but rather tried to eradicate it (see also Kesmanee 1989: 94-95). In spite of the aims underlying most Thai projects, Hmong people have been able to maintain a strong sense of autonomy and to preserve Hmong cultural identity.

International development agencies mainly promoted projects in opium poppy substitution and agricultural development. These projects included the United Nations (UN) Development Program, the UN Drug Abuse Control project, the US Department of Agriculture-supported Royal Project, the United States Agency for International Development (USAID) programs, projects by the World Bank like the Highland Agricultural and Social Development Project, conducted jointly with the Australian Development Assistance Bureau, the Norwegian Aid Church programs, and the long-term GTZ (Gesellschaft für Technische Zusammenarbeit) project called the Thai-German Highland Development Programme, which lasted for eighteen years (cf. Dirksen 1997: 331-340; McKinnon 1989: 337; Tapp 1986: 33-36; 62-66).

Most of the agencies and development projects had a pre-set agenda that did not accommodate local world-views and resource management objectives. The result was low participation among villagers and a failure to integrate local concepts and knowledge (cf. Kalland 2000: 328). An additional complication is that agricultural development based on new agricultural techniques and chemicals has made little effort to promote sustainable development. This problem is not limited to northern Thailand, but is an issue in other parts of the world where such development projects continue to be implemented. As a result, developing economies throughout the world face overwhelming challenges in achieving economic growth and alleviating poverty while promoting sustainable management of natural resources (cf. Coxhead and Jayasuriya 2003: 2).

There is also an increasing consensus that development projects working under the auspices of market economics have tended not to favour the equal participation of women (Bossen 1989: 340). Among the Hmong in Thailand, the majority of projects trained only men in new agricultural techniques and provided mainly men with support in commodities and credits, and failed to promote independent productive, managerial, and commercial activities that could also be carried out by women. Development projects thus bolstered male Hmong authority and economic control while further relegating women to the category of economic dependents.

In combination with the state integration programs, the national and international development projects initiated among the Hmong since the 1960s have had a significant influence on the Hmong economy and overall lifestyle (Leepreecha 2001: 35; cf. Durrenberger and Tannenbaum 1990: 1). In spite of the many millions of dollars that have been spent on development efforts, the Hmong and other ethnic mountain groups did not benefit as much as they might have from this extension work. Moreover, the newly developed and introduced methods of cultivation are better suited to lowland environments than to mountain agriculture (Kesmanee 1989: 94-95). In mountainous areas, the water supply is often intermittent, and fertilizer and pesticides are often unaffordable. The new agricultural methods have thus created new problems for the environment and region's inhabitants (cf. Kunstadter and Chapman 1978: 6). Many projects that introduced new crops and technology to Hmong agriculture failed to elicit public participation. They also did not provide technical support to open access to markets, assist with the control of pests, or train in the proper application of agricultural chemicals that are hazardous to human health (Kunstadter 2000: 168). The projects replaced opium poppy cultivation with the cultivation of new crops, but abandoned the farmers to deal alone with problems of marketing, rapidly changing crop prices, and environmental and health effects.

In Mae Sa Mai, the Royal Project (RP), a government agency, also affected Hmong farming methods. The small Royal Project extension bureau provides Hmong farmers with seeds for certain crops and training in new agricultural techniques. King Bumiphol, who is widely known for his sympathy for the mountain peoples, established the Royal Project in 1969. Alternative crops, mostly temperate cash crops, have been introduced to replace poppy cultivation, especially among the Hmong, who were one of the Royal Project's main target groups.

In Mae Sa Mai, the Thai-British Forest Restoration Research Unit (FORRU) has also affected resource use systems within the village, as I shall discuss further below. The most important influence in Mae Sa Mai, however, has been international seed and agrochemistry companies. Modern Hmong agriculture uses seeds, multinutrient fertilisers (especially nitrogen-phosphorus-potassium mixtures), and other agrochemicals. International agrochemistry companies import most of these. Company representatives pay regular, personal visits to Hmong villages to promote their products. The companies also employ Hmong farmers to disseminate information to remote Hmong villages about their products, including details on improved varieties of seeds, growth hormones, and chemical fertilisers. A Dutch company that markets hybrid carrot seeds employs a few Hmong men in Mae Sa Mai to conduct field experiments with the seeds. The company's goal is to optimise hybrid yields while preventing degradation of soil quality by the application of a mixture of chicken dung, rice husks and peanut shells as a natural fertilizer.

The use of imported hybrid seeds and chemicals are indicative of Hmong involvement in the market economy and of the increased monetary cost of production (cf. Sutthi 1989: 128-129). The Royal Project supports farmers by providing seeds and free extension services on plant production methods. In return, the farmers must agree to sell their crops to the Royal Project after harvest. Many Hmong from Mae Sa Mai believe that this makes the Royal Project unattractive because they can obtain an equal or even higher price on the lowland markets on their own. Many Hmong also express doubt about the methods the Project uses to grade crops by size, colour, ripeness and trace chemical content. The Project only purchases grade A crops. Grade B and C crops then can only be sold with difficulty at the markets in Chiang Mai. For this reason, the Hmong would prefer to sell their complete harvest to the Royal Project, not just the best part of it. Because of these issues, only approximately one-third of Mae Sa Mai households are members of the Royal Project. The most important benefit provided by the Project is the opportunity to receive credits at low rates after farmers have proved they are a faithful member (credit rates start at thirty percent and can go down to eight percent). The credits are given out by the BAAC. Non-members can also receive seeds and fertilizer from the Project, but not the low-rate credits.

Transformations in the Hmong economy

Under the influence of state agencies and international development programs, the Hmong economy rapidly abandoned the opium poppy, dry rice and maize-based agriculture, which continued to be practiced well into the 1980s, in favour of permanent, commercial forms of chemical-intensive cultivation. Especially since the 1980s, with the improvement of the road network in the uplands and highlands and the changes that resulted from development projects, the Hmong economy and demographic structure began to change at an increasing pace (Kunstadter 2000: 189-190). This change included the abandonment of old crops, the introduction of new cash and subsistence crops, and the alteration of basic agricultural techniques. The major effect was the reduced demand for labour and the reduced amount of land devoted to agricultural cultivation as a result of the use of agricultural chemicals. When agricultural practices change to require a smaller labour force, demographic change also results. Having a large number of children is no longer an economic asset but becomes an economic burden due to the cost of education. The result is that state family planning projects have become more successful among the Hmong, as I noted above. Despite a decline in population growth and a reduction in the amount of land needed for agriculture, there is still a shortage of fertile soil. This is the result of sedentarisation and intensive land use, in which the land is heavily exposed to agricultural chemicals and permitted only a short or no fallow period.

Another result of the transformation of the Hmong economy is that many Hmong from my research sites have become more entrepreneurial. Many have contracted debts from kin, the Royal Project, or the Bank for Agriculture and Agricultural Cooperatives (BAAC) to plant export commodities on their best land. In Mae Sa Mai, twelve of the twenty-nine households surveyed had current debts in an amount ranging from 3.000 to 420.000 baht. In Ban Phui, fifteen of the twenty households surveyed had debts ranging from 10.000 to 400.000 baht. The villagers also buy pickup trucks on a loan basis from car companies. In Mae Sa Mai, farmers also invest in perennials such as litchi and persimmon, hoping that these crops will provide a good income for their children as well. Even though the Hmong do not possess legal title to the land under cultivation, sedentarised Hmong farmers make long-term investments in their fields hoping to improve yields and profits and increase the likelihood that their children will be able to make a living from agriculture in the future. The Hmong strive for high profits from agriculture to cover their children's education costs and the increasing cost of industrially made consumer goods. As I noted above, the goal of Hmong production continues to be the most successful and profitable use of natural resources.

Many Hmong claimed in interviews that they have "inventive power" and a desire for economic experimentation, especially in comparison to other mountain groups, but that they lack the funds needed to implement business ideas in the lowlands. The Hmong believe there is one major impediment to economic activities outside the agricultural sector: the lack of land titles as security for bank loans and, thus, the inability to obtain higher credits from the banks. For example, Hmong men have ideas about setting up trade networks, large plantations, and garages in the lowlands but lack the money needed for an initial investment. In addition, Hmong farmers realise they are not independent players on the national and world markets because they cannot influence prices. They also say they are not diversified enough to be successful on a large scale, which again demonstrates that their central concern is an increase in economic profits.

In other words, changes in the Hmong resource use system have not changed the Hmong's overall goal of maximising success in their area of settlement. New modes of production increase profits that can be reinvested in symbols of wealth and the worship of ancestral and other spirits to secure future well-being. Hmong do not invest profits only in education, cars, DVD players and other goods, but also in "traditional institutions" like ancestor spirits and clan networks. The Yang clan lineage leader from Mae Sa Mai, Nyaj Sua, emphasised that even more pigs are sacrificed now than in the past in rituals to appease the *dab* and host the increased number of guests who are able to visit due to the improvements in roads and infrastructure.

Thus the introduction of a new economic system did not totally eradicate the old one. The Hmong communities I studied are neither completely "traditional" nor completely "modern". Instead, Hmong in both Mae Sa Mai and Ban Phui should be understood as local actors who make decisions about which of the many outside influences they accept and adopt and which aspects they do not integrate into their own system. As I show below, the Hmong are not passive farmers who only react to input from the outside. Instead, they decide to take advantage of certain potentials while ignoring others.

New forms of agriculture in Mae Sa Mai and Ban Phui

Hmong economic activities are still largely focused on agriculture, which plays an integral role in Hmong culture, as research among Hmong groups around the world demonstrates (cf. Géraud 1993: 414). A survey about specialty crop production among Hmong in Minneapolis (U.S.A.) showed that the "most common reason for these Hmong to become a gardener or farmer was because it was a hobby or part of their culture" (Olson et al.

2003: 2). Agriculture and Hmong identity are intimately linked because cultivating the (mountain) fields is understood as the main way to secure the Hmong's survival. Hmong say that they are proud of their fields. Diligent farming is still a highly valued trait even though some people in my research sites already earn their living from activities other than agriculture. Yeeb Thoj, a fifty-three-year-old woman from Mae Sa Mai, stated this when she spoke about Win Huj, who earns most of his income outside agriculture:

> "He is a good man and works hard even though he does not go much to the fields anymore. Normally good people who live according to the Hmong custom know how to work the land. They go to their fields early in the morning and return late in the evening. But new fields cannot be cut anymore like in the past so people are forced to do other work as well. Many things are changing." (Source: field interview, H-C-MSM 21)

Occupations are changing, as is the cultural knowledge that adheres to them. Knowledge of opium poppy cultivation, swiddening, different soil types, and bioindicator plants has been rendered obsolete now that new fields can no longer be cut out of the forest. It is now more important to know which cash crops grow well in a particular microclimate near the village than to know which soil types in the forest are best for dry rice swiddens. To find the right crops for the right plots, Hmong in both villages in my study experiment with vegetables and fruit and pass along their knowledge to others. Hmong farmers have learned about the ecological problems associated with planting the same crops year after year on the same plot of land. In order to restore the soil's fertility, for example, it is useful to plant peanut bean, even though its market price is low. The Hmong today still make intensive use of land, but do so in a more strategic manner by designating certain crops for specific plots of land for specific purposes (cf. Masipiqueña, Persoon and Snelder 2000: 179). As Nandini Sundar has noted regarding the change of knowledge among Indians who abandoned shifting cultivation:

"Local knowledge changes as local environments change and as people become implicated in new projects. This is obviously an uneven process, as memories of past practices continue to hold good for a while and as knowledge is transmitted through cultural practices which continue to take place even when the features of the world they refer to no longer exist in the same way." (2000: 83)

Hmong farmers broaden their knowledge constantly by learning new techniques of modern agriculture that use improved hybrid seeds and agricultural chemicals. Traditional Hmong agriculture was defined by the cultivation of three main crops, opium poppy, dry rice and maize. Today, it is defined by the variety of cash crops under cultivation. In Mae Sa Mai, approximately 1.100 *rai* are devoted to litchi, making it the main crop in the village. In Ban Phui, cabbage and red onion are the major crops. In villages near Mae Sa Mai other crops such as carrots (in Nong Hoi) and flowers (in Bouak Chan) play the most important role. Factors like elevation of fields, water supply, soil quality, access to markets and retailers, and input and support from outside agencies play an important role in determining which crops are primarily grown in each area.

Three systems of plant cultivation exist in parallel in the villages studied. These cropping systems can also be found among other ethnic groups in northern Thailand (Sutthi 1989: 126-128). In the mono-cropping system, the same plant is grown in a field year round. This crop might be, for example, rice, cabbage, or beans. In a sequential cropping system, plants are grown in rotation in a single year. The first rotation, for example, could be a rice crop, followed by red bean as a second crop, and cabbage as a third crop. The third is the mixed cropping system, which involves growing several crops at the same time in one field. This could be, for example, dry rice as the major crop, soybeans, tomatoes or corn as a secondary crop, and "traditional" Hmong vegetables (green leaf vegetables, beans, pumpkin, peas) as minor crops at the sides of the field. One farmer can apply all three systems at the same time, dividing his plots according to location, microclimate, water resources, and soil quality.

Cultivation of cash crops in Mae Sa Mai and Ban Phui

The most common cash crops among the Hmong of northern Thailand are maize, cabbage, red bean, chilli, ginger, opium, leaf lettuce, carrot, castor bean and cotton (Kunstadter 2000: 178). These crops, as well as many others, are cultivated in my research sites. The great variety of crops cultivated in the two Hmong villages in my study is a result of input from state and development agencies, as well as the result of experimentation with new crops to determine which vegetables and fruit are most suited to their area and obtain the highest profit at market. For the majority of the farmers interviewed, the market price is the most important factor in selecting crops for cultivation. New crops are experimented with constantly. For example, in Mae Sa Mai I was asked by the Hmong informants whom I befriended for a few kilograms of German potatoes for a field trial in the Hmong fields. A visiting German friend then did bring some potatoes of the "Linda" species, which obtained good yields and continue to be cultivated in my host village.

In his analysis of Hausa farmers and intercropping plans in Western Africa, Paul Richards notes that the range of skills and strategies employed by farmers extends beyond simple applied knowledge into a "set of improvisational capacities called forth by the needs of the moment" (1993: 62). In his analysis of "performance knowledge", Richards observes how Hausa farmers adjust to drought by planting and replanting different seed mixes until they achieve germination or available resources are exhausted. He suggests that local knowledge is constantly changing and intrinsically interactive and needs to be recognised as grounded in multiple domains, logic and epistemologies (1993: 62). He thus calls attention to the range of skills and practices that a group like the Hausa, or the Hmong, whether collectively or individually, can manipulate in order to create relevant local knowledge within a particular cultural sphere (see also Ellen and Harris 2000: 18).

To give another example from the Hmong, farmers from Ban Phui realised that red onion grown in the lowlands obtained a good market price.

About three to four years ago, they began to experiment with red onion cultivation, learning from their own and others' experiences. Thus far, red onion – which has two harvests, the flower and the onion – has proven a very profitable crop. Because of drastic price variations in national and international markets, this could change at any point. Since the advent of the technology-intensive "green revolution" in the 1960s, prices for agricultural products fluctuate constantly on the world market, as the list of profits below shows. These rapid changes in turn heighten farmers' uncertainties (cf. Kunstadter and Chapman 1978: 6).

Thai researcher Waranoot Tungittiplakorn, who has studied cash crop development and adoption among the Hmong in villages near Nan and Hot in northern Thailand, summarises her findings as follows:

"Government intervention, roads, and market agents are important factors that jump-started the adoption of cash crops in these two villages. However, the rapid development and diffusion of cash crops are facilitated by the clan network and the increase in mobility since the beginning of cabbage production. [...] Through the clan network, innovation is rapidly being transferred from one village to another." (1998: 147)

In my research sites, male Hmong farmers were frequently visited by kin from other provinces or travelled long distances to other Hmong villages to maintain clan relations and exchange knowledge about special aspects of Hmong culture, and to exchange information about newly introduced crops. Agricultural knowledge important to the Hmong is thus disseminated rapidly and frequently in the northern Thai Hmong Mountains.

Of course, in addition to adopting new crops, Hmong farmers abandon crops that do not bear good yields, are susceptible to pests, or do not obtain a market profit. Approximately thirty years ago in Mae Sa Mai, the main crops were cabbage (three harvests per year), perennials such as *Arabica* coffee and litchi, and Chinese peach and other "traditional Hmong crops" (see above). After the price for coffee dropped, chrysanthemum flowers and the "western peach" were added to the range of cash crops. The foreign peach species did not grow as well as the small native ones so new crops like leaf lettuce, pepper, leek, and a number of carrot varieties were introduced. About twenty years ago, opium poppy cultivation gradually began to wane, while dry rice and maize continued to be grown on the fields around the village. One important fact to remember is that perennials such as litchi and persimmon take five to ten years to begin to bear fruit, so intermediary crops like cabbage, carrots, leek, cucumber, yams, taro, dry rice, and corn need to be grown among the small trees to provide an income during the first years. In Mae Sa Mai, the Royal Project continues to promote cultivation of litchi trees as a secure source of income and to "green the area and to prevent soil erosion," as Khun Nikhon from the Mae Sa Mai Royal Project station explained (personal communication, 21.06.2001, Mae Sa Mai). Within the next few years in Mae Sa Mai, fields with steep slopes will either need to be reforested or cultivated with perennials like litchi and persimmon. If these measures are not carried out, the Royal Forestry Department will claim these areas for their own conservation programs. Hmong villagers agree that growing fruit trees is an investment in the future that could one day help sustain their children. As the statistics below demonstrate, the profit margin for litchi cultivation among Mae Sa Mai households is generally quite low, in part because harvests are highly susceptible to pests and bad weather. Farmers in Ban Phui achieve higher profits with cabbage and onion cultivation because they can be harvested several times a year. In spite of its popularity, which is linked to environmentalist and "modernising" ideas that are professed both by Hmong villagers from Mae Sa Mai and Thai officials from the Royal Project and the RFD, litchi cultivation grosses the second lowest profits after cabbage (Schoenleber 2002: 51).

After opium poppy cultivation came to a close at the end of the 1980s, most Ban Phui villagers cultivated a Hmong maize variety along with lesser, secondary crops like bamboo, plum, litchi, and coffee. In the early 1990s, visiting Royal Project agents promoted the cultivation of red beans. These measures were followed by the introduction of different varieties of cabbage, carrots, and leaf lettuce. Toward the end of the 1990s, the humanitarian organisation "Care International" worked for five years in the village to support farmers in the cultivation of persimmon trees. However, as in many other Hmong communities throughout northern Thailand, cabbage is still the main crop in Ban Phui in spite of its low profit per kilogram: cabbage sold to retailers directly at the field obtains one to two baht per kilogram; at the lowland market, it obtains between 0.5 baht and four to five baht per kilogram, depending on its availability at the time (see also Kunstadter 2000: 177). In spite of this low return, cabbage is popular because it is resistant to pests, able to grow in low quality soil, needs watering only once per week, can be grown three to four times per year, and remains fresh for four days after harvest. In Ban Phui, cabbage is grown mainly during the rainy season when insects are less of a problem. Because of the cooler temperatures during the cold season from December to February, insects are more of a problem in Ban Phui than in Mae Sa Mai (personal communication with entomologist Peter Schütz from the Thai-German "Uplands Program", 13.01.2002, Chiang Mai). Because of its popularity, Hmong villagers themselves describe cabbage as the "Hmong crop". Pickup trucks loaded with more than 1.500 kg of cabbage are a common sight near Hmong settlement areas.

Economic survey data

The following section and the section on additional economic activities and household income and expenditures are largely based on my economic survey data. To gain insight into the variety of Hmong economic activities extended survey interviews were conducted in twenty-nine households in Mae Sa Mai (October to December 2001) and in twenty households in Ban Phui (January to February 2002). In the survey, I treated each household as a single economic unit despite the fact that nuclear families sometimes cultivate their own land for profits. However, as long as these nuclear families are members of an extended household, they continue to contribute a portion of their income to the residential unit and remain economically involved in household activities – for example, helping on the fields of the household head, sharing jointly-used vehicles and machines, and sharing food.

The two survey samples are reasonably representative of households in the two villages because households of all clans, income categories, and sizes were interviewed. The survey interviews included questions about composition of household members, household goods, incomes and expenses, crops cultivated, yields, revenues, sizes of fields, wages earned and revenues drawn from other economic activities. In most cases, more than one household member joined the interview, and thus both women and men of all ages were questioned about their activities and their household data. Despite extensive interviews on revenues, yields, income from labour, and major expenses, it proved quite difficult to evaluate economic profits from agricultural and other activities and to compare assets for the survey households. This is in part because Hmong farmers do not calculate gross annual profits for each individual crop. Gross margins are understood as revenues from crops minus all variable costs invested in the growing and marketing of the crop, including machinery, (hired) labour, tools, seeds, agricultural chemicals, land rental, and payment of credits.

Since variable costs in the Hmong cultivation system are quite diverse and are often not clearly recorded or remembered, accurate calculation of gross margins is difficult. Even literate farmers do not normally maintain a written record of their agricultural activities, including input and output. As the Hmong themselves admit, they lack a "culture of writing" (see also Olson et al. 2003: ii, 19). Often it is even difficult to assess the number of *rai* cultivated by each household because land is sometimes lent to other villagers or borrowed and rented from villagers inside and outside the settlement. Some land is not under cultivation at all, or is planted with a perennial that requires input costs but has yet to bear fruit. In such cases, many Hmong farmers do not include the plot in the calculation of that year's economic activity. Because of these ambiguities and distortions in the economic figures, it was impossible to conduct a cost-benefit analysis and gross margin calculation on the basis of the survey data. Most Hmong farmers are only concerned to know whether a particular crop's profits are high enough to pay back loans, cover daily costs and sustain the family until the next yield is due. As my key informant, Yeeb Yaj, explained:

> "Why should we write down anything? We cannot change the prices anyway. Sometimes we are lucky and we get good prices. Sometimes we are not so lucky, and the crops turn bad before harvest or we have to throw the harvest away at the market because profits are too low. We cannot change that by writing anything down. We just have to work hard and try out as many things as possible." (Source: field interview, H-C-MSM 3)

When one villager successfully markets a newly introduced crop, other farmers often follow suit and plant one to three *rai* in the new crop to acquire experience in cultivating and marketing the new vegetable or fruit. Because of rapid changes in market price and the price decline that results from increasing availability, it is rarely possible to repeat high profits with a new crop.

Perennials

Perennials such as litchi, persimmon, and coffee are advantageous in a number of respects. First, these trees are a long-term investment into the land that might secure income for future generations. Second, planting of fruit trees meets the Royal Forestry Department's reforestation requirements. Finally, profits can be considerable if fruit is harvested at a time when lowland market supplies are low. For example, the litchi harvest in Mae Sa Mai is ready about a week before litchis mature in the lowlands, other northern Thai provinces (like Nan), and China. Since China is the main importer of Thai litchi, the prices are high when demand is high and local supplies are low. In Mae Sa Mai, where litchi is usually harvested in May, off-season litchi trees are also grown on higher elevations. Off-season litchi can be harvested in December, when supplies of litchi are generally low and prices high. Perennials, which are also grown to a certain extent in Ban Phui, are a long-term agricultural investment. Their cultivation leads to a deeper economical and emotional attachment of farmers to their fields, particularly in comparison to the age of swidden agriculture, when fields were abandoned after several years. Even though most Hmong farmers do not own legal title to their fields, their investments and their long-term dependence on yields increases their commitment to the land.

The cultivation of perennials also entails risks and disadvantages. Perennials do not produce yields for several years after planting, and farmers are not able to respond flexibly and easily to dramatic price fluctuations on the (world) market. For example, price fluctuations made the cultivation of coffee, introduced thirty years ago, unprofitable. Perennials are also susceptible to pests and poor weather, which can damage an entire harvest. For example, a thirty-minute hailstorm in April 2001 destroyed more than half of Mae Sa Mai's litchi harvest, affecting the majority of village households, for whom litchi was the most important source of income. In addition, a large number of trees were affected by a species of beetle that is pesticide-resistant because its destruction takes place in the inside of the tree. As these examples demonstrate, outside factors can nullify profits from perennials and thus endanger a household's key source of income for that year.

Annuals

The most important advantage of annuals is that crops that have proven unprofitable can be easily abandoned and replaced by more promising ones. In addition, crops like cabbage can be harvested three to four times per year, which increases chances for obtaining a good market price. Crops like red onion can be harvested twice a year, since first the flowers and two months later the crop can be sold. Shallots can be placed in dry storage and sold when surplus is low and prices are high. The disadvantages of annuals include the high variability of market price, and a large investment of money, agricultural chemicals, and water. Most Hmong farmers employ a variety of forms of irrigation, including ditch fed, rain fed and sprinkler irrigation, depending on the steepness of the field, water resources, and the funds available for investment into irrigation techniques. Pests and other natural hazards may also affect cash crop yields, and investments can be lost when crops cannot be harvested. During my fieldwork, many Hmong farmers in Mae Sa Mai and Ban Phui had were again undertaking large scale experiments with potato cultivation, spurred, for example, by the fact that potatoes can be sold at a good profit on a contract basis to the "Rito Lay" Potato Chips Company in Lampang (located ninety kilometres southeast of Chiang Mai). Potatoes were first introduced to Hmong agriculture in the beginning of the 1960s by Chinese traders, who purchased the harvest (Geddes 1976: 167; Lee 1981: 223). However, when prices rapidly collapsed, potatoes were abandoned as a commercial crop. During my research stay, some of the farmers in Mae Sa Mai and Ban Phui lost their potato harvest because of fungus problems. This meant that investments of between 3.000 and 5.000 baht in potatoes, chemicals and irrigation were lost. However, because farmers were able to obtain profits of forty-five baht per kilogram in 2001-2002, they continue to experiment with potatoes in spite of these difficulties.

Wet rice cultivation

One interesting feature of Hmong agriculture in Mae Sa Mai, and to a certain extent in Ban Phui, is wet rice cultivation. Dry rice is only grown on fields as small as 0.3 to three *rai* in order to provide households with enough "traditional" rice for the New Year ceremonies and other rituals. Hmong generally prefer to plant arable land with marketable cash crops rather than with commodities for home consumption. In both settlement areas in my study, wet rice cannot be grown on the mountainous slopes. Instead, paddy fields are rented from Thai owners in the lowlands (Mae Sa Mai) or from neighbouring Karen communities (Ban Phui). Input costs for wet rice cultivation include the rental of the fields (300 baht/*rai*/seven months), ploughing the fields twice by the Thai or Karen owner (700 baht/*rai* total), water charges (seventy baht/*rai*), the cost of cleaning the channels along the fields (150 baht/year), costs for agricultural chemicals (approximately 220 baht/*rai*), rice seeds (twenty kilograms/*rai*), labour (eighty baht/person/day) for transplanting (1.5 persons/day/*rai*), weeding twice (1.5 persons/day/*rai*) and for harvesting (three persons/day/*rai*), and transportation costs to the fields, which can lie between thirty and forty kilometres away from the mountain village.[119] For example, one of the households surveyed in Mae Sa Mai, which had a good paddy harvest, spent a total sum of 11.470 baht to grow wet rice on seven *rai*, rented from Thai lowland owners near Mae Rim in the year 2000. The harvest amounted to 3.600 kilograms husked rice, which equals approximately 36.000 baht.[120] At the markets in Mae Rim and Chiang Mai, forty-five kilogram sacks of husked jasmine rice can be bought for 450 to 480 baht. However, many households in Mae Sa Mai do not have such profitable paddy harvests; for some households, it would be cheaper to purchase rice from the lowland markets.

Investing labour and money in rice paddy cultivation on fields rented from lowland Thai and neighbouring Karen communities is not always profitable. Poor weather conditions, pests and labour shortages (especially in times of rituals) may result in low yields that do fail to cover input costs or provide the household with enough rice for the year. The Hmong I interviewed explained the continued cultivation of paddy rice in spite of its relatively low profitability by citing a number of factors. First, wet rice is the staple crop of the Hmong, making it important to insure a household's rice stock throughout the year. Although purchasing wet rice in the lowlands or

---

[119] Hmong farmers claim that they are not experienced in ploughing fields with machines, so they employ Thai or Karen people who own the machines to conduct this task.
[120] It is estimated by the villagers that the average rice consumption is 200 kilograms per head per year (see also Mischung 1990: 319).

from Karen neighbours might be cheaper, a household would need to have a stable disposable income each month in order to purchase rice monthly on the market. When harvests are poor or profits are low, this disposable income might not be available each month. The Hmong thus choose to invest both money and labour in rice paddy cultivation to increase the likelihood that rice yields will be sufficient for the entire year (see also Durrenberger and Tannenbaum 1990: 77). A second reason for the continued cultivation of wet rice is the Hmong's emotional attachment to this subsistence crop, which has a long history in Hmong farming. Many Hmong informants stated that they had always grown either dry or wet rice and intended to continue to grow it as a subsistence crop. Self-grown rice is believed to provide a margin of security within an unstable cash crop economy. It also provides a surplus that can be retained against future hardship (see also Cooper 1984: 158-159). Third, many villagers stated that "it is more fun to have self-grown rice" because the planting and harvesting is done communally by large (lineage) groups. This demonstrates that cultivation of particular crops is not always or only founded on rationality and profitability, but may also be founded on other socio-cultural factors. E. Paul Durrenberger and Nicola Tannenbaum (1990: 97) support this finding in their analysis of Shan and Lisu agriculture in northern Thailand:

> "[...] production decisions are not a separate domain, dissociated from other kinds of decisions such as those which inform levels of religious expenditure, aspirations for the future, and culturally defined standards of living. Rather, they are one aspect of ongoing decisions about the conduct of life." (Durrenberger and Tannenbaum 1990: 97)

The Hmong in Mae Sa Mai and Ban Phui also grow a great variety of subsistence crops for home consumption in quantities of one *ngan* (400 m^2) or less. Unlike the Karen, who grow these crops in village gardens, the Hmong plant them along the borders of cash crop fields or on small patches of land not suitable for cash crop cultivation. "Hmong crops", as they are called, include mainly varieties (of pumpkin, green leaf vegetables, ginger, maize, cucumber, for example) that were cultivated in China or in other outposts in the history of Hmong migration, and are not cultivated by other local mountain groups. These crops are highly valued, are grown as side-crops without the application of agricultural chemicals, and are not sold. Seeds are stored for the next year.

Agricultural chemicals

Agricultural chemicals such as herbicides, insecticides, fungicides, hormones, adherents and fertilizer are applied to control insects, weeds, and fungus, to increase yields, speed crop growth and decrease the amount of labour required. The intensified use of chemicals follows the larger trend in Thailand, where agrochemical use has increased rapidly in recent years (Kunstadter et al. 2001: 313; Kesmanee 1989: 91). Many farmers, including the Hmong, do not wear the recommended gloves, mouth coverings, and other protective clothing. Often they apply higher than recommended concentrations to their fields. Many use mixtures or "cocktails" of hormones, insecticides and adherents. An entomologist from the Thai-German "Uplands Program" stated in an interview that wearing gloves while handling the chemical products could substantially reduce the potential hazards. Most of the information on health risks is given to the Hmong by stores selling the products, and via radio and television warnings. However, the extension workers and company agents who promote the use of chemicals in the villages generally do not educate on their risks (see also Kunstadter et al. 2001: 315). Often safety warnings are unintelligible even by the literate since multinational corporations have not translated the container labels into Thai. Hmong farmers interviewed in my surveys either were not aware of the health risks associated with agricultural chemical use or did not care about the risks. However, people complain about negative effects on health, including symptoms such as headaches, itching, nausea, muscle weakness, dizziness, blurred vision, and an accelerated greying of the hair. Neeb Lyooj Xyooj, a forty-three-year-old man from Mae Sa Mai, who is interested in sustainable agriculture and who works for the nursery run by FORRU in the village, complained as follows:

> "We have no choice. We have to make a living from agriculture. We need to apply chemicals if we want to compete on the lowland markets. It is not fair. Everyone tells us that we do not use our natural resources in a sustainable way. But, I ask you, what other choice do we have? International companies come here and teach us to grow crops with the help of chemicals. Why don't your Western companies come here and teach us how to grow crops without so many chemicals? I think because they want to sell their products. We have no choice but to buy and use them." (Source: field interview, H-E-45)

Fields

Even though no legal land titles can be held in the National Parks and the Forest Protection Areas, the Hmong have their own system of land ownership. When swidden agriculture was still practiced, the land belonged to the person who had cleared the area (Cooper 1984: 247). When yields declined, the land was abandoned and available for general use. Now that the Hmong have started permanent settlements, land is inherited from one generation to the next. Other options for acquiring land are purchasing or renting it within the catchment from other villagers, and purchasing or renting it outside the catchment from Thai lowland and Karen farmers. In Mae Sa Mai, people directly linked to the first settlers in the area own most land. Land holding size is smaller for families who arrived after 1970, and is minimal for the few families who settled in Mae Sa Mai after the establishment of Suthep-Pui National Park in 1974. From 1974 on, only a few new settlers arrived in the village; the last household established by a family not directly related to a village inhabitant was founded in 1995. This explains in part why families who have lived longest in the village are generally wealthier and have more fertile land than families who arrived later. About ninety percent of the agricultural land area of Mae Sa Mai is under cultivation. Very little land is left fallow, partly because of Park regulations. Households who lack sufficient labour to till all of their plots either make the land available for free to relatives or rent it for a small sum to other villagers.

A number of households in Mae Sa Mai have as little as two *rai* of land to cultivate after plots were divided among the sons, or inherited land with low soil fertility. The largest farm has forty *rai* under cultivation (see also figure ten and eleven below). According to my survey data, the mean area of land cultivated per household is 12.65 *rai* in Mae Sa Mai, and 46.94 *rai* in Ban Phui. In Ban Phui, the smallest farm is five *rai* and the largest is 151.5 *rai*.[121] Of the households surveyed in Mae Sa Mai, twenty-five percent have about eight *rai*, fifty percent have about ten *rai* and twenty-five percent have more than 16.25 *rai*. In Ban Phui, twenty-five percent of the households surveyed have around 15.5 *rai*, fifty percent have around thirty *rai* and twenty-five percent have more than seventy-five *rai*. The discrepancy in fertile land available for cultivation in Mae Sa Mai and Ban Phui is one of the reasons that agricultural profits are generally higher in the latter village. In addition, as seen above, low yearly litchi yields can also minimise revenues while the growing of temporary crops such as cabbage and red onion that can be harvested several times a year can result in higher profits.

In Ban Phui, approximately ninety-five percent of the fields are under cultivation. Hmong villagers believe that the land that "belongs" to the settlement will meet its needs for the next ten years. Despite this fact, additional land is rented from neighbouring Karen villages. Hmong informants often stated that they did not understand why the Karen do not use their land "optimally", as demonstrated by the fact that they leave wet rice fields fallow during dry season. Hmong farmers, in contrast, are in need of land for cultivation all year round. As one of my key informants and father of the village headman, Nyaj Xeeb Yaj who is sixty years old and from Ban Phui explained to me:

---

[121] In his 1982 study of a Hmong village, Nicholas Tapp (1989: 42) demonstrates that commodities were not very diversified and that largest plots had 30 *rai*.

"Hmong need large areas of land. This is why we only have three small Hmong villages in this area. There is not enough land for another Hmong village here. And now we do not even have enough land for the three existing Hmong communities. It's funny that our three villages have about the same amount of land as the ten surrounding Karen villages. Our fields are spread over the whole area while Karen fields are quite small. Karen also grow crops on fields as small as half a *rai*. But for us Hmong, it is not worth it to grow anything on half a *rai*. We always need a lot of land and a lot of money that is why we also have to rent fields from Karen." (Source: field interview, H-JB 32)

Figure 9: Crops grown in fields larger than 0.25 rai (Mae Sa Mai and Ban Phui)

crops	area under cultivation (in rai)	Mae Sa Mai number of households		Ban Phui number of households	
		2000	2001	2000	2001
♦ crops grown for sale					
avocado	0.30–3.00	3	3	0	0
baby corn	0.50–1.75	2	3	0	0
beet root	0.25	2	2	0	0
carrot	0.75–7.00	5	7	1	1
cabbage	1.00–45.00	3	3	20	20
coffee	3.00–5.00	3	3	0	0
corn	0.25–0.50	3	4	0	0
green salad	0.50	2	2	0	0
lamyai	3.00	2	2	0	0
leek	0.25–1.00	2	3	0	0
litchi	0.30–35.00	26	26	11*	10*
mango*	9.00	1	1	0	0
red onion	2.00–47.00	0	0	15	15
orange	3.00–5.00	0	0	3	3
peach	2.00	1	1	0	0
persimmon*	3.00–6.00	2	2	4	4
radish	3.00	1	1	0	1

		Mae Sa Mai		Ban Phui	
crops	area under cultivation (in rai)	number of households		number of households	
		2000	2001	2000	2001
♦ crops grown for sale					
salee	1.00–2.50	0	0	2	2
potato	3.00–6.00	1	2	4	4
♦ rice grown not for sale					
dry rice	0.30–3.00	6	6	2	2
wet rice	1.50–24.00	15	16	2	2

Source: own survey; N=49 (MSM, BP); *young trees, no fruit yet

As the table shows, in Ban Phui crops are not grown on fields of half a *rai*. However, farmers in Mae Sa Mai cultivate plots as small as 0.25 *rai* with crops like avocado, beetroot, commercial corn, leek and litchi. Land cultivated by one nuclear family is not necessarily located in a single place, but may be scattered around the village depending on how it was obtained (through inheritance, purchase or rental). The chart illustrates that farmers in Mae Sa Mai cultivate, along with litchi, a greater variety of commercial crops. Villagers in the more remote Ban Phui focus on growing cabbage and red onion. Due to the impact of the RFD villages like Ban Phui recently began litchi cultivation; most of these trees do not yet bear fruit.

In addition to crops grown on land belonging to the village, in the past ten years, about forty Ban Phui households have rented wet rice fields from Karen farmers that are usually left uncultivated during the dry season. The Hmong plant them with "trial" cash crops such as potato, radish and tomato and pay 1,000 baht per *rai* for a three months term. These rentals are also risky because yields can be lost due to events like poor weather, fungus, and insects. The high input costs spent on rent, seeds, chemicals and transport to the Karen fields are then lost. Hmong farmers continue to rent this extra land because the soil in their own fields is partly degraded and suited only for growing "robust" crops like cabbage and not for more "demanding" kinds of vegetables, as the village headman Mbua Yim explained to me.

In the surveys, my interviewees were able to easily and precisely state an income figure achieved from the sale of their crops in the previous year. However, they had more difficulty giving precise numbers for the size of plots under cultivation and the yield of different crops. As I discovered, the figure for income generated by each crop was considered important and useful information. Other variables such as relation of yield to size of field and input costs were of lesser importance. Ethnohistorian Jean Michaud (1997: 223-224) also observed that when the Hmong practiced swidden agriculture, farmers only calculated the yield of their fields but not their field size. Michaud believes this was related to the fact that fields only had limited legal status and their exact extent was not fixed on paper.

Location of fields

In my research sites, fields that belong to one household tend to be scattered in location and at times are cultivated by close kin rather than the owners. Some fields are located far from Mae Sa Mai and Ban Phui since some villagers have inherited, rented or purchased fields in the lowlands and in other areas populated by the Hmong. The wide distribution of field location and the rental of fields from other Hmong farmers and groups in the mountains and lowlands are all factors that contributed to the lack of precision in estimates of field size and land amount under cultivation. However, a sample of Hmong fields that were remeasured was approximately the size previously indicated by their owners.

Most fields are located in the vicinity of the village. The amount of time spent to cover the distance between the village and the plots is generally between a ten-minute walk and a thirty-minute drive. If the household owns a motorcycle or car, people generally prefer to drive to the fields, which makes it easier to carry farm equipment and a lunchtime meal. Since many farmers cultivate plots that are not located next to each other, they also spend time driving from one field to the next. Some villagers in Mae Sa Mai and Ban Phui have rented or purchased fields from Karen and Thai owners that are a thirty-minute to one-hour drive away from their village. My neighbour, Vaam Zeej, inherited fields in Doi Samoen, about three hours away. He visits the fields irregularly and employs local Hmong farmers to till the soil. About ten families from Ban Phui own plots on a mountain range west of the village where they grow cabbage during rainy season in addition to fields near the village. Since these fields are a forty-five minute drive from the village and hard to reach during the rainy season, the owners jointly move to their relatively elaborate field huts for three months to cultivate the land. The farmers interviewed said that they would not stay in the mountain fields by themselves but only as a member of a group that provides social proximity and "spiritual" security. It is believed that the proximity of a group of people is always necessary to withstand the occasionally malevolent power of the *dab*, which are thought to be numerous outside the settlements in the wild and 'untamed' region of the forests and mountains. As this example demonstrates, the Hmong tend to think in dichotomies between "inside" (house, village) and "outside" (outside village boundaries, outside the "Hmong terrain"), and between Hmong and non-Hmong people.

Relation of field sizes, yields and profits

The amount of yields depends only conditionally on field size. As survey data shows, large fluctuations in yields can occur due to changing weather conditions, parasitic attacks, pests such as mycosis, or increased soil salination, to cite only a few examples. Revenues on yields can also vary because they depend on highly fluctuating market prices, which are derived according to surplus, product quality and prior price arrangements with retailers. As the figures ten and eleven below demonstrate using the example of litchi (Mae Sa Mai) and cabbage and red onion (Ban Pui), revenues can vary greatly from plot to plot.

Figure 10: Relation of cultivated land size (litchi) to revenues in Mae Sa Mai, 2001

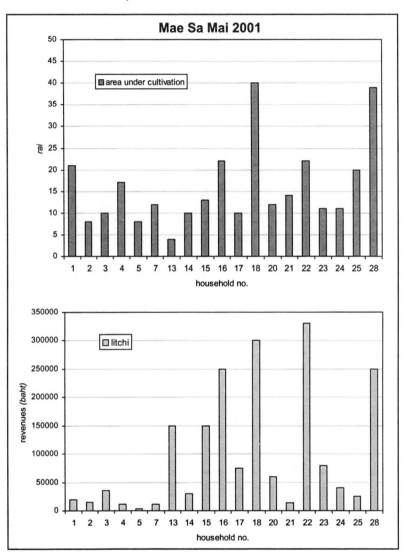

Source: own survey, only households with reliable data

Figure 11: Relation of cultivated land size (cabbage, onion) to revenues in Ban Phui, 2001

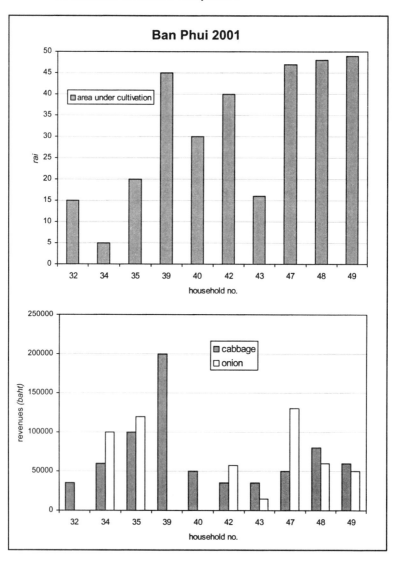

Source: own survey, only households with reliable data

The conditions of crop production and the marketing of yields entail a large amount of uncertainty and risk and, as a result, varying profits for farmers. Returns can differ greatly from household to household even when fields of a similar size are cultivated. For example, revenues for litchi in Mae Sa Mai in 2001 ranged from a profit of 311.000 baht to losses totalling 16.000 baht (see also Schönleber 2002: 53). Lack of liquidity often prevents optimal planning and development of farming systems. Even literate farmers do not keep written records of their activities on topics such as input and output. Instead, Hmong strategy to guarantee sufficient income is to diversify the cultivation structure to minimise the risk of low yields and prices. This strategy of agricultural diversification is practiced to a greater extent in Mae Sa Mai than in Ban Phui, where land resources are still reasonably sufficient and where crops such as cabbage and red onion grow well. Due to minor climatic and soil differences, cabbage and red onion yields are lower in Mae Sa Mai than in Ban Phui. In addition, litchi production is promoted in Mae Sa Mai for several reasons, even though revenues are not necessarily higher than for temporary crops.

Marketing

As producers of agricultural products, the Hmong are involved in a complex web of interdependence among a variety of actors at the local, regional, national and international level. The Hmong must increasingly compete with other ethnic minority groups like the Karen and Yao, who are also adopting cash crop cultivation, with Thai lowland farmers, and with farmers from nearby China, where most agricultural goods are produced at a fraction of the cost of production in Thailand. Large trucks from China are driven to the central markets in Bangkok, where cheap Chinese cash crops like spring onion and cabbage compete directly with locally produced crops, including commodities from the mountainous areas of northern Thailand. In addition, crops that are mainly sold to export companies, like litchi, coffee and flowers must be competitively priced on the world market so that companies do not search for alternatives elsewhere. In other words, as producers, the Hmong are dependent on stable and reasonable prices on national and international markets and on good cooperation with lowland retailers for the marketing of their crops.

Hmong villagers market their agricultural products in a variety of ways, depending on the location of their fields, the time of harvest, offers by local retailers, contracts with large-scale traders and the Royal Project, and transport facilities. Farmers who do not have a pickup truck or who need to sell their produce as fast as possible (for example, litchi perishes quickly after harvest), sell their harvest to local retailers directly at the fields. Prices paid for crops on location are usually half or less than half of what is paid at markets or trade centres in town. However, good prices are not always guaranteed at the market and trade centres, particularly when supplies are high or when retailers have agreed among themselves not to exceed a specific kilogram price for certain crops on that day. When that happens, Hmong farmers have to either accept low profits or risk waiting for a better price in the next few days.

Hmong villagers often stay overnight at trade centres, waiting and bargaining for better rates. In the meantime, the commodities gradually lose their freshness. For example, crops like cabbage and carrot can be sold up to four days after harvest, leek two to three days after harvest, and litchi needs to be sold immediately following harvest. When market prices are too low and retailers cannot be convinced to pay more than, for example, half a baht to two baht per kilogram for leek, crops are either left to rot near the market and trade centre or are not harvested at all. Problems occur when retailers from the lowlands drive up to Mae Sa Mai and Ban Phui and enter into agreements prior to harvest to purchase, for example, 1000 kg of carrots for five baht per kilogram. Hmong farmers then harvest the carrots, wash, package and drive them to markets in Chiang Mai (MSM) or Mae Chaem (BP) only to be informed by the retailers that the carrot surplus is too great that day, and only 500 kilograms of carrots can be purchased at the agreed price while the rest of the yield will obtain only one baht per kilogram.

Usually the Hmong farmer is forced to comply with these methods because they must dispose of the crops while still fresh and must insure that at least their input costs are covered. Costs are incurred for seeds, irrigation, chemicals and external labour, and for market-proof preparation and packaging. Vegetables and fruit need to be sorted according to grades, some varieties must be washed (like carrots, potatoes, radish) or stripped of rotten leaves (like cabbage, leaf lettuce, leek) and either wrapped in plastic or packed in boxes. Thus the preparation of the harvest for sale requires additional labour and money that must be covered by profits.

Earnings from crops can vary greatly. For example, the same commodity sold within a span of two months might obtain between one-half and ten baht per kilogram. Extreme fluctuations occur due to fluctuating world market prices, powerful export companies levelling prices, and changes in the supply and demand structure. To give a specific example from the time of my fieldwork, I examined the price obtained for litchi in Mae Sa Mai: In the middle of April 2001, 120 baht per kilogram were paid for the first litchis harvested. By the end of April, prices had already dropped to eighty baht per kilogram. By the beginning of May, only thirty baht per kilogram were paid. By the end of the season in late May, when the surplus for the crop was high on the market, grade A litchi (litchi with a red shell) earned only twenty-five baht per kilogram. Grade B litchi (brown fruit shell) received only fifteen baht per kilogram throughout the harvest. Loose litchi not hanging on the branch was graded as C, and did not earn more than three to two baht per kilogram.

Most Hmong farmers spoken to generally criticised the strong lobby of lowland retailers and export companies. Prices paid for crops often disregard farmer's variable input costs, but meet demands dictated by companies and trade centres in Bangkok or the world market instead. Hmong people see themselves as the weakest link in a commodity web that they can neither understand to its full extent let alone control. Most farmers do not know to where their products are finally sold: to other Thai provinces, to markets in Bangkok, throughout Asia or to other parts of the world.

In Ban Phui, most villagers market a portion of their produce through local Thai retailers. These retailers then sell the crops to regional wholesalers in different provinces or to companies in Chiang Mai and Bangkok. Some Hmong farmers from Ban Phui who lack the funds to invest in seeds for cultivation are provided with seeds by retailers in return for selling their entire yield to the retailer at a reduced profit. Villagers who own cars (about seventy-three percent of the households) usually bring their cabbage yield to Mae Chaem, Chom Thong, Chiang Mai, and even Lamphun (approximately 150 kilometres away) in search of good prices. Farmers also choose to sell crops like cabbage, carrots and shallots to retailers who wait with eighteen-ton-trucks along the national highway from Hot (about 100 kilometres southwest of Chiang Mai) to Chiang Mai. Profits along highways are usually higher than for crops sold to assemblers directly at the fields, but generally remain lower than at trade centres or markets in Chiang Mai. The large trucks transport the commodities to central markets in Bangkok and other provinces, where they must compete with an increasing influx of cheap agricultural products from China.

The marketing options of Mae Sa Mai Hmong are more varied than for farmers in the more "remote" Ban Phui. The reasons are the Royal Project station and the proximity of Chiang Mai with its trade centres, markets, companies and retailers. A further advantage is the fact that Mai Sa Mai farmers grow litchi, which is a highly valued commodity at markets in Thailand and throughout Asia. Processing and export companies urge large-scale production. The majority of farmers from Mae Sa Mai sell their products at trade centres and consumer markets in Chiang Mai. Other options include selling crops to rural assemblers who come to the village, selling crops to retailers with large trucks along the national highway between Chiang Mai and Fang (located about seventy kilometres west of Chiang Rai), and hiring a transport company to send crops such as litchi directly to Bangkok. A few villagers also drive their produce themselves directly to central markets in Bangkok, particularly if they can rely on close kin networks for support in accommodation and market information in the capital.

Marketing in Chiang Mai includes several options. Hmong villagers either go to the central Muang Mai market where they sell their crops to either retailers or individual consumers. Others drive to the large flower market along the highway, where retailers wait with their 18-ton-trucks to drive crops to Bangkok. Another option is to rent a parking space for thirty baht per day in one of the trading halls run by lowland Thai businessmen. There crops are sold directly from the Hmong pickup trucks, either in quantity to retailers or in small amounts to individual consumers. Thai retailers function either as middlemen who sell the crops to large-scale traders, drive the produce themselves to markets in other districts and provinces, or sell the crops to national or international contract companies.

According to personal observations and activity protocols from Mae Sa Mai and Ban Phui, the economic role of women also differs between the two villages. Women from Ban Phui either stay at home to care for the children and the household or accompany their husbands to the fields and the markets. However, they never undertake an economic activity on their own, and would never market their crops without their husbands present. This is different for women in Mae Sa Mai, who drive to trade centres and markets in Chiang Mai to sell agricultural products by themselves, accompanied by male relatives other than their husbands. Couples from Mae Sa Mai do not always work together like in Ban Phui. Instead, wives may also help on fields of lineage relatives while husbands and teenage children work on their own fields. On the one hand, women in Mae Sa Mai have the freedom to move about and decide more freely than women in Ban Phui. But they also have to assume more economic responsibility and contribute more to the household's income by working on other people's fields or going to the markets in Chiang Mai.

Some Hmong villagers from Mae Sa Mai and Ban Phui also work as retailers themselves. They sell agricultural products from remote Hmong settlements where most people do not own cars and are unable to market their produce on a large scale on their own. Some local Hmong assemblers also employ villagers in remote areas to grow certain cash crops on a contract basis, which they later sell in Chiang Mai or to retailers along the highways. The Hmong from Ban Phui also market agricultural products from remote Karen villages because fewer Karen farmers in the region own cars, and they have less contact to retailers from the lowlands. However, the number of Hmong retailers at the wholesale markets in Chiang Mai remains low due to high rents for stalls, which are also difficult to obtain.

Even though the Hmong have widespread clan networks throughout Thailand, the villagers in the study do not maintain the extensive trading networks that would allow them to receive better prices at lowland markets. In Mae Sa Mai, only five people from the Xiong clan maintain trading offices in Chiang Mai and Bangkok. Villagers, mostly Xiong, sell their agricultural produce to these offices. In Ban Phui, only one villager owns a similar business. Xauv Yam Thoj, a forty-two year old man from Mae Sa Mai, explained in an interview that some Hmong have already attempted self-marketing strategies in Chiang Mai and even in Bangkok, but failed due to large input costs and the powerful and well-organised competition from Thai retailers. These established retailers are able to keep their own costs low thanks to personal networks at lowland markets. Hmong farmers cannot compete with these large-scale networks and thus remain dependent on marketing structures under outside control. Hmong networks are too small in comparison to powerful Thai and international trading associations (cf. Dessaint and Dessaint 1992: 107).

During interviews on this topic, I asked why widespread Hmong networks were not used to exchange information on market prices in the same manner that they are employed to disseminate knowledge of new crops. I was informed that this kind of communication takes place only in a very informal and unstructured manner (see also Badenoch 2004: 14). Xauv Yam Thoj from Mae Sa Mai explained the lack of exchange of market price information and the lack of economic cooperation by citing the importance of clan networks. He argued that reciprocal clan networks should not be endangered by economic activities in which Hmong farmers would act in direct competition with each other (Source: field interview, H-C-MSM 21; see also Durrenberger and Tannenbaum 1990: 98). Exchanging information about the cultivation of certain crops to enable the farmers to act more independently of agricultural inputs from the outside is considered unacceptable. Structured exchange of market prices and even marketing cooperation is regarded as potentially harmful to good clan relations, for example, if one farmer obtains higher profits than another farmer with whom he had cooperated. Thus Hmong men strive for maximum independence, both from outside influence as well as from other Hmong. As was the case in the era of opium poppy cultivation, nuclear families still form the most important economic unit in modern Hmong agriculture. Each family acts on its own behalf and does not endanger unity via its economic activities, but instead supports the important overall social and religious structures. Economic activities and profits are supposed to sustain important kin networks and good relations to supernatural agents of the Otherworld, not endanger them. At the same time, kin networks and spirits are expected to enhance the wealth of individuals and society.

Further economic activities

Labour

Traditionally, Hmong households supplied their own labour, exchanged labour with other households or hired labour from other ethnic groups, but Hmong never engaged in wage labour themselves (Kunstadter 2000: 180). Villagers interviewed agreed that this is largely still true today: Hmong work their own fields, exchange labour with kin on a monetary or reciprocal basis, engage in wage labour for other Hmong (and sometimes for lowland Thai) while refusing to work for other ethnic mountain groups such as the Karen and Lua' (see also Dessaint and Dessaint 1992: 99-100). Hmong villagers work for economic success, but are not willing to give up too much self-determination. Hmong thus prefer to work for each other rather than for members of other groups. Working for Thai lowlanders is considered acceptable because the Thai have acquired an economic standard for which many Hmong strive. However, it is not acceptable to work for other groups such as the Karen, who are regarded as economically "inferior". This behaviour also serves to maintain a strong Hmong group within Thailand. It is acceptable for the Karen to work for the Hmong and submit to Hmong authority while the reverse is not considered acceptable. The Hmong strive to maintain clear boundaries with other mountain groups to preserve their identity and culture and to constitute a "place of their own" in the mountainous areas.

In addition to hiring seasonal workers from other groups, the Hmong also help each other on their cash crop fields in the mountains and their leased paddy fields in the lowlands during work peaks associated with planting and harvesting. In most cases, people of the same lineage assist each other either on a reciprocal or monetary basis. As I described above, sometimes members of a single household are paid for labour when they work on fields belonging to one of the household's independent farm units. Teenagers who do not attend school are also employed and involved in the reciprocal network of labour exchange. Labour of close kin is paid for when the needed help exceeds what the nuclear family can return to its closest relatives. While work on the fields is exchanged on both a monetary and reciprocal basis, assistance during rituals and celebrations is provided along terms of reciprocity only. Men assist each other in carrying out rituals and killing sacrificial animals. Women help each other with the preparation of food. Only the wife of the host then serves this food to the men attending a ritual.

Only Hmong men, either on a daily or a monthly contract basis, carry out wage labour for Thai employers. In my research sites, long-term employment was non-existent apart from a few men from Mae Sa Mai who worked for the nearby Queen Botanical Garden as plant and herb specialists for four to five years. However, even these men were not employed on a long-term contract basis, but rather were paid by day. Other jobs for Mae Sa

Mai villagers include day labour for Thai road construction companies, promotion of fertilizers and hybrid seeds for Thai and international companies, work on litchi fields for retailers who have bought the harvest, and work for the FORRU nursery in the village. In Ban Phui, job opportunities are limited because of the village's remoteness, and the majority of villagers only work their own fields. In Mae Sa Mai, when men engage in wage labour, women take over most of the household and farm work. Men only take off from their paid occupation to attend important rituals or to help their wives with planting, weeding and harvesting during agricultural work peaks.

Souvenir fever

In the 1970s, the Hmong also began to sell souvenirs in more distant locations in other provinces in Thailand. Mae Sa Mai villagers travelled to many locations, including Bangkok, Phatpong, Nonthaburi, Isaan and Koh Samui, to sell souvenirs to tourists and local Thai. At first, handicrafts made by Hmong refugees living in camps along the Thai-Lao border were sold. After the camps were closed and the refugees dispersed in the 1990s, the Hmong began to sell souvenirs purchased from Burmese immigrants (see also Leepreecha 2001: 41). People from Mae Sa Mai speak of a "souvenir fever" that "raged" among villagers from the mid-1970s until the mid-1980s. Many Hmong believed they had found a profitable business that could generate income outside from agriculture. Hmong cultivation changed greatly around that time, and was extremely uncertain because of the ban on poppy cultivation and swidden agriculture and the increasing land shortage.

In the mid 1970s, villagers from Mae Sa Mai became increasingly involved in the souvenir business at the Chiang Mai Night Market, like people from neighbouring Hmong communities. The Night Market takes place each evening from six p.m. to midnight along one of Chiang Mai's main roads in the city centre. Each evening, a great number of stalls are set up along the road offering commodities ranging from fake Levi's jeans, illegally copied music compact discs, and traditional tourist souvenirs including local spice assortments, candles, jewelry, and batik sarongs. Many small market stalls are still run by the Hmong today. Larger stalls are owned by Thai, and increasingly Akha walk around the market with vendor trays. People of other ethnic groups still do not sell at the Night Market. Most customers are international tourists who use Chiang Mai as a starting point for "hilltribe trekking adventures" in the Golden Triangle, which are promoted by many Thai travel agencies in town.

Once a few Hmong had ventured to new places to sell souvenirs, relatives followed and took advantage of existing Hmong support structures. For example, members of the Yang clan of Doi Pui started their souvenir business in Bangkok at the end of the 1970s. Yang clan members from Mae Sa Mai followed and were supported by their kin. These clan networks exist in Bangkok today. Yang clan members from Doi Pui and Mae Sa Mai still sell souvenirs in Bangkok on the big Chatuchak weekend market, on Silom Road, in Chinatown, in the main tourist destinations in Southern Thailand such as Koh Samui and Phuket. In Bangkok, the Hmong know where their kin usually set up their makeshift stalls along the roads and at the markets, and know that they can always rely on their help in case of need. Villagers join to rent small rooms that house five or more persons in Bangkok and other tourist centres. Souvenir articles bought from Burmese immigrants and handmade items such as carved soaps, story cloths, cushions, handbags and trousers with Hmong embroidery are sold. Many Hmong vendors spend most of the year in distant locations in an attempt to supplement their agricultural income. Even if they only return to Mae Sa Mai once a year, their social and ritual centre remains the village, not their "temporary" place of residence. They return to Mae Sa Mai for New Year and other special occasions, send remittances home, sometimes leave their children with grandparents or other kin, and continue to be regarded as full members of the household and village community. When they return to the mountain settlement, a shamanic ritual is usually held to insure their well-being and to welcome them home.

Yiv Xyooj, the daughter of one of the Mae Sa Mai shamans, recounted her life story, which reveals that even young children were involved in the souvenir fever. Her account also demonstrates that the souvenir business can generate a fairly good income and can permit alternative roles for women different from those under traditional agriculture. Nonetheless, her descriptions emphasise that the quality of life continues to be regarded as superior in the mountain village than in the lowlands, despite shortages of money:

" [...] I have three children, two daughters and one son. I get the three-month injection at Pong Yaeng because my husband and I do not have the money for more children. I got married when I was seventeen years old. I was the one who wanted to get married; my parents did not arrange the marriage. My husband is also from Mae Sa Mai. I met him in Bangkok when I was living there to sell souvenirs. [...] I did not finish fifth grade in the Mae Sa Mai school because I went to Bangkok to sell souvenirs with my father when I was thirteen years old. My mother did not go with us because she stayed in the village with my brothers and sisters. In Bangkok, we rented a small room together with other Hmong. For two years in Chinatown and then for two years on Silom Road, we sold dolls that we bought in Chiang Mai. I also sold souvenirs with my husband for about half a year, but then we returned to the village because my husband prefers to work in the fields over selling souvenirs. [...] I liked selling souvenirs because I could sell well; I earned 1.000 baht per day but my husband only made 100 baht per day. [...] I think if you do good business in Bangkok, then the city is good. But life in Mae Sa Mai is better even though there is no money here. When I lived in Bangkok, I only met people from Mae Sa Mai; I did not know any Thai. The money I earned, I sent home to the village to support my family. [...] Now I am back in the village, and my husband and I work in the fields a lot, we only stay at home a little. We grow cabbage, lettuce, spring onion, carrot, and sweet salad. My husband is the one who makes all the decisions, I only work in the fields." (Source: field interview, H-SNI-MSM 6)

The account shows that in Mae Sa Mai, female roles depart from the traditional role of women as wives who are economically inferior and socially obedient to their husbands. Women are also involved in the production and marketing of commodities. Women sell souvenirs at the Night Market in Chiang Mai and at the Mae Sa Elephant camp, a tourist attraction located about fourteen kilometres from the village on the main road to Chiang Mai. Hmong women in nearby Mae Rim also sew long skirts from black cloth, which are then decorated by Mae Sa Mai women with kauri, silver buttons, small bells and snippets of traditional Karen fabric. These skirts are sold by Hmong villagers from Mae Rim at the Chatuchak weekend market in Bangkok. At this market, there is one alley filled with Hmong shops where the Hmong social network supports spatially widespread economic activities.

Villagers from Ban Phui were not involved in the souvenir fever, nor do they sell at the Chiang Mai Night Market. This is due to several reasons. First, Ban Phui is quite far away from Chiang Mai, and its daily activities are largely centred in the Mae Chaem area. Second, the village's fields are still large enough and fertile enough to support all residents, even though villagers complain about the scarcity of land. For this reason, alternate income activities are less urgent than in Mae Sa Mai. Third, because of its focus on agriculture, socio-cultural structures and norms in Ban Phui remain more "traditional". Ban Phui villagers are still unable to imagine a life apart from farming in favour of economic activities that would entail daily interaction (also by Hmong women) with strangers and foreigners. However, moral norms and economic beliefs available to Ban Phui children began to change since boys and girls have started attending schools in Mae Chaem and other lowland cities. Parents understand that their children need to be given the opportunity to work outside the village and apart from agriculture since land resources will continue to degrade and diminish in the future.

Small-scale activities

Many Hmong villagers from Mae Sa Mai and Ban Phui also undertake a variety of small-scale activities to support the household. Animal husbandry is not a significant source of household income. Instead chickens, pigs and ducks are raised largely for ritual purposes and for special festivities like a child's return home from boarding school during vacation. Meat for everyday use is either purchased at lowland markets or in small village shops. Chicken eggs are not collected for consumption, but are left to hatch or used in shamanic curing rituals and other ceremonies. Animal fodder, including corn, vegetables of inferior quality, and banana trunks from the forest, is collected and prepared by women as part of their daily household chores. None of the households examined in Mae Sa Mai or Ban Phui engages in animal husbandry as an independent farm activity. In the past, Hmong people raised horses and cows, although this is no longer practiced in the villages studied. Horses have been replaced by pickup trucks. Cattle traditionally played an important role for the Hmong since they were a means of both economic and spiritual security. Cattle were a form of wealth that could be sold in times of need. Cows are still the main sacrificial animal in mortuary rites. It is important that the dead be accompanied by a herd of cows into the land of the dead to facilitate rebirth. Sacrificial cows are bought from Thai lowland farmers. In Mae Sa Mai, no farmer owns horses or cows. In Ban Phui, no resident raises horses, although six farmers own between three and thirty cows each. Cows are no longer raised on a large scale because village land is either needed for cultivation or is under protection.

Men earn additional income by the production of brooms from "elephant grass" (*pennisetum purureum schum*) and through transportation services provided to villagers who need to reach the city or transport commodities to the markets. A few men still engage in the traditional Hmong crafts of blacksmithing and silver smithing. Blacksmiths produce machetes of all shapes and sizes, which are used for household and agricultural work and are worn by men as a sign of their masculinity and Hmong identity. Silversmiths produce the typical Hmong necklaces, earrings and bracelets that are worn during the Hmong New Year and are an important sign of wealth. A single, massive silver necklace with elaborate pendants in the front and the back, up to 500 grams in weight, can cost up to 7.000 baht.

Most women regard their laborious craft of stitching and embroidering not as an economic activity but as a spare time activity to which they devote at least one to two hours per day. Traditional Hmong dresses are made to provide family members each Hmong New Year with elaborate and new Hmong clothes, which are an important sign of Hmong identity and wealth. Immediately following each Hmong New Year, new cloth is bought at the Chinese shop in Chiang Mai for sewing and embroidering new clothes for the next New Year celebration twelve months in the future. Plaited skirts, which involve painstaking embroidery of up to eight metres of material, may take two years to make.

Most of the small-scale activities do not generate substantial income for the households but are important in other ways. For example, in addition to their regular household and fieldwork, many women spend a considerable amount of time each day feeding animals and embroidering clothing. These activities contribute to the household in religious and social rather than financial form. Animal husbandry is important for the provision of sacrificial animals for the large number of rituals. Most Hmong prefer to sacrifice animals they have raised since they are believed to taste better than animals from markets raised at fattening units. Self-raised animals are thus a more valuable commodity to offer to the ancestors and other spirits than bought ones. Hand stitched and embroidered traditional Hmong clothes are a symbol of cultural identity handed down from one generation to the next. Stitching patterns vary from family to family and contain elements of Hmong history, even though many meanings in the patterns have been lost over the past decades, if they ever existed. Activities such as blacksmithing and silversmithing are of both economic and socio-cultural value, since their products are linked to Hmong identity and group specific status symbols.

Another economic activity that must be mentioned here even though its scope is difficult to estimate is illegal trafficking in metamphetamines and heroin. The survey data in both villages studied include some households whose expenses are much higher than their official earnings; the presence of material objects such as new pickup trucks and electronic devices suggests that these households had not revealed the full extent of their income. According to many Hmong informants and local NGO workers, there continues to be some drug trafficking in many Hmong villages and settlements of other ethnic groups in northern Thailand. This illegal activity distorts economic survey data to an unknown extent.

Household income and expenditures

Survey interviews demonstrate the difficulty of ascertaining exact figures of household income and expenditures (see also Michaud 1997: 223). Hmong interviewees had different categories and priorities than I had as an ethnographer interested in precise figures. Villagers are interested mainly in profits and market prices for their products, while I aimed to acquire as detailed and precise information as possible about *all* variables, including expenditures, labour force investments, and sources of income throughout the year. Most informants only cared whether profits sufficed to sustain the family over the next few weeks and months. Vaab Kwv, a forty-year-old woman from Ban Phui, stated in an interview:

> "We always spend what we earn. After we have earned some money by selling one of our harvests, we have to pay back loans. Then there is only little left for our families. We can never save money. Sometimes we get good profits but then we have to pay for hospital costs or someone dies in the family and all money is spent on the mortuary rites. Or our cars break down and we have to buy a new one. A used pick-up truck costs at least 140.000 baht. It is a constant struggle. As soon as we get some money, it is spent." (Source: field interview, H-C-BP 15)

Lack of liquidity is an immense problem in the Hmong farming system, as many informants complained in survey interviews. Most households immediately spend what they have earned on a harvest by repaying loans, covering daily costs, and paying for extra costs such as hospitals or rituals. Only a few households who have no extra expenses such as medicinal treatment and expensive rituals are able to accumulate some bank savings. Survey data shows that the mean of household income from agriculture and labour in Mae Sa Mai is 88.333 baht per household for the year 2000 and at 88.886 for 2001. In Ban Phui, the mean income for households is higher at 157.500 for the year 2000 and at 134.705 for 2001. In Mae Sa Mai, the lowest income was minus 21.000 baht, and the highest was 332.000 baht. In Ban Phui, the lowest income was minus 5.800 baht and the highest 280.000 baht. As mentioned above, these figures must be regarded as rough estimates acquired during survey interviews. Unfortunately, economic household data is not detailed enough to calculate all the variable costs that should be deducted from revenues to illuminate the gross margins of the households surveyed. The data nonetheless demonstrates that revenues vary greatly and are higher in Ban Phui overall than in Mae Sa Mai in spite of the latter village's better access to markets. However, this advantage is apparently minimised by the lack of land resources and the erosion of soil fertility and by unstable yields from perennials.

The agro-economist Nicole Schoenleber, who worked for the Thai-German "Uplands Program", devoted four months to a quantitative study of land use systems in the Mae Sa area. By means of a standardised questionnaire, she interviewed twenty-one households in Nong Hoi and thirteen residential units in Buak Chan. Both settlements are Hmong villages located near Mae Sa Mai. Interview data was processed for gross margin calculation to analyse farm income. The data cited in the figure below agrees with my own findings. In particular, profits can vary greatly between the households within a single village. Also, revenues correlate only roughly to the amount of land under cultivation because harvests differ depending on weather conditions, attacks by parasites, and the location, fertility and soil quality of the fields. In addition, income is largely subject to market prices that fluctuate greatly.

Figure 12: Gross margin calculation for two Hmong villages near Chiang Mai

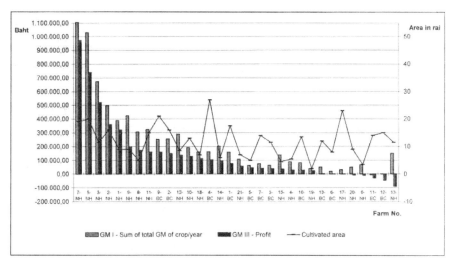

Source: Schoenleber 2002: 54; GMI = revenues of crop production, GM III: profit after deduction of variable and fixed costs

According to the expenditure data, many of the households surveyed spend most of their income on rituals, school education of the children, vehicles and machines, agricultural inputs, house-building/repair, medical treatment, and last but not least on food and clothes. Hmong rituals can be very cost intensive, especially due to the fact that they are performed on a regular basis. In most of the smaller rituals one to two chickens, rice, whiskey, paper money, and incense sticks are offered which cost about 300 baht in total. Shamanistic rituals include 150 to 200 baht as payment for the shaman, and 200 to 400 baht for several chickens, and circa 600 baht for a pig. The most expensive yearly ritual is the New Year Celebration lasting several days during which elaborately and newly made costumes are worn by the whole family (for about 3.000 baht per costume). Pigs, rice, whiskey, beer, paper money, incense sticks, and additional food for guests can amount to 10.000 baht per household. Daylong mortuary rituals are the most costly rituals of the Hmong during which hundreds of people are hosted and several oxen sacrificed on the last day. Expenses can add up to 100.000 baht.

Educational expenses for children place a further burden on the household economy. Traditional Hmong society was marked by the notable absence of any formal education system and high rates of illiteracy. This can also be seen by the fact that most people in my study sites over thirty years of age did not attend secondary school and can read and write only with difficulty. This has changed; today most parents value formal education and send their children to school as long as possible (cf. Yang Dao 1993: 83, 98-99). About one-fifth of annual household income is spent on the children's education. Expenses for education depend, of course, on the age of the child and the location of the school. They generally include a daily allowance of several baht, transportation costs, room and board, money for books, and sometimes also school fees. Of the twenty-nine households surveyed in Mae Sa Mai, twenty living units send some of their children to schools in the lowlands. Of the twenty households interviewed in Ban Phui, only six do so. Again, this discrepancy can be explained by the fact that arable land is still comparatively plentiful in the Ban Phui area, and its residents are not equally compelled to search for alternative non-farming occupations, as are the residents of Mae Sa Mai. Nevertheless, Ban Phui residents also value formal education as a viable perspective for the future. As the deputy of Ban Phui, who is thirty-nine years old, said about the education of his children:

> "Before we die we have to see that our children can make a living outside of agriculture. There will not be enough land for everyone in the future, so we must ensure that our children will be able to earn money with other activities than farming. In my generation we have already lost part of our cultural knowledge; when our children go to the lowlands to work there we will lose even more. But we also have to see that we survive." (Source: field interview, H-SNI-BP 22)

Most parents try to send their children to free lowlands schools like missionary schools, the temple schools, and the schools run by the Social Welfare Department. These schools can be located as far as a couple hundred kilometres away from the mountain villages, so parents have to cover transportation costs and take off work to drive their children to the schools and retrieve them for the holidays.

A considerable part of a household's income is also spent on food. At least half of daily meals contain foodstuffs bought in stores. A mean of sixty baht per household per day is spent in the small village stores where women buy fresh meat, vegetables and snacks for the children. Of course, these numbers can vary and depend on the size of a residential unit. Generally households that have just harvested and marketed crops or who have money at their disposal supplement their daily meals with pork and other foodstuffs bought at the village stores and the markets. Less affluent households cook their meals largely with forest products and "Hmong crops" grown alongside their cash crop fields. These crops are grown without the application of agricultural chemicals for home consumption.

In addition to the money spent at small shops owned by Hmong or Thai, most of the money earned by villagers is spent *outside* the mountain settlements in the lowlands. Cars, motorcycles and other commodities like sprayers, sewing machines, televisions and stereo are bought (usually on credit with monthly rates) at stores in Chiang Mai (MSM) or Mae Chaem/Chom Thong (BP). To give an example, a new eighty cubic centimetre-motorbike costs about 26.000 baht, while a used Toyota pickup costs between 140.000 to 200.000 baht and more. Since the felling of trees is prohibited in the forest protection areas, building materials also have to be bought in the lowlands unless villagers risk being caught illegally cutting wood. Since Ban Phui villagers are more affluent than residents from Mae Sa Mai, they can spend more money on house construction. In Ban Phui, between 2.000 and 300.000 baht (mean value: 102.105 baht) is spent on houses that are up to fifteen years old (mean value: 5.1 years). Houses in Mae Sa Mai are generally older, and were built up to thirty-two years ago (mean value: 12.5 years). They also cost less, with a minimum cost of 5.000 baht and a maximum cost of 200.000 baht (mean value: 54.160 baht). The survey again demonstrates that Mae Sa Mai and Ban Phui households have highly variable incomes and funds available to purchase daily commodities.

Importance of material wealth and traditional structures

Accumulating wealth improves the living standard of a family and household and is a measure of devotion to past generations and family ancestors. Wealth is converted into status and social prestige by the acquisition of material objects and through the display of generosity towards the Hmong community during rituals. Striving for surplus and wealth thus remains an important objective of Hmong agricultural production. To pay for cost-intensive rituals, households sometimes sell their cars or unofficial land-use rights to fellow Hmong or Thai lowland residents. Hosting a great number of visitors during rituals is a social norm, and it is socially expected that Hmong will visit in large numbers the sometimes daylong festivities. For many people, this entails long distance travel and risks diminished yields when crops are neglected for a number of days. Loss of income also occurs when people cannot go about their business activities at Chiang Mai's Night Market or their work as day labourers. Also, people who are employed on a monthly basis risk losing their jobs when they need to take several days off work. Despite possible income losses, it is expected by kin that they stop working in order to be able to attend rituals.

Hmong economic dynamics are still anchored in the kinship structure, and power between the clans is based on a local equilibrium, as Jean Michaud notes in a statement about the integrity of Hmong culture and its ability to adapt economically while preserving important Hmong traditions:

> "They demonstrate that despite ongoing economic modernisation in Ban Suay, villagers appear determined to maintain the political equilibrium of custom, which has shown considerable flexibility in adapting to new circumstances, or at the very least, to preserve a

system of traditional local authority parallel to that which prevails outside the village. Traditional beliefs are tenacious (persistent), cultural practices persistent, social life continues to be modelled on ancestral ways and inter-Hmong marriage remains the preference. In fact, enforced dependence on the market economy presently appears to be confined within well circumscribed limits, and does not seem to interfere directly with Hmong tradition." (1997: 231)

Wealth, demonstrated by the acquisition of a nice car or a house, and proper social and religious behaviour and knowledge about Hmong culture is the path to obtaining a good reputation, social prestige and influence in the Hmong society. Although in the past, most Hmong men were supposed to know about all aspects of Hmong culture, and especially Hmong rituals, nowadays men do not have the time, energy and desire to learn everything. Instead, they specialise in some parts of knowledge, and acquire some of their status through material success and the acquisition of signs of wealth like cars, mobile phones and attractive homes.

Summary

The economic activities pursued by the Hmong after the introduction of radical changes to their agricultural system are described above in detail. An analysis of these activities and potentials offers insight into economic structures and activities that constitute an important part of Hmong cultural spatiality. It reveals the manner in which the Hmong position themselves socio-economically in contrast to other mountain groups, to Thai lowland society, and to the outside world. I also examined which potentials and "niches" were exploited, and which opportunities were ignored, and why. After a short summary of the changes that Hmong economy underwent in the past decades, these potentials and their socio-cultural meanings were discussed.

Before the replacement of opium poppy cultivation and the ban on swidden agriculture, traditional Hmong economy was characterised by the cultivation of three major crops: opium poppy, dry rice, and maize. Minor crops such as local varieties of peach, beans, green leaf vegetables and hemp were grown at the sides of the fields in the forest. Extensive swiddening resulted in a constant move to new areas of cultivation in the search for new arable land. Good profits from opium poppy cultivation and characteristics of the crop such as a high value-to-weight ratio, its low perishability, and its high cash value facilitated continuous migrations throughout northern Thailand. Traditional Hmong semi-sedentary agriculture was based on people and rather than land and was thus characterised by a low emotional attachment to a specific territory. Instead of preserving land and other natural resources for future use, Hmong cultivation included large areas within the Hmong Mountains and movement to new land when the previous soils were degraded. As such, Hmong agriculture was a very land-extensive system. Large areas were also needed to sustain families with many children, which in return were necessary for labour intensive poppy cultivation. Population movement was the traditional Hmong solution to balance population and land resources while allowing production, wealth and population to increase.

The substitution of opium poppy cultivation and of swidden agriculture by modern forms of farming, including the planting of market oriented cash crops and the use of agricultural chemicals, was promoted and facilitated by national and international agencies. The extension work resulted in a drastic change in Hmong cultivation methods and in an intensified connection of Hmong economy to national and international markets and its fluctuating demands and prices. In comparison with other mountain groups, the Hmong seem to have better adapted to the change from subsistence to commercial agriculture, perhaps because they had been experienced in marketing and selling opium for more than a century. The Hmong experiment with new crops, taking in information and developing their own system of planting and marketing. Due to new crops and new agricultural techniques, less labour and land is needed. The main crops grown by Hmong farmers can change from season to season, from location to location. Another effect of the economic changes among the Hmong is an enhanced economic and emotional attachment to the land under cultivation. This is due to the fact that migration is no longer an option and that investments in crops such as perennials install the Hmong on a long-term basis in one settlement area.

Due to a growing land scarcity in northern Thailand, family planning has become more popular among the Hmong, who realise that the future of their children cannot be based on mountain agriculture but rather on education and employment in the lowlands. A number of Hmong already work for Thai traders, institutions and lowland companies. Hmong work for Thai since they are regarded as having an equal or higher socio-economic status. However, many Hmong still claim that they would never work for people of other ethnic mountain groups and uphold clear interethnic boundaries. They do not wish to be too dependent on other mountain groups, although they are willing to employ Karen and Shan and even learning their languages for their own benefit. Potential economic cooperation and employment linked to outside groups such as the Thai and international employers are considered acceptable as long as these activities do not make the Hmong too dependent on "outsiders". Employment in the lowlands is seen as a future option for the children, who are encouraged to obtain the formal education, which their parents did not. Because of the lack of formal training and the difficult access to employment in the lowlands, a number of Hmong, especially the villagers of Mae Sa Mai have found alternative, non-farming activities. These activities are mainly located in the souvenir business and make use of the extensive Hmong networks. Villagers from Ban Phui, where land is still sufficient, look for alternative income by either cultivating Karen fields in addition to their own or by functioning as retailers for Karen crops. The precise extent of drug trafficking as an extra source of household income remains unclear for both villages.

Even though Hmong economy is characterised by a high rate of transition and adaptability to new circumstances, typical Hmong aspects are nonetheless retained as an expression of a special Hmong identity that is consciously maintained in distinction from other groups. "Traditional"

Hmong crops are still cultivated for special occasions and to preserve Hmong "cultural heritage". Agriculture and Hmong identity are intimately linked, since cultivating the mountain fields is still seen as the most important way to secure the Hmong's economic and socio-cultural survival. Hmong assign a high socio-cultural value to their fields, and diligence in farming is still a highly valued norm, even though a number of villagers already earn their income from activities other than agriculture.

Striving for surplus and wealth remains an important objective of Hmong agricultural production. It sustains Hmong life in the mountains, ensures a "proper" and worthy appreciation of ancestral and other spirits, and enables the maintenance of clan networks by means of large celebrations visited by large numbers of local and distant kin. Roland Mischung (1990: 310) also believes that "outside" economic activities have a key function of sustaining the Hmong as a minority within the Thai majority society and maintaining the spiritually defined microcosm of the house, the village community, and the delocalised kin groups.

In the past decades, the dependence of the Hmong on the outside world and the socio-economic differences among the Hmong have increased. These developments parallel changes in local communities around the world as they adapt new technologies and become more connected to the international market system. The Hmong households employ varying and mixed strategies of survival. Many economic activities, even at a minutely small scale, are experimented with and attempted. Differences in income arise because of fluctuating market prices and as a result of innovation and diligence. Some farmers are more inventive and open to experimentation. This can result in high profits, for example when a farmer successfully attempts the cultivation of a new crop. Unlike other mountain groups in Thailand, the Hmong also pursue activities spatially delocalised from their home villages and accept long-term separation from their children, parents and village if economic activities like the cultivation of far-away mountain fields, the sale of souvenirs in Bangkok can earn a relatively good income.

In short, the Hmong in the villages studied try to secure their livelihoods through different income strategies that sustain their income while preserving core values of Hmong culture like respect for the ancestors and the maintenance of kinship structures (cf. Michaud 2004: 6). Not all decisions made in the Hmong economy thus appear "rational" from the outside. For example, the cultivation of paddy rice on leased lowland fields is often more cost and labour intensive than purchasing rice at lowland markets. Nonetheless, socio-cultural reasons, including the ideational meaning of self-grown rice and the fact that "it is more fun" to grow rice than to buy it, play an important role in the choice of certain economic activities. Decisions in local economies about commodities to be produced and activities to be followed always depend on social and cultural factors. Market-oriented competition over scarce resources and goods are not the only factor in small economies like that of the Hmong (cf. Rössler 1999: 145). Rather, balance with the religious sphere, the maintenance of extended Hmong clan networks, and a preference for actions connected to the Hmong - as a strategy of cultural survival in Thailand - also influence decisions and activities in the economic sector.

For example, during day-long Hmong rituals, the labour force is removed from agricultural production and made available to participate in these rituals and important networking events. People are aware of the fact that income is lost through these practices; at worst, entire yields may be lost when mortuary rites occur at harvest times. However, for many Hmong it is more important to engage in the rites to honour the ancestors and to insure that the *plig* of the dead is properly launched on its journey to its Chinese origins than to strive for economic success at these moments. For this reason, we cannot speak of "economic irrationality" in traditional production systems; instead, local belief systems must be taken into account (cf. Rössler 1999: 145). Marshall Sahlin's (1972) oft-criticised but nonetheless valuable analysis of domestic modes of production already attempted to explain reasons behind a so-called economic "underproduction" on the basis of socio-cultural factors. Traditional resource use systems mostly incorporate the belief in supernatural beings because spiritual quality is also regarded as a valued asset.

Hmong economic activities reveal a coexistence of tradition and modernity. Newly introduced economic activities still incorporate traditional religious and social values and normative models of action (cf. Géraud 1993: 401). It might even be argued that the transformed form of agriculture, which is now oriented towards national and international markets, has been instrumental in the reproduction of Hmong traditional social structure. Instead of leading to a de-structuration of the community, new forms of agriculture even ensure social cohesion; Hmong can be "modern" by means of their new economic activities and at the same time "traditional" in the socio-cultural domain by drawing on kin networks and religious spirituality.

The Hmong farmers recognise that they are not independent players on the national or world markets because they are not sufficiently diversified and lack the investment capital to gain positions of power. In addition, they depend mostly on lowland traders for the marketing of their crops and are subject to fluctuating prices. This perceived dependency on other agents within the national and international market economy enhances the need of Hmong minority society to constitute a spatiality that is determined and controlled by the Hmong themselves and that can exist in parallel to outside spheres. By choosing certain strategies and opting for certain economic potentials while ignoring others (like the formation of agricultural information networks), the two Hmong communities studied play an active role in their relation with the larger economic system. The Hmong integrate as best as possible in the large-scale market economy by cultivating and marketing diverse cash crops and working as labourers. They also chose to exploit economic niches open to them, like the souvenir business. These niches are intrinsically linked to the Hmong networks in Thailand and provide the Hmong with alternative economic activities that can exist independent of Thai and larger scale economic structures. Instead, they contribute to the constitution of Hmong spatiality that exists parallel to other groups and institutions.

10 Hmong Perceptions of the Environment and Spatial Orientation

As seen in the previous chapters, Hmong culture is characterised by a long history of movement to new territories as well as by an economy based on agriculture aimed at reaping maximum profits. F. G. Keen's has emphasised that Hmong economic organisation is based on people, not on land. According to Keen, who echoes many other scholars, the Hmong view land as an expendable commodity, not as a natural asset to be maintained for future generations. One of the questions this chapter seeks to answer is whether the relationship F.G. Keen described between the Hmong and their land has remained valid or whether it has changed along with the transformation of resource-use systems and settlement patterns. The ways in which a group relates to natural resources and the natural environment, as well as the ways in which people orient themselves in their natural habitat, can reveal aspects of their perception of their lifeworld and the meanings which they attach to it. Applying Gidden's structuration theory, perceptions and meanings of the environment then also have repercussions on modes of behaviour and actions conducted in the physical-material space.

For many years, literature on the Hmong questioned whether they had any attachment to their immediate environs whatsoever. A well-known Hmong proverb captures the interconnectedness between the Hmong and natural elements on the one hand, and the love of freedom on the other:

Lub ntuj yos noog lis.
(literally: World sky belong to birds.)
Lub roob yos hmoob lis.
(literally: Mountains belong to Hmong.)

Tub dleb yos tsem lis.
(literally: Water belong to fish.)

Translation:
The sky is for the birds,
the mountains are for the Hmong,
The rivers are for the fish.

A Hmong elder, fifty-eight years old, from Ban Phui discussed the proverb's meaning with me, explaining how the proverb shows freedom is just as important for the Hmong people as for birds that can fly freely in the sky and fish that can swim freely in the rivers. The "natural place" of the Hmong lies in the mountains, where they pursue a free and undisturbed life. Next to the mountains, the sky and rivers comprise important assets for the Hmong, who survive on what the mountains as well as the sky and rivers offer them. The Hmong believe both elements provide water and are inhabited by supernatural beings that can affect earthly life. The proverb stresses that the Hmong perceive themselves as "mountain people"; however, it does not clarify the ways in which they relate to their specific environment.

Because, inter alia, it secures economic existence, local people often imbue the environment with cultural meaning. Both the meaning and use of land and relations between the natural resources and social structure of communities contribute to a complex cultural spatiality (Lovell 1998a: 72). The environment always includes a cultural concept of the spatial constituted through cultural practice that, in turn, also has an impact on social practice (cf. Rössler 2003: 181, 212; Krauß 2001: 54; Lovell 1998: 11-18). In the sense of Bourdieu's structured structures, "landscape is implicated in people, and people in the landscape" (Gow 1995: 55). The local environment thus represents a lived space: it is both context and content, enacted and material (Rodman 1992: 650). It is known by means of movement through it, lived experiences, stories about past use and perception, and via the traces of people's movement and agency in it (Ingold 2000: 9). Along these lines, Barbara Bender asserts:

"Landscape is never passive. People engage with it, rework it, and contest it. It is part of the way in which identities are created and disputed, whether as individual, group or nation-state. Operating at the juncture of history and politics, social relations and cultural perceptions, landscape is a concept of high tension. It is also an area that forces the abandonment of conventional disciplinary boundaries and creates the potential for innovative cross-fertilization." (2003: 324)

Although the Hmong perceive themselves as "people of the mountains", their traditional forms of pioneer swiddening and intensive agricultural production have earned them the reputation of "resource depleters" who exploit rather than conserve their natural resources. Driving through the mountainous areas of northern Thailand seems to confirm this impression. Hmong villages are identifiable from far away: Settlement areas are still mostly characterised by far stretching mountainous cash crop fields and denuded hills. In contrast, Karen villages are mostly surrounded by dense secondary forest and comparably small areas of land are farmed in the vicinity of these villages.

This chapter examines the *de facto* relationships of Hmong at my research sites with their environment and natural resources. In my previous chapter, I discussed the use of natural resources and aspects of Hmong action within their environments. Here, I address the questions of how the Hmong perceive of the immediate geographical space around them and what meanings they assign to their territory of settlement. It is also important to assess how sedentarisation has affected the manner in which the Hmong interact with their land and manage natural resources. Last but not least, for a better understanding of a group's spatiality it is also important to understand how the Hmong orientate themselves in their environment. Do they have special markers or are they not anchored to the landscapes of their settlement areas in any way? Answering these questions sheds more light on Hmong cultural spatiality because, as Tim Ingold (2000: 9) has noted, "ways of acting in the environment are also ways of perceiving it".

In ecological anthropology, environmental as well as cultural determinism belong to paradigms of the past (cf. Ellen 1996: 17; Dickens 1992: 15). It has long been acknowledged that – next to environment and culture – other aspects, like context or history, influence the use of natural resources and perception of environments. Social and environmental variables interact in subtle and complex ways and disentangling the relationships between them requires enormous care (Ellen 1979: 8). Every environment offers multiple opportunities, while simultaneously imposing constraints for perceptions and actions within it. No environment or culture is simple, uniform, or static, but each can encompass considerable complexity, diversity, and dynamism. This variability in space and time within and among cultures and their ecosystems, as well as the ways in which they interact with and influence each other, now comprise the heart of ecological anthropology.[122] The Hmong communities are a useful example for this variability and dynamic interaction between culture and environment.

As Tim Ingold (2000: 9) indicates, to get to the bottom of people's own perceptions of the world, we need to overcome the division between the natural real and the culturally imagined. It is beyond the scope of this chapter and book to explain the full extent of the interaction and relation of Hmong culture with its ecosystems. Instead, I place emphasis on the ways in which the Hmong people at my research sites relate practically and interact with their environment. This chapter also explains how this relation has changed within the past decades along with altered circumstances. It goes

---

[122] In the 1990s, cultural ecology and ecological anthropology was increasingly applied to practical environmental problems and issues, given the continuing urgency of environmental problems. As a result, a specialisation called "environmental anthropology" has gradually emerged. In contrast to other approaches within ecological anthropology, it tends to be far more inclusive, diverse, interdisciplinary, dependent on research teams, comparative, and applied. Despite the shift in scope, there are still numerous continuities in this new form of ecological anthropology that have always been at the centre of attention in cultural ecology, including the emphasis on local communities, culture, ecosystems, systems analysis, process, change, and history (see e.g. Crumley 2001; Molnar and Molnar 2000; Townsend 2000; Little 1999).

without saying that factors such as the ban on opium poppy and swidden cultivation, the process of sedentarisation, the impact of national and international agencies, newly introduced agricultural techniques, the improvement of the northern Thai infrastructure, the declaration of protection areas by the state, and growing scarcity of fertile lands, as well as the increased integration of Hmong economy into the market economy have all affected how the Hmong interact in their environment and relate to their natural resources.[123]

Traditional relation to the landscape and natural phenomena

As we have seen in the chapter on Hmong religion, the Hmong perceive their landscape as teeming with entities that range from a hazy idea of supernatural energy to clearly visualised and named spirits. Each mountain, river, rock, stone, tree, or field, has some supernatural "quality", as do animals, birds, fish, insects, humans, and even artefacts like stools, doors and hearths. As in many other local cultures, the natural and supernatural do not form separate domains, but rather parts of a unified system of Hmong knowledge (see also Ellen 1996: 16).

In particular, the Hmong conceptually divide the landscape outside the villages into constituent entities credited with their own ongoing forms of being. This can be seen, for example, in rules about how to deal with certain natural places that the Hmong view as the domains of other creatures. Hence, it is considered wrong for menstruating women to "pollute" a river by washing in it, but quite permissible to remove water from the river and then wash in it. It is not water as a substance that is pollutable, but the river as an entity, which belongs to the evil and powerful dragon *Zaj*. Or to give other examples, if people pass by a cave without making an offering to the "cave spirit", they might be hit by him and, as a result, driven mad. People also believe that they can get rashes, stomachaches and headaches from the

---

[123] See also Tim Ingold (1979: 283-289) on cultural adaptation to ecological change.

"spirit of termites" if they disturb a termites' nest. Termites are considered very dangerous for the total of Hmong culture, and people therefore try to avoid these insects at all costs. People can only guard against these various spirits connected to multiple natural phenomena and the "wild" sphere outside the villages by (a) avoiding certain locations, (b) not "disturbing" certain places through forbidden actions, and (c) making offerings and speaking prayers to soothe the *dab*. For instance, when I walked through the environs of the villages, I always noticed burnt incense sticks, rice or other offerings placed at certain places such as large rocks, landmarks or watersources. These document the widespread belief in supernatural entities and their connection to certain locations in the Hmong landscape.

Besides seeing places as connected to spiritual beings, the Hmong also perceive the landscape as marked by the ancestors' graves, which are located in geomantically correct places. They extend across the whole of northern Thailand, since people have died in the course of the migrations. These graves keep the memory of both the ancestors and former settlement areas alive. The migration history of a lineage is recollected and passed on to the younger generation when the Hmong visit graves in the forest and mountain sites once a year in April to pay respect to their families' forefathers. Especially in the past, geomantic beliefs and practices helped the Hmong to anchor themselves in a mountainous landscape – the typical landscape of the Hmong – that may have even been unknown to them. Geomantic rules guided Hmong people's behaviour and thus helped them in their processes of place making in a foreign area.

In general, the geographical landscape serves as an idiom for the maintenance of personal memories and religious, genealogical, historical, or geomantic information. As such, landscape is an important mnemonic device for maintaining social relationships in general and the history of Hmong migration, settlement and cultivation within Thailand in particular. At the same time, it serves to establish the rights of Hmong communities to exploit the resources of a given area even when legal land titles do not exist. Apart from the fact that the Hmong connect natural phenomena to spiritual beings and honour certain places because of their relation to ancestors, the relationship between the Hmong people and their land is a generalised one (cf. Culas 2000: 42). Thus, Hmong people do not have specific Hmong names for features of their settlement areas or for their villages. As my "teacher" Vaam Zeej from Mae Sa Mai explained, "The Hmong think big. They do not need names for rivers or places. They only think of the mountains." (Source: field interview, H-LB-67)

In contrast to the Karen people, who have Karen names for both their villages and places around their settlements like river bends, trees, large rocks or fields in the forest, the Hmong have given no particular names to the area around the villages studied. In the vicinity of Mae Sa Mai, an assembly of large rocks is located on one of the mountaintops. The Thai have named this place *Pha Gong* because a sound can be heard when the rocks are hit. The Hmong people say that *Pha Gong* mountain is a mythical landmark because the rocks resemble a shell, a turtle and the divination horns used for oracles. Furthermore, one of the rocks contains signs said to be the footprints of the god-like creature *Yawm Saub* and his wife *Puj*, the King and Queen of Heaven. From time to time, the Hmong hold rituals and offer sacrifices to the spirits of this place and to the deities. They believe it is a sacred place where one should not misbehave or utter bad words. Yet although the location is important to the Hmong people from Mae Sa Mai, they do not have a Hmong name for it, using the Thai one instead. Similarly, in Ban Phui, Nyaj Xeeb Yaj explained "the Hmong are not interested in giving small names to small areas because Hmong are only interested in big things" (Source: field interview, H-JB-78). Thai authorities therefore name villages. The name Mae Sa Mai, for example, is derived from the Mae Sa river nearby that runs through the Mae Sa valley. Many Hmong villages have the Thai appendix *kau* for "old" and *mai* for "new" if the Hmong have erected a new village in the vicinity of an old one. Holly Peters-Golden (2002: 82) reports that Hmong villages in Laos also lack specific Hmong designations, but are instead named by the Laotian authorities. Rather than using Hmong names for their settlement areas, the Hmong typically speak of

Hmoob ntshuab roob, the Hmong Mountains. The concept of the Hmong Mountains relates to the "big things" or "big mountains", as recurring expressions of my informants elucidate. The Hmong are not interested in naming small landmarks in the surroundings of their settlements because only the totality of Hmong villages and regions in the mountainous areas, within and outside Thailand, counts. Just as the Hmong consider it insufficient for two or three singular Hmong families to settle somewhere, they believe claiming only one or two areas, as Hmong is inadequate. For the Hmong people, only a large assembly of people in a large area can guarantee the survival of their culture and their relatively independent way of life.

Self-critique and dilemma of development

Most of the Hmong people are aware of the fact that they have a bad reputation as resource depleters and that scientists, state agencies and the Thai public have long criticised their ways of cultivation. And indeed, the Hmong have never been particularly protective of their natural environment. With no regard for sustainability, they took advantage of whatever an area's natural resources had to offer in terms of opportunities for subsistence crops and, more importantly, for cash crops to generate silver or cash income (Ovesen 1995: 63). If the natural resources of one area were depleted, people moved on to new cultivation areas. During my fieldwork, both older and younger Hmong often criticize this practice. For example, an eighty-eight-year old woman from Ban Phui, Laug Tsab, noted:

> "To protect the environment is quite difficult to do in practice. Hmong people have never learned how to do it. My generation did not do it, maybe your generation and the next generation can form groups and protect the environment better than we did. We believe in *dab*, but we cannot see them. And we also have to work and eat in the fields." (Source: field interview, H-E 34)

Many Hmong villagers see that they are now faced with a dilemma. Due to sedentarisation and protection laws that prohibit cutting new fields in the forests, they depend on the natural resources and fields they currently have at their disposal. It is clear that to some degree these resources must be managed sustainably if the Hmong want to conserve them for their children's use in the future. The villagers consequently face a problem shared by many small-scale farmers in developing countries: They need to exploit depletable resources that are the only directly productive capital to which they have access. At the same time, they need to conserve these assets in order to sustain their livelihoods for the future (cf. Coxhead and Jayasuriya: 2003: 16). Many Hmong farmers, men and women alike, know that the use of agricultural chemicals causes, *inter alia*, environmental problems. They also understand that their intensified use of arable farmland is beyond the level that can still be considered sustainable. Intensified land cultivation leads to an increase of environmental problems such as soil erosion, high level of residual toxins in the soil and nutrient leaching (cf. Chotichaipiboon 1997: 105). Increasing contamination of ground water due to excessive use of chemical fertilizers and pesticides in watershed areas further affects the availability and quality of water. For example, one watersource in Mae Sa Mai has already dried up due to overuse. As explained earlier, the Hmong conducted a ritual to appease *Zaj*, the owner of all water, and ask him for forgiveness and water.

To solve the dilemma of degrading natural resources, land shortage and parallel population growth, the Hmong people of the research areas place an increased emphasis on their children's education for future employment in the lowlands and on modern family planning methods to reduce the overall birth rate. Peter Kunstadter et al. (2001: 314) have ascertained that the Hmong population still grew by as much as five percent per year in the 1980s (cf. Kunstadter 1983: 24). The Hmong people recognise that they need to reduce these rates if they want to survive depending primarily on their land resources in the mountainous areas. As shown above, many women now employ contraception techniques or even get sterilised after giving birth to three to five children.

As further measures to tackle the degradation and diminution of natural resources, Hmong farmers in both villages studied have started to introduce protective measures on their fields. For example, to avoid soil erosion and nutrient loss during rainy season, terraces are built on steep slopes. Some people have even stopped cultivating steep slopes and permitted the afforestation organised by the village conservation groups. Planting hedgerows in mountainous fields protects against soil loss, particularly from steep areas cultivated with short-term crops. The Hmong also practice intercropping in order to cover empty soil. As mentioned earlier, two or more different crops are either planted at the same time in the same field or different crops are planted in alternating orders in one field. Besides avoiding soil erosion and degradation, some farmers opt to reduce their consumption of chemical fertilizer. People have begun to reuse chicken dung as fertilizer. When I wondered about the bad smell near a Nyaj Xeeb's field hut in Ban Phui, he explained, it is because "we do not move anymore". The Hmong purchase the chicken dung from Thai traders for 100 baht per fifty kilogram sack.

Declaration of protection areas and changed environmental awareness

The Hmong people reside mainly within the numerous environmental protection areas in northern Thailand. They traditionally had no concept of sustainable land use, but must now find ways to follow conservation laws or risk resettlement and constant conflict with RFD officials. To minimise pressure from Thai officials and the public, ten to fifteen years ago, the Hmong at my research sites began to protect forested areas surrounding their villages on their own initiative. They have been supported in this effort through educational training from local NGOs such as IMPECT (Inter Mountain Peoples Education and Culture in Thailand Association), the

Royal Project and diverse international agencies. Men between the ages of seventeen to forty constitute the main target group for these programs, since some have attended Thai schools, speak Thai and are self-confident enough to interact with people from the lowlands. As a result, the younger Hmong generation has learned that they must adapt the behaviour and attitudes of their people to the drastic changes in overall environmental conditions in northern Thailand.

Zoov Nlaam Xyooj, a thirty-four-year old man and one of the founders of Mae Sa Mai's Conservation Group who has participated about twenty times in environmental training by the RFD, emphasises that Hmong people urgently need to react to pressures from outside: "There have been problems with the RFD so people from Mae Sa Mai need to do something on the official level." (Source: field interview, H-E 41) There were also recurrent conflicts with staff from the Doi Suthep-Pui National Park seven years ago when villagers were frequently arrested and mistreated by officials. In one quarrel, a National Park officer was shot dead by a Hmong villager.[124] Since then arrests occur only seldom. The Conservation Group in Mae Sa Mai has thirty-six active members all of whom are male. Women, especially married women, are not allowed to partake in the group's activities because moral norms do not allow "large scale" interaction between women and male non-kin. Group activities include training other villagers to live in "accordance with nature", apply more sustainable methods in agriculture or maintain the large protection zone around the *ntoo xeeb*, the sacred tree above the village. It is primarily the young Hmong men who work as volunteers or day labourers for the Britain-based Forest Restoration Research Unit (FORRU). They collect seeds from various native trees, care for the seedlings at the tree nursery within the village and help monitor the planted seedlings. About twice a year, seedlings from the nursery are transplanted. FORRU organises the planting days both as social and educational events in which numerous

---

[124] Nicholas Tapp (1989: 117) describes a similar incident of open violence towards a government official in his study site.

villagers participate. Unmarried and married women are also allowed to take part in these activities because they are carried out communally. The areas FORRU restores as forest ecosystems lie in the vicinity of Mae Sa Mai. The villagers themselves must leave them uncultivated and declare them protection zones, a process often interlaced with conflict between people who have different environmental attitudes and economic interests.

Conflict has also arisen between the younger and older male generations because the elders remained long unconvinced that forests needed to be restored at the cost of arable land. However, gradually members of the older generation recognised that the Hmong people could not continue as before and needed to learn from the new generation. This is a difficult process in a patriarchal and hierarchical society, which normally requires young people to obey and respect the old. Nonetheless, the elders are slowly yielding to new environmentalist ideas promoted by the younger generation and outside institutions. As a consequence, a new environmental awareness is being progressively incorporated into Hmong local knowledge and education systems.

As a result of this new environmental awareness, which I could ascertain in both study sites, Hmong spare land for self-initiated reforestation and forest conservation around their villages, especially on the mountain ridges and near the water sources. People declare, manage and protect these conservation areas by themselves and according to their own rules (cf. Pye 2003:1247). Villagers in Mae Sa Mai, Ban Phui and many other Hmong settlements (see appendix) were disappointed and angered by state afforestation programs with fast growing, but water-diluting and easily perishable pine and eucalyptus trees (Delang 2002: 494). As a consequence, they formed their own resource committees to draft rules on forest conservation, demarcate protection areas and afforest degraded land with a huge variety of local plants and trees. New agricultural techniques necessitate less manpower and land, thus enabling the Hmong to devote some of their land to protection and afforestation, in spite of the general shortage of fertile land.

Community rules on forest conservation include making firebreaks and organising fire patrols during dry season. They also include a clear definition of village boundaries to protect the area from encroachment by outsiders and control villagers' use of natural resources, especially of trees. If a fire occurs, as one did on the first day of my research in Mae Sa Mai, village fire volunteers, usually one man from each household, gather to stop the fire as fast as possible. The Hmong people from both Mae Sa Mai and Ban Phui force themselves to adhere to the new regulations and must pay fines in case of misconduct. For example, penalties between 500 to 3.000 baht, depending on the size of the tree, must be paid for illegally cutting trees in protected areas. The fines for shooting wildlife range from 300 to 1.000 baht, depending on the size and species of animal. Scouts from the Resource Conservation Committees irregularly monitor the protected areas to find offenders.

Of course, many landowners are not relinquishing their fields and former resource use practices without protest. However, social pressure in the villages seems to be strong enough to make most farmers concede to the protection plans and force them to give up some of their fields for conservation purposes. This is, of course, not a smooth process. For example, replanted trees in Mae Sa Mai have already been destroyed clandestinely in order to clear the land for cultivation again. But after more than ten years of self-initiated forest protection, many villagers have begun to realise the positive effects of conservation, namely that small water sources no longer desiccate during dry season, the climate is cooler during hot season and fewer problems occur with Thai authorities from the National Park, the Royal Forestry Department and the Royal Project.

As a result of international and national development projects, environmental NGOs and strong pressure from the RFD and Thai public, the Hmong's environmental awareness has increased and people have started to protect forest areas around their villages. This is a way of proving to the RFD and public that the Hmong are indeed able to protect valuable national assets and also a way of avoiding further open conflict with government officials. Furthermore, it represents an attempt to prevent the establishment of further national parks in Hmong settlement areas. Through new conservation practices, Hmong are also trying to finally rid themselves of their negative image as opium producers and resource depleters. Bouam Maim Xyooj who is sixty-three years old and from Mae Sa Mai said:

"We want to be part of the Thai nation and protect the environment together. In the past we did not care because the land did not belong to us. Even now it does not belong to us. But now we are Thai. We settle here and love the place. We old people still want to go everywhere, but actually the Hmong people have to stay. We now have to be humble and protect nature. We need to develop because we are fifty years behind the Thai people." (Source: field interview, H-E 24)

This changed approach to natural resources and land is not only a phenomenon at my research sites but can be found in other Hmong villages as well. During my visit to twenty Hmong communities in Chiang Mai and Mae Hong Son Province I realised that most of the villages had established self-declared protection areas (see appendix). Additionally, in 1997, twenty Hmong communities from Chiang Mai and Kamphaeng Phet Provinces joined to form the "Hmong Environment Networking Group". The group encourages natural resource conservation in Hmong villages, integrates traditional local knowledge into forest conservation and generally improves the public image of the Hmong by setting good examples. As of 2002, the Group had grown to cover over thirty-five villages, some of which are also located in the Province of Tak (Leepreecha 2004: 345).

Importantly, it is difficult to clearly distinguish between aspects of resource protection activities stemming from local Hmong knowledge and traditional beliefs and those initiated by outside institutions and pressures. Especially among young people, I would attribute the changed environmental awareness to myriad factors: Degrading natural resources, fixed settlement areas, environmental education, project influences, pressures, conflicts on different levels, the bad reputation of the Hmong, the determination to prevent further protection zones by the State, the desire for positive public recognition and identification with the land, as well as the urge to become part of the Thai nation. Many Hmong people no longer view land and forests as depletable resources, but as assets to be conserved.

Traditional and new forms of conservation: Sacred forest areas

In discussions about the traditional relation of the Hmong to their land, many informants pointed out critically that in the past, the Hmong did not know how to value natural resources. According to customary practice, people only maintained a protection area around the sacred tree (*ntoo xeeb*), the location of the greatest local divinity. This area was small (a few *rai*), and villagers did not discuss it much with strangers because of its sanctity and taboos existing around the tree. "This place cannot be found on any map, only on the map of our minds" proclaimed the female shaman of the Yang clan in Ban Phui.

The local divinity, either called *thwv tim* or *xeeb teb xeeb chaws* in Hmong, must remain "undisturbed". For example, dead people cannot be buried at or near the site of the spirit. Ritual leaders of the village community prohibit disturbing the tree and the area around it in any way. Neeb Lyooj, who runs the nursery for FORRU, explained:

> "One river has one spirit, which is the owner of the river. One mountain has one spirit, which is the owner of the mountain. All the spirits together are joined in the sacred tree. They are not the owner of the tree but just live there." (Source: field interview, H-R1 28)

Consequently, it remained unclear to me, as well as to many of my Hmong informants, whether *thwv tim* is a singular divinity or an amalgamation of all owner spirits (*xeeb teb*) of a terrain's river, mountains, caves, fields and so on. Shamans call the divinity *zaab zeej tim tswv* (literally: all together have one king spirit) which hints at the fact that *thwv tim* is indeed one great spirit of a locality.

The head of the Xiong clan, Nplaj Thoj, renowned for his profound knowledge of Hmong oral history and rituals, is the ritual expert of Mae Sa Mai who performs the yearly ritual for the *thwv tim* at the *ntoo xeeb*. During one of our numerous conversations about aspects of Hmong culture he explained:

> "In fact, Hmong people have always protected nature to some degree since we have always had our sacred tree and the protected area around it. But we did not tell anybody about this tree because we did not want the place to be disturbed by people from outside. But then the country started to develop and the Royal Forestry Department came. The Hmong people needed to cooperate and openly show that they could also protect the land, not only destroy it. Young people made the villagers understand that they need to protect more forest and the water sources. Life is water and every year we make sacrifices to the *xeeb teb* of the water source. In the past we worked in the fields, the whole year for poppies and vegetables. Unlike the Karen, the Hmong cut everything and did not leave any tree stumps to recover. But now life needs to be changed along with the times, we need to adapt to new situations and requirements. […] Our Hmong traditions have to be strong and continued, but all other things have to be adapted to modern times." (Source: field interview, H-S1 39-40)

Nplaj Thoj's statements underscore that attitudes towards resource protection have changed due to outside pressures, but are also grounded in local religious concepts and the belief that the landscape is "inhabited" by spiritual beings. In the past, Hmong have not revealed or promoted the institution of the sacred tree – including the protected area, which ensures the greatest local divinity remains undisturbed – to outsiders. However, according to Nplaj Thoj and other elders I spoke to, the *ntoo xeeb* ritual has been performed by the Hmong people for at least 200 years. All twenty

Hmong Perceptions of the Environment and Spatial Orientation 339

Hmong communities I visited on my tour around northern Thailand also had a *ntoo xeeb* and a religious expert who conducts the annual ritual.[125]

In 1996, the Tribal Research Institute estimated (cited by Leepreecha 2004: 342), that about half of the 242 Hmong villages in northern Thailand still perform the yearly ceremony. Few authors have thus far mentioned or discussed the institution of the "spirit of the place" or the *ntoo xeeb* ritual. Exceptions are William Geddes (1976: 93-94) and Nicholas Tapp (1989a: 61-62), who mention the sacred tree, and Nusit Chindarsi (1976: 135-136), who dedicates a single page to the "tiertee tier seng spirit ceremony". However, the *ntoo xeeb* tree offering ceremony and protected areas around it have become part of the Hmong self-definition in relation to natural resources preservation. These days, the Hmong speak more openly about the existence of this tree than they apparently did in the past. Prasit Leepreecha (2004) is the first scholar to discuss the ritual, its meanings and cultural redefinition for forest conservation in detail.

The sacred tree (*ntoo xeeb*)

In former times, when the Hmong erected a new village and settled in a new area, they had to find a tree, *ntoo xeeb*, or prominent stone to assign the greatest local divinity, the *thwv tim* of the settlement area, a locality for worship and offering. Some communities also postponed the assignment of the *thwv tim* until they faced a serious problem, for example, misfortune, draught, or illness (see also Leepreecha 2004: 340-341).

The *ntoo xeeb* is mostly a large, durable hardwood tree located on a mountaintop. It is believed that the greatest local spirit has to reside in a place well above the village and the people. The tree is fenced in and protected from disturbance by humans or animals. Strong taboos exist

---

[125] Hmong anthropologist Prasit Leepreecha (2004: 342) reports that Hmong communities in lowland areas have mostly abandoned the *ntoo xeeb* ceremony due to the lack of big trees and ritual experts who still have the religious knowledge to perform such a ceremony. Usually, the responsibility for practicing the *ntoo xeeb* rite is passed down to ritual experts from generation to generation.

against cutting down, hitting, or burning the tree and against shooting birds or animals in its vicinity. In other words, any activity, except for rituals, is strictly forbidden around the *ntoo xeeb*. The Hmong believe that people who illegitimately disturb the place, and thereby insult the local divinity, will face disaster and misfortune.

In Mae Sa Mai, the sacred tree is located about two kilometres above the village on top of a hill between two small streams that flow towards the village.

When the village Ban Phui was founded in 1972, the place's divinity was assigned to a big stone, called *pob zeb xeeb*, located on the mountaintop behind the village. Because the Karen and Thai had previously used the area around the rock for cultivation, only grass was growing there.[126] Due to the sanctity of the place, the Hmong villagers started to keep the place undisturbed and let trees and bushes grow again naturally. A few years after its establishment, the village was confronted by inexplicable misfortune and illness. Villagers believed the location of the local divinity was unfavourable and subsequently moved it to a large tree. However, a branch of this tree broke off during a storm about ten years ago. As a consequence, the villagers had to find a new, undamaged tree for the location of the supernatural being. Since Ban Phui might become part of the Mae Tho National Park in the near future, people are yet again contemplating the relocation of the *thwv tim* to a completely different area, which is less fertile than the current site. Due to land problems and the imminent introduction of stricter conservation laws, villagers want to cut new fields before the enlargement of the village's cultivation area becomes impossible. If the divinity is in fact moved again, the ritual leaders will have to cautiously explain the repositioning to the local divinity in order to prevent supernatural punishment for this further disturbance.

---

[126] One of Prasit Leepreecha's informants, a Hmong community leader from northern Vietnam, reports that his ancestors performed both the *ntoo xeeb* ritual and ceremony making offerings to the big stone (*pob zeb xeeb*). At present, his people have stopped believing in the supernatural as their forebears had done. Consequently, they no longer hold any of these rituals (Leepreecha 2004: 348).

The *ntoo xeeb* ritual

Nplaj Thoj offering at the *ntoo xeeb*

Once a year, on the last day (fifth day) of the Hmong New Year celebration, the ritual leader and male representatives of all village households perform a special *ntoo xeeb* offering ceremony. Early in the morning, the participants walk up the mountain together to the tree. Before starting the ritual, the area is cleared of branches and any other debris, the fence around the tree is repaired and a pig slaughtered. The pig is put on a wooden platform standing close by the tree. The ritual leader and all men then assemble around the tree to attend the prayer by the ritual leader. The leader beats a gong to communicate with the *thwv tim* and, through the ox horn oracle, ascertains whether the divinity will accept the sacrifices. The spirit is asked to protect the villagers from anything bad and support them in their economic success. Joss sticks, candles and paper money, contributed in large quantities by each household, are burned and whiskey, tea, oranges and flowers put on the platform as additional sacrifices. After the ritual, all people gather outside the fenced-in area to have lunch together. The pig – apart from the head, the backbone and tail – is removed from the platform and barbecued on sticks over a fire, the main reason for this ritual's great popularity among young boys. In general, women are also allowed to participate in the ritual. I myself attended it once in Mae Sa Mai. However, the legitimate representatives of a household must be male, which means widows who live only with their children usually send one of their sons instead of attending themselves.

Despite the fact that almost forty percent of the villagers in Mae Sa Mai have converted to Christianity, all households still send a representative to attend the *ntoo xeeb* ceremony (see also Leepreecha 2004: 344). The reason for this communal participation is threefold: First, *thwv tim* as the major local supernatural spirit is believed to govern *all* villagers, animals, mountains, rivers, trees and other natural resources of the area. Every household, notwithstanding its religious affiliation, is expected to pay its respect and make offerings to this local divinity. Since the ritual allows the people to invigorate claims over the area's resources that are governed by the divinity, Christians are also interested in taking part in the ceremony. Second, one member of all households is supposed to be present at the ceremony because it symbolises and strengthens the village's cohesion. The ritual represents one of the few occasions where the whole village is ritually assembled and acts as one unit. For this reason, people who do not belong to the village community are not allowed to step inside the fenced-in area of the tree but can only participate in the ceremony by joining the meal after the ritual. These days, the Hmong people from Mae Sa Mai always invite representatives from the Royal Project, the RFD or the National Park to take part in the ritual outside the fenced in area. Villagers want to demonstrate publicly that they are also engaged in forest protection.

Redefinition of *ntoo xeeb* for forest conservation

In 1985, after villagers had reduced the forest around Mae Sa Mai to a minimum and encroached ever more frequently on the protected area around the *ntoo xeeb*, a turning point in the function of the sacred tree occurred.

Nplaj Thoj, who already performed of *ntoo xeeb* ritual at the time, fell ill frequently. This was connected to the illegitimate and frequent disturbance of the local divinity, and Nplaj Thoj and the village elders therefore decided to enlarge the protection area around the tree to about 100 *rai*. Five years later, this protection area was enlarged by another 2.400 *rai* and declared a community conservation forest. The conservation area is now protected by a firebreak zone, largely fenced in and demarcated by signs in Thai language explaining protection rules.

An extraordinary sacrificial ceremony at Mae Sa Mai's sacred tree took place in 1998, on the occasion of the fiftieth anniversary of the King's coronation. In other parts of the country, the Buddhist ceremony *buad pa* (Thai: forest ordination), which included wrapping trees in yellow cloth, was held in honour of the King. The ceremony was based on the belief that honouring large trees can avert misfortunes incited by nature (Isager and Ivarsson 2002: 410). Hmong villages were asked to participate in this activity. However, many refused to take part because the Buddhist ritual did not accord with Hmong beliefs and their own ritual around the sacred tree (Leepreecha 2004: 344, 347). Instead, during that reign's anniversary year, about 300 people from outside the village of Mae Sa Mai were officially invited to take part in the *ntoo xeeb* ceremony. Participants included the *Nai Amphoe* (district officer) of the Mae Rim District Office; reporters from nationwide television, radio stations and newspapers; university academics; several state representatives; and NGO workers (especially from IMPECT and the Hmong Association in Chiang Mai); as well as community leaders from both highland and lowland villages. Due to nationwide broadcasting, the ceremony became known throughout Thailand. Representatives from other Hmong villages still visit Mae Sa Mai to learn from the village's conservation committee about sustainable resource management and the redefinition of the *ntoo xeeb* ceremony for conservation purposes. The committee also teaches its visitors how to publicise the ritual and sacred forest to construct a positive image for Thai state agencies, in particular the RFD, and the public (Leepreecha 2004: 344-345).[127]

> "The performance of the Hmong *ntoo xeeb* tree offering ceremony is part of self-definition of natural resources preservation in the Hmong community. The evidence implies that the Hmong are struggling to create a cultural space for themselves in the Thai nation state, after having been labelled forest destroyers for decades. Local people have proved to state authorities and outside peoples that they are well equipped to handle the problem of natural resources diminution by themselves, if their local wisdom is recognised by state authorities." (Leepreecha 2004: 346)

The Hmong in northern Thailand have chosen to redefine the *ntoo xeeb* ritual for the purposes of natural resource protection, as well as to fight the prevailing negative image of Hmong as the primary resource depleters in mainstream Thai society. Members of the "Hmong Environment Networking Group" travel to other Hmong villages to promote the idea of establishing large protection forests around the *ntoo xeeb*, which are likely to be supported and respected by most villagers. Group members teach Hmong villagers ways of redefining the traditional Hmong *ntoo xeeb* ceremony for the sake of conserving natural resources, strengthening village cohesion and obtaining positive recognition from the state authorities and public. Thus, the "Hmong Environment Networking Group" and their members partake in a conscious definition of Hmong spatiality within Thailand. It is characterised by strategies against both natural resource depletion and negative mediations of the Hmong in Thai majority society, as well as for strengthening the unity of Hmong in Thailand.

The belief in thwv tim and redefined, annual performance of the *ntoo xeeb* ceremony contribute to a deeper anchoring of the Hmong people in their settlement area. While the belief in the "owner spirit" has always

---

[127] See also Ikuya Tokoro's paper (2003) on the transformation of shamanic ritual in the southern Philippines as yet another example how a ritual can become an arena of tacit political struggle.

existed, the enlarged protected community forest area adds a new dimension to the sacred tree. People consciously refrain from cultivating this forest area of their now permanent settlement regions and engage in conscious protection measures that, due to the sanctity of the place, must be largely supported by all residents of the village.

Spatial orientation

Upon entering a Hmong village, most Hmong visitors know where the *ntoo xeeb* is located – on the forested mountainside "behind" the village. Besides this marker and other geomantic principles (already referred to in chapter six) that help Hmong situate themselves in a foreign settlement, the Hmong also orient themselves in their environment according to general north, south, east, and west coordinates. These coordinates are represented in cosmological thought by the *dab* for all "corners" of the sky: *dab paab npeg* (side above all = north), *dab paab ntsaa* (down side = south), *dab hnub tuaj* (sunrise = east) and *dab hnub npoob* (sunset = west). These coordinates are both topographical coordinates and cultural conceptions of the world. For example, standing in Mae Sa Mai and looking towards the mountain range lying in the south opposite the small hills to the north, the Hmong villagers nonetheless speak of the mountain in the south as being located "downwards" while the small hills in the north are "upwards". Just as the Yupno in Papua New Guinea have a general uphill/downhill orientation (Wassman 1993: 16; see also Senft 1992: 30), the Hmong have an upward/downward and upriver/downriver orientation. This includes an orientation beyond their immediate location and characteristics of their immediate environment. To speak in Hmong terms, people "think big".

The mountain opposite the small northern hills in Mae Sa Mai is located downward, like any other southern location, whether mountainous or not. A water source positioned, for example, in the east of the village, is connected to the "upward" direction because the Hmong believe all rivers originate in the "large mountains in China" (Himalayan). In other words, the Hmong conceptualise "up" and "down" or "upriver" and "downriver" within a broader framework, taking the topography of Thailand and of the wider Asian region into account. Following this logic, any place in the north, whether its immediate surroundings are characterised by small hills or even a valley, is upward and upriver. Hmong people always navigate with a map anchored by the absolute coordinate upward/upriver/north and downward/downriver/south.

As I observed in the course of my research, even when far away from their home settlements, many villagers displayed a keen sense of absolute orientation and direction. This demonstrates that most Hmong operate with a developed, inbuilt sense of up/down and north/south orientation. Despite this sense of orientation, some of the people I spoke to expressed a certain familiarity with a particular territory necessary for the exact use of an alignment. For example, many villagers claimed that they need to walk through a dense secondary mountain forest a few times before they can orientate themselves along north/south coordinates without seeing the position of the sun (when going hunting at night, for example). On the whole, the Hmong have a geo-centred reference system rather than the ego-centred system found in many Western societies (see also Brown and Levinson 1993: 50-53).[128] Discussing examples from Mexico, India, Nepal and Papua New Guinea, cognitive anthropologists Penelope Brown and Stephen Levinson (1993: 67), assert that most members of local societies occupying a mountainous terrain generally possess an inbuilt compass and geo-centred reference system. According to them, this system constitutes a "perfectly natural solution to the problem of spatial reference" in such a terrain. For instance, among the Tzeltal in Mexico, who also live in a mountainous area, the main spatial frame of reference is also "uphill" and "downhill" (Brown 2002: 185).

---

[128] In the Western-European tradition of thought, space is egocentrically organised and understood in the framework of Euclidian geometry. Three bodily reference points help specify location: the first one separates right and left, the second one front and back and the third, above ground and below ground level (Senft 1992: 5).

Hmong Perceptions of the Environment and Spatial Orientation 347

Ego-centred and geo-centred orientation systems constitute fundamentally different strategies of spatial conception, focusing either on local configurations regardless of outside points of reference or on orientations within a larger frame of reference, such as a landscape (Brown and Levinson 1993: 47). Of course, these systems can be used, along with an object-centred or ego-centred system, in tandem. For example, when I asked the Hmong villagers in a test to describe the location of objects placed before, besides, behind, above, and underneath them and others present in the setting, respondents referred to the items both in an ego-centred and also object-centred manner. At the same time, they related to locations in and beyond the village through geo-centred reference points.

The Hmong acquire this geo-centred system of location and orientation socio-culturally through a shared mental model. This model is represented by the Hmong Mountains and extends beyond the boundaries of the villages and northern Thailand. As represented in the cosmological view of the world, the Hmong Mountains is a religious conception. It is a social conception because it unites all Hmong people within a single spatiality. And finally, it is a geo-spatial conception that incorporates the mountainous areas of Asia (and beyond) where Hmong people originated and currently live. In addition to this geo-centred reference system, the Hmong at my research sites also position themselves geo-politically in the North of Thailand according to concepts of "the mountains" (*hmoob npem roob*, literally: Hmong up mountain) and "the lowlands" (*chaw qis*). This system exists parallel to the north/upward/upriver and south/downward/downriver orientation and forms part of the Hmong Mountains-concept. The mountain-lowland dichotomy reflects the socio-political situation of the Hmong as *one* of the mountain groups in opposition to Thai lowland society. The Hmong see themselves as belonging to an overall group of ethnic mountain minorities that all occupy the mountainous areas of Thailand and face similar socio-economic and political problems, described in chapter two. The annual May rallies in front of Chiang Mai's City Hall openly enact the ethnic mountain groups' joint identity, as do the combined efforts of Hmong and

Karen villagers in the Ban Pui area to prevent incorporation into the Mae Tho National Park.

Summary

During the times of swidden agriculture and opium poppy cultivation connected to frequent relocations within northern Thailand, the Hmong people maintained a generalised relation to the land and its natural resources. Despite the fact that farming mountain fields is an integral part of Hmong culture, people exhibited no special regard for sustainable cultivation methods. When the resources of one area were depleted, people moved on to new regions. They had no particular Hmong names for certain features of the landscape or for their frequently relocated and abandoned villages. Irrespective of this generalised relation to land and settlement areas, the Hmong cosmos accounts for the fact that the Hmong believe in a connection between the land, its different features and various supernatural entities. A disregard of geomantic rules and disrespect of the spiritual beings can have an impact on the villager's life. Nicholas Tapp correctly argues:

> "The natural environment and social order of the Hmong is therefore closely interpenetrated with the supernatural world of historical legend, shamanic ritual and domestic worship." (1989a: 91)

Through both the worship of supernatural beings and their ancestors, the Hmong are connected to their burial places in areas of former villages. Memories of and connections to these places are nurtured through yearly visits and ceremonies at the graves. These locations are individual points in the mental model of the Hmong people that interconnect them today with their ancestors, the history of migration and among themselves because of their common historical reference points. In other words, the Hmong are indeed attached to land, not to a small area of settlement but rather to the totality of locations where the Hmong have been temporarily living in the past and settling permanently at present. One of my key informants in Mae

Sa Mai, Yeeb Yaj, stated in this regard: "The Hmong think big, they think of the Hmong Mountains." (Source: field interview, H-E 45)

Because of rapid changes in their socio-economic situation, the Hmong are under great pressure from people inside and outside their society. These changes have, *inter alia*, resulted in a general shift in environmental awareness and self-initiated protection measures. Hmong now strive to find ways of sustaining their limited natural resources, ameliorating their image in the Thai public, preventing the foundation of further national parks on their territories, thwarting further conflict with the RFD, honouring the King and showing respect for the nation's policies.

At present, it is easier for the Hmong to protect resources because relatively seen, each household requires less land than before the introduction of new crops. Hybrid crops and agro-chemicals enable farmers to extract a higher yield from smaller pieces of land. Owing to these developments, the Hmong can afford to place certain areas under protection without endangering their livelihoods. The Hmong have chosen the *ntoo xeeb* ritual, the institution of the sacred tree and taboo area around it, to openly demonstrate their desire to integrate into the nation and participate in natural resource conservation. As Prasit Leepreecha concludes, the Hmong are determined to change their negative image as forest destroyers, publicise and redefine traditional forms of forest conservation and "create a cultural space for themselves in the Thai nation state" (2004: 346).

With their natural environment, the Hmong display a geo-centred reference system that includes an apparently inbuilt sense of up/down, north/south and upriver/downriver orientation in relative terms. This geo-centred system of location and orientation forms part of the mental model of the Hmong Mountains. It is based on the cosmological division of the north, south, east and west "corners of the sky" and belief that the Hmong populate an unbounded terrain in the northern mountain ranges of Southeast Asia. In addition to the geo-centred reference system, the Hmong divide geo-politically between "the mountains" and "the lowlands", conceptualising themselves as part of an overall group of ethnic mountain minorities that socio-economically and politically contrasts with Thai lowland society. The dichotomy perceived between mountain and lowland societies runs parallel to the notion that the Hmong belong to the Thai nation. The redefinition of the *ntoo xeeb* ceremony represents one example of Hmong society's efforts to gain public recognition as equal Thai citizens while maintaining and even strengthening important aspects of the Hmong socio-cultural system.

11 RHYTHM OF SPATIALITY: IMPORTANT VILLAGE SETTINGS

Previous chapters of this book have discussed the main political, religious and social structures of the Hmong, as well as their related practices. This part will scrutinise Hmong social practice more thoroughly as observed in most important village settings. German anthropologist Klaus Hesse (2003: 121) emphasises that the "rhythm of spatiality" is expressed in daily routine and within activities, events and rituals that recur daily, weekly or monthly. In order to reach a better understanding of the Hmong's "rhythm of spatiality" at my research sites, my fieldwork devoted in-depth attention to settings as locations of actions. As defined in the theoretical part of the book, a setting is a place or a zone in known or imagined space that is associated with specific activities, meanings and purposes. Settings should be explored in their meaning *for* action and examined for how they express a symbolic appropriation *through* actions. They thus comprise part of a spatial order, which represents an important basis of ideational conceptions, specific codes of social values and social and symbolic classifications. Classifications can be mythical or real. However, they are always socially produced and form part of a "collective consciousness" and knowledge (Hesse 2003: 126-127).

Through their collective consciousness and knowledge, members of a society can "read the built environment" of a place in order to know how to behave in specific settings. This embodied and shared cultural knowledge provides for a concurrence in the perspectives of people acting in particular settings. For the most part, settings therefore involve people with common understandings of spatial arrangements and behaviour. People emplace themselves through certain activities and are influenced in their actions by the underlying connotations of the setting. However, rules and patterns of behaviour must not be identical for all agents. As the example of the mortuary rites setting below clearly illustrates, one setting – even when consisting of a single room – can be divided into multiple sub-settings that have their own connotations and expected forms of behaviour. It is therefore necessary to take gender- and generation-specific and time-related features into account when analysing settings.

Importantly, cultural spaces are not identical with geographical locales. A locale can be reconfigured into different settings, depending on the people, their actions, norms and values and way to constitute spatiality. Visiting one and the same market in Chiang Mai with Hmong people is a totally different experience from a visit with, for example, Thai or Western people. In this sense, Margaret Rodman (1992: 647) speaks of a "multivocal dimension of place", which conveys the fact that a single place can be experienced quite differently by different people.

Since not all settings encountered in the field can be described exhaustively, this chapter analyses five settings exemplary for transporting a sense of the "rhythm of Hmong spatiality": the house, the neighbourhood square, the mortuary rites (in the neighbouring village), the market in Chiang Mai, and the wider world. The house setting consists of multiple sub-settings, such as the sleeping quarters, the eating table or the central post. This is the most detailed description here because it elucidates the Hmong's main behavioural principles, which generally apply to other settings. The settings selected are important, frequently recurring everyday settings which are also considered as important everyday settings by the villagers interviewed and which are often mentioned in the households' activity protocols. In their totality, they help draw a picture of the Hmong group's mental model and add a further tessera to understanding Hmong spatiality.

My description of representative settings is primarily based on participant observation, as well as interviews about the qualities, meanings and connotations of these settings. The central question guiding my research of settings was: Who does what, where, when, including/excluding whom, and why? I ascertained the setting "wider world" through interviews, as well as by cultural learning, since this setting is based on perceptions and meanings that are not concretely accessible. Instead, they are widely known through the media, relatives living abroad, international extension workers, tourists and researchers. Hmong villagers frequently discuss life in other parts of the world, compare it with their own and try to estimate its potential for the Hmong.

I describe the settings according to the categories of fixed (e.g. buildings, roads, fields), semi-fixed (e.g. equipment of a place, furniture, make-shift components of rituals) and non-fixed (e.g. people, their behaviour, actions and symbolic meanings) elements. People's diverse actions are discussed, including gender, age or time differences. My analysis endeavours to elucidate the social and spiritual qualities of Hmong settings, as well as their meanings and connotations.

The house

This section analyses the house as setting because of its significance among Hmong locations for daily social interaction and ritual practice. The Hmong house at once suggests and legitimates a set of expectations about the social system and people's relationships with one another. It is the primary locus of socialisation where children learn about proper social conduct, obligations and hierarchies so they can progressively engage in culturally appropriate activities. My chapter on social organisation highlighted that all people residing in a house form the smallest recognised and at the same time the strongest social unit in Hmong society, the "one-house people". Yet, households do not simply represent residential units, but a structural category and model of thought. The extended family mostly made up of several generations and twenty to forty people, acts as a unit in which people can always rely on each other. The individual member of a household and his or her needs and opinions are only secondary compared with the household's overall requirements. Through its structure and activities, the house secures the survival of the group. It has social and spiritual qualities because it is the most important locality for ancestor worship. In addition, the Hmong house is a representation of the cosmos; the construction of a Hmong house symbolises the recreation of the universe:

> "The Hmong house and its surroundings similarly form a ritual as well as a social space, in which different categories of the supernatural are symbolised by spirits associated with different parts of the house, which must be honoured at different times by particular rituals." (Tapp 1989a: 91)

Traditional house structures

Hmong house-building follows strict rules of spatial division and ordering that leave most houses structured along the same model and similar in appearance. Many houses in the villages studied are still built on the ground according to traditional house-building styles passed down from generation to generation.

Most Hmong houses still consist of a single, large, rectangular room which contains some divided off sleeping sections. The outer walls of a typical Hmong house are either made of wood or concrete and covered by zinc or polystyrene roofing. A veranda usually runs along the outside length of the house. It is used to store firewood or as a meeting place, with benches placed along the wall of the house. In the inside, the floor is made from packed earth. Houses usually have one to three doors. The main door is called *qhov rooj dab*, is located at the side of the veranda and of high ritual importance. Most households have more than one main door in order to enable comings and goings of a "profane" quality through a "secular" side door.

The Hmong house has five support beams, the most important one standing in the centre. This beam is home to the main domestic spirit which guards the house. The ancestor spirits of the household head dwell in the house's other pillars (Tapp 1989a: 63). When babies were still born at home, instead of in hospitals, the placenta of a boy was buried at the main post to honour the house spirit. The placenta of a girl was buried underneath the parent's bed to symbolise the close relation between parents and daughters, despite the practice of virilocal residence after marriage (cf. Lee 1996: 12; Chindarsi 1976: 15).

Each house has two fireplaces, which have both a practical and symbolic meaning. On the large ceremonial stove, usually located at the left hand side of the rectangular room, the Hmong cook food for rituals and large groups. This fireplace represents the whole community. The extended family living together in one household is represented by a small fireplace, usually located to the right of the main entrance, where daily meals are cooked and people assemble for conversation after dinner. However, when grave problems occur that also involve the Hmong community, these are discussed in front of the big hearth. Win Huj's mother Kaab (sixty-five years old) once told me while we were sitting at this fireplace: "Fire means truth because fire is strong and dangerous. We should not lie in front of the fire. A

Figure 13: House patterns

Model No. 1

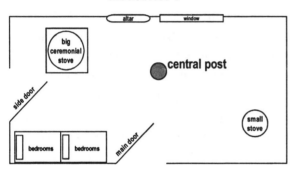

Model No. 2

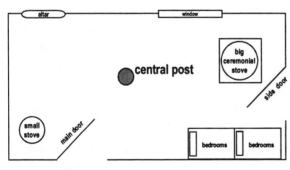

Source: drawing by Win Huj Yaj and Yeeb Yaj, Mae Sa Mai, 20 March 2002

disaster can happen if we lie in front of the big fire." (Source: field interview, H-S1-45) The two fireplaces represent both the household and Hmong community inside the house. The big, ceremonial hearth symbolically ensures the group's survival and adherence to traditional morals and norms, while the small oven symbolises the cohesion of the household. As described further below, the Hmong believe that benevolent house spirits inhabit both fireplaces that protect the house's residents when respected through offerings.

According to many of my informants and my own observations, the majority of Hmong houses are constructed according to a certain house pattern (see model number one). Only a small percentage is structured according to the second model, which in itself can have slight variations. In general the main fireplace is located in the left hand corner of the rectangular one-room house, viewed from the central door. Opposite the large, ceremonial stove is the bedroom of the household head (model number one). If the big stove stands on the right corner of the room, the whole interior of the house is restructured accordingly (model number two). Nusit Chindarsi (1976: 15) also illustrates these two main house patterns in a drawing. My assistant Win Huj and my neighbour Yeeb Yaj have jointly drawn these two models of Hmong houses for me.

Besides the two cooking hearths, there is also a resting and storage platform jutting out from the right-side wall inside the centre room, near the main entrance door. One to three altars (altars for the spirit of the house, the herb/medicinal spirit and the shaman spirit) hang on the long wall opposite this door. One to two bedrooms can be partitioned off from the main room by wooden planks to the left of the main door; another two can be built in the right-hand corner next to the platform. A large, rectangular wooden table with two long benches is normally placed at the side of the altar(s), where one to two windows are usually located. Besides two benches, which are mostly used during ceremonies or when guests are present, small stools are used as seats inside the house. These small stools can be easily moved in and out of the house to join, for example, circles of people gathered at the big fireplace in the evening or in front of the house for an afternoon conversation.

Household items are rarely stored in cabinets, but rather on the floor, in large baskets, on small shelves or on bamboo constructions above the big cooking stove. The Hmong keep food and woven mats above the hearth to prevent insects from destroying them. Rice sacks are mostly piled in one corner of the room. Most families own a sewing machine, a radio, a television set and DVD player, as well as a personal stereo. On the walls hang pictures of the King and the Royal family; photographs of household members in the traditional Hmong dress worn during New Year; pictures of male family members wearing uniforms connected to one of the village committees; old electricity bills; pictures of Chinese landscapes; Chinese calendars; and wall clocks. For the most part, houses are simply decorated with little furniture. In Mae Sa Mai, neon light illuminates the interiors of the houses. In Ban Phui, candles provide light during the dry season. Rudimentary toilet houses are located outside the main house.

The sleeping quarters of the house have the character of makeshift rooms because (a) the main room is the central area of the house, (b) families of older married sons will move into their own houses eventually, and (c) the inner house space has to be kept flexible so that it can be easily rebuilt for special events and ceremonies. For example, when Txwj Xaab fell ill from kidney failure, the interior of the central room was restructured in such a way to situate the patient's bed in the middle of the room. A greater number of people could thus be seated around it. For mortuary rites, which last for days, the Hmong clear the main room of most objects and sometimes even sleeping quarters in order to lay out the corpse at the place of the altar, attach the large sacred death drum at the side of the resting platform and host hundreds of people at once. During the mortuary rites, the inside of the house resembles a large hall more than a living quarter. Cooking for the numerous visitors is done outside the house.[129]

Most Hmong houses look similar due to the traditional structuring principles. However, house styles also evolve and slowly contribute to changing the appearance of Hmong villages. The majority of houses in Mae Sa Mai is still built along the main house pattern described above. However, some villagers from Ban Phui already invest their spare money in modern-style lowland houses built on stilts with elaborately decorated wooden stairs, balconies, and sometimes even tiled floors. These Hmong openly aim to display their wealth and signs of modernity. In contrast, most of the houses in Mae Sa Mai look shoddier and dilapidated, even those of fairly wealthy households. Here, more emphasis is put on the maintenance of the traditional house structure because Hmong culture in Mae Sa Mai, due to its proximity to Chiang Mai, is more exposed to overall changes than Ban Phui. Villagers from Mae Sa Mai instead tend to display their wealth through the purchase of cars, motorbikes, mobile phones, gold jewelry for daily use and elaborate silver jewelry worn during New Year.

Spiritual beings as an integral part of the house

Even when Hmong no longer adhere to handed-down forms of building houses, they still ensure that the five main house spirits can be connected to their locations: the main door, the small family fire stove, the big ceremonial fire stove, the main post, and the altar(s) on the wall. These five benevolent supernatural beings are, next to the ancestral spirits, an integral part of each Hmong house and secure the well-being of its members. Win Huj's father Txwj Xaab explained to me during an interview on Hmong beliefs:

---

[129] The size and length of mortuary rites depends on the age, sex, and number of children and status of the deceased. The most elaborate rites are held for elders with many children. The rites of Win Huj's father lasted five days and were attended by over 1.000 people, including a great number of Hmong kin from other provinces, such as Lampang, Nan, Phayao, Tak and Mae Hong Son.

"The spirits of the house protect the life in the house. The spirits belong to the people and the people belong to them. There are five main spirits of the house: First, the *dab qhov rooj*, the spirit of the door which resides at the side of the door inside the house; second, the *kug ncej cuab*, the spirit of the main post, third, the *dab qhov tsug*, the spirit of the big fire-stove for big pans; fourth, the *dab qhov cub*, the spirit of the small fire-stove for the family, and fifth, the *dab xwm kab*, the spirit of the altar that protects all members of the household. In some houses you can also find two other spirits: sixth, the *dab ntsuaj*, the spirit of herbs and medicine. You can only find this spirit in houses where women or men have the knowledge to worship it. Seventh, the *dab neeb*, the spirit of the shaman, which you can only find in the house of a shaman." (Source: field interview, H-R1 23-24)

A Hmong house is both a living quarter and place of spirits, ancestors and worship that unite all members of the household and protect them from malevolent outside influences. The stove spirits are less important than the other benevolent *dab* to which (male) members of a household make sacrifices in returning rituals that still adhere. The details of the ceremonies vary from clan to clan.[130] Sometimes, only small offerings are placed at the location of the *dab*, such as burning incense sticks or rice. On other occasions, special rituals are performed to ensure the goodwill and protection of the supernatural forces. For example, every three years, the Hmong have to perform a ceremony for the spirit of the centre post. This sacrificial rite, including the offering of a chicken or a pig, provides an essential safeguard for the *plig* of all household members. During the Hmong New Year celebrations, besides making offerings to the ancestors, the Hmong sacrifice a chicken, incense sticks and four cups of whiskey to the *dab xwm kab*, the spirit of the altar and all residents. During this rite, the head of household prays to invoke the altar spirit and places new white paper with chicken blood, feathers and golden paper on the wall altar (cf. Chindarsi 1976: 137-139). In addition, a ceremony for the spirit of the door

---

[130] For a detailed description of the ceremony of the door spirit and the middle post see Nusit Chindarsi 1976: 113-119, 125-130.

has to be performed once a year, especially when the household faces serious problems or any kind of misfortune. The Hmong believe that the door spirit looks after all people and animals in the house. The *dab* requires a sacrificial ceremony to protect all inhabitants and bring health and abundance to them. The ritual takes place at night and includes the offering of a pig and several chickens. As part of the ceremony, the household head ritually closes the door, saying that he is now going to feed the door spirit to keep good fortune inside the house and expel all misfortune. For the next three days, the door must be kept locked. Only residents can enter or leave the house via the window.

The door and the house as the representation of the cosmos

The door does not only play a central role in the ritual for the *dab qhov rooj* (door spirit). When ritual experts ask the lost spiritual essence of a person to return to a sick person in a *hu plig* ceremony, they usually call the *plig*, holding a chicken in their arms for sacrifice, standing at the threshold facing out of the door. The doorsill represents an important marker between the benevolent inside and the potentially malevolent outside world. The door is also the central location between the safeguarded inside and the untamed outside sphere when a shaman declares all houses belonging to his clan *ncaiv* (taboo) for the next three days. Then, signs are hung on the doors of each house to signify the special state to outsiders. Interestingly enough, household members are not taboo, but rather the houses as territorial entities, with the doors forming the main boundaries between the inner and outer spheres (Bumke 1971: 83).

The door, as a central feature of the house, can thus be seen as a sign of access and disclosure to the world. The door concretises and reflects the experience of transition. It separates the interior, subjective space of the Hmong from the exterior, objective space of all other beings (see also Bourdieu 1996: 91). During mortuary rites, the door is also a reminder of people's final threshold – the death's door. The dead are hurriedly carried over the threshold of the house on the final morning of the mortuary rites.[131] All items previously connected to the deceased and the death ritual are hastily destroyed, swept away and cleaned up. The Hmong view the door's threshold as the symbol for the transition of the dead from the sphere of the living to the sphere of the ancestors and supernatural beings, which are all believed capable of bringing harm to the living when angered. The soul of the dead must ask permission from the spirit of the door to pass from the house, the sphere of the living, to the Otherworld. If permission is denied or not requested, the soul of the dead might be prevented from passing safely towards the place of origin in China.

Consequently, the door can be seen as "the incarnation of the experience of *transition*, animating in a visible manner the dialectic of inside and outside" (Lang 1985: 204). The door is more than a physical thing; it marks the access to and disclosure of things. Just as the Hmong regard the human body as the "carrier" of the *plig*, they view the house as the "embodied carrier" of the ancestor spirits and the tame, benevolent *dab*. The house with all its meanings and connotations is an important expression of Hmong culture and way of life (cf. Rapoport 1969: 129). Moreover, as Nicholas Tapp contends, the Hmong house can truly be understood as "a reflection of the cosmos" (1989a: 63): The roof and beams represent the vault of heaven, the packed earthen floor stands for the world of nature and the sphere underneath. Between the sky and sphere underneath the earth lies the world of the people and their social life, represented by the household members and their actions. Symbolically and conceptually, the inside of the house is the Hmong world, the outside sphere an unknown territory potentially inhabited by malevolent *dab* that bring danger to people. In other words, the house is not only a representation of the cosmos but also of the centre of the world. In this respect, the geographical location of a Hmong house is of

---

[131] Mircea Eliade also devotes special attention to the sacred threshold of the church, understanding it as the partition of existential spaces: the profane outside and the sacred inside. He conceptualises the threshold as both a boundary and as a place where both worlds meet and communicate, where a "passage from the profane to the sacred world becomes possible". (1959: 25)

minor importance; it is always perceived and constituted as the centre on both the horizontal and vertical levels. The hearths, the main door and the main pole are symbols of this centre. Every time a new Hmong house is built – whether in Ban Phui, Chiang Mai or Fresno (California), this centre is established anew. The house thus represents both a place and an *action* that can occur anywhere in the world. This concept of 'centre' dissolves spatial boundaries and, in some instances, movement and migration. It instead includes a potential for movement that can exceed any boundaries and of a place making anywhere in the world where Hmong build houses (or apartments) according to the cosmological principles.

People's behaviour around the house

A household comprises a self-contained unit. The oldest, married man is usually the head of this unit and owner of the house, its material belongings and the land. Sons can only keep most of the profit from and cultivate on their own terms land they have already officially inherited. One part of the revenue is then contributed to the household and in times of need (sickness or death), sons may be forced to contribute all of their earnings or even sell their cars or land to pay for hospital or mortuary rites costs.

Within the rectangular one-room house, with its small sleeping quarters divided off for each nuclear family, there is scant privacy for the people living together. The head of household's regime and well-being of the whole household take priority over the affairs of nuclear families and individuals. Couples share their small sleeping compartment, and often their beds, with their children. Even if wooden planks or blankets separate the sleeping area off from the main room, privacy does not exist in terms of an insulated room shielded from outside noises. For example, when the household head receives visitors until late in the evening, all other relatives must either stay awake or sleep in spite of the noises of conversation and laughter. The physical and spatial closeness of all household members ensures that people can easily call on each other at all times, even in the middle of the night.

Individuals do not have to pass through doors or other barriers to communicate with each other; a shout suffices to get attention. When nuclear families have retired to their sleeping quarters, people can still address each other through the noise-permeable delimitations of their quarters. However, they do not enter sleeping areas without the consent or presence of its inhabitants.

Hmong expect the members of their households to support each other to the fullest extent possible. Earnings from privately owned cash crop fields belong to the nuclear families. However, it is a social norm for family members to help one another in times of need, for example, if someone falls ill or has an accident, or has a poor harvest. When one of the household members becomes seriously ill, the Hmong also expect at least two people to care for that person. Family and lineage members take turns sitting with the sick person all day and all night. For example, when Txwj Xaab became seriously ill during my fieldwork, the whole household barely slept for two months. People usually support each other through their presence.

Different behaviour around the house is expected according to hierarchies of age and gender. The young have to show respect towards old people and above all, have to honour the head of household. As the main performer of the sacrificial rites for the ancestors and the house spirits, the household head mediates between the supernatural sphere and the other residents. Disparities in terms of gender occur when women have to subordinate themselves to male kin because men are the legitimate descendants of the ancestors. Despite this rule and the subdued behaviour of women towards men on official occasions, female household members receive respect for their work and partake in decisions as much as their male counterparts. As mentioned earlier, many men seek their wives' advice, albeit in private when the couple has withdrawn to its sleeping quarters.

Prohibitions in accordance with customary laws regulate the relationship between the household head and his daughters-in-law. A married woman and her father-in-law are not allowed to enter each other's sleeping quarters together. The Hmong believe this regulation safeguards the incest taboo, viewing daughters-in-law in much the same positions as daughters (Lee no year: 4; Chindarsi 1976: 79). A daughter-in-law has to observe several additional behavioural directives around the house. For example, she is not allowed to climb the roof of the house. This would mean she surmounts the main post of the house and positions herself above the central beam, the location of one of the house spirits. She is also not allowed to trespass on the area between the post and the sleeping quarters of her parents-in-law; this area is known as the southern side of the big fireplace and the domain of the household spirits. The daughter-in-law's violation of these taboos would represent an open disrespect for the ancestors and house spirits, which could bring harm to her and all members of the extended family. These prescriptions for behaviour and prohibitions illustrate that daughters-in-law have a special role and position within the household: They are integral parts of the extended family and seen as daughters. However, since they come from the outside sphere, they are nonetheless perceived as potentially threatening to the harmony between consanguinal family members and the supernatural.

Hierarchies and differing role classifications within the extended family become especially apparent during meals. Meals in the house take place in multiple, slightly differing ways, only the two most important of which I describe here. When only the nuclear family comes together for lunch, for example, the meal is mostly eaten on a large mat laid out on the floor in the middle of the main room. The food is placed in the middle of the mat; husband, wife and children sit close together around the meal and eat together at one time. When most of the household members are present for breakfast or dinner, then the women of the household serve the men at the long table – rice, fried pork, cucumber soup, chilli paste or stir fried vegetables, for example.

Men mostly eat before the women and children. These usually eat in a "second round" and sit down on small stools around the hearth, especially in winter when this is the warmest place in the house. When male lineage members join the household for a meal, the women can display an open, self-confident behaviour, even teasing their close kin of the opposite sex. This changes immediately when men are present to whom the women are neither closely related nor with whom they interact on a daily basis. Then they must demonstrate a more reserved, restrained behaviour. They are expected to serve food and hot tea, remain quietly in the background and not interrupt or join the men's conversation. If male villagers from different lineages or clans gather in a household during the evening to discuss matters, the host's wife must serve the men tea and stay awake until the last guests have departed or her husband signals that she is not needed any longer.

A "normal day"

A "normal day" in a household starts around five o'clock in the morning. The female household members get up before the men and children to prepare the morning's meal. As mentioned earlier, all women are expected to get up early in order to prepare everything for the other household members and take care of the children and various household chores, including feeding the chickens and pigs. The head of household's wife usually does less work around the house than her daughters and daughters-in-law and these delegate part of their work to the children, typically the girls.

In the mornings between five and six o'clock, the one-hour Hmong radio program emanates from many houses. Due to the houses' thin wooden or bamboo walls, the sounds of the Hmong radio blend into one background tone throughout the village during broadcast time. In the evenings, the Hmong program is on air between seven and eight o'clock. The Department of Public Welfare established a "Hilltribe Radio Station" in Chiang Mai in 1968 that still broadcasts in languages such as Karen, Hmong, Akha, Lisu or Lahu twice daily in the mornings and evenings. The radio station broadcasts news about mortuary rites or weddings, greetings from kin living apart from each other and traditional sung Hmong poetry, which plays in the background while villagers go about their daily activities. The early morning hours the people leave for the fields, is also when the headman addresses the whole village via microphone and loudspeakers to announce important administrative information or upcoming meetings.

Activities of household members can vary during the day. When fields need to be only weeded or watered, husband and wife, sometimes accompanied by young children go to their cash crop fields by themselves. At planting or harvesting time, the whole household, sometimes accompanied by lineage kin, leaves before sunrise to undertake the work communally. In any case, the house, and therefore also the village, for the most part empties out during the day. Only older people, who are too weak to work in the fields every day, young mothers weaning their children and school children, stay behind. Children start school at eight in the morning and finish around four in the afternoon; they take their lunch along to school. Sometimes boys and girls run home during lunch break to check if a household member has stayed home and can give them two or three baht for snacks.

Children are generally raised to become independent and strong from an early age on. Girls in particular are expected to assist their mothers and the other women of the household with their daily chores, such as dishwashing, laundry, or housecleaning. Six-year old girls already take care of and carry around their baby brothers or sisters, while fathers teach their sons how to handle and work with a machete – one of the most important Hmong tools and found in several shapes in every house. Children are raised and educated by their biological parents, their grandparents, as well as their "younger" and "older" fathers and partners. Childcare is easily organised within the household, since there are many people available who are regarded as legitimate educators. In spite of this, children have the closest attachment to their biological parents, sharing a sleeping quarter with them after roaming around the house and playing with all its residents during the day.

My personal observation, interviews and activity protocols show that most household members are either in the fields, at the trading markets or working as labourers during the day. Only people who have no work in their fields, are weak, take care of young children or are currently unemployed remain home during the day. The activities of people spending the day at home vary according to gender. Women do their housework, cook meals and meet with other women in front of houses for conversation or joint embroidering. Sometimes they watch daily soap operas from China, which the children and men also enjoy. Men spending the day at home repair their farm tools; watch soap operas or international (sports) news (villages receive CNN and BBC); rest in the hot afternoon sun; or join women or other men in front of the houses for chats or cups of tea. In most houses, a big pot with imported Chinese tea-leaves simmers over the fire of the family stove and provides a constant supply of tea for family members and visitors. Some of my informants stressed that the big teapot symbolises the unity of the people on the one hand, and the open hospitality of the Hmong on the other. While the Thai lowland population rarely consumes tea, many Hmong drink tea daily and see this as a cultural trait connecting them to their forefathers in China.

Within the house, daytime is always calm and quiet, since most of the household members are away and the children are at school. The main door typically remains closed; visitors passing by either join people sitting on the veranda in front of the house or, if no one is outside, they knock at the less important, less official side door, which most houses have. Entering through this door keeps the visit informal and relieves the person present in the household visited of any hosting obligations, such as offering a seat, tea or a long conversation. As part of the extended family and, in a way, the household, lineage members in particular enter and leave the house freely via this door. They are also free to visit in the evenings when household members mostly stay by themselves and spend spare time together.

Around seven o'clock in the evening, most house doors in the village are not only shut, but also locked from the inside. People say they need to protect themselves from thieves and "illegal" people in the village (meaning drug dealers or immigrants from Burma). But Hmong also lock their doors because the family needs some time to itself in the evenings, and the locked door signals this to outsiders. Only people with important requests or problems visit in the evenings. Other visits of minor importance, for example those aimed at borrowing something or obtaining information on some matter, take place either early in the morning, during the day or before dinner. "Formal" behaviour, including various signs of respect displayed by both the host and guest, is expected only on certain occasions. Such behaviour might involve the male host's prostration to welcome the guest. It occurs, for example, during visits by people who are not closely related and close relatives with whom there is little contact, or when performing a ceremony.

To sum up, it is important to note that the house setting has diverse qualities during the course of the day and can be visited in different manners. The presence of most family members characterises the mornings and evenings. The morning is filled with many activities in preparation of the day's work. It is the time when villagers not belonging to the lineage can pass by informally to discuss matters or borrow a farm tool. The doors remain open and visitors only have to shout a greeting to be asked in. During the day, when most people are gone, the house is a quiet setting, both in terms of noise and people's activities. This is the time to rest, go about chores and converse with lineage kin or neighbours from other clans. The house becomes increasingly busy after four o'clock when the children return from school and their parents gradually return from their fields or the market. As in the morning, the house's doors stay open; people leave and enter the house through the side door frequently. Visitors can easily drop in; neither side expects formal behaviour. This changes at dinnertime. When the family eats, visiting lineage members or villagers are urged to join the meal. Families are socially expected to invite visitors to eat with them. However, it is polite to refuse this invitation, or even better, not to go to other people's homes during mealtimes and after dinner.

After dinner, when the house is closed, visitors have to knock formally at the (side) door and state the purpose of their visit to be let inside. Data from activity protocols and personal observation show that most extended families stay at home in the evenings, sitting together around the big hearth or watching television. Men play with their children; women embroider or go to sleep early after a long day's work. This is also when household members take turns bathing in the toilet house. Visits by other villagers or kin from neighbouring villages are rare and mostly restricted to "official" purposes, such as mortuary rites and other ceremonies, or illness.

The neighbourhood square

As the village is characterised by a relative lack of cohesion and communal village activities occur rather seldom, most villages lack a central village square or meeting place. In some villages, such as Ban Phui, the Thai administration has financed the building of a meeting hall. The hall is above all used for official events such as the announcement of village related matters, drug education programs and conventions held by agencies like the Public Health or Royal Forestry Department. When villagers assemble on their own terms, they do so in their private homes or, less formally, in the areas around their houses and in one of the neighbourhood squares. This square can be a free area encircled by houses, a large, open space in front of a lineage member's house or an open area around a large shady tree, as in front of "my" house in Mae Sa Mai. Houses in the Hmong villages are built in relative proximity to each other. Because they are not surrounded by gardens, like those of the Karen for example, dwellings compose clusters of four to six houses, which are then separated by a path, street or neighbourhood square.

The closeness of the houses adds to the manifold background noises heard inside a home. The neighbours' conversations, television sets, radios, or chants, prayers and accompanying rituals can be easily heard. The physical proximity of the houses, including the sounds of their inhabitants, is considered normal and even desirable. For the most part, lineage members live in one neighbourhood of the village, share many meals with one another, help on each other's fields, and in many respects act as a large extended family. In this respect, it is an advantage when lineage members live close together and can easily call on each other. The neighbourhood square between or in front of the houses constitutes their informal meeting place. This is where they cook large amounts of food communally for important ceremonies and prepare, wash and package crops for market. Newly built houses near the fields, which are not yet surrounded by many other homes, are considered "unsafe" and lonely "outside" dwellings located too far from the daily assistance of relatives and the community.

The Hmong conceptualise the house to accommodate the benevolent inside sphere. Everything beyond its walls belongs to the malevolent outside sphere. In certain respects, the village in general and the section populated by one lineage in particular represent the "buffer zone" between these two spheres. Because the neighbourhood neither belongs completely to the inside nor the outside space, it provides its inhabitants with an area still spiritually safeguarded from the "unknown other" outside its boundaries. Although village sections consist of separate dwellings belonging to the extended families, houses of one lineage are viewed as a collective *home*. The centre of this collective home is the neighbourhood square.

In most cases, a lineage group residing in one neighbourhood of ten to twenty houses has more than a single, informal meeting area. There are three such locations in the vicinity of Win Huj's family's house: One in front of "my" house, around the large jackfruit tree; one at the carport of my neighbour, Vaam Zeej; and one between Win Huj's house and Nyaj Sua's house. All three places are equipped with small wooden benches and, as required, small stools or mats, which people who join the setting bring along themselves.

People meeting at the square

People meeting informally in one of the neighbourhood squares typically reside in the area. Villagers who have their houses in other sections of the settlement usually do not attend these settings. When people living in other parts of the village pass by a square, they stop for a brief conversation, or simply nod their heads and continue on their way. The setting is also not structured to easily host "outsiders" during these informal meetings because its small benches are mostly occupied. Additional seating must be brought along personally.

Gatherings in the open squares are informal enough for any nearby resident to join and leave the place at all times. People can, for example, stay for a scant three minutes and leave without a word, sit down for two hours and join the conversation, or engage in another activity like embroidering, sharpening a knife or eating a snack. Women typically leave and join the square frequently, intermittently caring for their children, putting food on the stove or doing other household chores.

In Mae Sa Mai, where village sections are inhabited by different clans, it is common for neighbours of different clans to meet informally in the neighbourhood square. They spend afternoons with spare time together, for example. Neighbours belonging to different clans also invite each other to their lineage ceremonies, which would typically not be done. However, Hmong throughout the village invite only elders, regardless of clan affiliation, to attend rituals held inside the private homes. For the most part, only lineage members provide reciprocal help around the house or on the fields, not neighbours belonging to different clans. While people of different clan membership interact informally in the neighbourhood squares every day, they seldom visit each other in their homes. This would require an official event, such as a ceremony, a sick neighbour or an invitation to watch television together. The neighbourhood square gives Hmong of different clans, who are socially less close to each other than clan or lineage people, the opportunity to meet in an unpretentious way. People can come and go, join and leave again without any formal greeting or farewell. The whole setting is unconventional, but can instantly be "disturbed" in its familiarity through a visitor, for example an elder from another clan or outside visitor, whose behaviour must be formal and socio-culturally appropriate according to customary morals and norms.

In general, women populate the setting of the neighbourhood square more often than men. Women sometimes stay at home while their husbands drive the agricultural products to market, take care of the household's children and prepare the meals for the family. They thus have more opportunities to join the open area – and go about their task of embroidering Hmong costumes. The full traditional dress is only worn for the New Year.[132] A family then displays its social position and wealth by wearing painstakingly hand-stitched clothes. On "normal" days, villagers both in Mae Sa Mai and Ban Phui do not adhere traditional dress codes. Only some of the older people retain the complete traditional costume. Men usually only wear the baggy Hmong trousers, which are embroidered at the end of the trousers' legs. Women wear the Hmong jacket in combination with a blouse or t-shirt and trousers or a sarong. Most women always wear typical handmade Hmong silver jewelry, such as earrings and bracelets, which are finely ornamented and chased.

Returning to the setting, the neighbourhood square is, like the house, used for different purposes at different times of the day and year. Early in the morning, before and after breakfast, male lineage members generally populate the square for a short period of about half an hour. They meet to discuss their day's work and possible common rides into town while their wives prepare the children for school and attend to household chores. During the day, women use the square to prepare and pack agricultural products for the market, meet to embroider together, taking care of young children in the meantime. Most women who join the setting of the square bring along their embroidering material either tucked inside their belts or in a small basket. Completing the hand-sewn, elaborately decorated clothes for the whole family requires endless hours of work. Every Hmong mother teaches her daughters the craft of *paj ntaub* (literally: flower cloth) from an early age on. Women are socially expected to spend their "spare time" with this craft and display their diligence. For the most part, they keep busy or pretend to be

---

[132] For descriptions of the traditional Hmong costume see Lewis and Lewis 1984: 101-133.

busy with embroidering, although they sometimes fall asleep on their mats in the hot midday sun.

When the husbands are at the markets and children at school, the women mostly do not cook lunch for themselves. Instead, they buy a Thai noodle-soup or curry from one of the travelling Thai traders who frequently pass by the Hmong villages to sell their goods. These dishes, as well as snacks like ice cream in wheat buns or fried chicken claws, are shared among the women. Generally however, the women share food more openly when it originates from their own fields. They spend hours in the square eating, embroidering, resting and gossiping. Although a marginal discourse, the women's gossip about other villagers, especially about other sections of the community and people from other clans, helps define the social and moral boundaries of the neighbourhood and lineage. These conversations reinforce and reproduce dominant societal perceptions.

The village square setting primarily changes in the afternoon around four to five p.m. when children, men and couples who have been in the fields together return home and populate the neighbourhood. Men join the women underneath the tree or on the bench near the house, recount the day's events and relax in the friendly atmosphere of their kin and neighbours. People who join either bring their own small stools or use the motorbikes parked nearby for additional seating. Women and men, old and young, can informally meet. They do not have to observe the usual behavioural constraints regarding age and gender to their full extent. Instead, people of the opposite sex can tease each other or old and young can engage in a kind of joking relationship. This would be unthinkable in other settings, such as inside the spiritually important house. When people have tense muscles after a hard day's work in the fields, they even massage each other in the neighbourhood square. It is in this setting, the open, outside sphere filled with many people, that women with therapeutical knowledge can massage their half undressed male kin's people – a behaviour that would otherwise give rise to rumour and conflict.

The setting of the neighbourhood square is convenient for both parents and children. As within the house, children become accustomed to adults, learn to call lineage members by their classificatory kinship terms and to obey them the same as their biological parents. Children can roam around the neighbourhood freely and find their parents and other adults seated in the squares on small stools or mats, at their own height. In other words, adults are not located above but at children's level. Children either play with each other or train themselves in adult activities. At the age of eight or nine, girls start to embroider small parts of cloth and are instructed by their mothers. Boys let their cocks fight each other, just like their fathers.

Compared to girls, boys usually receive special treatment from all adults. While daughters must help with household chores, boys can play outside in the village square. When boys and girls get in fights, no matter who started the quarrel, the girls are usually reprimanded. When children ask their parents or grandparents for money to buy snacks, boys always receive one to two baht more than the girls. Despite these differences in upbringing, which can be easily observed in the frequent interactions between parents and children in the neighbourhood square setting, both boys and girls are trained in toughness. Hmong expect all children to become independent at an early age and learn to solve problems on their own.

Children do not receive instant assistance with difficult matters. Adults wait and see if they can find solutions for themselves. For example, one afternoon a four-year old girl had climbed a three-metre wall belonging to the school compound, located near the jackfruit tree of "my" house in Mae Sa Mai. Many people were assembled underneath the tree, but no one got up to help the crying girl off the high wall. Instead, they teased the girl and prodded her into finding a solution herself – she had climbed the wall, so she had to find a way down, which she finally did. Yet more than girls, boys are trained in toughness. Both female and male lineage members incite them when their cocks fight, when they hit banana trees until they fall down or box with their fathers. From an early age, boys are socialised to feel special and view themselves as predominantly masculine. Girls are taught to be strong but obedient to male dominance. Both are expected to show their utmost respect towards the generation of and above their parents.

The square around New Year[133]

Changes in the people and activities of the neighbourhood square unfold not only within the course of the day but also the year. Hmong frequent the open areas less during work peaks, when the planting or harvesting of crops keeps most of them busy from sunrise to sunset. Moreover, during the rainy season between May and October, when rain soaks everything outside, the neighbourhood square is seldom used. Most activities take place inside the houses then. However, at the end of the rainy season, the Hmong start to frequent the meeting places. They again become characterised by the busy activities of both adults and children. When the New Year ceremony (*tsiab peb caug*) at the end of December approaches, women are busy in the square finishing the family's costumes. Men meet to plan and organise the celebrations, boys and girls to train for spinning wooden tops. As part of the New Year's activities, the third day is devoted to contests in "traditional" Hmong games and crafts. Spinning tops is one contest during which men and boys officially compete against each other. The New Year Festival is one of the most important Hmong celebrations, usually lasting for five days. Utmost importance is assigned to the various sacrificial "thanksgiving" rituals for the spirit of the house, the ancestor spirits, the spirits of the crops, as well as for the *plig* of all household members involved in the New Year festivities. Rituals also serve to expel all evil and ill fortune. It is important for the Hmong to have a good start into the New Year, with the best clothes and food, abundant offerings to the spirits and ancestors and traditional Hmong activities. Everything that happens during these days will have a positive effect on the whole new year.

As the Festival approaches, alcohol from corn is distilled in large pans in the neighbourhood squares and adults meet after dinner to practice sung poetry. During the celebrations, adults compete against each other on a large

---

[133] This section does not attempt to give an overall account of the New Year Festival, but rather describe the activities of the neighbourhood square setting connected to New Year. For a detailed description of the ceremonies see, for example, Yang Dao 1992: 300-308 and Nusit Chindarsi 1976: 136-139.

village stage in the evenings. The whole atmosphere of the neighbourhood fills with busy and joyful anticipation of the upcoming event. A couple of days before the end of the Hmong year, calculated after the Chinese lunar calendar, all people from the neighbourhood meet in one of the open areas to cook sticky rice together in large pans. The cooked rice is then filled into a wooden dug-out form and beaten intermittently by two people. The grains of rice are stamped into a sticky "dough". At least ten people then communally divide the gluey, dough-like mass and pack small pieces into banana leaves. During the New Year's celebrations, these packages of sticky rice are grilled over the fire. This "cake" is a very popular desert available only at this time of the year. Hmong people visiting from neighbouring villages or afar are also served this delicacy and homemade corn "whiskey".

Once the New Year celebrations have started, people fill the open areas around the neighbourhood and cook rice and pork in peppered water over large fires for the ceremonies. Although each household performs the sacrificial rituals individually and, except for the *ntoo xeeb* ceremony, no communal village rite takes place, male villagers visit and join each other in the different neighbourhood squares and inside the houses for ceremonial meals. Women are typically not invited to eat and drink in houses not belonging to their own lineage, whereas many families throughout the settlement ask the men to join them. During the Festival, some spatial boundaries and restrictions common throughout the rest of the year are partly abandoned. Nevertheless, the generalised gender division, moral norms and high socio-cultural importance of men prevail during these cheerful festivities.

A ceremony in the village

In order to provide an example of another important setting, I have chosen to describe and analyse a typical ceremony in the village. The ceremony is significant both for its frequent recurrence in the community and because it illustrates the social and ritual levels on which most (male) villagers interact.

Rhythm of Spatiality: Important Village Settings 377

As mentioned earlier, the total village community only assembles on rare occasions. The settlement unit is also conceptually less important than the extended family and the (lineage) people of a neighbourhood. Village matters are only discussed by elders or other representatives in formal meetings (for the most part only when a problem has occurred). They are also addressed during numerous rituals in households to which elders and other respectable men of the village community are invited. Such ceremonies can be welcoming or farewell rituals for villagers coming home from or leaving for a longer period of time in Bangkok, for example. Hmong might also hold them to thank people for their support in solving problems like obtaining the Thai identity card for a household member or honouring an important guest in the village. Other occasions to kill a pig and invite villagers would be the announcement of a new position within the Thai administration, the "mature naming ceremony" for adult men, a good win in the illegal lottery or the purchase of a new car, which must be blessed by the shaman. Most aspects of the typical ceremonial setting described here can also be found in more elaborate rituals, such as the mortuary rites, marriages, or the lineage-centred *lwm tauj* (literally: clean the house with a broom) ritual, the so-called tofu day ritual when lineage members are not allowed to consume meat. The (sub)setting of a ceremony illustrates the ways in which seniority and hierarchy are maintained and confirmed within the villages. It also shows how single households subordinate themselves to the rules and norms of the Hmong community while trying to position themselves within the hierarchical Hmong society. Finally, it demonstrates the ways in which Hmong identity as well as the position and status of political and ritual leaders, are acknowledged and reinforced.

The ritual before the communal meal

As previously mentioned, most Hmong settlements do not have central meeting places. These are not needed because most of the villagers' social and ritual activities take place in and around individual houses. The central location of a typical ceremonial setting in a house includes the long table standing in front of the altar(s) along the wall opposite the main entrance door of the house. Minor locations are the seating platform inside the house and areas outside the dwelling where mostly young Hmong men, who do not have any office or high status, are seated for most of the time.

Before most of the invited male villagers arrive, a shaman or ritual expert – depending on the occasion – performs the actual rite in front of the house altar by sacrificing a pig, incense sticks, paper money, rice, whiskey and tea to the spirits of the house, the ancestors and the *plig* of the household members involved. The spirits of the house and the ancestors are invited to "come to eat" the pig and look after the *plig* of the persons involved in the ritual. As with most ceremonies, not much solemn attention is given to the religious performance itself. Generally only the household head, his wife and important lineage members attend. Other female household members may be present in the background, but leave during or shortly after the ritual to prepare the food.

After the actual rite, usually around noon, numerous male lineage members assemble in the square in front of the house for the communal preparation of the meat, skinning the pig and cutting it into pieces. This is accompanied by loud conversation and laughter. Men are always jointly responsible for killing the pig and preparing the traditional pork dish (pork cooked for twenty minutes in salted and peppered water) while the women provide the rice, serve the meal, clean up afterwards and take care of any remaining chores. Female lineage members support each other with their tasks, cook parts of the rice in their own homes when a house lacks a second large stove outside for the rice. They also help each other wash the dishes. The women assisting at the ceremony are usually the only women to attend the event because mostly only men from other parts of the village join the ritual meal. Elders, the clan's own shaman and men of all clans who hold important offices are the most essential guests of the ceremonies. Nonetheless households try to host as many men as possible in order to strengthen their position within the community. Few visitors and the absence of important dignitaries would signal the weak standing of the household head within the village.

The seating order

Most of the guests arrive after the religious performance. The most important people are asked to take a seat at the long table first. The rest, who cannot fit at the table, either sits around the family stove or on the platform and wait for the first "round" at the table to finish their food. All men not belonging to the first round sit down at the table to eat in a second or even third round. The last round is made up of women, if they have not already eaten outside the house. The first round is the formal one and necessitates the observance of many rules. It includes a ritualised form of drinking and eating to which subsequent rounds do not adhere.

Figure 14: Male seating order during ceremonies

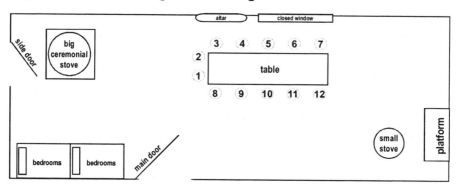

Source: own survey

The most important man, according to status and office, in the first round is viewed as the "chairman" of the ceremony and therefore seated at the head of the table. This place of honour (No. 1) occupies the left-hand side, near to the altar, next to the big fireplace and opposite the main door. The shaman and all other important people sit on the ceremonial head's left side. The most honourable men thus occupy the positions at the head of the table and along the wall.

A man's position at the table signifies his social position. Places are allocated by the host and elders alike; their decisions are guided by socially constituted perceptions of a man's Hmong traditional knowledge, adherence to Hmong mores and norms, socio-economic standing, his family's reputation, as well as any official positions he might hold. When most of these factors are positively valued, a man gains public recognition and invitation to occupy a high-status position. The allocation of a honourable place is a highly interactional activity through which social identities are negotiated and the ongoing social event framed in terms of spatial access (see also Duranti 1992: 660). This conscious relational positioning emplaces such qualities as status, position, office, function and/or spiritual powers. Hierarchy is thus spatially translated from an abstract phenomenon of social structuration into action (see also Dickhardt and Hauser-Schäublin 2003: 30).

As the Hmong, especially in Mae Sa Mai, have to deal with certain Thai officials, they are invited to official ceremonies in the village. For the most part, these officials come to show their respect towards the Hmong people with whom they directly cooperate. They stem, for example, from the Royal Project, National Park or district police, and are allocated places of relatively high social standard (number four to six seats in the diagram). In the past, when relations were characterised by tensions, mistrust and conflict, such visits of Hmong rituals by Thai men were unusual. As Hmong villagers increasingly interact with Thai people, they respect them for their education and relative economic success. Yet relationships between the two people primarily remain on a formal and superficial basis, as discussed in chapter seven.

Toasts and speeches before the meal

Before the actual meal starts, the women put fried pork on the table. Two (male) lineage relatives, who walk around the table from behind, serve the men seated two small cups of whiskey in the order of their seniority. The first man at the table delivers a brief speech, then drinks a toast to the person sitting next to him, finishes the two cups and passes them, in order of seniority, to his neighbour, who then repeats the procedure. While emptying the two cups of homemade corn "whiskey", one can also ask for help from others, thus passing cups to the men serving from behind or to other people sitting around in the room. Through this activity, men and women not seated at the table are integrated into the main aspect of the setting. Those toasting wish luck to and praise the seated neighbour and hosts and also emphasise the greatness, strength and unity of the Hmong people. Men further honour and glorify each other, strengthening Hmong self-confidence. As such, these ceremonies are important events that help to bolster Hmong identity and cohesion.

Seating order during a ceremony

After the speeches, ritualised drinking and eating of the pork "appetizer" women arrange the "real food", which must always contain rice, on the table according to customary rules: bowls of rice and pork soup stand in alternating order on the table. The men eat, drink non-ritualised rounds of whiskey and get up individually as soon as they have finished their meal. The men are expected to do so because seats are needed for the subsequent "informal" eating rounds not preceded by the speeches and formalised drinking. Women clean the table in the meantime and constantly replenish the food.

Sub-setting outside the house

After having finished eating, the men either retire to the platform to rest and drink some of the tea simmering over the family stove or leave the central part of the setting completely by going outside the house. The sub-setting outside the dwelling is less formal than inside. Here, people can move around freely, sit together in small groups and chat the afternoon away over further glasses of whiskey. After their work, the unmarried and married women also assemble in the neighbourhood square, typically somewhat apart from the men. Nonetheless, the men offer them drinks, which they usually turn down, since it is not appropriate for females to appear drunk in public.

The house's interior, as a representation of the cosmos, is closely connected to the supernatural sphere and behaviour, movement and actions are more restricted in the ceremony setting. Outside, people are no longer bound by behavioural restrictions connected to the setting. For example, they can leave at any time without much hassle. Children can play and make noise, since the serenity of the setting inside the house must not be observed. At the table, the atmosphere is more tense and regulated by rules of conduct. Outside the house, the honourable men mingle with the others and are less formal than inside.

Trips to mortuary rites in a neighbouring village

Besides visits to markets and necessary trips to hospitals or the administration in the lowlands, mortuary rites comprise the most important reason for Hmong people to travel longer distances. As seen in chapter seven, many villagers attend mortuary rites in other Hmong settlements about two to three times per year. Women travel less to other Hmong communities, as well as to the lowlands in general. Nonetheless, for them too, mortuary rites represent the most important reason to accompany men on visits to Hmong villages as far as one to three hours drive. For the most part, only men attend mortuary rites taking place farther away that require an overnight stay.

I explore the typical setting of a visit of mortuary rites in another Hmong village here rather than attendance of these rites in one of the villages studied to include travel as part of the setting. Attendance of mortuary ceremonies within one's own village differ from attendance of such rites in other villages. Within the settlement, people are present at the house of the deceased two or three times during the rites lasting over days. Women mostly attend with a few female kin's people. They tend to stay shorter than the men, who are joined by their "younger" and "older" brothers and expected to stay for the most part of the night. Husband and wife thus do not attend mortuary rites together, but in small groups made up of their own sex.

Trips to mortuary rites in other Hmong villages differ because women and men travel together in a larger group of kin's people. Contrary to mortuary rites in their own settlements, people only participate in the rites outside their villages once, but for at least half of the night. Important mortuary rites farther away than a three-hours drive are mostly visited by a group of men only. Due to the distance, they must spend one or two nights in the other community. Women, especially those with younger children, stay behind in the home village to take care of the rest of the family. Usually Hmong look unfavourably upon women travelling long distances alone with men. If women join in to visit mortuary rites, there are always at least three or four of them. This is different for older women, who have a more consolidated status. The Hmong would not dare question their integrity; hence, they can travel unaccompanied by other women to mortuary rites farther away and stay overnight in a clan relative's house.

The Hmong typically visit mortuary rites for the head of household of one's own clan's people, as well as for relatives of the wife's natal clan.

Above all, great numbers of Hmong attend mortuary rites of respected elders, but also of older women with the reputation of being honourable and knowledgeable. Within Hmong society, people are expected to demonstrate respect towards the family of the deceased and elders of the village by attending numerous mortuary rites. People support the mourning through their presence and through lengthy attendance, underscore that the deceased was a respected member of the Hmong community – a fact also important for the reputation of the living who remain behind. Traditional Hmong mortuary rites, which occur over days, can only proceed with the help of many people. Those who do not adhere to the moral norm of attending other families' mortuary rites are punished through social sanctions. In return, rites for the deceased of that person's family are poorly attended. In other words, the rest of the community eventually "punishes" disregard for social obligations.

Most Hmong place special emphasis on being present for the nighttime deathwatch, since the dark hours are the most difficult for the family in mourning. On the first night, the recitation of the "Showing the Way" (Hmong: *qhuab kev*) chant, which can last up to five hours, guides the soul of the dead to the Otherworld and finally to the ancestors in China. The chant spans the deceased's life stages and places in reverse order. The night before the burial is the time for settling the debts of the deceased and for a long prayer lasting for hours that is meant to teach the descendants how to act towards one another.[134] The Hmong understand this night in particular as an occasion to visit the house of the deceased in great numbers, with people coming from both the village and afar.

The journey

Most journeys to mortuary rites in other villages begin after a day's work in the early evening around six o' clock. Lineage members meet in one of the

---

[134] For a translation of the prayer see Nusit Chindarsi 1976: 148-157.

Rhythm of Spatiality: Important Village Settings

neighbourhood squares where the pick-up trucks are parked. The atmosphere is relaxed and joyful because most Hmong view a shared journey through the mountains to another Hmong village not only as a social obligation, but "fun" as well. The voyage, despite its sad occasion, permits a welcomed interruption of the daily routine and meeting of a large number of clan relatives and other Hmong people.

Both men and women typically dress in their traditional Hmong clothes when driving to mortuary rites. Costumes seldom include all the elaborate accessories, such as the heavy silver necklaces and breast garments worn during New Year. People underscore the importance of wearing the Hmong clothes to openly display Hmong identity and contribute to strengthening Hmong culture during events at which hundreds of Hmong relatives assemble. Most remarkable in this respect is Doi Pui, a Hmong village near Mae Sa Mai that is *the* hilltribe tourist destination in Thailand. Every day, tour buses drive up the Suthep mountain near Chiang Mai to provide international tourists with the opportunity to visit an "authentic" hilltribe community. However, this village is divided into two parts: The front part contains approximately forty or fifty souvenir stands where Hmong, as well as Thai and Chinese, traders peddle standard handicrafts and airport art. The back section of Doi Pui, which is not visited, resembles any other Hmong settlement, only somewhat richer due to the many new, Toyota pick-ups. While villagers there hardly wear any parts of their customary Hmong dress during the day for the tourists, they wear their full traditional dress, including all the accessories and elaborate hairstyle of the women, for mortuary rites – consciously displaying a Hmong identity that withstands the "invasion" of thousands of tourists each year.

Returning to my description of the mortuary rite setting: Improved infrastructure within northern Thailand and the fact that most extended Hmong families have at least one pick-up truck at their disposal facilitates attendance of multiple mortuary rites in Hmong communities. About ten to fifteen people travel together in one truck. Contrary to normal practice, children are not taken along because such trips usually last well into the night. The two most important men of the group sit together with the driver in the closed front cab, while the rest of the group sits on the load area in the back; women mostly wrapped in blankets because the breeze, especially at night, can be quite cold. Despite the (cool) wind and rumbling of the car over dirt roads, most of the rides to mortuary rites are accompanied by laughter and cheerful conversation in joyful anticipation of meeting many clan relatives.

When arriving after a one to three hour drive, the Hmong visitors usually find the village of the deceased already crowded with parked pick-up trucks from many Hmong communities. While most Hmong settlements are relatively quiet and unpopulated after dinnertime, villages with mortuary rites come alive for four or five nights. Extra light bulbs are installed in the village to guide visitors from all parts of northern Thailand to the house of the deathwatch. The sounds of the mortuary drum and *qeej* (reed pipe) can be heard from afar, as can the chattering of large numbers of people.

Spatial division of the house

Upon arriving at the house of the dead, the group travelling together divides according to gender. The men go towards the main door while the women enter the dwelling through the side door. The men donate about 100 baht each at the post set up in front of the main entrance to help the family with the high expenses for the mortuary rites. These contributions are listed in a book indicating the amount of money, the name, and the origin of the male donator. These notes show that visitors to Hmong mortuary rites usually come from thirty to forty different places within Thailand. Hmong relatives from other countries such as Laos, France or the U.S. are usually the exception and would only attend when a close lineage member has died. Women do not donate any money and are thus not included in the listing. Sometimes these lists are made public and hung on the outside wall of the house for everyone to see who has attended the rites and how much each person has donated. This practice highlights the strong social pressure to attend mortuary rites and support the family of the deceased socially and economically.

Figure 15: Spatial division of a Hmong house during mortuary rites

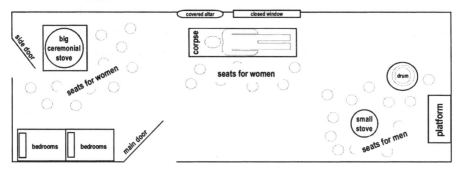

Source: own survey

All windows of the house of a dead are closed to keep out malevolent spirits who might want to enter "undetected" and harm the deceased in his or her passage to the Otherworld. Three aspects always characterise the atmosphere inside the house of the deceased: First, it is sad, with people mourning around the displayed corpse and women seated in rows for the deathwatch. The sound of the mortuary drum, located in the right part of the room and surrounded by *qeej* players, underpins the mournful climate. Both the sounds of the drum and the *qeej* are typical reverberations of mortuary rites, and these instruments are only played in this combination for the communication between the living and deceased (cf. Cooper et al. 1996: 42-45). Second, the atmosphere is very formal near the main entrance door where new male guests arrive and are formally received by five to ten of the deceased's male lineage relatives. As part of the formal greeting, the men prostrate themselves in front of the new arrival and move their hands towards the guests to honour them while speaking words of appreciation and thank. Most people interrupt the bowing after a short while, saying that they have accepted the honour and do not want to be positioned above their hosts any longer. The atmosphere is also quite formal in the left part of the room around the main stove where the women simply sit in great numbers in rows facing the corpse and the drum. Third, around the family stove and sitting platform, the atmosphere is rather joyous and excited. Only men sit and meet there for conversation and drinks. This relatively merry sub-setting partly overlaps with the sub-setting of the formal greeting of new arrivals in the very crowded part of the house around the main door. The informal and formal activities do not obstruct each other, but take place simultaneously. On the whole, the different sub-settings of the mortuary ceremony at night, the intermingling sounds of the special music and humming of countless voices transform the inside of the house into a very particular and intense setting.

Gendered activities

Women do not enter the house through the main entrance, as the men do, but through the side door. Shortly after the formal greeting, which only the men receive from the hosts, men and women meet up again in front of the deceased to pay their respects by looking, mourning loudly and even touching the corpse. Women generally remain in that area near the dead, either seated directly in rows in front of the deceased or in rows in the left side of the room, which is populated exclusively by a great number of women. Here, the atmosphere is livelier than near the corpse. Nevertheless, it remains quite formal because subdued behaviour is generally expected of women inside the main room during mortuary rites. Unlike the men, women are not offered a drink like tea or whiskey inside the house. While the men around the sitting platform on the right side of the main door gather and talk in quite cheerful groups, the women comply with their tasks by mourning the dead, taking care of the deathwatch and simply remaining in large numbers in the left part of the room. They speak only quietly. Men sit and drink together and exchange knowledge about ritual aspects, agricultural facts and

& nbsp;
# Rhythm of Spatiality: Important Village Settings

news about Hmong relatives who are not present. The conversations of Hmong men and women that take place during the night at mortuary rites facilitate the dissemination of knowledge and information throughout the Hmong Mountains.

Outside the house

Outside and all around the neighbourhood, the sub-setting has the atmosphere of a funfair: To host guests during the night and overnight guests for even several days, kin relatives of the dead have to provide food, drink and entertainment. Men sit together in one corner and play cards or board games for money. In one of the open squares, rows of women and men sit in great numbers in front of a dramatic Hmong love story filmed either in China or by American Hmong filmmakers in Thailand. Thai porn films are mostly shown for the men in a house nearby.

Besides gambling and film watching, many guests also entertain themselves by talking to Hmong relatives or by meeting new people during one of the many meals served on long tables outside the house. Hmong people, men and women alike, from different regions sit together, ask themselves about their clan backgrounds to find common relatives and ancestors and instantly link up in that way. Even a Yang man at a deceased's house in Nong Hoi Mai, a neighbouring village of Mae Sa Mai, immediately called me „sister" when he heard that I had been adopted into his clan. After having attended several mortuary rites in the vicinity of both of my research sites, I started to encounter Hmong people from different villages whom I had already met at previous mortuary rites. To a small extent, I was thus incorporated into the activities and relations constituting and interconnecting the Hmong Mountains.

The women typically want to drive home to their villages earlier than the men. They tend to tire early because they get up in the mornings to prepare breakfast for their families. For them the ceremony setting is more tiring and, after a while, more boring than for the men. Sitting at night in a crowded room without drink or the opportunity to move or speak much is more exhausting and less entertaining than the men's meeting, talking, laughing, and drinking. Sometimes the women succeed in convincing their men to leave the house of the ritual around two or three o'clock at night, but if the women are not careful the men steal away to "quickly" visit another clan relative in the village. After a while waiting, the people travelling together in one pick-up truck finally assemble and can drive home through the moonlit mountains and starry night.

The trip to a market in the lowlands

The market in the lowlands where Hmong people from the villages studied sell their crops from pick-up trucks to individual customers or wholesalers is an important setting because it forms both part of the villagers' frequent activities and shows the interface between the "Hmong world" and life in the lowlands. As already with my description of the mortuary rite setting, I include travel in my analysis of the setting of the lowland markets. The Hmong journey from the mountainous area to the markets is not merely a car ride but clarifies many aspects of the ways in which Hmong villagers act in lowland settings.

Hmong nuclear families from both Mae Sa Mai and Ban Phui visit markets in Chiang Mai to sell crops from their own fields when a trader has not been found beforehand or when they expect better profits through retail prices. The Hmong do not have permanent stands at the markets but request them when needed. Villagers try to obtain a communal location in one section of the markets where they can park their pick-up trucks together as vending places. Thus, there is a particular Hmong section at the Muang Mai market in Chiang Mai where Hmong people from different villages within Chiang Mai Province gather for their business. Hmong view proximity to other Hmong as a means of security in social terms, but not necessarily cooperation in economic terms. Each Hmong couple or group of people selling their crops together sell their wares on their own terms without any economic cooperation with other clan's people. It is more important to meet kin and non-kin from other places, exchange information about relatives and developments in the villages and assist each other when help is needed to guard the vending place. Thus, the typical Hmong setting at lowland markets helps constitute a special Hmong network within northern Thailand. Throughout northern Thailand, Hmong people successfully constitute typical Hmong settings, even outside their villages in the lowland, that serve as alternative "Hmong retreats" in a macro-setting dominated by non-Hmong people. In other words, people can travel to places such as Mae Chaem, Mae Rim, Chiang Mai or even Bangkok and always be able to move within particular Hmong settings that help maintain Hmong culture and identity.

In most cases, husband and wife sell crops like carrots, leek, or cabbage together right from their truck. However, women mostly stay in the "background", meaning that they pack and weigh the goods. The men interact directly with the customers because they usually speak better Thai. In addition, too much interaction between (married) Hmong women and unknown Thai men would be considered inappropriate, especially when the husband is around to negotiate prices. When male lineage members harvest one crop at the same time, they sometimes also drive to one of the lowland markets together to jointly sell their crops. In that case, the wives mostly stay behind in the village to take care of the children, the household, or other tasks in the fields. When people drive to the lowlands, either to market their crops, buy agricultural products or visit a doctor, they usually go with a number of people, seldom alone. There are several reasons for this.

First, the Hmong think economically and try to make the best possible use of the pick-up's load area. Villagers who do not own a car pay about fifty to 100 baht for one trip to lowland markets on the truck of an unrelated resident (depending on the distance and the load transported). Lineage members are mostly transported for free. Second, the Hmong view travelling together as a type of "security" because the Hmong truck is a place where people can rely on each other and act in similar ways. At the marketplace, the truck becomes the vending place that can be easily driven into and retrieved from the overall setting of the lowland market. It enables the Hmong farmers to market their products with relative freedom from lowland structures and facilitates the constitution of a Hmong setting at the marketplace.

The Hmong pick-up truck is therefore more than just a mode of transport; it is part of a Hmong spatiality that exists parallel to lowland spatiality. To be surrounded by many people of the own group entails social support and security in a foreign space, as outlined in the chapters above. When going to a market in the lowlands, most villagers make sure to wear at least one part of the traditional Hmong dress, men mostly the baggy Hmong trousers and women the jacket, to display their ethnic affiliation and be easily recognised by other Hmong people. The Hmong succeed in constituting an exclusively Hmong setting at lowland markets, which is a spatially separate area of the market where Hmong norms, values and modes of conduct prevail. For example, if one family cannot sell all its crops in one day, they transform the truck into an on-spot sleeping place where the people can spend the night and keep their vending space for the next day. Since a number of Hmong families have to stay overnight at the market, people remain assure they are surrounded, and thus protected from thieves, in their "Hmong setting" by their own people.

Even after establishing strong, permanent relations to traders from the lowlands, relations with the Thai are, apart from a few exceptions, mainly economical and do not extend into the private sphere. Hmong people stay among themselves at the markets and when they visit other places in town. For example, when Hmong villagers visit a Thai restaurant or noodle shop for lunch, other Hmong accompany them or they stop at places frequented by other Hmong. Word spreads quickly within the Hmong community about restaurants that are good, cheap, and, most of all, run by Thai people who are friendly towards the Hmong and prepare food according to Hmong requirements. In many of these eating establishments, cassette tapes by famous local Hmong singers or video tapes with Hmong movies from the "World Video Recording Company" (from Fresno, California) are on display for the Hmong customers because the Thai or Chinese owners have already adapted to the needs of their Hmong customers. In other words, most Hmong people would rather move around in Hmong settings in the lowlands than take advantage of the great variety of eating places a Thai city has to offer.

Hmong must also visit places in the lowlands other than the markets, such as administration offices or hospitals. Because they cannot easily "turn these places into" Hmong settings, they generally limit their stays to a bare minimum and visit in the company of relatives. This, of course, does not apply to Hmong men who hold a formal office and must interact with lowland people frequently, or to young Hmong, as explicated in chapter eight. However, most Hmong try to move around in the lowlands in predominantly Hmong settings and withdraw, when possible, to the mountainous areas as soon as they finish their business. Twenty or thirty years ago, they could not do this to the same extent because the lowlands were still as much as a day's walk from the villages. Geographical distances were difficult to overcome, not to speak of cultural barriers and prejudices. Today, the Hmong can easily drive to the lowlands. But despite the diminution of geographical barriers, many socio-cultural barriers seem to persist between most Hmong and Thai people. Prejudices continue on both sides, despite the frequent interactions between business partners and official representatives. Hmong villagers thus prefer to move around in the lowlands in settings that include many of their own people and Hmong behavioural norms.

The world outside of Thailand

In addition to the various settings and sub-settings important for Hmong daily life, another important setting exists that is not concretely accessible for most people: the world outside of Thailand. Only a few villagers have ever left the country, but most people are confronted daily with the outside world through television and radio; agricultural products and companies from Western countries; cash crops purportedly grown for the world market; tourists, extension workers and researchers; relatives visiting form the United States or France; and, last but not least, through stories told about ancient China, migration and the Hmong ancestors.

Hmong villagers take part in world news such as the destruction of the World Trade Centre, occurrences in the war in Iraq, the tsunami that devastated the south of Thailand and other Asian countries in December 2004, and results of popular soccer games such as between Manchester United and Liverpool via daily television broadcasting. Some people are even directly affected by an event such as the terrorist attack of September 11, 2001 or the December 2004 tsunami, since tourist numbers to Thailand have declined in the aftermath. As a result, Hmong villagers from Mae Sa Mai can sell less souvenirs to tourists in Chiang Mai, Bangkok and other destinations. People became deeply worried when the United States Army started to invade Iraq because they feared the whole world, including the North of Thailand, would become unsafe. Many Hmong men watch news on Thai or international broadcasting channels like CNN and BBC every evening to inform themselves about the rest of the world. Women do not watch the news as much as the men because they are busy with cooking, child-rearing and household chores during the news broadcasts at seven p.m. They are also usually less fluent in Thai than their husbands. And finally, they tend to be less interested in international affairs because they are busy with the maintenance of their own world.

Generally, the world outside of Thailand is divided into two spheres: The Hmong Mountains, which include China and other (Southeast Asian) countries where the Hmong live, and the rest of the world, represented by the West. People perccive countries where other Hmong people live as for the most part accessible, since they know they can rely on the Hmong clan networks in these countries. Many Hmong villagers say they have had the urge to visit places like France or the United States in the past. In the meantime however, they have realised that life in these countries is not necessarily easier or better than in Thailand. International news about mad cow disease in Europe or the terrorist attacks in the U.S. have changed this aspiration. Accounts from relatives living in these countries have also emphasised that Hmong life there is characterised by hard work and sometimes even poverty. Instead of wanting to visit relatives in the Western world, many Hmong people dream of travelling to China one day. Men and women alike stress that they do not have the urge to live but rather to travel there to see "the original" Hmong culture in their "homeland". They wish to visit their brothers and sisters in China, see how Hmong culture is "properly" performed and experience how it differs from their own way of living. Nicholas Tapp has also found this longing for China among the Hmong people of his Thai research site:

> "To revisit China is to go back in time, to go back to 'the village of the mother and father' where the soul of the deceased is led to be reborn, to revisit cousins who must be closer to the ways of the grandparents than one has been able to be oneself." (2001: 16)

While the Karen people in northern Thailand speak frequently of Europe and have the wish to travel there, Hmong have the greatest desire to visit China once in their lifetime, learn about their country of origin and compare Hmong life in China with their own in Thailand. China is both present in their every day lives through historical accounts and stories of migration from China to Southeast Asia and in daily Chinese soap operas, posters with Chinese landscapes, Chinese calendars hanging on the wall of the houses, old Hmong people and shamans speaking Mandarin in prayers as well as through sacrificial Chinese paper money or Chinese tea. Many Hmong dream of visiting their homeland at least once; yet only a few have the wish to live there permanently. Villagers perceive their lives in Thailand as less burdened by hardship than those of Hmong relatives in China, Vietnam, or Laos. Hmong kin from France and the United States, who visit clan's people in Thailand rather than Laos or other countries of the region, confirms their perception. On the one hand, they know that it is easier and more comfortable to travel within Thailand, on the other hand, they fear negative repercussions if they travel as Hmong people to Laos (Yang, Kou 2003: 285).[135]

Perceptions of countries where no Hmong people live are predominantly influenced by prejudices about Western countries, while other parts of the world are imagined rather vaguely, if at all. Many Hmong people have already had direct encounters with tourists, extension workers, missionaries, or researchers from the Western hemisphere who frequent the Hmong villages. Families who sell souvenirs to tourists in Chiang Mai or other places even have regular contact with people from many parts of the world whose behaviour influences the way their countries of origin are perceived. Most of my Hmong informants think people from Western countries are generally rich and well-fed, but somewhat unclean, unfriendly and unreliable. Many complained that tourists apparently have the money to pay for the airfare to Thailand, but bargain for every Thai baht at the tourist markets. They view Westerners as rich, but believe they live without many morals. For example, the Hmong pointed out their allegedly high rates of divorce and "illicit" children. They also mention the lack of support from kin's people, who simply send their elderly to old-age homes. Young tourists who come to Hmong villages searching for drugs do not necessarily improve these relatively negative images of Western countries and their people.

Summary

In the theoretical part of this book, I argue that the dialectic between spatial structure and practice constitute cultural spatiality. This chapter has analysed settings in-depth in order to gain a thorough understanding of the ways in which people structure their locales of interaction, in both physical-material and socio-cultural ways. It has also explored the ways in which people behave, interact and give meaning to their surroundings. This analysis of

---

[135] The Lao PDR Government is reported to have maintained a "black book" of members of Hmong resistance groups overseas that can make entry into the country an arduous task because Hmong names are very common (Yang, Kou 2003: 285).

important Hmong settings has attempted to tease out the connotations of settings and their inherent cues for the behavioural patterns on which structural or cultural codes depend, and vice versa. The totality of the settings, reflected in the "rhythm of spatiality", constitutes the mental model of the Hmong, represented by the concept of the Hmong Mountains.

The household is the smallest and most significant social unit in Hmong society. As a consequence, the house, as physical object *and* action, expresses this centrality. Hmong houses are physically structured along certain recurring patterns that provide (a) the places for the five (to seven) important house spirits, (b) the places for ancestor worship and other sacrificial rituals that include the altar, the centre post, the hearths and the door, and (c) the place for both the extended family and, if needed, for a large number of people attending a ceremony. Just as individuals and nuclear families have to subordinate themselves to the household head and interests of the lineage, the space of the individuals and nuclear families within the house becomes subordinate to the overall needs of the household, the Hmong community *and* the supernatural agents. Both individuals and nuclear families are only granted small private areas in the *one-room* house; these areas might have to be abandoned altogether in cases of a special event, sickness or mortuary rites.

The people, the ancestors and the house spirits comprise the inhabitants of a single house. They all belong together and have an effect on each other's existence. In other words, within the house both the supernatural and the living, the vertical and the horizontal are interconnected in one entity. The house can thus be seen as a microcosm of the universe and, as such, the centre of male-dominated power where the status hierarchy of the cosmos is reproduced ritually. The delineation of inner spaces, such as the house as a safe place, suggests that these spaces are also projected as intensely moral realms. As part of the house, rituals, the reference to the ancestors and spirits, the spatial differentiation between men and women carry implicit references to honour, hierarchy, morality, and the cosmological worldview. This is made especially explicit during ceremonies in the house when men and women have different, complementary tasks to fulfil; when status and hierarchy are reinforced by the seating and eating order, as well as by the spatial division of the house; and, last but not least, when the inside of a house becomes characterised by a formal and respectful behaviour that contrasts with an outer sphere where people can display more informal behaviour.

Whereas the house represents the cosmos and "centre of the world", the house's exterior represents the wild and untamed outer sphere populated by malevolent spirits and non-Hmong people. The door and threshold must be understood as the physical boundary between these two spheres. On the one hand, the Hmong need to safeguard the benevolent inner sphere of the house from the potentially malevolent outside. On the other hand, both spheres need to be interconnected. This inside-outside dichotomy and perception of the world is also reflected in the way the Hmong make place in the lowlands when they visit the markets or other locations there: The spatial proximity of a number of Hmong people, either at the markets or in the restaurants, constitutes an inside sphere which protects the people, but which allows them to interact with the outside lowland domain. The pick-up truck might, in this case, even be compared with the threshold of the house, connecting, but also separating the Hmong lifeworld with the outside world.

I would argue that the settings of the neighbourhood, the ritual in the village and the mortuary rites in a neighbouring settlement all form substantial aspects of Hmong spatiality in Thailand. In neighbourhood settings, mostly related lineage members interact with one another on a daily basis. Everyday practices such as the use of classificatory kin terms (older brother, younger father etc.), frequent informal visits to each other's houses, informal meetings in the squares and mutual socio-economic assistance reinforce the physical as well as socio-cultural proximity of lineage members. The lineage or neighbourhood area represents an important place for Hmong socialisation and communal child rearing. Moral norms and social values are enacted in the village square every day, thus providing Hmong with culturally specific knowledge. The social proximity of people from one neighbourhood or lineage compensates for the relative lack of cohesion of the whole village. Nevertheless, village matters can be dealt with because each household and lineage has legitimate representatives who contribute to the maintenance of Hmong hierarchy, power and identity. This occurs, for example, in ritualised meals and mortuary rites, in which signs of respect are exchanged. When people attend a ceremony in the village, it is not the whole village community that is important, but rather the respectable men (from inside *and* outside the village if visitors are present) who are invited to eat the ritual meal. These honourable men guarantee, through their status and knowledge, the continuance of the Hmong group in general. The preservation of the village community is thus not as important as that of the Hmong people, who struggle to survive socio-culturally despite their minority status.

During mortuary rites in one of the villages, attended by a great number of people from many destinations, spatial boundaries of the Hmong villages are even "unmade" for the benefit of the spatially unbound clan and Hmong networks. During the nights of the rites, Hmong retell their personal history by the "showing of the way" ritual and sending back of the soul of the deceased to its ancestral home in China via its "life stations". But they also literally enact the Hmong Mountains in the typical Hmong settings inside and outside the house of the departed through its sounds, smells, tastes, activities, and the presence of traditionally dressed Hmong people from all parts of the region. This Hmong spatiality, which exists parallel to the spatiality of the lowlands or other ethnic mountain groups, is constituted through the extensive stories exchanged about ancestors, living relatives and current socio-economic and religious practices. Strong social pressure causes the Hmong to attend mortuary rites, especially for respected people. Attendance ensures the safe passage of the dead to the Otherworld and offspring's well-being. However, it also guarantees the durability and interconnectedness of the people and clans and hence, of the entire Hmong group.

Typical Hmong settings characterised by the attendance of at least a few and, more often than not, many people provide the Hmong group with the social support essential for their socio-cultural survival as an ethnic minority group. These settings give the Hmong security and support in maintaining their culture despite their increasing interaction with Thai lowland society. So far, as the setting of the market exemplifies, the Hmong have succeeded in preserving their own, parallel settings in the lowlands and sustaining special spaces for their culture. With the ever-increasing participation of Hmong people in the lowland market economy, the Hmong Mountains might successfully expand to include settings in the lowlands as well.

CONCLUSION: THE HMONG MOUNTAINS AND THE CONSTITUTION OF HMONG CULTURAL SPATIALITY

> "The Emperor has ten thousand soldiers, but the Hmong have ten thousand mountains"
> (Yang, Kou 2003: 297)

The theoretical part of this treatise defined and conceptualised cultural spatiality as both an aspect and outcome of socio-cultural practice. This approach to cultural spatiality is a clear move away from the view that people simply *construct* spaces. Instead, it envisions a dialectic between spatial structure and socio-cultural practice in which spatiality is at once constituted through and constitutive of actions. As such, it includes all aspects of human agency, experiences and outside influences. The concept of cultural spatiality also allows an access to the phenomenon of space beyond the physical-material. Instead, it encompasses socio-culturally enacted localities, whether these are real, imagined or only potential spheres of socio-economic, religious, symbolic, or political action. In this regard, cultural spatiality provides a broader perception of locality and community. As in the case of the Hmong, people can be anchored via processes of place making in both local settlements and a diaspora spread over five continents. They can be simultaneously anchored "here" and "there", in this world as well as in the Otherworld. Furthermore, discussion of Hmong spatiality draws our attention to the inadequacies of simple dichotomies like traditional and modern, local and global, urban and rural. Such dichotomies are not salient for capturing the complex ways in which people constitute their lifeworlds by integrating and transforming influences from the global, national, or regional levels and turning them into inherent parts of their own culture, which can also have larger-scope effects.

This work has brought further attention to the fact that field sites are no longer simply localised in traditional terms of place, but comprise part of multiple and larger contexts. As one of the ethnic mountain groups settling in northern Thailand, the Hmong are exposed to the expansion of state and international control of the geopolitical spaces of the North of the country, as well as to a new (inter)national perception of their habitat and natural resources. Like other ethnic groups, they have become part of a national and international environmentalist discourse to which they have responded by staking out self-managed protection areas and redefining the *ntoo xeeb* ritual. A ritual formerly aimed at reinvigorating a community's relation with the most important local divinity has been modified to such an extent that it can be used for participation in national and global resource protection efforts, as well as for better integration into the Thai nation. The Hmong are, however, not only affected by changed environmental awareness and perceptions of the mountainous areas in Thailand. The increasing geographic reach of the world market has also influenced their culture. Even geographically remote villages such as Ban Phui, formerly connected only very sparsely or intermittently to the national and world economies, have become more completely integrated into the marketplace. Infrastructure development, the freer flow of people and commodities, growth of incomes and exploitation of opportunities even in remote areas by both Thai and Hmong traders have hastened this process. Expanding markets also create new opportunities for income generation for villagers and, in so doing, alter the value of region-specific resources such as forests or agricultural land. Villagers strictly adhere to the most important cornerstones of Hmong socio-cultural practice, religious beliefs and the kinship system. However, they are very open to change and adaptation in the economic field, as long as they do not threaten the core aspects of Hmong culture.

Both market expansion and the impact of state policies and international agencies strongly influence the way the Hmong use their natural resources.

Conclusion

They also inflect how Hmong position themselves within a socio-economic and political frame in which they can only exert little power. In the increasingly "contested spaces" – contested in environmental, geopolitical and economic terms – of mountainous areas in northern Thailand, the Hmong people have to position themselves in such a way that enables their integration into the larger system. At the same time, they have to find a place for themselves to avoid total assimilation by Thai society and the risk of losing socio-cultural distinctiveness. The Hmong Mountains signify the "place" the Hmong people have constituted to maintain their socio-cultural distinctiveness. This concept, which my book has explored in depth, comprises an essential part of the group's cultural spatiality. It is a mental model of the Hmong lifeworld and is not static or defined by an essence or "purity". Rather, it has evolved during the course of a long history of migration, dispersal and settlement in Thailand. Through people's embodied practices, it is constantly evoked, transformed and adapted to new circumstances.

The question should no longer be whether or not mountainous areas are the natural habitat of the Hmong and whether or not the migratory aspect is ingrained in Hmong culture. Instead, it should be acknowledged that the Hmong themselves understand mountainous areas and migration as an integral part of their culture and identity, whether they live in rural, mountain areas or in urban settings. First, people (temporarily) living and working in urban areas are still considered to belong spiritually to the household of origin in the mountain village. Second, the mountains are an important facet of Hmong cosmology and history. Mountainous landscapes, conceptualised as *the* habitat that "naturally belongs" to the Hmong, are "mirrored" in Hmong conceptions of the mountainous Otherworld. Some versions of the myth of origin even tell of a mythical creation of the mountains connected to the foundation of the different clans. Furthermore, the sphere above the sky and underneath the earth (the Otherworld), as well as the earth (*yaj ceeb*) itself, are believed to be populated by a variety of supernatural spiritual forces. One of these – *Zaj*, the dragon – is even thought to be represented in the mountains' topography: The dragon's contours and veins form the lines of natural energy running along the mountain ridges and watercourses. Based on the lines of energy, geomantic practice requires the correct siting of Hmong villages, houses and graves in the "mountainscapes", a practice that helped anchor the Hmong even in unknown (mountainous) territories in their out-migrations from China.

Most large-scale Hmong migrations culminated in Thailand. However, a correct village or burial site remains important for both the living and their ancestors, for as Nicholas Tapp has aptly stated, it is "upon the welfare of ancestors that the fortunes of their descendants depend". The Hmong are convinced that disrespect of ancestors or incorrectly conducted rites can have an effect on their own well-being, their agricultural yields, weather, fortune, health of the family, and the community. Thus, to respect and make sacrifices to the supernatural world also represents the worship of Hmong society in the Durkheimian sense and ensures the affluence and well-being of the living. We cannot speak of the "economic irrationality" of the Hmong economic system when the Hmong abandon their fields, for example, to participate in rituals for days. Hmong production aims at accumulating as much wealth as possible, both to provide for the living and accrue the financial resources to pay appropriate respect to hierarchically higher-situated ancestors.

The Hmong believe that their ancestors, as well as other supernatural beings, affect their lives and vice versa. Thus, the Hmong incorporate all spaces – unknown and known, on earth, above the sky or underneath the earth – into spheres where Hmong people, their souls, and their ancestors' spirits reside and are interconnected. Hmong religious topography is a cardinal point that does not only extend to the horizontal, but also to the vertical level. Furthermore, past, present and future are interconnected through the ancestors, the living and the belief in reincarnation, or in other words, through the cycle of life. It is therefore legitimate to speak of a time-space-continuum in the Hmong lifeworld that – by means of religious belief – interconnects the "here" and "there" and the past, present, and future. The shaman is the intermediary between the world of the living and the supernatural agencies; he or she allows direct communication between the two spheres. Through the shaman's trance and his or her obvious contact with the spiritual beings, the Otherworld is visibly enacted and becomes tangible for the living. In a practical sense, shamans connect spaces to the same extent that ritual experts connect the ancestors with the living on a daily basis.

The Hmong cosmos integrates the world above the sky, the earth and the sphere underneath the earth into one. The Hmong house, as the centre of Hmong socio-cultural life and activity, reflects this cosmos. The idea of the house as a "centre" is not conceptualised as a point in a horizontal disc on the earth, but rather incorporates the vertical. The actual physical-geographical location of a Hmong house is of minor importance, it is always perceived and constituted as the centre. The hearths, the main door and the main pole supporting the roof of the house symbolise this centre of the world. This centre is always established anew when Hmong people erect new houses, no matter whether they are in Mae Sa Mai, in Chiang Mai or in Saint Paul (U.S.A.). In short, the house does not represent a place, but an *action* that can occur anywhere in the world. This concept of centre unmakes spatial boundaries and in a way, unmakes movement and migration. Instead, it includes the potentiality of a movement that can exceed any boundaries and of place making or siting culture wherever Hmong houses are constructed. As Caroline Humphrey writes for the Mongol nomads which also holds truth for the Hmong:

> "The ritualized journey is thus a spatial liminality, into and out of the otherness of 'travelling that is not travelling' – paradoxically an otherness which serves to reassert the nomadic way of life – thereby negating movement in the everyday world. The time axis, which is universal, and thus locates each household at the centre of the cosmos among the nomads, is the *axis mundi*." (1995: 142-143, italics in original)

Hmong people, by way of conceptualising their world, mostly do not think in terms of "here" and "there", since both spheres belong to one. "There" is always a potential "here" because the Hmong "centre" of socio-cultural activity can be constituted anywhere. Instead of differentiating between "here" and "there", Hmong people distinguish between "inside" and "outside". The house represents the Hmong cosmos and comprises the "inside". All spheres around it symbolically belong to the "outside". Everything and every place that is non-Hmong belong to the "outside" and is potentially harmful to the well-being of the people, whereas the "inside" provides security and social satisfaction. The house is the centre of the world. Nonetheless, it always needs an assembly of "centres" to actually build an "inside" sphere on which the stateless Hmong people can rely in a foreign environment.

Group social proximity is needed to withstand the occasionally malevolent power of the *dab*, who are believed to be numerous outside the settlements in the wild and "untamed" region of the forests, mountains, and beyond. The social proximity of a significant number of Hmong transforms an area or place into a "Hmong space" that provides socio-cultural and spiritual security and clearly defines the boundary between inside and outside, between the Hmong and the non-Hmong peoples. This manner of constituting Hmong spatiality already existed in the era of semi-sedentary swidden agriculture and can still be observed today, whether in the mountain fields of Ban Phui, the weekend market in Bangkok, or "Hmong areas" in the United States.

Place making through interconnecting spheres and people

Hmong cultural spatiality is marked by an interconnection of this world and the Otherworld, of the past, present, and future, as well as all potential places of settlement around the globe. As supernatural beings in general and ancestor spirits in particular are believed to impinge on the domain of the living, they need to be incorporated into interrelations existing among the

Conclusion

Hmong. Supernatural agents are as much a part of Hmong networks as the people. Through these Hmong-specific networks in particular, enacted daily in rituals and other socio-cultural practices, the stateless Hmong people make place in Thailand and throughout the diaspora. The Hmong make use of their social capital in the Bourdieusian sense to find alternative ways of siting culture, existing in a realm dominated by Hmong and their lifeworld instead of by other peoples. As a diaspora group with a history of expulsion and independent movements, the Hmong people "think big". For them, it is not enough to site their culture in one locality only. Rather, their culture represents the totality of the mountainous areas of China, Vietnam, Laos, Burma, Thailand and other countries seen to potentially belong to the Hmong Mountains; places of migration are still remembered, passed on and enacted during the rituals at the ancestors' graves. This large (imagined) area, with the Chinese homeland as a starting point, secures the socio-cultural survival of the stateless Hmong as much as the remembered points of former settlement and far-flung clan networks of the present interlink people and places of the Hmong Mountains. The clan system offers latent potential for the mobilisation of solidarity, an important criterion in the search of marriage partners, and a principle for the determination of social proximity. Lineage connections and affinal kinship relations must be understood as nodal points in the spatially unbound networks of the Hmong (Mischung 1990: 297).

The Hmong at my research sites are largely integrated into a market economy and interact with the Thai lowland and neighbouring populations to an increasing extent. Yet Hmong social networks remain characterised by an endosociality that represents an important strategy for socio-cultural survival. By placing emphasis on the continuance of religious beliefs and practices, as well as on the maintenance of spatially unrooted clan networks, the Hmong constitute a spatiality existing parallel to spatial practices of the Thai majority society, for example. By collecting a relatively large number of people and seeking their spatial proximity – whether in a temporary settlement in the forest fields of Ban Phui or at the large Chatuchak

Weekend Market in Bangkok – Hmong endosociality entails a high level of security, satisfaction and intensity in the social life of the people. Within a Hmong group, people can mutually support each other in conducting the important rituals that sustain the balance between the living and supernatural agents. They can provide each other with social security, which is partly denied by Thai lowland society. Kinship structures clearly regulate the degree to which degree people can rely on each other, endowing each member with a specific position within attenuated clan networks. Even people unknown to each other can immediately position themselves within this network. They do not need to slowly build up trust as an individual, but can rely on the reputation of the ancestors, extended family and lineage. Strong inter-clan relations are also reinforced by the practice of clan-exogamous but group endogamous marriages. The natal clan of a wife remains important even after her adoption into the patrilineal clan of her husband.

Clan relationships are maintained through personal visits, and most importantly, through numerous attendances of mortuary rites, New Year celebrations and other rituals in the home and other villages. While it can be argued that the role of local settlements has grown in importance through processes of sedentarisation, boundary-exceeding clan networks have also gained in strength and salience through the overall improvement of infrastructure and communication systems. Social relations largely based on kinship span the mountainous areas, the towns and cities in the lowlands, the capital and even other countries where Hmong people reside. When villagers from my research sites travel outside their area, they do so in clearly established conduits within which they mainly meet their own kind, either belonging to the lineage/clan or other local Hmong. They travel in groups in their open pick-up trucks, which can literally be seen as "mobile Hmong settings". When they stay overnight, they stay in other Hmong's houses. There is a concerted practice of endosociality, which makes living as well as travelling with the Hmong a special and unique experience. It is possible to travel with Hmong people through Chiang Mai or other Thai lowland areas without personally meeting any non-Hmong. Ephemeral encounters with Thai people remain limited to visits of markets and small food shops. However, the Hmong even prefer to conduct such visits in locations already visited by other Hmong.

Endosociality entails a high level of security and intensity in religious and social life for the villagers. A Hmong can always be sure to be hosted by a fellow Hmong when travelling throughout the mountainous areas or even the lowlands. The cores of these social networks are kinship-based, often part of lineage or clan relationships. But in spite of this completely Hmong-dominated core, the level of commerce with the outside world is relatively high and interactions with other peoples relatively frequent. The Hmong villages are economically dependent on and politically integrated into the Thai state and global system. However, that integration does not wholly determine local strategies of social survival, even if it sets limits to their viability and the Hmong understand themselves as part of the Thai nation. Just like any other group, the Hmong negotiate their identities situationally. These identities are defined by heterogeneity, diversity, and multiplicity, although a common understanding of Hmong-ness based on the exodus from the homeland in China and central values of Hmong culture always occupies the core.

Intra-ethnic differences

As we open ourselves to the world of things and places, we give them meaning through our actions and experiences. At the same time, these things and places construct our sense of identity through our interactions with them. Appropriation is rooted, therefore, in a concerted action through which we appropriate aspects of our world as anchors for our self-identity. Especially in Hmong society, self-identity can take heterogeneous forms due to hierarchical structures and gender differences in space and time. As far as hierarchy goes, status is acquired through spirituality, profound religious and historical knowledge, respectable behaviour rooted in moral norms and possession of authority within one's own clan. These high-status positions are mostly reserved for elderly men who have accumulated a certain degree of knowledge and garnered enough respect by others. In the past, young men were largely barred from higher positions in the hierarchy. This has changed in part because relatively young men can hold office in the Thai administration and thus hold power positions outside the traditional political structure. Young males can also be respected due to their knowledge acquired in the formal education system, a system that for a long time the Hmong did not deem of any value.

With the increasing scarcity of land, the Hmong have come to view formal education as the major conduit for their children to obtain non-agricultural occupations in the lowlands. It goes without saying that the identities of young Hmong people who attend lowland schools in an inter-ethnic framework differ from those of their parents and grandparents. While the grandparents, and in most cases the parents as well, have still experienced the times of opium poppy cultivation and frequent relocations of villages and people throughout northern Thailand, children are born and raised in sedentarised settlements with decreasing natural resources. Instead of migrating like their parents, they partake in *movements* between the mountainous areas and the lowlands, sometimes only temporarily for a few months, sometimes more permanently for a few years. These movements can be seen in spatial as well as inter-ethnic terms. In the mountain villages, the children form part of their Hmong community and are surrounded by Hmong people; in the lowlands they are students at Thai schools who have to adapt to the Thai setting, but are also trained early on by their parents to seek assistance from other Hmong children and develop a Hmong consciousness that will prevail away from home.

Experiences and partial identities differ not only between generations, but also between the sexes. As the description of typical village settings clearly demonstrates, Hmong spatiality is not only gendered in place but also in time. Women and men mostly occupy different places inside as well as outside the houses, have different scopes of movement and complementary roles within Hmong society. The men are the ones who are responsible for the ritual maintenance of the patriline. They control and determine economic and political affairs as well as ceremonies and prayers; they communicate with the ancestral and household spirits. Women's roles are embedded in the domains of motherhood and procreation – two domains that are highly valued by Hmong society and without which the clan's genealogical line could not be continued. Even though men exert control over women as a consequence of the patrilineal and hierarchical system, discussions of Hmong gender relations should not underestimate informal forms of women's power and influence or the fact that both sides clearly depend on each other.

How do these differences in the life experiences and identity formations of the different generations and sexes inflect the ways in which people respond to the world around them? Furthermore, how do differences, especially economic ones, between the two villages investigated affect the concept of mental models of the Hmong lifeworlds? This book has argued that the sum of classes and sub-classes of settings in which people are practically involved constitute a mental model such as the Hmong Mountains. To varying degrees, young and old people, female and male, villagers from Mae Sa Mai and Ban Phui are all ensconced in settings inside and outside the villages. They have disparate positions and tasks, are confronted by various experiences and influenced by dissimilar contexts. For example, young people think that they are more deeply Hmong-Thai than their parents. Women are less involved in the maintenance of spatially boundless networks than men. Villagers from Ban Phui tend to understand the Hmong Mountains in a more "classical" sense of the term that incorporates the mountainous lifeworld of the Hmong from China, Vietnam, Laos, Burma and Thailand. In contrast, villagers from Mae Sa Mai have already extended this concept to include groups in the diaspora because of their deeper involvement with "cultural entrepreneurs" and Hmong organisations in the city and abroad. These intra-generational, intra-gender and intra-village differences all form part of a cultural spatiality constituted by *all* facets of socio-cultural practice and experience. Simultaneously, this spatiality has a structuring effect on the actions of people. Following Bourdieu's concept of habitus, it is the totality of practices, experiences and spatial structure more than singular actions that determine the ways in which people are alive to the world around them.

Despite these variations and a spatiality marked by a constant process of transformation, findings from both villages may still hold true, to a certain extent, for Hmong in the diaspora, as some publications on Hmong groups in other countries suggest. In the United States, Hmong people have resettled in a wave of secondary migration to be closer to their clan's people in spatial terms. Hmong people living in Germany assembled in two small villages near Stuttgart. In both cases, it seems the Hmong followed the same networking and support principles as the Hmong on Silom Road in Bangkok or Hmong villagers in their forest fields in Ban Phui. It is also clear that many Hmong, whether young or old, female or male, adhere to similar religious and social principles, even if their scope of knowledge and action varies. Through their habitus and participation in Hmong ways of life, the Hmong are, regardless of their different positions in society and individual actions, part of a cultural spatiality constituted through socio-cultural practice that links the Hmong to each other and features of the spatially boundless physical and supernatural world.

Village transformations

Trying to pinpoint the main characteristics of Hmong cultural spatiality necessitates careful scrutiny of the cultural variation that stems from people's different roles and positions in society and from development and change. Comparison of the villages studied clearly elicits certain similarities between the settlements. Yet they also differ in key respects. On the one hand, Ban Phui is geographically more "remote" and more "traditional" in the sense that household and village structures have been less influenced by outside agencies. On the other hand, Ban Phui is (still) less affected by land shortages and can thus obtain higher agricultural profits than Mae Sa Mai, a village subject to many development and research efforts. Despite the fact that villagers from Mae Sa Mai have better and faster access to lowland markets and grow perennials with supposedly stable harvests, farmers from Ban Phui can generate more income through their agricultural activities than people from the former settlement.

In short, Ban Phui still has enough land to sustain its villagers through agriculture, mainly relying on cabbage and red onion cultivation. Strong profits enable villagers to invest in a considerable amount of animals and vehicles, machines and modern-style houses. Investments in large animals, such as cows, can be seen as traditional forms of securing economic safety, while the acquisition of vehicles, machines and modern-style houses reflect the village's degree of involvement in the market economy and modern developments. In contrast, Mae Sa Mai has less agricultural land at its disposal than the second village studied. Mae Sa Mai has a larger population and has been part of the Suthep-Pui National Park since 1978. As such, there are clear restrictions on land use and diverse outside pressures to place certain forest areas under self-protection. Despite the diversity in what villagers grow and in their marketing strategies, their profits remain below those in Ban Phui. Farmers grow many varieties of cash crop but, except for litchi, only in relatively small plots because they lack land. Even when harvests of different crops are good, revenues are not necessarily high because of strongly fluctuating market prices. Hmong villagers from Mae Sa Mai consequently have less spare money at their disposal for new vehicles, machines and modern-style houses and must search out more for off-farm employment and activities.

Since the 1980s, Mae Sa Mai villagers have been involved in the souvenir business, which capitalises on the people's spatial mobility and willingness to relocate in search of a better living. As seen above, these movements are feasible since people understand themselves as still belonging to the household, the "centre" in the mountain village to which they are socially and spiritually linked through their connection to the house spirits. Mae Sa Mai villagers also take advantage of a spatial mobility by sending their children to secondary schools in the lowlands, which in turn creates opportunities for them there. Children either spend most of the year separated from their parents or return only over the weekends. They nonetheless remain connected to Hmong society and the community and, even in the lowland schools, are part of a Hmong network.

The new forms of Hmong economic action, increasingly apparent in the lowlands, raise important questions for the future of Hmong culture in Thailand. Will villagers from Mae Sa Mai still be able to maintain their socio-religious connections to the "centres" in mountain villages or will they erect new ones in the lowlands? Will they still be able to preserve strong clan networks and spatial proximity of members as they have in the past? Or, will villagers from Ban Phui withstand changes that new forms of home construction imply for their socio-religious anchoring in place? Will they always continue to erect a hearth and centre post in tiled living rooms or will they eventually abandon this practice and thereby lose places central to the maintenance of Hmong culture? Up to the present, a strong religious system and extensive kinship ties have provided stability for Hmong society in Thailand and other countries. Transformations in life circumstances, such as sedentarisation and large-scale integration into a market economy, have thus far been offset by a strengthening of clan networks facilitated by improved modes of transportation and communication. Conscious processes of identity management, which emanate mainly from Hmong-Americans, but also cultural entrepreneurs in Thailand, have also bolstered these networks.

The Hmong Mountains: Strategy of survival

During my fieldwork, I asked people who mentioned the Hmong Mountains to describe the mountains to me or even draw a picture of them. I was well aware that, as a mental model, the Hmong Mountains could not be straightforwardly externalised. At most, descriptions or drawings would enable me to grasp only facets of this model. Some of my informants

Conclusion

succumbed to drawing mountainous areas that were geomantically suitable for constructing a village or situating a burial site. When describing the Hmong Mountains in narratives, informants either told me that "mountains are mountains" or "took me along on a narrated route", which included all the places where Hmong interact with each other in the mountainous areas or in the lowlands: the neighbouring village; the burial place of ancestors near or far; former places of settlement throughout northern Thailand; places of clan relatives in other provinces; but also the Chinese shop, the "Hilltribe Radio Station", the Hmong church or the Hmong Association in Chiang Mai.

Describing the full content and meaning of the Hmong Mountains is a difficult task for the Hmong. The model exists primarily in the subconscious, is enacted through everyday practices and behaviour and substantiated through everyday experiences. Because the model is so closely connected to socio-cultural practice, participating in and observing locales of action proved more useful in fieldwork than asking about people's knowledge.

Mental models should not be seen merely as the re-representation of the totality of classes of settings, but also mapped in relation to power. Hmong succeed in mentally attaining power over their area of settlement, which they do not control politically or own legally. When Hmong villagers speak of the Hmong Mountains, they always do so in relation to the larger group of Hmong, whether they believe this group resides only in Asia or also in other parts of the world. This interconnection with a larger social unit gives them strength and power in relative terms.

The constitution of Hmong spatiality, represented by the mental model of the Hmong Mountains, provides the Hmong with an alternate space within Thailand. This space runs parallel to the relationship of subservience and subordination in Thai society and gives Hmong people the possibility of distinguishing themselves as a minority with their "own place in the world." Hmong researcher Kou Yang (2003: 297) mentions a saying from a Chinese elder who worked with the Hmong in the middle of the last century that still applies to the Hmong in my research sites:

"The Emperor has ten thousand soldiers, but the Hmong have ten thousand mountains"

The knowledge that Hmong are spread and interconnected throughout the mountainous areas, to which they are in many ways related, gives this people a culturally constituted medium in political action. Through this medium, they can confront marginalization in diffuse and ambiguous relations between the local, regional and global and compensate for their statelessness. In this regard, the Hmong face the same challenges as other ethnic mountain groups like the Karen, the Akha or the Yao, or other localised groups throughout the world. For instance, Japanese anthropologist Hiromu Shimizu observes the following for the Pinatubo Ayta and other ethnic groups in the Philippines:

> "The common problem of these groups is how to secure a geographical space in which to make a living as well as a socio-political position in which they can enhance their human, civil, and ancestral rights, given that they can no longer live in the isolation from the outside world nor maintain the basic resources necessary for their livelihood. The urgent issue for them is to find a way to avoid being absorbed totally and helplessly within the political and economic system of the modern world, at the very bottom of the hierarchical social order." (2003: 199)

The concept of the Hmong Mountains as "transnational mountain-spaces" stands for a cultural spatiality that is socio-culturally constituted by the Hmong as an alternative spatiality or an "in-between space" of dislocation, minority and existential identification. This spatiality allows the Hmong to survive socio-culturally within a geopolitical space they do not determine and over which they have only limited means of power. Hmong cultural spatiality should be seen as being a strategy of survival in relation to power structures in Thailand. Spatiality thus always relates to a socio-cultural positioning within a space, which can be powered or governed by others. In other ways, the study of cultural spatiality teaches us that we can no longer think of power simply in terms of demand and control, as Pierre Bourdieu indicates. Rather, we need to acknowledge that power can also be constituted through an alternative redefinition of the spatial.

In Thailand, the Hmong have started to imbue places such as the mountainous areas or protected forest areas with meanings that exist alongside those of majority society. By relating to and enacting these places in a different way than members of Thai society, villagers turn these places into their own on a socio-cultural level and incorporate them into their cultural spatiality. This spatiality transcends the only superficially marked boundaries between territories; the places of villages, cities and nations, the horizontal and the vertical levels, as well as time. Represented by the mental model of the Hmong Mountains, it stands within a broad spectrum of human notions and actions, symbols and competition over contested spaces.

Is Hmong culture emplaced?

This book has devoted attention to the ways in which the Hmong constitute cultural spatiality by means of spatially boundless socio-cultural practices and interrelations. Theoretical debates about globalisation and processes of deterritorialisation have questioned whether cultures can still be perceived as located within any fixed places or whether global links and influences have become more important than certain localities. The following citation from Hmong scholar Gary Yia Lee seems to support the latter notion:

> "A Hmong is a Hmong when he or she reaches out to other Hmong. We are not one single homogenous group located in one single geographical area, but a multi-ethnic and multilingual community living with many people in many countries." (1996: 32)

The Hmong in the two villages studied indeed display a spatially boundless mental model of the Hmong Mountains that is not connected to one single geographical area. However, I would argue that Hmong culture remains emplaced. Mental models should be seen as one way of establishing culture on "site". The exact nature of this "site", its extent and its relation to real or imagined localities needs to be ascertained from case to case. The Hmong provide a useful example for clarifying how people constitute contexts of spatiality and anchor themselves in space through dynamic processes of place making and siting culture. The Hmong are characterised by an identity and cultural spatiality based on social interaction, interrelations and boundless entities. Despite their statelessness, they are not a people without any relation to particular localities.

First, the Hmong are anchored in space by means of their cosmological view of the world. They perceive mountainous areas their people's natural habitat. Second, as is typical of diaspora groups, the Hmong refer to a mystified, ancestral homeland in China, a place construed as the origin of all Hmong people to which the souls of the dead must return. Third, the Hmong are anchored in the geography of northern Thailand and neighbouring areas through their ancestors' former places of settlement, which the Hmong still partly visit as burial sites and preserve as important in recurring narrations about the recent history of migration. When Hmong people meet each other, they seek commonalities on both a clan and historical level. Former settlement sites thus contribute to a networking and an anchoring of the people in space. Fourth, the Hmong are anchored in the houses to which they belong as members of an extended family *and* as members ritually connected to the household spirits. This house as the "centre" of the Hmong cosmos can be anywhere in the world; it always remains *the* essential locality of Hmong culture and practice. It provides the Hmong with an "inside" place to which they are strongly attached, both ritually and socially, no matter where this house is geographically located. Fifth, the Hmong in Thailand have become linked to a new dimension of place, a dimension long non-existent in Hmong society: a geographical location. Through enforced processes of settlement, Hmong villagers have become gradually attached to their current village sites. This applies especially to the young Hmong who have not experienced large-scale migrations, but more minor moves to the lowlands. Young people are exposed to outside (environmental) training and opinion-building. Faced with rapidly dwindling resources, they have learned to appreciate the "land" next to the people. Older people succumb in turn to these "new" forms of relation to the spatial. To conclude, Hmong cultural spatiality is connected to and anchored in more than one locality. It is connected to localities that do not necessarily coincide with geographical places but are, nonetheless real and very important to the people. Although outsiders cannot easily perceive the ways in which the Hmong are spatially anchored in the world, this does not mean that places do not possess a central importance for them (see also Kokot 2002: 105). Rather, the Hmong identify with places as sources of life and reference points from their particular positions in the more "global network of human relations" (Hastrup and Olwig 1997: 12). Like the concept of the Hmong Mountains, the boundaries of the (partially imagined) Hmong community that extends across five continents are not spatial; they are grounded in the social networks, which constitute this broadly dispersed group.

Towards a Theory of Cultural Spatiality

One further point of consideration is an examination of how the study of Hmong cultural spatiality can contribute to the development of a theory of cultural spatiality. Cultural spatiality, as an overarching principle, structures people's worlds and influences their behaviour and actions. Although people act according this principle, it is largely taken for granted and thus often remains invisible in (anthropological) analysis. Especially in times where the local, regional, national and global levels have become more intertwined and affect each other to an unknown extent, it is important to ascertain how people are alive to the world around them. The concept of cultural spatiality helps to assess the main facets of a contemporary reality in which cultures are increasingly delocalised, but also re-localised and attached to places that can be geographically real, imagined or only potential sites of action.

The example of the Hmong has elucidated that cultural spatiality can transcend marked boundaries between territories. It can be anchored in multiple localities, which may only come into existence as enacted in people's praxis (for example, the Hmong house and its meanings). Hmong cultural spatiality also draws our attention to the ways in which people can constitute a spatiality that includes more than one spatial dimension and more than one time. Diffuse relations to the regional, national and global cannot fully account for people's everyday lives, which also include complex relations to the supernatural, as well as the past and future. These interrelations among the Hmong, both explicit and subtle, spatial structures and socio-cultural practices, resist easy categorisation or explanation. Rather, they necessitate thorough documentation and analysis of the socio-cultural practices found in a group's typical settings or "locales." The study of settings facilitates the analysis of human praxis; settings are linked to practices, relations and behavioural patterns and also to places, even when they include imagined, supernatural or potential spheres of action.

The study of Hmong cultural spatiality broadens our theoretical knowledge about the nature of cultural spatiality by eliciting the ways in which socio-cultural phenomena can be spatial, but not bound to essentialist concepts of place. The cultural spatiality of a people, whether belonging to a diaspora group or one only found in a single geographical region, is constituted through the dialectic relationship of human practices and relations and spatial structure. Thus, while the socio-cultural practices and spatial structure constructed by this practice may vary from group to group, the nature, extent and boundaries of the spatial may also differ greatly, even for people inhabiting the same territory. Cultural spatiality does not coincide with actual physical locations of a people, but rather reveals how people live and find their place in the world. The concept of the Hmong Mountains provides a vivid example for this.

APPENDIX: HMONG VILLAGES VISITED IN NORTHERN THAILAND

Villages listed in order of visits in February and July 2001. Information on the settlements was provided either by the village headmen or their deputies.

Pha Nok Kok

Foundation of village:	1973;
Population:	380, White Hmong;
Households:	64 (with an average of approximately 6 persons per household);
Congregations:	56 households Seventh Day Adventist, 5 households traditional Hmong religion (7,8 %), 3 households Protestant;
Cultivation:	Litchi, cabbage, salad, leek;
Tourism:	Daily tour groups to the "Hill-Tribe Museum" of the village, souvenir-stalls along the main road;
Projects:	Pilot-project of the RFD concerning "community forests";
Environmental Protection:	In the 1990s, villagers have turned three areas around the settlement into conservation zones. A sacred tree does not exist, as the majority of the people are Seventh Day Adventists.

Bouak Chan

Foundation of village:	1972;
Population:	760, White and Green Hmong;
Households:	95 (with an average of approximately 8 persons per household);

Congregations:	75 households traditional Hmong religion (78,94 %), 10 households Seventh Day Adventists, 10 households Catholic;
Cultivation:	Flowers, cabbage, carrots, leek, litchi;
Tourism:	None;
Projects:	Royal Project;
Environmental Protection:	Surroundings of the village have been declared a "*Phaa Sa Nguan Haeng Chaat*" (Forest Protection Area) by the Royal Forestry Department. Villagers have turned three areas around the settlement into conservation zones; in one of these zones is the sacred tree of the village located. The rest of the land is under intensive use and cultivation.

Doi San

Foundation of village:	1981;
Population:	350, White Hmong;
Households:	57 (with an average of approximately 6 persons per household);
Congregations:	50 households traditional Hmong religion (87,71 %), 7 households Seventh Day Adventists;
Cultivation:	Rice and maize for subsistence, small quantities of ginger for sale;
Tourism:	Infrequent visits of individual tourists;
Projects:	None;
Environmental Protection:	In 1997, villagers extended the conservation area around the sacred tree.

Appendix

Nong Hoi Kau

Foundation of village:	1951;
Population:	700, Green Hmong;
Households:	113 (with an average of approximately 6 persons per household);
Congregations:	98 households traditional Hmong religion (87 %), 15 households Protestant
Cultivation:	Carrots, cabbage, leek, pepper;
Tourism:	Weekly visits by tourists, a few souvenir-stalls along the road;
Projects:	Royal Project;
Environmental Protection:	In 1998, surroundings of the village have been declared a "*Phaa Sa Nguan Haeng Chaat*" (Forest Protection Area) by the RFD. Villagers have turned three further areas into conservation zones; in one of these zones is the sacred tree of the village located. The rest of the land is used extensively.

Nong Hoi Mai

Foundation of village:	1977;
Population:	900, Green Hmong;
Households:	97 (with an average of approximately 9 persons per household);
Congregations:	94 households traditional Hmong religion (96,9 %), 3 households Protestant;
Cultivation:	Mainly cabbage, also carrot, leek, pepper;
Tourism:	Very little;
Projects:	Royal Project;

Environmental Protection:	In 1997, villagers put forest surrounding the village under protection; fines have to be paid to the village committee in case of, for example, felling trees illegally. A sacred tree is located in the forested mountain above the village.

Chang Khian

Foundation of village:	1972;
Population:	800, White Hmong;
Households:	80 (with an average of approximately 10 persons per household);
Congregations:	60 households traditional Hmong religion (75 %), 10 households Protestant, 10 households Catholic;
Cultivation:	Litchi for sale, several kinds of vegetables for subsistence;
Tourism:	Tour groups from Hmong village Doi Pui during dry season;
Projects:	Research Project by the Faculty of Agriculture (Chiang Mai University) on "Arabica" coffee plants;
Environmental Protection:	The village is part of the Suthep-Pui National Park. Villagers do not have a sacred tree nor have they declared own protection zones.

Doi Pui

Foundation of village:	1968;
Population:	1.300, Green Hmong;
Households:	110 (with an average of approximately 12 persons per household)
Congregations:	100 households "traditional" Hmong religion (90,90 %), 10 households Protestant;
Cultivation:	Litchi, carrots, cabbage, leek, salad, onion;

Tourism:	Since 1970, daily tour groups visit the village from nearby Chiang Mai. Doi Pui is a well-known "hilltribe" tourist destination in Thailand. Villagers maintain a large number of souvenir stalls for the tourists in one part of the settlement;
Projects:	None;
Environmental Protection:	The village is part of the Suthep-Pui National Park. Villagers have a sacred tree but have not enlarged the protection zone around it, as done in other Hmong villages.

Huai Khwang

Foundation of village:	1976;
Population:	315, Green Hmong;
Households:	75 (with an average of approximately 4 persons per household);
Congregations:	67 households traditional Hmong religion (89,33 %), 8 households Catholic;
Cultivation:	Litchi, carrots, cabbage, onion for sale; rice and maize for subsistence;
Tourism:	Infrequent visits by tourists, villagers can daily sell souvenirs in nearby tourist resorts;
Projects:	Royal Project;
Environmental Protection:	In 1998, surroundings of the village have been declared a "*Phaa Sa Nguan Haeng Chaat*" (Forest Protection Area) by the RFD; villagers maintain an extended protection zone around the sacred tree.

Huai Sieo

Foundation of village:	1981;
Population:	270, Green Hmong;

Households:	34 (with an average of approximately 8 persons per household);
Congregations:	28 households Protestant, 6 households Catholic;
Cultivation:	Not enough land for commercial agriculture, only for small-scale subsistence cultivation;
Tourism:	None;
Projects:	Royal Project;
Environmental Protection:	In 1998, surroundings of the village have been declared a *"Phaa Sa Nguan Haeng Chaat"* (Forest Protection Area) by the RFD; villagers do not have a sacred tree as the settlement lies relatively low for a Hmong village (500 meters above sea level) and is thus not surrounded by forests or mountains.

Pha Khia Nai

Foundation of village:	1972;
Population:	800, Green Hmong;
Households:	104 (with an average of approximately 8 persons per household);
Congregations:	74 households traditional Hmong religion (71,15 %), 12 households Protestant, 10 households Seventh Day Adventist, 8 households Catholic;
Cultivation:	Litchi, carrot, cabbage, onion, strawberry;
Tourism:	Visits by tourists are seldom;
Projects:	Social Welfare Department, Police School;
Environmental Protection:	Villagers protest against the establishment of a national park by the Royal Forestry Department including their settlement area. In 1992, villagers have expanded the protection area around the sacred tree to amount to 4.000 *rai* of land.

Mae Chi

Foundation of village:	1978;
Population:	461, Green Hmong;
Households:	51 (with an average of approximately 9 persons per household);
Congregations:	41 households Catholic, 6 households Seventh Day Adventist, 5 households traditional Hmong religion (9,8 %);
Cultivation:	Carrot, cabbage, strawberry;
Tourism:	None, only passing trekking groups;
Projects:	Social Welfare Department, RFD;
Environmental Protection:	Villagers protest against the establishment of a national park by the RFD including their settlement area. They stopped farming in two areas in order to prevent the park. With the foundation of the village, a sacred tree and a conservation zone around the tree have been set up that is still ritually maintained by the Hmong adhering to the traditional religion.

Mae Tala

Foundation of village:	1936;
Population:	245, Green Hmong;
Households:	26 (with an average of approximately 9 persons per household);
Congregations:	25 households traditional Hmong religion (96,15 %), 1 household Catholic;
Cultivation:	Carrot, cabbage for sale; rice and maize for subsistence;
Tourism:	None;
Projects:	Social Welfare Department, Public Health Department, RFD;

Environmental Protection: After the foundation of the village, a sacred tree and protection zone were established; in 1995 this zone was extended to now include 100 *rai* of land.

Doi Samoen

Foundation of village:	1935;
Population:	420, Green Hmong;
Households:	48 (with an average of approximately 9 persons per household);
Congregations:	42 households traditional Hmong religion (87,5 %), 6 households Catholic;
Cultivation:	Carrot, cabbage, potatoes for sale; rice and maize for subsistence;
Tourism:	Tourists pass through the village often on their way to Wat Chan, location of a "Hilltribe" Museum;
Projects:	Social Welfare Department;
Environmental Protection:	After the foundation of the village, a sacred tree and protection zone were established; in 2000 this zone was extended to now include 150 *rai* of land.

Hui Luk

Foundation of village:	1978;
Population:	3.000, 2.000 Green Hmong and 1.000 lowland Thai and Lahu;
Households:	178 Hmong households (with an average of approximately 11 persons per household);
Congregations:	163 households traditional Hmong religion (91,57 %), 15 households Catholic;
Cultivation:	Carrot, maize, flowers, potatoes;

Appendix

Tourism:	Tourists come every day, souvenir-stalls along the road;
Projects:	Royal Project, Social Welfare Department;
Environmental Protection:	The RP helps to protect the extended conservation area around the sacred tree since 1995. Before the protection zone around the tree was extended in the 1990s, the area was used for the growing of dry rice. Both on the King's and Queen's birthdays, trees are planted each year in the conservation zone.

Chun Yen

Foundation of village:	1980;
Population:	200, White Hmong;
Households:	35 (with an average of approximately 6 persons per household);
Congregations:	28 households traditional Hmong religion (80 %), 6 households Protestant, 1 household Catholic;
Cultivation:	Maize, cotton flowers for sale;
Tourism:	Tourists come every day, souvenir-stalls along the road;
Projects:	None;
Environmental Protection:	None;

Na Pa Paek

Foundation of village:	1935;
Population:	360 Green Hmong, 810 Shan;
Households:	45 Hmong households (with an average of approximately 8 persons per household);
Congregations:	35 households traditional Hmong religion (77,77 %), 10 households Protestant;

Cultivation:	Cabbage for sale, rice and maize for subsistence;
Tourism:	Tourists come every day, souvenir-stalls along the road;
Projects:	Royal Project, Highland Agriculture Project, and Public Health Department;
Environmental Protection:	The village used to have a sacred tree but after the death of the village shaman no villager had the knowledge to perform the yearly *ntoo xeeb* ritual. In 1982, the protection area around the tree was enlarged to 500 *rai* and is now maintained with the support by the RFD.

Tho Mae Tho

Foundation of village:	1952;
Population:	1.040 Green Hmong, other groups in the village: Karen, Shan, and Pa-U;
Households:	130 Hmong households (with an average of approximately 8 persons per household);
Congregations:	123 households traditional Hmong religion (94,61 %), 7 households Protestant;
Cultivation:	Cabbage and carrot for sale, rice and maize for subsistence;
Tourism:	None;
Projects:	Royal Project, Highland Agriculture Project, and Royal Forestry Department;
Environmental Protection:	When the settlement was founded, the protection area around the sacred tree measured 50 *rai*. In 1987, this area was extended by the villagers to 5.000 *rai*.

Appendix

Ban Microwave

Foundation of village:	1976;
Population:	465, Green Hmong;
Households:	48 (with an average of approximately 10 persons per household);
Congregations:	45 households traditional Hmong religion (93,75 %), 3 households Protestant;
Cultivation:	Cabbage and carrot for sale, rice and maize for subsistence;
Tourism:	Visiting tourists every day during dry season as village is part of a guided trekking tour;
Projects:	Royal Forestry Department, Faculty of Agriculture (CMU), Army Development and Education Program, TV Channels 3 and 9 maintain a transmitter in the village;
Environmental Protection:	Village is part of the Nam Tok Mae Surin National Park. The villagers themselves protect 30 *rai* of land around the sacred tree.

Puat Thai

Foundation of village:	1938;
Population:	120, Green and White Hmong;
Households:	13 (with an average of approximately 9 persons per household);
Congregations:	10 households traditional Hmong religion (76,92 %), 3 households Protestant;
Cultivation:	Cabbage, carrot, potatoes, tomatoes, maize for sale, rice for subsistence;

Tourism:	The village has been provided with electricity in 1999, since then tour groups no longer have the settlement on their agenda;
Projects:	Care, Social Welfare Department;
Environmental Protection:	The village does not have a sacred tree (the Vang majority clan claims not to worship a local spirit) but started to conserve 1.000 *rai* of land in 1998 to act before the Royal Forestry Department would enforce state protection laws on the village.

Lau Li

Foundation of village:	1959;
Population:	1.500 Green Hmong, Chinese, Karen and lowland Thai also live in the village;
Households:	120 Hmong households (with an average of approximately 13 persons per household);
Congregations:	110 households traditional Hmong religion (91,66 %), 10 households Protestant;
Cultivation:	Cabbage, carrot, red onion for sale, rice for subsistence;
Tourism:	During dry season trekking groups pass through the village, no selling of souvenirs;
Projects:	Royal Project, Public Health Department, Social Welfare Department;
Environmental Protection:	The settlement is part of the Mae Tho National Park. The village does not have a sacred tree but started to conserve an area of 500 *rai* in 1992 to openly demonstrate own environmental protection efforts.

BIBLIOGRAPHY

Abadie, Maurice
1924 *Les Races du Haut-Tonkin de Phong-Tho à Lang-Son*. Paris: Ancienne Maison Challemel.

Agnew, John
1993 Representing Space: Space, Scale and Culture in Social Science. In *Place, Culture, Representation*, edited by James Duncan and David Ley. London, New York: Routledge, pp. 251-271.

Amanor, Kojo Sebastian
2002 Indigenous Knowledge in Space and Time. In *Cultivating Biodiversity*, edited by Michael Stocking. London: ITDG, pp. 126-131.

Anderson, Benedict
1983 *Imagined Communities: Reflections on the Origin and Spread of Nationalism*. London: Verso.

Appadurai, Arjun
1988 Putting Hierarchy at its Place. In *Cultural Anthropology*, Vol. 3, No. 1, pp. 36-49.
1991 Global Ethnoscapes: Notes and Queries for a Transnational Anthropology. In *Recapturing Anthropology: Working in the Present*, edited by Richard J. Fox. Santa Fe: School of American Research Press.

Ardener, Shirley
1993 Ground Rules and Social Maps for Women: An Introduction. In *Women and Space: Ground Rules and Social Maps*, edited by Shirley Ardener. Oxford (USA): Berg, pp. 1-29.

Badenoch, Nathan
2004 Social Organization in the Upland Landscape of Northern Thailand: Hmong Responses to Resource Scarcity. *Paper presented at the International Conference "Impact of Globalisation, Regionalism and Nationalism on Minority Peoples in Southeast Asia"*. Chiang Mai (Thailand), 15-17 November 2004.

Banijbatana, Dusit
1978 Forest Policy in Northern Thailand. In *Farmers in the Forest: Economic Development and Marginal Agriculture in Northern Thailand*, edited by Peter Kunstadter, E.C. Chapman, and Sanga Sabhasri. Honolulu: University of Hawaii, pp. 54-60.

Barnard, Alan and Jonathan Spencer
2003 Culture. In *Encyclopedia of Social and Cultural Anthropology*, edited by Alan Barnard and Jonathan Spencer. London, New York: Routledge, pp. 136-143.

Barnes, Robert H.
1993 Everyday Space: Some Considerations on the Representation and Use of Space in Indonesia. In *Alltagswissen, Les Savoirs Quotidiens, Everyday Cognition*, edited by Jürg Wassmann and Pierre R. Dasen. Freiburg: Universitätsverlag Freiburg, pp. 159-178.

Barrett, Mark E.
2003 Correlates of Illicit Drug Use in Karen Villages in Northern Thailand. In *Substance Use and Misuse*, Vol. 38, No. 11-13, pp. 1616-1649.

Barth, Fredrik
1969 Introduction. In *Ethnic Groups and Boundaries*, edited by Fredrik Barth. London: George Allen and Unwin, pp. 9-38.
2002 Toward a Richer Description and Analysis of Cultural Phenomena. In *Anthropology beyond Culture*, edited by Richard Fox and Barbara J. King. Oxford, New York: Berg, pp. 23-36.

Basso, Keith
1996 Wisdom Sits in Places: Notes on a Western Apache Landscape. In *Senses of Place*, edited by Steven Feld and Keith Basso. Santa Fe, Mexico: School of American Research Press, pp. 53-90.

Bender, Barbara
1995 Introduction: Landscape - Meaning and Action. In *Landscape: Politics and Perspectives*, edited by Barbara Bender. Providence, Oxford: Berg, pp. 1-18.
2003 Landscape. In *Encyclopedia of Social and Cultural Anthropology*, edited by Allen Barnard and Jonathan Spencer. London, New York: Routledge, pp. 323-324.

Bibliography

Bender, Mark
1988 Hxak Hmub: An Introduction to an Antiphonal Myth Cycle of Miao in Southeast Guizhou. In *Contributions to Southeast Asian Ethnography*, Vol. 7, pp. 95-128.

Benko, Georges
1997 Introduction: Modernity, Postmodernity and the Social Sciences. In *Space and Social Theory: Interpreting Modernity and Postmodernity*, edited by Georges Benko and Ulf Strohmayer. Oxford, Malden (Massachusetts, USA): Blackwell, pp. 1-44.

Bernatzik, Hugo. A.
1947 *Akha und Meau: Probleme der angewandten Völkerkunde in Hinterindien*. 2 Volumes. Innsbruck: Wagner.

Bertrais, Yves
1964 *Dictionnaire Hmong (Meo Blanc) - Français*. Vientiane: Mission Catholique.
1978 *The Traditional Marriage among the White Hmong of Thailand and Laos*. Chiang Mai: Hmong Centre.

Bhruksasri, Wanat
1989 Government Policy: Highland Ethnic Minorities. In *Hill Tribes Today: Problems in Change*, edited by John McKinnon and Bernard Vienne. Bangkok: White Lotus, pp. 5-31.

Blu, Karen
1996 "Where do you stay at?" Homeplace and Community among the Lumbee. In *Senses of Place*, edited by Steven Feld and Keith Basso. Santa Fe, New Mexico: School of American Research Press, pp. 197-227.

Bollig, Michael, Julia Pauli, and Michael Schnegg
2000 Zwischen Toolbox und Dichter Beschreibung: Ethnologische Methoden in Wissenschaft und Praxis. In *Ethnoscripts*, Vol. 2, pp. 66-78.

Bossen, Laurel
1989 Women and Economic Institutions. In *Economic Anthropology*, edited by Stuart Plattner. Stanford: Stanford University Press, pp. 318-350.

Bourdieu, Pierre
1977 *Outline of a Theory of Practice*. Cambridge: Cambridge University Press.

1985 *Sozialer Raum und "Klassen": Leçon sur la Leçon. Zwei Vorlesungen.* Frankfurt am Main: Suhrkamp Verlag.
1991 Physischer, sozialer und angeeigneter physischer Raum. In *Stadt-Räume*, edited by Martin Wentz. Frankfurt, New York: Campus Verlag, pp. 25-34.
1996 *Die feinen Unterschiede: Kritik der gesellschaftlichen Urteilskraft.* Frankfurt am Main: Suhrkamp Verlag.

Boyarin, Daniel and Jonathan Boyarin
1993 Diaspora: Generational Ground of Jewish Identity. In *Critical Inquiry*, Vol. 19, No. 4, pp. 693-725.

Brown, Penelope
2002 Language as a Model for Culture: Lessons from the Cognitive Sciences. In *Anthropology beyond Culture*, edited by Richard Fox and Barbara J. King. Oxford, New York: Berg, pp. 169-192.

Brown, Penelope and Stephen Levinson
1993 "Uphill" and "Downhill" in Tzeltal. In *Journal of Linguistic Anthropology*, Vol. 3, No. 1, pp. 46-74.

Bryman, Alan and Robert G. Burgess
1994 Developments in Qualitative Data Analysis: An Introduction. In *Analyzing Qualitative Data*, edited by Alan Bryman and Robert G Burgess. London, New York: Routledge, pp. 1-17.

Buchsteiner, Jochen
2004 Thaksins Würgegriff: In Thailand regt sich Kritik am Regierungssystem des Ministerpräsidenten. In *Frankfurter Allgemeine Zeitung*, Vol. 223, pp. 4; 24.09.2004.

Bulk, Jack
1996 American Hmong on the Move: An Explanation of Very Distinctive Secondary Migration Patterns. In *Hmong Forum*, Vol. January 1996, pp. 3-28.

Bumke, Peter J.
1971 *Die Miao: Sozialgeschichte und politische Organisation einer segmentären Gesellschaft und die Auswirkungen der thailändischen Minderheitenpolitik.* Wiesbaden: Otto Harrassowitz.

Bibliography

Bünte, Marco
2000 *Probleme der demokratischen Konsolidierung in Thailand.* Hamburg: Institut für Asienkunde.

Burawoy, Michael
2000 Introduction: Reaching for the Global. In *Global Ethnography: Forces, Connections, and Imaginations in a Postmodern World*, edited by Michael Burawoy, et al. Berkeley, Los Angeles, London: University of California Press, pp. 1-40.

Certeau, Michel de
1980 *L'Invention du Quotidien: Arts de Faire.* Paris: Union Générale des Editions.
1986 *The Practise of Everyday Life.* Berkeley: University of California Press.

Cha, Dia
2001 The Hmong 'Dab Pog Couple' Story and its Significance in Arriving at an Understanding of Hmong Ritual. *Paper presented at the 6th Annual Hmong National Conference.* Sacramento (USA), 30 March - 1 April 2001.

Chan, Sucheng (ed.)
1994 *Hmong Means Free: Life in Laos and America.* Philadelphia: Temple University Press.

Chandraprasert, Elawat
1997 The Impact of Development on the Hilltribes of Thailand. In *Development or Domestication? Indigenous Peoples of Southeast Asia*, edited by Don McCaskill and Ken Kampe. Chiang Mai: Silkworm Books, pp. 83-96.

Charoenpanij, Siracha
1989 The Thai Legal System: The Law as an Agent of Environmental Protection. In *Culture and Environment in Thailand*, edited by The Siam Society. Bangkok: D.K. Bookhouse, pp. 463-473.

Chatty, Dawn and Marcus Colchester
2002 Introduction: Conservation and Mobile Indigenous Peoples. In *Conservation and Mobile Indigenous Peoples: Displacement, Forced Settlement, and Sustainable Development*, edited by Dawn Chatty and Marcus Colchester. New York, Oxford: Berghahn Books, pp. 1-20.

Chindarsi, Nusit
1976 *The Religion of the Hmong Njua.* Bangkok: The Siam Society.

1983 Hmong Shamanism. In *Highlanders of Thailand*, edited by John McKinnon and Wanat Bhruksasri. Kuala Lumpur et al.: Oxford University Press, pp. 187-193.

Chotichaipiboon, Tawin
1997 Socio-Cultural and Environmental Impact of Economic Development on Hill Tribes. In *Development or Domestication? Indigenous Peoples of Southeast Asia*, edited by Don McCaskill and Ken Kampe. Chiang Mai: Silkworm Books, pp. 97-116.

Classen, C.
1991 The Sensory Orders of "Wild Children". In *The Varieties of Sensory Experience*, edited by David Howes. Toronto: University of Toronto Press, pp. 47-60.

Clifford, James
1986 Introduction: Partial Truths. In *Writing Culture: The Poetics and Politics of Ethnography*, edited by James Clifford and George E. Marcus. Berkeley, Los Angeles, London: University of California Press, pp. 1-26.
1988 *The Predicament of Culture: Twentieth-Century Ethnography, Literature, and Art*. Cambridge (Massachusetts, USA): Harvard University Press.
1997 *Routes: Travel and Translation in the Late Twentieth Century*. Cambridge (Massachusetts, USA): Harvard University Press.

Clifford, James and George E. Marcus (eds)
1986 *Writing Culture: The Poetics and Politics of Ethnography*. Berkeley, Los Angeles, London: University of California Press.

Cohen, Abner
1969 *Custom and Politics in Urban Africa: A Study of Hausa Migrants in Yoruba Towns*. Berkeley: University of California Press.

Cohen, Robin
1997 *Global Diaspora: An Introduction*. Seattle: University of Washington Press.

Colchester, Marcus
1995 Indigenous Peoples' Rights and Sustainable Resource Use in South and Southeast Asia. In *Indigenous Peoples of Asia*, edited by Robert Harrison Barnes, Andrew Gray, and Benedict Kingsbury. Michigan: Association for Asian Studies, pp. 59-76.

Comaroff, Jean
1985 *Body of Power, Spirit of Resistance*. Chicago: University of Chicago Press.

Condominas, Georges
1991 *From Lawa to Mon, from Saa' to Thai: Historical and Anthropological Aspects of Southeast Asian Social Spaces*. Canberra: Australian National University.

Conquergood, Dwight
1989 *I am a Shaman: A Hmong Life Story with Ethnographic Commentary*. Minneapolis: Center for Urban and Regional Affairs, University of Minnesota.

Cooke, Fadzilah Majid
2003 Maps and Counter-Maps: Globalised Imaginings and Local Realities of Sarawak's Plantation Agriculture. In *Journal of Southeast Asian Studies*, Vol. 34, No. 2, pp. 265-284.

Cooper, Robert
1978 Unity and Division in Hmong Social Categories in Thailand. In *Studies in ASEAN Sociology: Urban Society and Social Change*, edited by Peter Chen and Hans-Dieter Evers. Singapore: Chopmen Enterprises, pp. 297-320.
1979 The Yao Jua Relationship: Patterns of Affinal Alliance and Residence among the Hmong of Northern Thailand. In *Ethnology*, Vol. 18, No. 2, pp. 173-181.
1983 Sexual Inequality among the Hmong. In *Highlanders of Thailand*, edited by John McKinnon and Wanat Bhruksasri. Kuala Lumpur et al.: Oxford University Press, pp. 173-186.
1984 *Resource Scarcity and the Hmong Response*. Singapore: Singapore University Press.
1986 The Hmong of Laos: Economic Factors in Refugee Exodus and Return. In *The Hmong in Transition*, edited by Glenn L. Hendricks, Bruce T. Downing, and Amos S. Deinard. New York: Center for Migration Studies, pp. 23-40.
2004 Rape: Perceptions and Processes of Hmong Customary Law. In *Hmong/Miao in Asia*, edited by Nicholas Tapp et al. Chiang Mai: Silkworm Books, pp. 421-438.

Cooper, Robert et al.
1996 *The Hmong*. Bangkok: Art Asia Press.

Corlin, Claes
2000 The Politics of Cosmology: An Introduction to Millenarianism and Ethnicity among Highland Minorities of Northern Thailand. In *Civility and Savagery: Social Identity in Thai States*, edited by Andrew Turton. Richmond: Curzon Press, pp. 104-121.
2004 Hmong and the Land Question in Vietnam: National Policy and Local Concepts of the Environment. In *Hmong/Miao in Asia*, edited by Nicholas Tapp et al. Chiang Mai: Silkworm Books, pp. 295-320.

Coxhead, Ian and Sisira Jayasuriya
2003 *The Open Economy and the Environment: Development, Trade and Resources in Asia*. Cheltenham (U.K.), Northampton (USA): Edward Elgar.

Crabtree, Andy
2000 Remarks on the Social Organization of Space and Place. Electronic Source: <http://www.mundanebehaviour.org/issues/vlnl/crabtree.html>, 03.09.2000.

Cromley, Ellen K.
1999 Mapping Spatial Data. In *Mapping Social Networks, Spatial Data, & Hidden Populations*, edited by Jean J. Schensul et al. Walnut Creek: Alta Mira, pp. 51-124.

Crumley, Carole L. (ed.)
2001 *New Directions in Anthropology and Environment: Intersections*. Thousand Oaks (USA): Alta Mira Press.

Culas, Christian
1994 The Cultural Change and the Structures of Social Organisation of the Hmong in Thailand. *Final Research Report for the National Research Council of Thailand*, Aix en Provence: Institut de la Recherche sur l'Asie du Sud-Est.
2000 Migrants, Runaways and Opium Growers: Origins of the Hmong in Laos and Siam in the Nineteenth and Early Twentieth Centuries. In *Turbulent Times and Enduring Peoples: Mountain Minorities in the South-East Asian Massif*, edited by Jean Michaud. Richmond: Curzon Press, pp. 29-47.
2004 Innovation and Tradition in Rituals and Cosmology: Hmong Messianism and Shamanism in Southeast Asia. In *Hmong/Miao in Asia*, edited by Nicholas Tapp et al. Chiang Mai: Silkworm Books, pp. 97-126.

Culas, Christian and Jean Michaud
2004   A Contribution to the Study of Hmong (Miao) Migrations and History. In *Hmong/Miao in Asia*, edited by Nicholas Tapp et al. Chiang Mai: Silkworm Books, pp. 61-96.

Darlington, Susan M.
1998   The Ordination of a Tree: The Buddhist Ecology Movement in Thailand. In *Ethnology*, Vol. 37, No. 1, pp. 1-15.

Davis, Richard
1984   *Muang Metaphysics: A Study of Northern Thai Myth and Ritual*. Bangkok: Pandora.

Dear, Michael
1997   Postmodern Bloodlines. In *Space and Social Theory: Interpreting Modernity and Postmodernity*, edited by Georges Benko and Ulf Strohmayer. Oxford, Malden (Massachusetts, USA): Blackwell, pp. 49-71.

Dearden, Philip
1995   *Ecotourism, Parks and Biocultural Diversity: The Context in Northern Thailand*. Bangkok: Institute of Eco-Tourism, Srinakharinwirot University.

Delang, Claudio
2002   Deforestation in Northern Thailand: The Result of Hmong Farming Practices or Thai Development Strategies? In *Society and Natural Resources*, Vol. 15, pp. 483-501.

Descola, Philippe and Gisli Pálsson (eds)
1996   *Nature and Society: Anthropological Perspectives*. London, New York: Routledge.

Dessaint, William Y. and Alain Y. Dessaint
1992   Economic Systems and Ethnic Relations. In *The Highland Heritage: Collected Essays on Upland North Thailand*, edited by Anthony R. Walker. Singapore: Suvarnabhumi, pp. 95-110.

Dey, Ian
1999   *Grounding Grounded Theory: Guidelines for Qualitative Research*. San Diego: Academic Press.

Dickens, Peter
1992   *Society and Nature: Towards a Green Social Theory.* London: Harvester Wheatsheaf.

Dickhardt, Michael
2001   *Das Räumliche des Kulturellen: Entwurf zu einer Kulturanthropologischen Raumtheorie am Beispiel Fiji.* Münster, Hamburg, London: LIT Verlag.

Dickhardt, Michael and Brigitta Hauser-Schäublin
2003   Einleitung: Eine Theorie kultureller Räumlichkeit als Deutungsrahmen. In *Kulturelle Räume - Räumliche Kultur*, edited by Brigitta Hauser-Schäublin and Michael Dickhardt. Münster, Hamburg, London: LIT Verlag, pp. 13-42.

Diedrich, Richard-Michael
1999   You Can't Beat Us: Class, Work and Masculinity on a Council Estate in the South Wales Coalfield. *Unpublished PhD Thesis*, Hamburg: University of Hamburg.

Dirksen, Hagen
1997   Solving Problems of Opium Production in Thailand: Lessons Learned from the Thai-German Highland Development Program. In *Development or Domestication? Indigenous Peoples of Southeast Asia*, edited by Don McCaskill and Ken Kampe. Chiang Mai: Silkworm Books, pp. 329-357.

Donnelly, Nancy
1994   *The Changing Lives of Hmong Women.* Seattle: University of Washington.

Dorsch, Hauke
2000   *Afrikanische Diaspora und Black Atlantic.* Münster, Hamburg, London: LIT Verlag.

2004   Griots, Roots and Identity in the African Diaspora. In *Diaspora, Identity and Religion: New Directions in Theory and Research*, edited by Waltraud Kokot, Khachig Tölölyan, and Carolin Alfonso. London, New York: Routledge, pp. 102-116.

Dracklé, Dorle and Waltraud Kokot
1996   Neue Feldforschungen in Europa: Grenzen, Konflikte, Identitäten. In *Ethnologie Europas: Grenzen, Konflikte, Identitäten*, edited by Waltraud Kokot and Dorle Dracklé. Berlin: Dietrich Reimer Verlag, pp. 3-20.

Driessen, Henk
1996 What am I Doing Here? The Anthropologist, the Mole, and Border Ethnography. In *Ethnologie Europas: Grenzen, Konflikte, Identitäten*, edited by Waltraud Kokot and Dorle Dracklé. Berlin: Dietrich Reimer Verlag, pp. 287-298.

Dulyakasem, Uthai
1986 Shamans and Rebels: The Batchai (Meo) Rebellion of Northern Laos and North-West Vietnam (1918-21). In *Journal of The Siam Society*, Vol. 74, pp. 107-215.

Duncan, James
1993 Sites of Representation: Place, Time and the Discourse of the Other. In *Place, Culture, Representation*, edited by James Duncan and David Ley. London, New York: Routledge, pp. 39-56.

Duncan, James and David Ley (eds)
1993 *Place, Culture, Representation*. London, New York: Routledge.

Dunnigan, Timothy
1986 Processes of Identity Maintenance in Hmong Society. In *The Hmong in Transition*, edited by Glenn L. Hendricks, Bruce T. Downing, and Amos S. Deinard. New York: Center for Migration Studies, pp. 41-53.

Duranti, Alessandro
1992 Language and Bodies in Social Space: Samoan Ceremonial Greetings. In *American Anthropologist*, Vol. 94, No. 3, pp. 657-691.

Durham, William H.
2002 Cultural Variation in Time and Space: The Case for a Populational Theory of Culture. In *Anthropology beyond Culture*, edited by Richard Fox and Barbara J. King. Oxford, New York: Berg, pp. 193-206.

Durkheim, Emile
1994 *Die elementaren Formen des religiösen Lebens*. Frankfurt am Main: Suhrkamp. Transl. 1st edition.

Durkheim, Emile and Marcel Mauss
1963 *Primitive Classification*. Chicago: Chicago University Press.

Durrenberger, E. Paul
1996   The Power of Culture and the Culture of States in Thailand. In *State Power and Culture in Thailand*, edited by E. Paul Durrenberger. New Haven, Connecticut: Yale University, pp. 1-21.

Durrenberger, E. Paul and Nicola Tannenbaum
1990   *Analytical Perspectives on Shan Agriculture and Village Economics*. New Haven (Connecticut, USA): Yale University Southeast Asia Studies.

Eliade, Mircea
1959   *The Sacred and the Profane*. New York: Harcourt, Brace and World.
1968   *Le Chamanisme et les Techniques Archaïques de l'Extase*. Paris: Payot.

Ellen, Roy
1979   Introduction: Anthropology, the Environment and Ecological Systems. In *Social and Ecological Systems*, edited by Philip C. Burnham and Roy Ellen. London, New York, San Francisco: Academic Press, pp. 1-17.
1996   Introduction. In *Redefining Nature: Ecology, Culture and Domestication*, edited by Roy Ellen and Katsuyoshi Fukui. Oxford, Washington: Berg, pp. 1-36.

Ellen, Roy and Holly Harris
2000   Introduction. In *Indigenous Environmental Knowledge and its Transformations: Critical Anthropological Perspectives*, edited by Roy Ellen, Peter Parkes, and Alan Bicker. Amsterdam: Harwood Academic Publishers, pp. 1-33.

Elliott, Stephen, David Blakesley, and Vilaiwan Anusarnsunthorn
1998   *Forests for the Future: Growing and Planting Native Trees for Restoring Forest Ecosystems*. Chiang Mai: Biology Department, Science Faculty.

England, Philippa
1997   UNCED and the Implementation of Forest Policy in Thailand. In *Seeing Forests for Trees: Environment and Environmentalism in Thailand*, edited by Philip Hirsch. Chiang Mai: Silkworm Books, pp. 53-71.
1998   National Agendas in Malaysia and Thailand before and after the Adoption of the Authoritative Statement of Forest Principles at Rio. In *Land Conflicts in Southeast Asia: Indigenous Peoples, Environment and International Law*, edited by Catherine Iorns Magallanes and Malcolm Hollick. Bangkok: White Lotus Press, pp. 241-271.

Entrikin, Nicholas J.
1991 *The Betweenness of Place: Toward a Geography of Modernity.* Baltimore: Johns Hopkins University Press.

Evans, Grant R. (ed.)
1999 *Laos Culture and Society.* Chiang Mai: Silkworm Books.

Fadiman, Anne
1997 *The Spirit Catches You and You Fall Down: A Hmong Child, her American Doctors, and the Collision of Two Cultures.* New York: Farrar, Straus and Giroux.

Fairhead, James and Melissa Leach
1996 *Misreading the African Landscape: Society and Ecology in a Forest-Savanna Mosaic.* Cambridge: Cambridge University Press.

Falvey, Lindsay
2000 Self Sufficiency or Buddhism? Applied Agricultural Ethics in Thailand. In *Thai Culture*, Vol. 5, No. 2, pp. 15-18.

Feld, Steven and Keith Basso (eds)
1996 *Senses of Place.* Santa Fe, New Mexico: School of American Research Press.
1996a Introduction. In *Senses of Place.* Santa Fe, New Mexico: School of American Research Press, pp. 3-11.

Feuchtwang, S.
1974 *An Anthropological Analysis of Chinese Geomancy.* Vientiane: Vithagna.

Forsyth, Timothy
1999 Questioning the Impacts of Shifting Cultivation. In *Watershed*, Vol. 5, No. 1, pp. 23-29.
2001 Watersheds and Science: Why the Concern? *Paper presented at the "International Symposium on Watershed Management: Highland and Lowland in the Protected Area Regime".* Chiang Mai, Thailand, 23-26 March 2001.

Foucault, Michel
1986 Of Other Spaces. In *Diacritics*, Vol. 16, No. 1, pp. 22-27.
1991 Andere Räume. In *Stadt-Räume: Die Zukunft des Städtischen*, edited by Martin Wentz. Frankfurt a. Main, New York: Campus, pp. 65-72.

Fox, Jefferson
2000   How Blaming "Slash and Burn" Farmers is Deforesting Mainland Southeast Asia. In *Analysis from the East-West Center*, Vol. 47, pp. 1-8.

Fox, Richard G. and Andre Gingrich
2002   Introduction. In *Anthropology, by Comparison*, edited by Richard G. Fox and Andre Gingrich. London, New York: Routledge, pp. 1-24.

Freksa, Christian, Christopher Habel, and Karl F. Wender (eds)
1998   *Spatial Cognition: An Interdisciplinary Approach to Representing and Processing Spatial Knowledge*. Berlin: Springer Verlag.

Friedman, Jonathan
1994   *Cultural Identity and Global Process*. London: Sage.
1997   Simplifying Complexity: Assimilating the Global in a Small Paradise. In *Siting Culture: The Shifting Anthropological Object*, edited by Kirsten Hastrup and Karen Fog Olwig. London, New York: Routledge, pp. 268-291.
1999   The Hybridization of Roots and the Abhorrence of the Bush. In *Spaces of Culture: City, Nation, World*, edited by Mike Featherstone and Scott Lash. London, Thousand Oaks, New Delhi: Sage, pp. 230-256.

Ganjanapan, Anan
1997   The Politics of Enviornment in Northern Thailand: Ethnicity and Highland Development Programs. In *Seeing Forests for Trees: Environment and Environmentalism in Thailand*, edited by Philip Hirsch. Chiang Mai: Silkworm Books, pp. 202-222.
1998   From Local Custom to the Formation of Community Rights: A Case of Community Forestry Struggle in Northern Thailand. In *Human Flow and Creation of New Cultures in Southeast Asia*, edited by ILCAA. Tokyo: Institute for the Study of Languages and Cultures of Asia and Africa (ILCAA).
1998a The Politics of Conservation and the Complexity of Local Control of Forests in the Northern Thai Highlands. In *Mountain Research and Development*, Vol. 18, No. 1, pp. 71-82.
2000   *Local Control of Land and Forest: Cultural Dimensions of Resource Management in Northern Thailand*. Chiang Mai: Regional Center for Social Science and Sustainable Development.
2003   Globalization and the Dynamics of Culture in Thailand. In *Globalization in Southeast Asia: Local, National and Transnational Perspectives*, edited by Shinji Yamashita and Jeremy S. Eades. New York: Berghahn Books, pp. 126-141.

Geddes, William Robert
1970   Opium and the Miao: A Study in Ecological Adjustment. In *Oceania*, Vol. 41, No. 1, pp. 1-11.
1976   *Migrants of the Mountains: The Cultural Ecology of the Blue Miao (Hmong Njua) of Thailand*. Oxford: Clarendon Press.

Geertz, Clifford
1972   Deep Play: Notes on the Balinese Cockfight. In *Daedalus*, Vol. 101, pp. 1-37.
1973   *The Interpretation of Cultures: Selected Essays*. New York: Basic Books.
1988   *Works and Lives: The Anthropologist as Author*. Stanford: Stanford University Press.
1996   Afterword. In *Senses of Place*, edited by Steven Feld and Keith Basso. Santa Fe, New Mexico: School of American Research Press, pp. 259-262.

Géraud, Marie-Odile
1993   Les Hmong de Guyane Française. *Unpublished PhD Thesis (Microfiche by the University of Lille III)*, Montpellier: Université Paul-Valéry.

Geusau, Leo Alting von
1983   Dialectics of Akhazan: The Interiorizations of a Perennial Minority Group. In *Highlanders of Thailand*, edited by John McKinnon and Wanat Bhruksasri. Kuala Lumpur et al.: Oxford University Press, pp. 243-277.
2000   Akha Internal History: Marginalization and the Ethnic Alliance System. In *Civility and Savagery: Social Identity in Thai States*, edited by Andrew Turton. Richmond: Curzon Press, pp. 122-158.

Giddens, Anthony
1979   *Central Problems in Social Theory: Action, Structure and Contradiction in Social Analysis*. London: Macmillan.
1987   *Social Theory and Modern Sociology*. Cambridge: Polity Press.
1990   *The Consequences of Modernity*. Stanford: Stanford University Press.
2001   *The Constitution of Society: Outline of the Theory of Structuration*. Cambridge: Polity Press. Reprinted edition.

Glaser, Barney G.
1992   *Basics of Grounded Theory Analysis*. Mill Valley (California, USA): Sociology Press.

Glaser, Barney G. and Anselm L. Strauss
1975   *The Discovery of Grounded Theory: Strategies for Qualitative Research*. New York: Aldine de Gruyter.

Glick-Schiller, Nina and Georges Eugene
2001   *George Woke Up Laughing: Long Distance Nationalism and the Search for Home.* Durham: Duke University Press.

Gow, Peter
1995   Land, People, and Paper in Western Amazonia. In *The Anthropology of Landscape: Perspectives on Place and Space*, edited by Eric Hirsch and Michael O'Hannon. Oxford: Oxford University Press, pp. 43-62.

Gowan, Teresa and Seán Ó Riain
2000   Preface. In *Global Ethnography: Forces, Connections, and Imaginations in a Postmodern World*, edited by Michael Burawoy et al. Berkeley, Los Angeles, London: University of California Press, pp. ix-xv.

Grandstaff, Terry B.
1976   Swidden Society in North Thailand: A Diachronic Perspective Emphasizing Resource Relationships. *Unpublished PhD Thesis*, University of Hawaii: Honolulu.
1979   The Hmong, Opium and the Haw: Speculations on the Origin of their Association. In *Journal of the Siam Society*, Vol. 67, No. 2, pp. 70-79.

Gravers, Mikael
1994   The Pwo Karen Ethnic Minority in the Thai Nation: Destructive Hilltribe or Utopian Conservationists. In *Copenhagen Discussion Papers No. 23* Copenhagen: Centre for East and Southeast Asia, pp. 21-46.
2001   Ethnic Minorities in Thailand: Figures and Selected Bibliography. In *Forest in Culture, Culture in Forest: Perspectives from Northern Thailand*, edited by Ebbe Poulsen et al. Tjele: Research Centre on Forest and People in Thailand, Danish Institute of Agricultural Sciences, pp. 17-20.
2001a Karen Notions of Environment - Space, Place and Power in a Political Landscape. In *Forest in Culture, Culture in Forest: Perspectives from Northern Thailand*, edited by Ebbe Poulsen et al. Tjele: Research Centre on Forest and People in Thailand, Danish Institute of Agricultural Sciences, pp. 55-84.

Gray, Andrew
1995   The Indigenous Movement in Asia. In *Indigenous Peoples of Asia*, edited by Robert H. Barnes, Andrew Gray, and Benedict Kingsbury. Michigan: Association for Asian Studies, pp. 35-58.

Gregory, Derek
1997 Lacan and Geography: The Production of Space Revisited. In *Space and Social Theory: Interpreting Modernity and Postmodernity*, edited by Georges Benko and Ulf Strohmayer. Oxford, Malden (Massachusetts, USA): Blackwell, pp. 203-231.

Grøn, Ole
1991 A Method for Reconstruction of Social Structure in Prehistoric Societies and Examples of Practical Application. In *Social Space: Human Spatial Behaviour in Dwellings and Settlements*, edited by Ole Grøn, Ericka Engelstadt, and Inge Lindblom. Odense: Odense University Press, pp. 100-117.

Gupta, Akhil and James Ferguson
1992 Beyond "Culture": Space, Identity, and the Politics of Difference. In *Cultural Anthropology*, Vol. 7, pp. 6-23.
1997 *Culture, Power, Place: Explorations in Critical Anthropology*. Durham, London: Duke University Press.
1997a Culture, Power, Place: Ethnography at the End of an Era. In *Culture, Power, Place: Explorations in Critical Anthropology*, edited by Akhil Gupta and James Ferguson. Durham, London: Duke University Press, pp. 1-29.
1997b Beyond "Culture": Space, Identity, and the Politics of Difference. In *Culture, Power, Place: Explorations in Critical Anthropology*, edited by Akhil Gupta and James Ferguson. Durham, London: Duke University Press, pp. 33-51.
1997c Discipline and Practice: "The Field" as Site, Method, and Location in Anthropology. In *Anthropological Locations: Boundaries and Grounds of a Field Service*, edited by Akhil Gupta and James Ferguson. Berkeley, Los Angeles, London: University of California Press, pp. 1-46.

Hägerstrand, Torsten
1975 Space, Time and Human Conditions. In *Dynamic Allocation of Urban Space*, edited by Anders Karlqvist, Lars Lundqvist, and Folke Snickars. Lexington: Saxon House Lexington Book.

Hall, Sandra E.
1990 Hmong Kinship Roles: Insiders and Outsiders. In *Hmong Forum*, Vol. 1, pp. 25-39.

Hall, Stuart
1992 The Question of Cultural Identity. In *Modernity and its Future*, edited by Stuart Hall, David Held, and Tony McGrew. Cambridge: Polity Press, pp. 273-325.

Hang, Doua
1986 Tam Tuab Neeg: Connecting the Generations. In *The Hmong World*, edited by Brenda Johns and David Strecker. Abbotsburg (Australia): Yale Southeast Asia Studies, pp. 33-41.

Hann, Christopher M.
2002 All Kulturvölker now? Social Anthropological Reflections on the German-American Tradition. In *Anthropology beyond Culture*, edited by Richard Fox and Barbara J. King. Oxford, New York: Berg, pp. 259-276.

Hannerz, Ulf
1992 *Cultural Complexity: Studies in the Social Organization of Meaning*. New York: Columbia University Press.
1996 *Transnational Connections: Culture, People, Places*. London, New York: Routledge.

Hart, Keith
1996 Social Anthropology is a Generalizing Science: For the Motion (1). In *Key Debates in Anthropology*, edited by Tim Ingold. London, New York: Routledge, pp. 21-26.

Harvey, David
1995 *The Condition of Postmodernity: An Enquiry into the Origins of Cultural Change*. Oxford, Malden (Massachusetts, USA): Blackwell. Reprinted edition.

Hastrup, Kirsten
1993 The Native Voice - and the Anthropological Vision. In *Social Anthropology*, Vol. 1, No. 2, pp. 173-186.
2002 Anthropology's Comparative Consciousness. In *Anthropology, by Comparison*, edited by Richard G. Fox and Andre Gingrich. London, New York: Routledge, pp. 27-43.

Hastrup, Kirsten and Karen Fog Olwig
1997 Introduction. In *Siting Culture: The Shifting Anthropological Object*, edited by Kirsten Hastrup and Karen Fog Olwig. London, New York: Routledge, pp. 1-14.

Hauser-Schäublin, Brigitta
1997 *Traces of Gods and Men: Temples and Rituals as Landmarks of Social Events and Processes in a South Bali Village*. Berlin: Dietrich Reimer Verlag.
2003 Raum, Ritual und Gesellschaft: Religiöse Zentren und sozio-religiöse Verdichtungen im Ritual. In *Kulturelle Räume - Räumliche Kultur*, edited by Brigitta Hauser-Schäublin and Michael Dickhardt. Münster, Hamburg, London: LIT Verlag, pp. 43-87.

Hayden, Dolores
1995 *The Power of Place: Urban Landscapes as Public History*. Cambridge (Massachusetts, USA): Massachusetts Institute of Technology Press.

Heidegger, Martin
1986 *Sein und Zeit*. Tübingen: Max Niemeier Verlag.

Heimbach, E.E.
1979 *White Hmong-English Dictionary*. Ithaca, New York: Cornell University.

Hengartner, Thomas, Waltraud Kokot, and Kathrin Wildner
2000 Das Forschungsfeld Stadt in Ethnologie und Volkskunde. In *Kulturwissenschaftliche Stadtforschung*, edited by Thomas Hengartner, Waltraud Kokot, and Kathrin Wildner. Berlin: Dietrich Reimer Verlag, pp. 3-18.

Hesse, Klaus
2003 Kulturelle Räumlichkeit und Stadt: Das Beispiel Mandi (Himachal Pradesh, Indien). In *Kulturelle Räume - Räumliche Kultur*, edited by Brigitta Hauser-Schäublin and Michael Dickhardt. Münster, Hamburg, London: LIT Verlag, pp. 89-132.

Hirsch, Eric
1995 Introduction. Landscape: Between Place and Space. In *The Anthropology of Landscape: Perspectives on Place and Space*, edited by Eric Hirsch and Michael O'Hannon. Oxford: Oxford University Press, pp. 1-30.

Hirsch, Philip
1990 Forest, Forest Reserve, and Forest Land in Thailand. In *Geographical Journal*, Vol. 156, No. 2, pp. 166-174.
1997 Introduction: Seeing Forests for Trees. In *Seeing Forests for Trees: Environment and Environmentalism in Thailand*, edited by Philip Hirsch. Chiang Mai: Silkworm Books, pp. 1-14.

1997a Environment and Environmentalism in Thailand: Material and Ideological Bases. In *Seeing Forests for Trees: Environment and Environmentalism in Thailand*, edited by Philip Hirsch. Chiang Mai: Silkworm Books, pp. 15-36.

Humphrey, Caroline
1995 Chiefly and Shamanist Landscapes in Mongolia. In *The Anthropology of Landscape: Perspectives on Place and Space*, edited by Eric Hirsch and Michael O'Hannon. Oxford: Oxford University Press, pp. 135-162.

Ingold, Tim
1979 The Social and Ecological Relations of Culture-Bearing Organisms: An Essay in Evolutionary Dynamics. In *Social and Ecological Systems*, edited by Philip C. Burnham and Roy Ellen. London, New York, San Francisco: Academic Press, pp. 271-292.
1994 *Companion Encyclopedia of Anthropology: Humanity, Culture and Social Life*. London, New York: Routledge.
2000 *The Perception of the Environment: Essays in Livelihood, Dwelling and Skill*. London, New York: Routledge.
2002 Introduction to Culture. In *Companion Encyclopedia of Anthropology: Humanity, Culture and Social Life*, edited by Tim Ingold. London, New York: Routledge, pp. 329-349.

Iorns Magallanes, Catherine
1998 National Lands and Resources in International Law. In *Land Conflicts in Southeast Asia: Indigenous Peoples, Environment and International Law*, edited by Catherine Iorns Magallanes and Malcolm Hollick. Bangkok: White Lotus Press, pp. 181-240.

Iorns Magallanes, Catherine and Malcolm Hollick
1998 Introduction. In *Land Conflicts in Southeast Asia: Indigenous Peoples, Environment and International Law*, edited by Catherine Iorns Magallanes and Malcolm Hollick. Bangkok: White Lotus Press, pp. 1-20.

Isager, Lotte
2000 Forest and People in Thai Environmentalist Discourse. *Unpublished Working Paper No. 1*, Tjele: Research Centre on Forest and People in Thailand, Danish Institute of Agricultural Sciences.
2001 History and People of North Thailand. In *Forest in Culture, Culture in Forest: Perspectives from Northern Thailand*, edited by Ebbe Poulsen et al. Tjele: Research Centre on Forest and People in Thailand, Danish Institute of Agricultural Sciences, pp. 85-115.

Bibliography

Jensen, Jürgen
2004　Plural Societies and "Transnational" Social Spaces - Modern African Complexities. In *Social Spaces of African Societies: Applications and Critique of Concepts about "Transnational Social Spaces"*, edited by Jürgen Oßenbrügge and Mechthild Reh. Münster: LIT Verlag, pp. 35-75.

Johnson, Charles and Se Yang (eds)
1992　*Myths, Legends and Folk Tales from the Hmong of Laos*. St. Paul, Minnesota: Linguistics Department, Macalester College.

Jónsson, Hjörleifur
1996　Tai States, Forests, and Upland Groups. In *State Power and Culture in Thailand*, edited by E. Paul Durrenberger. New Haven (Connecticut, USA): Yale University, pp. 166-200.
1998　Dead Headmen: Histories and Communities in the Southeast Asian Hinterland: Political Culture in Southeast Asia. In *Facets of Power and Its Limitations: Political Culture in Southeast Asia*, edited by Ing-Britt Trankell and Laura Summers. Uppsala: Department of Cultural Anthropology Uppsala University, pp. 191-212.
2000　Traditional Tribal What? Sports, Culture and the State in the Northern Hills of Thailand. In *Turbulent Times and Enduring Peoples: Mountain Minorities in the South-East Asian Massif*, edited by Jean Michaud. Richmond: Curzon Press, pp. 219-245.

Julian, Roberta
2003　Transnational Identities in the Hmong Diaspora. In *Globalization, Culture and Inequality in Asia*, edited by Timothy J. Scrase, Todd Holden, and Scott Baum. Melbourne: Trans Pacific Press, pp. 119-143.

Kaae, Berit C. and Anny Toftkaer
2000　Tourism and the Doi Inthanon National Park. *Unpublished Report*, Tjele: Research Centre on Forest and People in Thailand, Danish Institute of Agricultural Sciences.

Kahn, Joel S.
1989　Culture: Demise or Resurrection? In *Critique of Anthropology*, Vol. 9, No. 2, pp. 5-25.

Kalland, Arne
2000   Indigenous Knowledge: Prospects and Limitations. In *Indigenous Environmental Knowledge and its Transformations: Critical Anthropological Perspectives*, edited by Roy Ellen, Peter Parkes, and Alan Bicker. Amsterdam: Harwood Academic Publishers, pp. 319-335.

Kant, Immanuel
1787   Kritik der reinen Vernunft. In *Immanuel Kants Sämtliche Werke in Sechs Bänden: Dritter Band*, edited by Insel Verlag. Leipzig: Insel Verlag.

Kearney, Michael
1995   The Local and the Global: The Anthropology of Globalization and Transnationalism. In *Annual Review of Anthropology*, Vol. 24, pp. 547-565.

Keen, F.G.B.
1966   *The Meo of North-West Thailand: The South-East Asian Hilltribe*. Wellington: Government Printer.
1978   Ecological Relationships in a Hmong (Meo) Economy. In *Farmers in the Forest: Economic Development and Marginal Agriculture in Northern Thailand*, edited by Peter Kunstadter, E.C. Chapman, and Sanga Sabhasri. Honolulu: University Press of Hawaii, pp. 210-220.

Keesing, Roger
1987   Anthropology as Interpretative Quest. In *Current Anthropology*, Vol. 28, pp. 161-176.

Kesmanee, Chupinit
1989   The Poisoning Effect of a Lovers Triangle: Highlanders, Opium and Extension Crops, a Policy Overdue for Review. In *Hill Tribes Today: Problems in Change*, edited by John McKinnon and Bernard Vienne. Bangkok: White Lotus Press, pp. 61-102.

Kessler, Manuela
2004   Ballspiele eines Tausendsassas. In *Süddeutsche Zeitung*, Vol. 134, pp. 3; 14.06.2004.
2005   Fluthilfe für den Milliardär. In *Süddeutsche Zeitung*, Vol. 27, pp. 12; 03.02.2005.

Keyes, Charles F.
1979   The Karen and Thai History and the History of the Karen in Thailand. In *Ethnic Adaptation and Identity: The Karen on the Thai Frontier with Burma*, edited by Charles F. Keyes. Philadelphia: Institute for the Study of Human Issues, pp. 31-54.
1987   Tribal Peoples and the Nation-State in Mainland Southeast Asia. In *Southeast Asian Tribal Groups and Ethnic Minorities: Prospects for the Eighties and Beyond*, edited by Cultural Survival. Cambridge (Massachusetts, USA): Cultural Survival, pp. 19-26.

King, Russell
1995   Migrations, Globalization and Place. In *A Place in the World? Places, Cultures and Globalization*, edited by Doreen Massey and Pat Jess. Oxford, New York: Oxford University Press, pp. 5-44.

Kokot, Waltraud
2000   Diaspora, Lokalität und Stadt: Zur ethnologischen Forschung in räumlich nicht begrenzten Gruppen. In *Kulturwissenschaftliche Stadtforschung*, edited by Thomas Hengartner, Waltraud Kokot, and Kathrin Wildner. Berlin: Dietrich Reimer Verlag, pp. 191-203.
2002   Diaspora und Transnationale Verflechtungen. In *Ethnologie der Globalisierung: Perspektiven kultureller Verflechtungen*, edited by Brigitta Hauser-Schäublin and Ulrich Braukämper. Berlin: Dietrich Reimer Verlag, pp. 95-110.

Kokot, Waltraud, Khachig Tölölyan, and Carolin Alfonso
2004   Introduction. In *Diaspora, Identity and Religion: New Directions in Theory and Research*, edited by Waltraud Kokot, Khachig Tölölyan, and Carolin Alfonso. London, New York: Routledge, pp. 1-8.

Korff, Rüdiger
2003   Local Enclosures of Globalization: The Power of Locality. In *Dialectical Anthropology*, Vol. 27, No. 1, pp. 1-18.

Korkeatkachorn, Wipaphan and Suntaree Kiatiprajak (eds)
1997   *Directory of Non-Governmental Organizations*. Bangkok: Thai Development Support Committee.

Krauß, Werner
2001   *"Hängt die Grünen!" Umweltkonflikte, nachhaltige Entwicklung und ökologischer Diskurs*. Berlin: Dietrich Reimer Verlag.

Kunstadter, Peter
1978   Introduction. In *Farmers in the Forest: Economic Development and Marginal Agriculture in Northern Thailand*, edited by Peter Kunstadter, E.C. Chapman, and Sanga Sabhasri. Honolulu: University of Hawaii, pp. 201-205.
1983   Highland Populations in Northern Thailand. In *Highlanders of Thailand*, edited by John McKinnon and Wanat Bhruksasri. Kuala Lumpur et al.: Oxford University Press, pp. 15-45.
1984   Cultural Ideals, Socioeconomic Change, and Household Composition: Karen, Lua', Hmong, and Thai in Northwestern Thailand. In *Households: Comparative and Historical Studies of the Domestic Group*, edited by Robert Netting, Richard Wilk, and Eric Arnould. Berkeley, Los Angeles, London: University of California Press, pp. 299-329.
2000   Changing Patterns of Economics among Hmong in Northern Thailand 1960-1990. In *Turbulent Times and Enduring Peoples: Mountain Minorities in the South-East Asian Massif*, edited by Jean Michaud. Richmond: Curzon Press, pp. 167-192.
2004   Hmong Marriage Patterns in Thailand in Relation to Social Change. In *Hmong/Miao in Asia*, edited by Nicholas Tapp et al. Chiang Mai: Silkworm Books, pp. 375-420.

Kunstadter, Peter and E.C. Chapman
1978   Problems of Shifting Cultivation and Economic Development in Northern Thailand. In *Farmers in the Forest: Economic Development and Marginal Agriculture in Northern Thailand*, edited by Peter Kunstadter, E.C. Chapman, and Sanga Sabhasri. Honolulu: University of Hawaii, pp. 3-23.

Kunstadter, Peter et al.
1987   *Hmong and Karen Health and Family Planning: Cultural and Other Factors Affecting Use of Modern Health and Planning Services by Hilltribes in Northern Thailand*. Bangkok: Ministry of Public Health.
1991   Rapid Changes in Fertility among Hmong of Northern Thailand. *Paper presented at the "Thai National Symposium on Population Studies"*. Salaya, Nakorn Pathom (Thailand), 21-22 November 1991.
2001   Pesticide Exposures among Hmong Farmers in Thailand. In *International Journal of Occupational and Environmental Health*, Vol. 7, No. 4, pp. 313-325.

Kuper, Adam
2002   Comparison and Contextualization: Reflections on South Africa. In *Anthropology, by Comparison*, edited by Richard G. Fox and Andre Gingrich. London, New York: Routledge, pp. 143-166.

Lakanavichian, Sureeratna
2001   Forest Policy and History. In *Forest in Culture, Culture in Forest: Perspectives from Northern Thailand*, edited by Ebbe Poulsen et al. Tjele: Research Centre on Forest and People in Thailand, pp. 117-129.

Lang, Hartmut
2003   Kultur-System-Globlisierung. In *Ethnologie: Einführung und Überblick*, edited by Hans Fischer and Bettina Beer. Berlin: Dietrich Reimer Verlag, pp. 413-427.

Lang, Hartmut, Peter Challenor, and Peter D. Killworth
2004   A New Addition to the Family of Space Sampling Methods. In *Field Methods*, Vol. 16, No. 1, pp. 55-69.

Lang, Richard
1985   The Dwelling Door: Towards a Phenomenology of Transition. In *Dwelling, Place and Environment: Towards a Phenomenology of Person and World*, edited by David Seamon and Robert Mugerauer. Dordrecht, Boston, Lancaster: Martinus Nijhoff Publishers, pp. 201-213.

Laungaramsri, Pinkaew
1999   The Ambiguity of "Watershed": The Politics of People and Conservation in Northern Thailand. A Case Study of the Chom Thong Conflict. In *From Principles to Practice: Indigenous Peoples and Protected Areas in South and Southeast Asia*, edited by Marcus Colchester and Christian Erni. Copenhagen: IWGIA & FFP, pp. 108-133.
2001   *Redefining Nature: Karen Ecological Knowledge and the Challenge to the Modern Conservation Paradigm*. Chennai: Earthworm.

Leach, Edmund
1954   *Political Systems of Highland Burma: A Study of Kachin Social Structure*. London: Bell.

Lee, Gary Yia
1981   The Effects of Development Measures on the Socio-Economy of the White Hmong. *Unpublished PhD Thesis*, Sydney: University of Sydney.
1986   White Hmong Kinship: Terminology and Structure. In *The Hmong World*, edited by Brenda Johns and David Strecker. Abbotsburg (Australia): Yale Southeast Asia Studies, pp. 12-32.
1986a   Culture and Adaptation: Hmong Refugees in Australia. In *The Hmong in Transition*, edited by Glenn L. Hendricks, Bruce T. Downing, and Amos S. Deinard. New York: Center for Migration Studies, pp. 55-71.

1988 Household and Marriage in a Thai Highland Society. In *Journal of the Siam Society*, Vol. 76, pp. 67-73.
1996 Cultural Identity in Post-Modern Society: Reflections on What is a Hmong? In *Hmong Studies Journal*, Vol. 1, No. 1, pp. 1-38.
no year Hmong World View and Social Structure. Electronic Source: *<http://www.global.lao.net/laostudy/hmrelate.htm>*, 12.10.2000.

Leepreecha, Prasit
2001 Kinship and Identity among Hmong in Thailand. *Unpublished PhD Thesis*, Washington: University of Washington.
2004 *Ntoo Xeeb*: Cultural Redefinition for Forest Conservation among the Hmong in Thailand. In *Hmong/Miao in Asia*, edited by Nicholas Tapp et al. Chiang Mai: Silkworm Books, pp. 335-351.

Lefebvre, Henri
1996 *The Production of Space*. Oxford, Cambridge (Massachusetts, USA): Blackwell.

Leifer, Michael
2001 *Dictionary of the Modern Politics of South-East Asia*. London, New York: Routledge. 3rd edition.

Lemoine, Jacques
1972 *Un Village Hmong Vert du Haut Laos: Milieu Technique et Organisation Sociale*. Paris: Centre National de la Recherche Scientifique.
1983 *L'Initiation du Mort chez les Hmong*. Bangkok: Pandora.
1986 Shamanism in the Context of Hmong Resettlement. In *The Hmong in Transition*, edited by Glenn L. Hendricks, Bruce T. Downing, and Amos S. Deinard. New York: Center for Migration Studies, pp. 337-348.
1996 The Constitution of a Hmong Shaman's Powers of Healing and Folk Culture. In *Shaman*, Vol. 4, No. 1-2, pp. 143-165.

Levinson, Stephen
1992 *Pragmatics*. Cambridge: Cambridge University Press.

Lévi-Strauss, Claude
1969 *The Elementary Structures of Kinship*. Boston: Beacon Press.

Lewellen, Ted
2002 Groping Toward Globalization: In Search of an Anthropology Without Boundaries. In *Reviews in Anthropology*, Vol. 31, pp. 73-89.

Lewis, Gilbert
2002   Magic, Religion and the Rationality of Belief. In *Companion Encyclopedia of Anthropology: Humanity, Culture and Social Life*, edited by Tim Ingold. London, New York: Routledge, pp. 563-590.

Lewis, Paul and Elaine Lewis
1984   *Peoples of the Golden Triangle*. London: Thames and Hudson.

Little, Paul
1999   Environmentalists and Environmentalisms in Anthropological Research: Facing a New Millennium. In *Annual Review of Anthropology*, Vol. 28, pp. 253-284.

Lohmann, Larry
1993   Land, Power and Forest Colonization in Thailand. In *Global Biology and Biogeography Letters*, Vol. 3, pp. 180-191.

Long, Norman
1996   Globalization and Localization: New Challenges to Rural Research. In *The Future of Anthropological Knowledge*, edited by Henrietta. L. Moore. London: Routledge, pp. 37-59.

Lovell, Nadia
1998   Introduction: Belonging in Need of Emplacement? In *Locality and Belonging*, edited by Nadia Lovell. London, New York: Routledge, pp. 1-24.
1998a Wild Gods, Containing Wombs and Moving Pots: Emplacement and Transience in Watchi Belonging. In *Locality and Belonging*, edited by Nadia Lovell. London, New York: Routledge, pp. 53-77.

Lyman, Thomas Amis
1968   Green Miao (Meo) Spirit-Ceremonies. In *Ethnologica*, Vol. 4, pp. 1-27.
1974   *Dictionary of Mong Njua: A Miao (Meo) Language of Southeast Asia*. The Hague, Paris: Mouton.
2004   A Note on the Ethno-Semantics of Proverb Usage in Mong Njua (Green Hmong). In *Hmong/Miao in Asia*, edited by Nicholas Tapp et al. Chiang Mai: Silkworm Books, pp. 167-178.

Malinowski, Bronislaw
1944   *A Scientific Theory of Culture and Other Essays*. Chapel Hill: University of North Carolina Press.

Maniratanavongsiri, Chumpol
1999 People and Protected Areas: Impact and Resistance among the PgaK'Nyau (Karen) in Thailand. *Unpublished PhD Thesis*, Toronto: University of Toronto.

Marcus, George E. and Michael Fischer (eds)
1986 *Anthropology as Cultural Critique*. Chicago: University of Chicago Press.

Marlowe, David
1969 Upland Lowland Relationship: The Case of the Sgaw Karen of Central Upland Western Chiang Mai. In *Tribesmen and Peasants in Thailand*, edited by Peter Hinton. Chiang Mai: Tribal Research Institute, pp. 53-68.

Masipiqueña, Andres B., Gerard A. Persoon, and Denyse Snelder
2000 The Use of Fire in Northeastern Luzon (Philippines): Conflicting Views of Local People, Scientists, and Government Officials. In *Indigenous Environmental Knowledge and its Transformations: Critical Anthropological Perspectives*, edited by Roy Ellen, Peter Parkes, and Alan Bicker. Amsterdam: Harwood Academic Publishers, pp. 177-211.

Massey, Doreen
1996 *Space, Place and Gender*. Cambridge, Oxford: Polity Press. Reprinted edition.

Matisoff, James A.
1983 Linguistic Diversity and Language Contact. In *Highlanders of Thailand*, edited by John McKinnon and Wanat Bhruksasri. Kuala Lumpur et al.: Oxford University Press, pp. 56-86.

McCargo, Duncan
1997 *Chamlong Srimuang and the New Thai Politics*. London: Hurst.

McCaskill, Don and Ken Kampe
1997 From Tribal Peoples to Ethnic Minorities: The Transformation of Indigenous Peoples: A Theoretical Discussion. In *Development or Domestication? Indigenous Peoples of Southeast Asia*, edited by Don McCaskill and Ken Kampe. Chiang Mai: Silkworm Books, pp. 27-60.

McElwee, Pamela
2002 Lost Worlds and Local People. In *Conservation and Mobile Indigenous Peoples: Displacement, Forced Settlement, and Sustainable Development*, edited by Dawn Chatty and Marcus Colchester. New York, Oxford: Berghahn Books, pp. 296-312.

McKay, Deirdre
2003 Cultivating new Local Futures: Remittance Economies and Land-Use Patterns in Ifugao, Philippines. In *Journal of Southeast Asian Studies*, Vol. 34, No. 2, pp. 285-306.

McKinnon, John
1989 Structural Assimilation and the Consensus: Clearing Grounds on which to Rearrange our Thoughts. In *Hill Tribes Today: Problems in Change*, edited by John McKinnon and Bernard Vienne. Bangkok: White Lotus, pp. 303-359.

McKinnon, John and Wanat Bhruksasri (eds)
1983 *Highlanders of Thailand*. Kuala Lumpur et al.: Oxford University Press.

McKinnon, John and Jean Michaud
2000 Montagnard Domain in the South-East Asian Massif. In *Turbulent Times and Enduring Peoples: Mountain Minorities in the South-East Asian Massif*, edited by Jean Michaud. Richmond: Curzon Press, pp. 1-25.

Mecklenbräuker, Silvia, Werner Wippich, and Monika Wagener
1998 Spatial Information and Action. In *Spatial Cognition: An Interdisciplinary Approach to Representing and Processing Spatial Knowledge*, edited by Christian Freksa, Christopher Habel, and Karl F. Wender. Berlin: Springer Verlag, pp. 39-61.

Melhuus, Marit
2002 Issues of Relevance: Anthropology and the Challenges of Cross-Cultural Comparison. In *Anthropology, by Comparison*, edited by Richard G. Fox and Andre Gingrich. London, New York: Routledge, pp. 70-91.

Michaud, Jean
1996 Social Change and Tourism in a Hmong Community. *Paper presented at the 6th International Conference on Thai Studies: "Traditions and Changes at Local Marginal Levels"*. Chiang Mai (Thailand), 14-17 October 1996.
1997 Economic Transformation in a Hmong Village of Thailand. In *Human Organization*, Vol. 56, No. 2, pp. 222-232.

2004   Hmong Economic Adaptation in Northern Vietnam: A Few Theoretical Considerations. *Paper presented at the 4th EUROSEAS Conference*. Paris (France), 3-5 September 2004.

Milton, Kay
1993   Introduction: Environmentalism and Anthropology. In *Environmentalism: The View from Anthropology*, edited by Kay Milton. London, New York: Routledge, pp. 1-17.
1996   *Environmentalism and Cultural Theory: Exploring the Role of Anthropology in Environmental Discourse*. London, New York: Routledge.

Mischung, Roland
1984   *Religion und Wirklichkeitsvorstellungen in einem Karen-Dorf Nordwest-Thailands*. Wiesbaden: Franz Steiner Verlag.
1986   Environmental "Adaptation" among Upland Peoples of Northern Thailand: A Karen / Hmong (Meo) Case Study. *Unpublished Report Presented to the National Research Council of Thailand, Bangkok*, Frankfurt: University of Frankfurt, Frobenius Institute.
1988   Welchen "Wert" haben ethnographische Daten? Grundsätzliche Überlegungen und Erfahrungsbeispiele zu Ideal und Praxis völkerkundlicher Feldforschung. In *Giessener Beiträge zur Entwicklungsforschung*, Series 1, Vol. 16, pp. 75-99.
1990   Geschichte, Gesellschaft und Umwelt: Eine kulturökologische Fallstudie über zwei Bergvölker Südostasiens. *Unpublished Habilitation*, Frankfurt/Main: University of Frankfurt.
1999   Über Diskursmoden in der Ethnologie. In *Wozu Ethnologie? Festschrift für Hans Fischer*, edited by Waltraud Kokot and Dorle Drackle. Berlin: Dietrich Reimer Verlag, pp. 155-175.
2004   Erfahrungen mit "übersinnlichen" Fähigkeiten in Festland-Südostasien. In *Hexen im Museum - Hexen heute - Hexen weltweit*, edited by Wulf Köpke and Bernd Schmelz. Hamburg: Museum für Völkerkunde, pp. 340-347.
no year Versuch einer Synthese der Geschichte der Hmong. *Unpublished Paper*, Hamburg: University of Hamburg.

Molnar, Stephen and Iva M. Molnar
2000   *Environmental Change and Human Survival: Some Dimensions of Human Ecology*. Upper Saddle River (New Jersey, USA): Prentice Hall.

Montoya, Miguel
2002   Colonizing Farmers and Lumber Resources in the Ticoporo Reserve. In *Conservation and Mobile Indigenous Peoples: Displacement, Forced Settlement, and Sustainable Development*, edited by Dawn Chatty and Marcus Colchester. New York, Oxford: Berghahn Books, pp. 21-35.

Moore, Henrietta L.
1996   *Space, Text, and Gender: An Anthropological Study of the Marakwet of Kenya*. New York, London: The Guilford Press.

Moréchand, Guy
1968   Le Chamanisme des Hmong. In *Bulletin de l'Ecole Français de l'Extrême Orient*, Vol. LIV, pp. 53-294.

Mottin, Jean
1980   *The History of the Hmong (Meo)*. Bangkok: Rung Ruang Ratana Printing.
1982   *Allons Faire le Tour du Ciel et de la Terre: Le Chamanisme des Hmong vu dans les Textes*. Bangkok: White Lotus.

Muanpawong, Suntariya
2000   Public Participation in Thai Environmental Law. In *Tai Culture*, Vol. 5, No. 2, pp. 35-45.

Murdock, George Peter
1967   *Social Structure*. New York: Macmillan. 4th edition.

Niranjana, Seemanthini
2001   *Gender and Space: Femininity, Sexualization and the Female Body*. New Delhi, Thousand Oaks, London: Sage.

Nohlen, Dieter
1991   Minderheit. In *Lexikon Dritte Welt: Länder, Organisationen, Theorien, Begriffe, Personen*, edited by Dieter Nohlen. Reinbek: Rowohlt, pp. 461.

O'Connor, Richard A.
1996   Rice, Rule, and the Tai State. In *State Power and Culture in Thailand*, edited by E. Paul Durrenberger. New Haven (Connecticut, USA): Yale University, pp. 68-99.

2000 Who are the Tai? A Discourse of Place, Activity and Person. In *Dynamics of Ethnic Cultures Across National Boundaries in Southwestern China and Mainland Southeast Asia: Relations, Societies, and Languages*, edited by Hayashi Yukio and Yang Guangyuan. Chiang Mai: Ming Muang, pp. 35-50.

Olson, Kent et al.
2003 *Results of a Farm and Market Survey for Hmong Specialty Crop Farmers in the Minneapolis, St. Paul Metro Area*. St. Paul: Department of Applied Economics, University of Minnesota.

Olwig, Karen Fog
1997 Cultural Sites: Sustaining a Home in a Deterritorialized World. In *Siting Culture: The Shifting Anthropological Object*, edited by Kirsten Hastrup and Karen Fog Olwig. London, New York: Routledge, pp. 17-38.
2004 Place, Movement and Identity: Processes of Inclusion and Exclusion in a "Carribean" Family. In *Diaspora, Identity and Religion: New Directions in Theory and Research*, edited by Waltraud Kokot, Khachig Tölölyan, and Carolin Alfonso. London, New York: Routledge, pp. 53-71.

Otto, Ton and Henk Driessen
2000 Protean Perplexities: An Introduction. In *Perplexities of Identification: Anthropological Studies in Cultural Differentiation and the Use of Resources*, edited by Ton Otto and Henk Driessen. Aarhus: Aarhus University Press, pp. 9-26.

Ovesen, Jan
1995 *A Minority Enters the Nation State: A Case Study of a Hmong Community in Vientiane Province, Laos*. Uppsala: Uppsala University.
2004 The Hmong and Development in the Lao People's Democratic Republic. In *Hmong/Miao in Asia*, edited by Nicholas Tapp et al. Chiang Mai: Silkworm Books, pp. 457-474.

Paerregaard, Karsten
1997 Imagining a Place in the Andes: In the Borderland of Lived, Invented, and Analyzed Culture. In *Siting Culture: The Shifting Anthropological Object*, edited by Kirsten Hastrup and Karen Fog Olwig. London, New York: Routledge, pp. 39-58.

Painter, Michael
1995 Introduction: Anthropological Perspectives on Environmental Destruction. In *The Social Causes of Environmental Destruction in Latin America*, edited by Michael Painter and William H. Durham. Ann Arbor: University of Michigan Press, pp. 1-24.

Peters-Golden, Holly
2002 *Culture Sketches: Case Studies in Anthropology*. Boston et al.: Mc Graw Hill. 3rd edition.

Piaget, Jean and Bärbel Inhelder
1967 *The Child's Conception of Space*. New York: Norton.

Pickles, John
1985 *Phenomenology, Science and Geography: Spatiality and the Human Sciences*. Cambridge: Cambridge University Press.

Pile, Steve
1997 Introduction: Opposition, Political Identities and Spaces of Resistance. In *Geographies of Resistance*, edited by Steve Pile and Michael Keith. London: Routledge, pp. 1-32.

Postert, Christian
2003 Soziale Morphologie und Ritueller Zyklus der Person bei den Hmong in Laos und Thailand. *Unpublished PhD Thesis*, Münster: Westfälische Wilhelms-Universität.
2004 From Culture Circle to Cultural Ecology: The Hmong/Miao as reflected in German and Austrian Anthropology. In *Hmong/Miao in Asia*, edited by Nicholas Tapp et al. Chiang Mai: Silkworm Books, pp. 39-60.

Pred, Allan
1983 Structuration and Place: On the Becoming of Place and the Structure of Feeling. In *Journal of the Theory of Social Behavior*, Vol. 13, No. 1, pp. 45-68.
1990 *Making Histories and Constructing Human Geographies*. Boulder, Oxford: Westview.

Pye, Oliver
2003 Thailand: Militär, Wald und Widerstand. In *Blätter für deutsche und internationale Politik*, Vol. 10, pp. 1245-1247.

Quang, Vuong Duy
2004　The Hmong and Forest Management in Northern Vietnam's Mountainous Areas. In *Hmong/Miao in Asia*, edited by Nicholas Tapp et al. Chiang Mai: Silkworm Books, pp. 321-331.

Quincy, Keith
1988　*Hmong: History of a People*. Cheney, Washington: Eastern Washington University Press.

Rapoport, Amos
1969　*House Form and Culture*. Englewood Cliffs: Prentice-Hall.
1982　*The Meaning of the Built Environment: A Nonverbal Communication Approach*. Beverly Hills, Thousand Oaks, London: Sage.
2002　Spatial Organization and the Built Environment. In *Companion Encyclopedia of Anthropology: Humanity, Culture and Social Life*, edited by Tim Ingold. London, New York: Routledge, pp. 460-502.

Rapport, Nigel and Joanna Overing
2000　*Social and Cultural Anthropology: The Key Concepts*. London, New York: Routledge.

Ratliff, Martha
2004　Vocabulary of Environment and Subsistence in the Hmong-Mien Protolanguage. In *Hmong/Miao in Asia*, edited by Nicholas Tapp et al. Chiang Mai: Silkworm Books, pp. 147-165.

Rehbein, Boike
2004　*Globalisierung in Laos: Transformation des ökonomischen Feldes*. Münster, Hamburg, London: LIT Verlag.

Rehbein, Boike and Jürgen Rüland and Judith Schlehe (eds)
2006　*Identitätspolitik und Interkulturalität in Asien*. Münster, Hamburg, London: LIT Verlag.

Relph, Edward
1985　Geographical Experiences and Being-in-the-World: The Phenomenological Origins of Geography. In *Dwelling, Place and Environment: Towards a Phenomenology of Person and World*, edited by David Seamon and Robert Mugerauer. Dordrecht, Boston, Lancaster: Martinus Nijhoff Publishers, pp. 15-31.

Renard, Ronald D.
1994 The Monk, the Hmong, the Forest, the Cabbage, Fire and Water: Incongruities in Northern Thailand Opium Replacement. In *Law and Society Review*, Vol. 28, No. 3, pp. 657-664.
1997 The Making of a Problem: Narcotics in Mainland Southeast Asia. In *Development or Domestication? Indigenous Peoples of Southeast Asia*, edited by Don McCaskill and Ken Kampe. Chiang Mai: Silkworm Books, pp. 307-328.
2001 *Opium Reduction in Thailand 1970-2000: A Thirty-Year Journey*. Chiang Mai: Silkworm Books.

Reynolds, Craig J.
1998 Globalization and Cultural Nationalism in Modern Thailand. In *Southeast Asian Identities: Culture and the Politics of Representation in Indonesia, Malaysia Singapore and Thailand*, edited by Joel S. Kahn. Singapore: Institute of SEA Studies, pp. 115-145.

Richards, Paul
1993 Cultivation: Knowledge or Performance? In *An Anthropological Critique of Development*, edited by Mark Hobart. London: Routledge, pp. 61-78.

Rigg, Jonathan
1995 *Counting the Costs: Economic Growth and Environmental Change in Thailand*. Singapore: Institute of Southeast Asian Studies.
1997 *Southeast Asia: The Human Landscape of Modernization and Development*. London, New York: Routledge.

Rodman, Margaret C.
1992 Empowering Place: Multilocality and Multivocality. In *American Anthropologist*, Vol. 94, No. 3, pp. 640-656.

Rodseth, Lars
1998 Distributive Models of Culture: A Sapirian Alternative to Essentialism. In *American Anthropologist*, Vol. 100, No. 1, pp. 55-69.

Roß, Norbert
1997 Ökologie und Religion: Einige Methodische und theoretische Überlegungen zu einem Kognitiven Ansatz. In *Ethnologische Studien*, edited by Ulrich Köhler. Münster: LIT Verlag, pp. 177-192.
2001 *Bilder vom Regenwald: Mentale Modelle, Kulturwandel und Umweltverhalten bei den Lakandonen in Mexiko*. Münster, Hamburg, London: LIT Verlag.

Rössler, Martin
1999   *Wirtschaftsethnologie: Eine Einführung*. Berlin: Dietrich Reimer Verlag.
2003   Landkonflikt und politische Räumlichkeit: Die Lokalisierung von Identität und Widerstand in der nationalen Krise Indonesiens. In *Kulturelle Räume - Räumliche Kultur*, edited by Brigitta Hauser-Schäublin and Michael Dickhardt. Münster, Hamburg, London: LIT Verlag, pp. 171-220.

Rubel, Paula G.
2003   Travelling Cultures and Partial Fictions: Anthropological Metaphors for the New Millennium? In *Zeitschrift für Ethnologie*, Vol. 128, No. 1, pp. 3-24.

Ruey, Yih-Fu
1960   The Magpie Miao of Southern Szechuan. In *Social Structure in Southeast Asia*, edited by George Peter Murdock. Chicago: Quadrangle Books, pp. 143-155.
1972   The Miao: Their Origin and Southward Migration. In *China: The Nation and Some Aspects of its Culture: A Collection of Selected Essays with Anthropological Approaches*. Taipei: Yee Wen Publishing Company, pp. 141-157.

Safran, William
2004   Deconstructing and Comparing Diasporas. In *Diaspora, Identity and Religion: New Directions in Theory and Research*, edited by Waltraud Kokot, Khachig Tölölyan, and Carolin Alfonso. London, New York: Routledge, pp. 9-29.

Sahlins, Marshall
1993   Goodbye to Tristes Tropes: Ethnography in the Context of Modern World History. In *The Journal of Modern History*, Vol. 65, No. 1, pp. 1-25.

Said, Edward W.
1978   *Orientalism*. New York: Pantheon.

Sander, Ingvar
2000   Umweltpolitik in Thailand: Chancen für eine ökologische Modernisierung. In *Thailand: Aktuelle Wandlungsprozesse in Politik, Wirtschaft, Umwelt und Gesellschaft*, edited by Ingvar Sander and Gerhard Reinecke. Hamburg: Institut für Asienkunde, pp. 143-153.

Sathirathai, Suthawan
1995 Roles of Property Rights on the Adoption of Conservation Practices in Northern Thailand. In *TEI Quarterly Environmental Journal*, Vol. 3, No. 2, pp. 41-54.

Sathitpiansiri, Satawat and Nipatvej Suebsaeng
2001 Desk Reviews: Hill Tribe Situation in Thailand 2001. *Unpublished Document*, Chiang Mai: Tribal Research Institute.

Sato, Jin
2003 Public Land for the People: The Institutional Basis of Community Forestry in Thailand. In *Journal of Southeast Asian Studies*, Vol. 34, No. 2, pp. 329-346.

Savina, Francois Marie
1930 *Histoire des Miao*. Hong Kong: Nazareth: Imprimerie de la Société des Missions Etrangères de Paris. 2nd edition.

Saykao, Pao
1997 Hmong Leadership: The Traditional Model. *Paper presented at the "Hmong Community Leadership Conference"*. Ohio (USA), 27 March 1997.

Schechner, Richard
2002 Ritual and Performance. In *Companion Encyclopedia of Anthropology: Humanity, Culture and Social Life*, edited by Tim Ingold. London, New York: Routledge, pp. 613-647.

Schein, Louisa
1999 Diaspora Politics, Homeland Erotics, and the Materializing of Memory. In *Positions*, Vol. 7, No. 3, pp. 697-729.
2004 Vocabulary of Environment and Subsistence in the Hmong-Mien Protolanguage. In *Hmong/Miao in Asia*, edited by Nicholas Tapp et al. Chiang Mai: Silkworm Books, pp. 273-290.

Schmidt-Vogt, Dietrich
1999 *Swidden Farming and Fallow Vegetation in Northern Thailand*. Stuttgart: Franz Steiner Verlag.

Schnegg, Michael and Hartmut Lang
2002   Netzwerkanalyse: Eine praxisorientierte Einführung. Methoden der Ethnographie, Heft 1. Electronic Source: <*http://www.methoden-der-ethnographie.de*>, 12.12.2002.

Schoenfelder, Maren
2000   Vom Forschungsareal zum Forschungsgegenstand: "Raum" und seine Bedeutung für die Ethnologie. *Unpublished Master Thesis*, Hamburg: University of Hamburg.

Schoenleber, Nicole
2002   Economical and Ecological Analysis of Farming Systems in the Mountainous Area of Northern Thailand. *Unpublished Master Thesis*, Stuttgart: University of Hohenheim.

Schweizer, Thomas (ed.)
1989   *Netzwerkanalyse: Ethnologische Perspektiven.* Berlin: Dietrich Reimer Verlag.
1996   *Muster sozialer Ordnung: Netzwerkanalyse als Fundament der Sozialethnologie.* Berlin: Dietrich Reimer Verlag.
1999   Wie versteht und erklärt man eine fremde Kultur? Zum Methodenproblem der Ethnographie. In *Kölner Zeitschrift für Soziologie und Sozialpsychologie*, Vol. 51, No. 1, pp. 1-33.

Scrase, Timothy J., Todd Holden, and Scott Baum
2003   Social and Cultural Transformation in Asia: A Critical Assessment. In *Globalization, Culture and Inequality in Asia*, edited by Timothy J. Scrase, Todd Holden, and Scott Baum. Melbourne: Trans Pacific Press, pp. 269-285.

Senft, Gunter
1992   Everything we always thought we knew about Space - but did not bother to question. *Working Paper No. 10*, Nijmegen: Cognitive Anthropology Research Group.

Shields, Rob
1997   Spatial Stress and Resistance: Social Meanings of Spatialization. In *Space and Social Theory: Interpreting Modernity and Postmodernity*, edited by Georges Benko and Ulf Strohmayer. Oxford, Malden (Massachusetts, USA): Blackwell, pp. 186-202.
2002   A Resumé of Everyday Life. In *Space and Culture*, Vol. 5, No. 1, pp. 4-8.

Bibliography

Shimizu, Hiromu
2003 Diaspora and Ethnic Awakening: The Formation of Cultural Consciousness among the Ayta of Mt. Pinatubo. In *Globalization in Southeast Asia: Local, National and Transnational Perspectives*, edited by Shinji Yamashita and Jeremy S. Eades. New York: Berghahn Books, pp. 179-201.

Singer, Mona
1997 *Fremd.Bestimmung: Zur kulturellen Verortung von Identität*. Tübingen: Edition Diskord.

Skeat, Walter W.
1980 *A Concise Etymological Dictionary of the English Language*. New York: Perigree.

Smalley, William A., Chia Koua Vang, and Guia Yee Yang (eds)
1990 *Mother of Writing: The Origin and Development of a Hmong Messianic Script*. Chicago, London: University of Chicago Press.

Smelser, Neil J.
1996 The Methodology of Comparative Analysis of Economic Activity. In *Comparing Nations and Cultures: Readings in a Cross-Disciplinary Perspective*, edited by Alex Inkeles and Masamichi Sasaki. Englewood Cliffs, New Jersey: Prentice Hall, pp. 90-100.

Smith, Christina
1996 *The Hmong, 1987-1995: A Selected and Annotated Bibliography*. Minnesota: Refugee Studies Center.

Soja, Edward W.
1980 The Socio-Spatial Dialectic. In *Annals of the American Geographers*, Vol. 70, No. 2, pp. 207-225.
1989 *Postmodern Geographies: The Reassertion of Space in Critical Social Theory*. London: Verso.

Stock, Brian
1994 Reading, Community and Sense of Place. In *Place, Culture, Representation*, edited by James Duncan and David Ley. London, New York: Routledge, pp. 314-328.

Stott, Philip
1991 Mu'ang and Pa: Elite Views of Nature in a Changing Thailand. In *Thai Constructions of Knowledge*, edited by Manas Chitakasem and Andrew Turton. London: School of Oriental and African Studies, pp. 142-154.

Strauss, Anselm L. and Juliet Corbin
1990 *Basics of Qualitative Research: Techniques and Procedures for Developing Grounded Theory*. Thousand Oaks: Sage.

Sundar, Nandini
2000 The Construction and Destruction of "Indigenous" Knowledge in India's Joint Management Forest Programme. In *Indigenous Environmental Knowledge and its Transformations: Critical Anthropological Perspectives*, edited by Roy Ellen, Peter Parkes, and Alan Bicker. Amsterdam: Harwood Academic Publishers, pp. 79-100.

Sutthi, Chantaboon
1989 Highland Agriculture: From Better to Worse. In *Hill Tribes Today: Problems in Change*, edited by John McKinnon and Bernard Vienne. Bangkok: White Lotus, pp. 107-142.

Symonds, Patricia V.
1991 Cosmology and the Cycle of Life: Hmong Views of Birth, Death and Gender in a Mountain Village in Northern Thailand. *PhD Thesis (published in revised version in 2004)*, Providence: Brown University.
2004 *Calling in the Soul: Gender and the Cycle of Life in a Hmong Village*. Washington: University of Washington Press.
2004a Following Hmong Cultural Pathways for the Prevention of HIV/Aids: Notes from the Field. In *Hmong/Miao in Asia*, edited by Nicholas Tapp et al. Chiang Mai: Silkworm Books, pp. 353-374.
no year From Gendered Past to Gendered Future: Hmong Women Negotiating Gender Inequity in Northern Thailand. *Unpublished Paper*, Providence: Brown University.

Tambiah, Stanley J.
1984 *The Buddhist Saints of the Forest and the Cult of Amulets*. Cambridge: Cambridge University Press.

Tanabe, Shigeharu and Charles F. Keyes
2002 Introduction. In *Cultural Crisis and Social Memory: Modernity and Identity in Thailand and Laos*, edited by Shigeharu Tanabe and Charles F. Keyes. Honolulu: University of Hawaii Press, pp. 1-39.

Tanner, Adrian
1991 Spatial Organization in Social Formation and Symbolic Action: Fijian and Canadian Examples. In *Social Space: Human Spatial Behaviour in Dwellings and Settlements*, edited by Ole Grøn, Ericka Engelstadt, and Inge Lindblom. Odense: Odense University Press, pp. 21-39.

Tapp, Nicholas
1986 *The Hmong of Thailand: Opium People of the Golden Triangle*. London: Anti-Slavery Society.
1988 Geomancy and Development: The Case of the White Hmong of North Thailand. In *Ethnos*, Vol. 53, pp. 228-338.
1989 *Sovereignty and Rebellion: The White Hmong of Northern Thailand*. Oxford, New York, Singapore: Oxford University Press.
1989a Hmong Religion. In *Asian Folklore Studies*, Vol. 48, pp. 59-94.
1996 The Kings who could fly without their Heads: "Local" Culture in China and the Case of the Hmong. In *Unity and Diversity: Local Cultures and Identities in China*, edited by Tao Tao Liu and David Faure. Hong Kong: Hong Kong University Press, pp. 83-98.
2001 *The Hmong of China: Context, Agency, and the Imaginary*. Leiden, Boston, Köln: Brill.
2002 Hmong Confucian Ethics and Constructions of the Past. In *Cultural Crisis and Social Memory*, edited by Shigeru Tanabe and Charles F. Keyes. London: University of Hawaii Press, pp. 95-110.
2002a Diasporic Returns: The Sociology of a Globalised Rapprochement. In *Beyond China: Migrating Identities*, edited by Shen Yuanfang and Penny Edwards. Canberra: Centre for the Study of Chinese Southern Diaspora: Australian National University, pp. 11-28.
2004 The State of Hmong Studies (An Essay on Bibliography). In *Hmong/Miao in Asia*, edited by Nicholas Tapp et al. Chiang Mai: Silkworm Books, pp. 3-37.

Tapp, Nicholas and Gary Yia Lee (eds)
2004 *The Hmong of Australia: Culture and Diaspora*. Canberra: Pandanus Books.

Taylor, Jim
1997 "Thamma-Chaat": Activist Monks and Competing Discourses of Nature and Nation in Northeastern Thailand. In *Seeing Forests for Trees: Environment and Environmentalism in Thailand*, edited by Philip Hirsch. Chiang Mai: Silkworm Books, pp. 37-52.

1998   Community Forests, Local Perspectives and the Environmental Politics of Land Use in Northeastern Thailand. In *Land Conflicts in Southeast Asia: Indigenous Peoples, Environment and International Law*, edited by Catherine Iorns Magallanes and Malcolm Hollick. Bangkok: White Lotus Press, pp. 20-55.

Thayer, Millie
2000   Traveling Feminisms: From Embodied Women to Gendered Citizenship. In *Global Ethnography: Forces, Connections, and Imaginations in a Postmodern World*, edited by Michael Burawoy et al. Berkeley, Los Angeles, London: University of California Press, pp. 203-233.

Thrift, Nigel
1983   On the Determination of Social Action in Space and Time. In *Environment and Planning 1: Society & Space*, Vol. 1, pp. 23-57.
1996   *Spatial Formations*. London, Thousand Oaks, New Delhi: Sage.
2003   Space. *Paper presented at the Conference "Passages: On the Global Construction of Locality"*. Berlin (Germany), 14-15 November 2003.

Tilley, Christopher
1994   *A Phenomenology of Landscape: Places, Paths, and Monuments*. Oxford: Berg.

Tokoro, Ikuya
2003   Transformation of Shamanic Rituals among the Sama of Tabwan Island, Sulu Archipelago, Southern Philippines. In *Globalization in Southeast Asia: Local, National and Transnational Perspectives*, edited by Shinji Yamashita and Jeremy S. Eades. New York: Berghahn Books, pp. 165-178.

Tomforde, Maren
1997   Die Hausa-Diaspora in Westafrika unter besonderer Berücksichtigung der Rolle der Frau. *Unpublished Master Thesis*, University of Hamburg: Hamburg.
2003   The Global in the Local: Contested Resource-Use Systems of the Karen and Hmong in Northern Thailand. In *Journal of Southeast Asian Studies*, Vol. 34, No. 2, pp. 347-360.
2003a   Participation of Ethnic Mountain Groups in Sustainable Highland Development in Northern Thailand. In *Sustainable Upland Development in Southeast Asia*, edited by Rogelio Serrano and Romulo Aggangan. Laguna, Los Baños (Philippines): PCARRD.

Tomforde, Maren and Norbert Placzek
1996 Bericht über ein Feldforschungspraktikum in dem Karen-Dorf Mü Ka Klö in Nordwest-Thailand vom 05.08.1995 - 12.09.1995. *Unpublished Report*, Hamburg: University of Hamburg.

Townsend, Patricia K.
2000 *Environmental Anthropology: From Pigs to Policies*. Prospect Heights (Illinois, USA): Waveland Press.

Trotter, Robert T.
1999 Friends, Relatives, and Relevant Others: Conducting Ethnographic Network Studies. In *Mapping Social Networks, Spatial Data, & Hidden Populations*, edited by Jean J. Schensul et al. Walnut Creek: Alta Mira, pp. 1-50.

Tuan, Yi-Fu
1977 *Space and Place: The Perspective of Experience*. Minneapolis: University of Minnesota.

Tungittiplakorn, Waranoot
1998 Highland Cash Crop Development and Biodiversity Conservation: The Hmong in Northern Thailand. *Unpublished PhD Thesis*, Victoria (Canada): University of Victoria.

Turton, Andrew
1976 North Thai Peasant Society: A Case Study of Rural and Political Structures at the Village Level and their Twentieth-Century Transformations. *Unpublished PhD Thesis*, London: University of London.

Uhku, Maling
1997 Narcotic Trade and Addiction in the Kachin Hills of Myanmar: An Impact of Political Mismanagement and Economic Chaos. In *Development or Domestication? Indigenous Peoples of Southeast Asia*, edited by Don McCaskill and Ken Kampe. Chiang Mai: Silkworm Books, pp. 610-631.

Vaddhanaphuti, Chayan and Karan Aquino
1999 Citizenship and Forest Policy in the North of Thailand. *Paper presented at the 7th International Conference on Thai Studies : "Thailand: Civil Society?"*. Amsterdam (The Netherlands), 4-8 July 1999.

Vandergeest, Peter
1996 Property Rights in Protected Areas: Obstacles to Community Involvement as a Solution in Thailand. In *Environmental Conservation*, Vol. 23, No. 3, pp. 259-268.
2003 Racialization and Citizenship in Thai Forest Politics. In *Society and Natural Resources*, Vol. 16, pp. 19-37.

Vang, Lue
1998 A Cultural Interpretation of Thai Hmong: Beliefs, Traditions and Values about Education and Leadership. *Unpublished PhD Thesis*, San Francisco: University of San Francisco.

Vang, Lue and Judy Lewis
1990 *Grandmother's Path, Grandfather's Way: Oral Lore, Generation to Generation*. Rancho Cordova (California, USA): Zellerbach. 2nd edition.

Vatikiotis, Michael R.J.
1996 *Political Change in Southeast Asia: Trimming the Banyan Tree*. London, New York: Routledge.

Vienne, Bernard
1989 Facing Development in the Highlands: A Challenge for Thai Society. In *Hill Tribes Today: Problems in Change*, edited by John McKinnon and Bernard Vienne. Bangkok: White Lotus, pp. 33-60.

Walker, Anthony R.
1992 North-Thailand as Geo-Ethnic Mosaic: An Introductory Essay. In *The Highland Heritage: Collected Essays on Upland North Thailand*, edited by Anthony R. Walker. Singapore: Suvarnabhumi, pp. 1-93.

Wassmann, Jürg
1992 Worlds in Mind: The Experience of an Outside World in a Community of the Finisterre Range of Papua New Guinea. *Working Paper No. 9*, Nijmegen: Cognitive Anthropology Research Group.
1993 Finding the Right Path: The Route Knowledge of the Yupno of Papua New Guniea. *Working Paper No. 19*, Nijmegen: Cognitive Anthropology Research Group.

Waters, Malcolm
1995 *Globalization*. London: Routledge.

Bibliography

Weber, Max
1980   *Wirtschaft und Gesellschaft: Grundriss der Verstehenden Soziologie.* Tübingen: J.C.B. Mohr. 5th edition.

Weichhardt, Peter
1990   *Raumbezogene Identität: Bausteine zu einer Theorie räumlich-sozialer Kognition und Identifikation.* Stuttgart: Franz Steiner Verlag.

Weiner, James
2002   Between a Rock and a Non-place: Towards a Contemporary Anthropology of Place. In *Reviews in Anthropology*, Vol. 31, pp. 21-27.

Werlen, Benno
1995   *Sozialgeographie alltäglicher Regionalisierungen. Band 1: Zur Ontologie von Gesellschaft und Raum.* Stuttgart: Franz Steiner Verlag.
1997   *Sozialgeographie alltäglicher Regionalisierungen. Band 2: Globalisierung, Region und Regionalisierung.* Stuttgart: Franz Steiner Verlag.
2003   Kulturelle Räumlichkeit: Bedingung, Element und Medium der Praxis. In *Kulturelle Räume - Räumliche Kultur*, edited by Brigitta Hauser-Schäublin and Michael Dickhardt. Münster, Hamburg, London: LIT Verlag, pp. 1-11.

Winichakul, Thongchai
1994   *Siam Mapped: A History of the Geo-Body of a Nation.* Chiang Mai: Silkworm Books (reprinted 1998).

Winslow, Deborah
2002   Space, Place, and Economic Anthropology: Locating Potters in a Sri Lankan Landscape. In *Theory in Economic Anthropology*, edited by Jean Ensminger. Walnut Creek, Lanham, New York: AltaMira Press, pp. 155-181.

Wyatt, David K.
1984   *Thailand: A Short History.* New Haven et al.: Yale University Press.

Yamashita, Shinji
2003   Introduction: "Glocalizing" Southeast Asia. In *Globalization in Southeast Asia: Local, National and Transnational Perspectives*, edited by Shinji Yamashita and Jeremy S. Eades. New York: Berghahn Books, pp. 1-17.

Yang Dao
1975   *Les Hmong du Laos face au Développement.* Vientiane: Edition Siosavath.
1990   The Longest Migration. In *Hmong Forum*, Vol. 1, pp. 3-7.

1992   The Hmong: Enduring Traditions. In *Minority Cultures of Laos: Kammu, Lua', Lahu, Hmong, and Mien*, edited by Judy Lewis. Rancho Cordova, California: Southeast Asia Community Resource Center, pp. 250-323.
1993   *Hmong at the Turning Point*. Minneapolis: Wordbridge Associates.

Yang, Kao-Ly
2004   Problems in the Interpretation of Hmong Clan Surnames (Hais Txog Kev Nrhiav Hmoob Cov Xeem). In *Hmong/Miao in Asia*, edited by Nicholas Tapp et al. Chiang Mai: Silkworm Books, pp. 179-215.

Yang, Kou
2003   Hmong Diaspora of the Post-War Period. In *Asian and Pacific Migration Journal*, Vol. 12, No. 3, pp. 271-300.

Yang, Tou T.
2003   Hmong of Germany: Preliminary Report on the Resettlement of Lao Hmong Refugees in Germany. In *Hmong Studies Journal*, Vol. 4, No. 1, pp. 1-14.

Market, Culture and Society
edited by Hans-Dieter Evers, Rüdiger Korff, Gudrun Lachenmann, Joanna Pfaff-Czarnecka, Günther Schlee, and Heiko Schrader

Günther Schlee (ed.)
Imagined Differences
Hatred and the construction of identity
The book addresses key concepts of modern anthropology like "difference" and "identity" in the light of ethnographic evidence from various local settings stretching from Morocco to Indonesia. As the antagonistic and destructive aspects of social identification are also discussed, the book is a contribution to conflict theory, it provides elements of orientation in a world marked by a proliferation of ethnic movements and of nationalisms which become more narrow and more aggressive.
Bd. 5, 2. Aufl. 2004, 296 S., 25,90 €, br.,
ISBN 3-8258-3956-7

Hans-Dieter Evers; Rüdiger Korff
Southeast Asian Urbanism
The Meaning and Power of Social Space
Southeast Asian Urbanism is based on the results of over two decades of field research on cities and towns of Thailand, Sri Lanka, Indonesia, Malaysia, the Philippines and Singapore. The connections between micro and macro processes, between grassroots interactions and urban structures, between social theory and empirical data are analysed to provide a vivid picture of the great variety of urban forms, the social creativity in the slums of Bangkok, Manila or Jakarta, the variety of cultural symbolism and the political and religious structuration of urban space. The book is written in the tradition of German or European sociological research from Marx and Weber to Habermas and Bourdieu. The work on Southeast Asian urbanism was carried out within the research programme of the Sociology of Development Research Centre of the University of Bielefeld in Germany, but also during teaching and research assignments at Chulalongkorn University, the National University of Singapore, the Science University of Malaysia, the National University of Malaysia, Andalas University, Padang, the Population Studies Centre at Gadjah Mada University, the University of Indonesia, the University of the Philippines and the Institute of Southeast Asian Studies, Singapore. The book will be of interest to urban anthropologists, political scientists and sociologists, to students of Southeast Asian history, culture and society, to urban planners and policy makers.
Bd. 7, 2. Aufl. 2004, 280 S., 25,90 €, br.,
ISBN 3-8258-4021-2

Nursyirwan Effendi
Minangkabau Rural Markets
Trade and Traders in West Sumatra, Indonesia
This book is a study on traditional markets and their functions in the market society of Minangkabau, West Sumatra Indonesia. It contains detailed empirical findings on the forms of marketplaces, trade and traders, local people (mostly peasants) experiences dealing with market situation and the function of local values in the market that is embedded in the Minangkabau culture. The interacting pictures of marketplaces and indigenous social practice within and beyond them are mostly delineated.
Bd. 9, 2005, 168 S., 20,90 €, br.,
ISBN 3-8258-4387-4

Heiko Schrader
Lombard Houses in St. Petersburg
Pawning as a Survival Strategy of Low-Income Households?
The book is an outcome of a research project on pawnshops in Saint Petersburg, which took place in 1999/2000 in cooperation with the Center of Independent Social Research. It relates to the function of pawnshops in the life strategies of low-income households. The research investigated different topics with various methods: a reconstruction of the history of Russian pawnshops based on secondary materials and government reports; a description of the current pawnshop landscape in Saint Petersburg based upon secondary material and own information; a question-

LIT Verlag Münster – Berlin – Hamburg – London – Wien
Grevener Str./Fresnostr. 2 48159 Münster
Tel.: 0251 – 62 032 22 – Fax: 0251 – 23 19 72
e-Mail: vertrieb@lit-verlag.de – http://www.lit-verlag.de

naire of 100 pawnshop customers focusing on demographic data of the respondents and their households, the living conditions, the income situation, the importance of pawnshops in their life strategies, the use of credit, alternative sources of credit, defaults, and the like; five pre-structured deep interviews of pawnshop customers who already had lombard experience in Soviet times to work out differences and similarities, as well as the psychological component of pawning; open pre-structured interviews with pawnshop directors on their companies' business, their target group and the pawnshop market; and finally a profile of one successful private firm in the market and the biography of its chairman. In addition to an institutional analysis the book aims at a description of the milieu of pawnshop customers, which is shaped by an ongoing crisis of the Russian economy and society.
Bd. 10, 2001, 192 S., 20,90 €, br.,
ISBN 3-8258-5109-5

Heiko Schrader; Markus Kaiser; Rüdiger Korff (Hg.)
Markt, Kultur und Gesellschaft
Zur Aktualität von 25 Jahren Entwicklungsforschung. Festschrift zum 65. Geburtstag von Hans-Dieter Evers
In "Markt, Kultur und Gesellschaft – Zur Aktualität von 25 Jahren Entwicklungsforschung" nehmen die AutorInnen Bezug zu gegenwartsbezogenen Themen der Entwicklungssoziologie und Sozialanthropologie. Im Gegensatz zur "Großen Theorie" sind die Beiträge durch eine empiriegeleitetes "Theorizing" mit mittlerer Reichweite gekennzeichnet.
Bd. 11, 2001, 256 S., 24,90 €, br.,
ISBN 3-8258-5291-1

Gudrun Lachenmann; Petra Dannecker (Hg.)
Die geschlechtsspezifische Einbettung der Ökonomie
Empirische Untersuchungen über Entwicklungs- und Transformationsprozesse
Bei der Betrachtung von Globalisierungs- und entsprechenden Lokalisierungsprozessen wird in der neueren Wirtschaftssoziologie das Konzept der Einbettung der Ökonomie in die Gesellschaft (Karl Polanyi, Mark Granovetter) wieder aufgegriffen. In diesem Buch ist die leitende Annahme, dass der geschlechtsspezifische Blickwinkel auf ökonomisches Handeln und Veränderungsprozesse paradigmatisch für die Einbettung der Wirtschaft in die Kultur und Gesellschaft ist. Die Vorstellung der geschlechtsspezifischen Strukturierung der Wirtschaft wird fortgeführt im Hinblick auf die Notwendigkeit der Verbindung des produktiven mit dem reproduktiven Sektor und den Zusammenhang von Subsistenz- und Marktwirtschaft. Dazu werden neue Konzeptualisierungen vorgeschlagen, mit denen das Ineinandergreifen und die Konstruktion sozialer Welten und Räume analysiert werden können. Außerdem werden die entscheidenden Verflechtungen zwischen verschiedenen ökonomischen Handlungsfeldern im Sinne einer "Frauenökonomie" z. B. von städtischen Hauswirtschaft über die verwandtschaftlich organisierte landwirtschaftliche Produktion bis zu Fernhandelsnetzen aufgezeigt. Die Beiträge zu einer empiriegeleiteten Theoriebildung in Form von Fallstudien aus Afrika, Asien und Lateinamerika beruhen auf intensiver Feldforschung und Kontextualisierung.
Bd. 12, 2002, 384 S., 25,90 €, br.,
ISBN 3-8258-5649-6

LIT Verlag Münster – Berlin – Hamburg – London – Wien
Grevener Str./Fresnostr. 2 48159 Münster
Tel.: 0251 – 62 032 22 – Fax: 0251 – 23 19 72
e-Mail: vertrieb@lit-verlag.de – http://www.lit-verlag.de

Maximilian Martin
Globalization, Macroeconomic Stabilization, and the Construction of Social Reality
An Essay in Interpretive Political Economy
Globalization is a forceful phenomenon. It is also a buzzword. What is the systematic relationship between experts' models and the way globalization reshapes economy and society? How do paradigmatic statements such as the Washington Consensus impact on social reality? And how do real-world outcomes such as the collapse of the Argentine economy change the way we theorize economic relationships? Based on fieldwork in the Caribbean and inspired by the work of Thomas Kuhn and Michel Foucault, the author argues that to understand globalization, we must analyze material and symbolic factors and their dialectical interaction simultaneously. Part one analyzes how economic thinking and policy in Latin America have evolved historically. To uncover the mechanisms that produce economic thinking and policy, the author formulates a new social theory: interpretive political economy. Integrating research in anthropology, economics, and sociology, he examines four levels of social reality: meaning structures, discourse, practice, and material conditions. Part two provides in-depth case studies on Cuba and the Dominican Republic. What does the rise of economic surveillance mean for globalizing socialism and neopatrimonial capitalism? Does thinking about social relations in the language of the market affect these relations in any systematic way?
Bd. 13, 2004, 488 S., 39,90 €, br., ISBN 3-8258-7526-1

Boike Rehbein
Globalisierung in Laos
Transformation des ökonomischen Feldes
Welche sozialen und kulturellen Folgen hat der Prozess der Globalisierung – insbesondere die Ausbreitung der Marktwirtschaft – an der globalen Peripherie? Am Beispiel von Laos zeigt der Autor die Vielschichtigkeit des Prozesses auf, ohne dabei auf theoretische Konsistenz zu verzichten. Er stützt sich auf eine intensive Auseinandersetzung mit der Theorie Pierre Bourdieus und viele Jahre soziologischer, linguistischer und kulturanthropologischer Forschung in Laos. Durch seine interdisziplinäre Ausrichtung ist das Buch eine wahre Schatzkiste und das bislang umfassendste Werk über Laos in deutscher Sprache.
Bd. 14, 2004, 312 S., 29,90 €, br., ISBN 3-8258-7894-5

Spektrum
Berliner Reihe zu Gesellschaft, Wirtschaft und Politik in Entwicklungsländern
hrsg. von Prof. Dr. Georg Elwert†, Prof. Dr. Volker Lühr, Dr. Ulrike Schultz und Prof. Dr. Manfred Schulz
(Freie Universität Berlin)

Verda Kaya
Lehmburgen und Wellblechdächer
Architektur und Lebensform bei den Dagara in Ghana
"We shape our buildings, thereafter they shape us" – dieses Zitat von Winston Churchill stellt die Ethnologin Verda Kaya ihrer Arbeit voran, in der sie die Wechselwirkung zwischen Architektur und Lebensform bei den Dagara in Ghana analysiert. Das Haus wird als Konsumobjekt aufgefaßt, das verschiedene Lebensstile reflektiert und nicht nur Auskunft über seine Bewohner, sondern auch über gesellschaftliche Transformationsprozesse gibt. Ausgangspunkt der Betrachtung sind Missionierung und Kolonialisierung, die mit ihren Prozessen der Urbanisierung, sozialen Differenzierungen und der Elitenbildung zur Entstehung neuer Architekturformen beigetragen haben. Anhand von Wohnbiographien, zahlreichen Interviews, Fotos und Grundrissen verschiedener Dagara Häuser wird dargestellt, wie der Übergang von „traditioneller" Architektur zu „modernen" Bauweisen und -formen veränderte Wertvorstellungen und Bedürfnisse widerspiegelt.
Bd. 70, 2002, 176 S., 17,90 €, br., ISBN 3-8258-4760-8

Ulrich Goedeking
Politische Eliten und demokratische Entwicklung in Bolivien 1985–1996
Von Eliten in Lateinamerika können Anstöße ausgehen zu demokratisierenden Reformen und zum Wandel einer autoritären und klientelistischen politischen Kultur. Das Beispiel Boliviens zeigt, wie eine liberale Unternehmerelite mit einem unorthodoxen politischen Bündnis zum Reformakteur wurde. Theoretische Annahmen, die Eliten auf die strategische Wahrung ihrer Interessen festlegen, greifen zu kurz. Entscheidend sind die Vorstellungen und das daraus resultierende Handeln politischer Eliten. Reformanstöße von Elitenseite allein aber reichen nicht aus. Nur wenn Nichteliten Reformen zu ihrer Sache machen, können diese langfristig wirken.
Bd. 72, 2003, 288 S., 25,90 €, br., ISBN 3-8258-4860-4

Rita Schäfer
Gender und ländliche Entwicklung in Afrika
Eine kommentierte Bibliographie
Diese kommentierte Bibliographie bietet einen umfassenden Überblick über den Forschungsstand zur Frauen- und Geschlechterforschung in ländlichen Gebieten Afrikas. Die Zusammenstellung basiert auf der Auswertung von über 100 ethnologischen, soziologischen, agrarwissenschaftlichen und entwicklungspolitischen Fachzeitschriften. Darüber hinaus wurden zahlreiche Monographien und Sammelbände integriert. Einzigartig ist die Dokumentation der veröffentlichten und unveröffentlichten Beiträge afrikanischer Wissenschaftlerinnen und Entwicklungsexpertinnen zur Thematik. Indem diese Bibliographie europäische, amerikanische und afrikanische Literatur einbezieht, informiert sie mit über 1500 Titeln und Kommentaren in umfassender Weise über Forschungserkenntnisse unterschiedlicher Fachgebiete und Erfahrungen aus Entwicklungsprojekten. Mit ihrer interdisziplinären Perspektive richtet sie sich an Wissenschaftler/-innen, Studierende und Mitarbeiter/-innen in der Entwicklungszusammenarbeit.
Bd. 75, 2., aktualis. u. erw. Aufl. 2003, 472 S., 30,90 €, br., ISBN 3-8258-5053-6

Doreen Montag
Gesundheit und Krankheit im Urubamba-Tal/Peru
Die emische Kategorisierung von Krankheit als Determinante der Heilerwahl und Vermittler zwischen traditioneller und Biomedizin
Urubamba liegt im heiligen Tal der Incas, am Ostabhang der Anden. Seine Bewohner haben Zugang zur traditionellen und Biomedizin. Das vielfältige Angebot an medizinischen Leistungen prägt die Inanspruchnahme im Krankheitsfall eines Urubambinos. Die Wahl des adäquaten Heilers eines bestimmten Deutungsmusters ist theoretisch konfliktverbunden. Wie gehen die Urubambinos damit um? Gibt es für Sie eine Trennung zwischen der traditionellen und der Biomedizin? In diesem Buch wird der theoretischen Darstellung einer Konfliktbildung bei der Auswahl unterschiedlicher Heilsysteme dem aktuellen Umgang der Urubambinos mit dem Aspekt Krankheit gegenübergestellt. Die Akteursgruppen der Patienten, traditionellen Heiler und Ärzte und ihre emische Kategorisierung von Krankheit und Gesundheit stehen dabei im Vordergrund.
Bd. 82, 2002, 136 S., 15,90 €, br., ISBN 3-8258-5701-8

Inga Scharf da Silva
Umbanda
Eine Religion zwischen Candomblé und Kardezismus. Über Synkretismus im städtischen Alltag Brasiliens
Die Umbanda als urbane Religion definiert sich auf repräsentativer Ebene durch Dachverbände und auf der religiösen Alltagsebene durch die autonomen *terreiros*, dem religiösen Raum, als synkretistisch und undogmatisch. In Anlehnung an Freyres Konzept der *Rassendemokratie* vom Anfang des 20. Jahrhunderts zur Legitimation eines brasilianischen Nationalcharakters, stellt sie sich als eine typisch

LIT Verlag Münster – Berlin – Hamburg – London – Wien
Grevener Str./Fresnostr. 2 48159 Münster
Tel.: 0251 – 62 03 22 – Fax: 0251 – 23 19 72
e-Mail: vertrieb@lit-verlag.de – http://www.lit-verlag.de

brasilianische Religion dar. Die Vorstellung einer einheitlichen Nation hat sich in postmodernen Zeiten jedoch geändert. Heutzutage akzentuieren die verschiedenen sozialen Gruppen ihre Unterschiede und kritisieren die vorher kaschierte Diskriminierung.
Bd. 83, 2004, 264 S., 15,90 €, br.,
ISBN 3-8258-6270-4

Manfred Schulz; Uwe Kracht (Eds.)
Food and Nutrition Security in the Process of Globalization and Urbanization
The reader in two volumes examines key issues of food and nutrition security under the driving forces of globalization and urbanization. The different sections and chapters present approaches to food security throughout the world in a historic as well as a systematic perspective. The methods applied are both qualitative and quantitative (two econometric models and one cluster analysis). Although much has been written on food security, a systematic treatment of a historical-empirical and theoretical-analytical view is a recent development, and we have therefore chosen a 'holistic' approach. The first volume contains contributions of a more historical-empirical nature; the second volume is policy oriented. Each volume is essentially self-contained and can be read in its own right, according to the reader's interest. The current work builds on our 1999 volume on "Food Security and Nutrition – The Global Challenge". Our new reader comprises 62 articles by 71 authors. It is written for a broad audience, including scientists, experts, consultants, practitioners of development aid and students. The reader constitutes one of the most comprehensive compendia of its kind.
Bd. 84, 2005, 912 S., 69,90 €, gb.,
ISBN 3-8258-6709-9

Haile Gabriel Dagne
Das entwicklungspolitische Engagement der DDR in Äthiopien
Eine Studie auf der Basis äthiopischer Quellen
Die vorliegende Studie stellt die politischen Hintergründe und Rahmenbedingungen für ein weitreichendes Engagement der DDR in Äthiopien von 1976 bis 1990 dar und behandelt den Drang Äthiopiens nach einer Annäherung an den Osten. Bei der Recherche äthiopischer Quellen ist zu berücksichtigen, dass Quellen, vor allem in den Bereichen Militär und Sicherheit generell nicht für die Öffentlichkeit zugänglich sind. Zum einen ist die Einflussnahme der DDR auf Politik, Ideologie, Militär sowie die innere Sicherheit Äthiopiens Thema der Arbeit. Zum anderen sind aber auch die Bestrebungen der beiden Länder in der Gestaltung der entwicklungspolitischen Zusammenarbeit und der Durchführung von Projekten in den Bereichen Landwirtschaft, Industrie, Geologie, Bergbau, Transport, Kommunikation, Handel, Kultur, Bildung und Gesundheit Gegenstand der Studie.
Bd. 87, 2004, 120 S., 15,90 €, br.,
ISBN 3-8258-7519-9

Ute Siebert
Heilige Wälder und Naturschutz
Empirische Fallbeispiele aus der Region Bassila, Nordbénin
Eignen sich heilige Wälder in Bénin mit ihren religiösen Tabus in besonderem Maße für Naturschutz? Viele internationale Naturschutzprogramme rücken die Rolle von religiösen Normen und „traditional lifestyles" als Basis für Naturschutz in den Vordergrund. Diese Ethnografie über die dynamische Beziehung zwischen Menschen, Wäldern und Waldgöttern setzt sich mit diesem Naturschutz-Trend auseinander und leistet gleichzeitig einen Beitrag zur ökologischen Anthropologie. Aus multiperspektivischer Sicht werden anhand fünf empirischer Fallstudien zahlreiche lokale Akteure mit ihren Interessen im politischen, ökonomischen und rechtlichen Kontext des ländlichen Bénins analysiert.
Bd. 88, 2004, 376 S., 29,90 €, br.,
ISBN 3-8258-7610-1

LIT Verlag Münster – Berlin – Hamburg – London – Wien
Grevener Str./Fresnostr. 2 48159 Münster
Tel.: 0251 – 62 032 22 – Fax: 0251 – 23 19 72
e-Mail: vertrieb@lit-verlag.de – http://www.lit-verlag.de

Volker Lühr; Arne Kohls; Daniel Kumitz (Hg.)
Sozialwissenschaftliche Perspektiven auf Afrika
Festschrift für Manfred Schulz
Der hier vorliegende Band steht unter dem Motto Sozialwissenschaftliche Perspektiven auf Afrika, da dank des Kahlschlags an deutschen Universitäten die Perspektive der sozialwissenschaftlichen Afrikanistik alles andere als gewiss ist. Die versammelten zwölf Beiträge behandeln afrikanische oder für Afrika relevante Themen aus unterschiedlichen Bereichen und Blickwinkeln, vereinen Einsichten und Aussichten. Der in vorherrschenden Darstellungen der afrikanischen Gegenwart oft unterstellten Perspektivlosigkeit Afrikas setzen wir eine andere Sicht entgegen.
Bd. 89, 2004, 288 S., 29,90 €, br., ISBN 3-8258-8280-2

Martin Kipping; Stefan Lindemann
Konflikte und Kooperation um Wasser
Wasserpolitik am Senegalfluss und internationales Flussmanagement im Südlichen Afrika
Wodurch entstehen Konflikte um Wasser? Was kann sie überwinden helfen? Wann kommt es zu zwischenstaatlicher Kooperation in internationalen Flussgebieten? Unter welchen Bedingungen ist sie erfolgreich? In „Konflikte und Kooperation um Wasser" entwerfen Martin Kipping und Stefan Lindemann neue Perspektiven für die Forschung sowie für Außen- und Entwicklungspolitik. Aus zwei unterschiedlichen theoretischen Blickwinkeln – der Debatte um Ressourcenkonflikte einerseits und der Regimetheorie andererseits – untersuchen die Autoren die Wasserpolitik am Senegalfluss und internationale Flussregime im Südlichen Afrika.
Bd. 90, 2005, 240 S., 19,90 €, br., ISBN 3-8258-8465-1

Magnus Treiber
Der Traum vom guten Leben
Die eritreische *warsay*-Generation im Asmara der zweiten Nachkriegszeit
„...Eritrea is the saddest place of all", sagt Biniam und schüttelt den Kopf. Doch, obwohl die Preise ständig steigen, Militär das Land im Würgegriff hält und jeder Freund auch ein Spitzel sein kann, ist Biniam nicht bereit, seinen Traum vom guten Leben aufzugeben.
Bd. 92, 2005, 312 S., 29,90 €, br., ISBN 3-8258-9054-6

ZEF Development Studies
edited by Prof. Dr. Hans-Dieter Evers (Center for Development Research (ZEF), University of Bonn)

Shahjahan H. Bhuiyan
Benefits of Social Capital
Urban Solid Waste Management in Bangladesh
The theory of social capital cannot be universally applied unless it is contextualised according to the local conditions of a given society. Based on extensive field research in Dhaka and Chittagong the author shows that collective action works well when the public has confidence in the prevailing law and order situation.
The *ZEF Development Studies* are edited by the Department of Political and Cultural Change, ZEF-Zentrum für Entwicklungsforschung/Center for Development Research, University of Bonn.
Bd. 1, 2005, 288 S., 19,90 €, br., ISBN 3-8258-8382-5

LIT Verlag Münster – Berlin – Hamburg – London – Wien
Grevener Str./Fresnostr. 2 48159 Münster
Tel.: 0251 – 62 032 22 – Fax: 0251 – 23 19 72
e-Mail: vertrieb@lit-verlag.de – http://www.lit-verlag.de